THE PHYSICS OF EXPERIMENTAL METHOD

THE PHYSICS OF
EXPERIMENTAL METHOD

by

H. J. J. BRADDICK, Ph.D.
Reader in the University of Manchester

with a Foreword by
Professor P. M. S. BLACKETT, F.R.S.

CHAPMAN and HALL LTD

LONDON

First published 1954
Reprinted with revisions 1956
Second edition 1963
Reprinted with minor corrections 1966

Printed in Great Britain at the Aberdeen University Press

FOREWORD

FAR fewer good textbooks suitable for the advanced student
have been written on the methods of experimental physics
than on special branches of physical knowledge. Threlfall's
On Laboratory Arts, published in 1898, must have been
one of the first in English and Strong's *Modern Physical
Laboratory Practice* perhaps the most up-to-date and comprehensive. Dr. Braddick's book, though it has much in
common with these, has three special features which should
make it of special value to the advanced student. The first
is that it lays great emphasis on the fundamental physical
principles of measurement, on the reduction of observations
and on the statistical analysis of errors. Secondly, it em-
phasises the essential dependence of physical measurement
on the properties of various key materials and their proper
use in the construction of apparatus or in the design of instruments. Thirdly—and this point is of great practical importance
to both the teacher and student—the scope of the book is
limited to matters which are both useful to, and can be reasonably expected to be mastered by, the average advanced student.
In fact, Dr. Braddick's book contains what every such student
ought to know.

Of course, there is and must be much that is arbitrary
in the selection of topics and, like all good books, for such
I emphatically think it is, it bears the stamp of the author's
personality. Trained in the great school of experimental
atomic science under Rutherford and now an active research
worker in the closely related field of Cosmic Rays, Dr. Braddick
is a gifted designer of apparatus and instruments with, in-
cidentally, outstanding practical achievement during the
1939-45 War in the design of aircraft instruments.

Long experience of teaching of experimental physics in
one of the larger experimental schools in the country has given
Dr. Braddick an unrivalled opportunity to learn just what the
student must learn in order to become an independent and
original experimental physicist. Another author with different

experience and aptitudes would no doubt have given the book a somewhat different bias. But the bias that is Braddick's seems to me excellently suited to the needs of a large fraction of the young experimental physicists of to-day—and not of physicists only. For it is a common-place that many if not most experimental sciences tend as they advance to make increasing use of what traditionally have been called physical measurements. This is certainly true of Chemistry, Biology, Physiology, Mineralogy, Petrology, Medicine and, of course, Engineering. It is, no doubt, with this consideration in mind, that Dr. Braddick named his book not *The Method of Experimental Physics*, but chose the wider and apter title *The Physics of Experimental Method*. I feel that there are few experimental scientists who will not profit from Dr. Braddick's experimental wisdom. For all who have to plan experiments or design apparatus must know much or even most of the contents of this book—whatever the subject matter of their research.

It is not only in the scientific research laboratory that precise physical measurements are essential : increasingly they are becoming an essential part of modern industrial production methods. Manufacturing processes are increasingly controlled by the use of data provided by scientific measuring instruments, often of great delicacy and complication. Not only are standard instruments to furnish continuous records of electric currents and potentials, temperatures and pressures, or gas composition by infra-red spectrometer and so on, an essential part of many modern production units, but often specially designed instruments of non-standard type have to be built for specific purposes. Here is a field where Dr. Braddick's emphasis on instrument design may be invaluable to the young industrial scientist working, for instance, in a laboratory attached to a production unit. Improved instrumentation is undoubtedly one of the important avenues to more efficient production.

In the public estimation of the gigantic achievements of pure science, nourished on the many admirable popular expositions, there is a natural tendency to view these achievements as resulting primarily from the speculative genius of a few great thinkers. It is easy to forget the innumerable achievements of precise experimentation, of subtle instrument design and of supreme manipulative skill, which have furnished the facts on which these great theoretical generalisations are founded. The craft of the experimental scientist, which at its highest becomes indeed the Art of Experimental Science, remains the basis of modern science and so of our knowledge of the world we live in.

Nearly a hundred years ago, Liebig expressed the matter with admirable clarity :

" The development of culture, that is, the extending of man's spiritual domain, depends on the growth of inventions which condition the progress of civilisation. . . . How do we find things out about the world ? Not by sitting in an arm-chair and thinking about them, but by observing nature and making experiments. What we know about the world depends on what we can do—and this depends on the instruments at our disposal, the materials we have available to make the in-struments and the skill of our hands by which we use the instruments."

Braddick's book will serve its purpose if it helps the young experimenter to master the fascinating art of ex-perimentation.

P. M. S. BLACKETT

October, 1953

AUTHOR'S PREFACE

TO SECOND EDITION

THE plan of the book remains unaltered but many changes have been made in detail to cover changes in experimental methods and their relative importance. A section has been added on the production and measurement of magnetic fields. The topics dealt with in this are mostly not very new, but references to them are rather scattered. The Electronic Method chapter now contains an elementary account of transistors and an attempt to appraise their laboratory uses. A new chapter on spectral radiation detectors covers a subject in which there have been recent advances and which has important applications outside the physical laboratory.

I am grateful to my son for checking the whole of the proof-reading.

H. J. J. BRADDICK

AUTHOR'S PREFACE

THE methods of experiment used in physical investigations become more varied at the same time as our knowledge of physical facts and laws grows more extensive. The time available to a student learning physics does not, however, increase correspondingly, and inevitably the new facts and generalisations take precedence over details of experimentation. The student beginning research therefore finds it increasingly difficult to choose methods and to plan details of his experiments.

In large research schools this difficulty is met by guidance from the staff and by discussion between students, but the more isolated worker may well find it serious.

For several years we have given in Manchester a lecture course on " Physics of Experimental Method " as part of the laboratory training of degree students. It is intended to call the attention of students to some of the principles of experiment and to some of the available techniques. This book has the same aim : it is not intended to compete with books which give fully detailed accounts of particular procedures, and references to such books are freely given. There is a fairly extensive list of references, which gives some preference to easily accessible books and papers, and to those which act as keys to further reading.

Some of the mathematical methods which form working tools for the experimental physicist are described in a long appendix to Chapter II, written by Mr. J. Maddox of the Manchester University Theoretical Physics department, who has had much experience in advising experimental workers on such matters.

I am glad to record my gratitude to Professor Blackett for encouraging me in writing this book, to several of my colleagues and friends on whose knowledge and time I have drawn for advice and criticism, and to my wife who has given not only sympathy but very active assistance.

I am very grateful to a number of people who have called attention to mistakes or obscurities in the first impression.

H. J. J. BRADDICK

CONTENTS

CONTENTS

CONTENTS

CONTENTS

CONTENTS

CONTENTS

CONTENTS

THE PHYSICS OF
EXPERIMENTAL METHOD

CHAPTER 1

INTRODUCTION

The Place of Experiment in Physical Science

The method of experimental science depends essentially on guiding speculation by experience, and on frequent comparison between deductions from hypothesis and the observed behaviour of objects. A scientific experiment is a deliberately arranged series of events intended to reveal as clearly as possible some regularity in the behaviour of objects—a so-called natural law.

In principle, every event, even in a well thought-out experiment, is more or less closely connected with every event in the outside world, and unpredictable variations in the behaviour of experimental systems must arise for this reason (cf. Ch. 2). It is, however, characteristic of physics, more than of any other science, that it deals with relatively simple systems and is able to secure for them a relatively high degree of isolation from the outside world. This end is secured by an elaboration of experimental technique which goes beyond that usually employed in any other science. An excellent example of the use of advanced technique to simplify the fundamental situation occurs in the frequent use of high vacuum in experimental work with molecular and atomic particles. By exhausting the air from a vessel it is possible to secure for a molecule a free path of several centimetres or several metres, in which it is practically free from any interaction with its neighbours, and in which the effect of electric or magnetic fields, of radiation, or of deliberately arranged collisions can be studied. A very large part of the advance made in atomic physics since the 1890s may be directly traced to the use of this device.

In some sciences other than physics, this drastic simplification is not a practical method of investigation. For example, many systems studied in the biological sciences are very complicated, and we can make only small changes in conditions

1

without destroying the processes we wish to study. In such cases we must ensure that conditions, other than those deliberately varied, are kept as constant as possible, and verify their constancy as far as possible by " control experiments ". In meteorology and in sociology, it is nearly impossible to produce *experimental* changes, and we have to separate causes and effects from a mass of observations of phenomena occurring outside our control. Field trials in agriculture, and many large-scale experiments on industrial plant occupy an intermediate position ; experimental variations can be made, but their effects are overlaid with those of uncontrolled changes taking place all the time. These sciences depend for the analysis of their data on an elaborate statistical technique ; for the separation of variables, which is impossible on a small set of data, may be accomplished by analysing a large number of observations.

Statistical methods are much more important in these cases than in most physical research, but from time to time these methods must be used in a physical investigation. As one might expect, they are often useful in the borderlands between physics and such sciences as meteorology, and we may give an example from cosmic ray research. The cosmic rays are affected by the earth's magnetic field and by complicated and imperfectly known interactions in the atmosphere. One method of inferring some of their properties is to observe the time variation of the ray intensity at the earth's surface, and to correlate its changes with the movements of the earth, with changes in the geomagnetic field, and with atmospheric changes. In this way it has been found, for example, that a comparatively small part of the radiation is influenced by the sun and may originate there. The mathematical methods used (those of multiple correlation) were largely devised for use in biological and sociological investigation.

While the refined statistical techniques are borrowed by physicists from the biologist's armoury, it is obvious that the experimental techniques devised in the physical laboratory can be applied in other fields : this is clearly true of those devices which extend the scope of human senses—(e.g. the microscope, the electron microscope, in biology), or the control of environment (e.g. the high temperature furnace in experimental geology). In certain cases (e.g. the study of nerves and muscles by the use of valve amplifiers and sensitive thermal detectors), it has been possible to simplify conditions considerably, following the trend of experiments in pure physics. Very important results have been obtained in this way, and it is likely that it will continue to be a profitable line of development in the biological sciences.

Pure laboratory physics has an important two-way connection with industry. The time between a laboratory discovery in pure physics and its application to industrial technique may nowadays be very short, though it is sometimes very long if economic and social changes are involved. Often empirical development for industrial purposes precedes and inspires scientific understanding, as has happened with the photographic emulsion and with semi-conductors.

The industrial development of laboratory physics is well recognised, but it is perhaps less clearly realised that laboratory physics depends to a large and increasing extent on the use of the products of specialised industry—a spectacular example is the employment in experimental apparatus of thermionic valves in numbers which would be impossible without an *industrial* source of these tools. Besides these special products the progress of laboratory experiments depends on supplies of industrial materials and on the general level of industrial technique. At every moment in the history of physics the speed and direction of progress has been controlled very largely by the technique available.

It may be useful to attempt a classification of experiments in pure physics as they present themselves to the contemporary worker. There is first the exploratory experiment usually devised on the basis of a very naïve theory, or a pure " hunch "—a historical example is Becquerel's experiment which resulted in the discovery of radioactivity. He tried whether uranium compounds (chosen because of their fluorescence, which was later found to be irrelevant) emitted a penetrating radiation which would blacken a photographic plate as did the then recently discovered X-rays. Experiments of this type merge into another class ; those which are devised

3

under the guidance of a more definite hypothesis which is confirmed, rejected, or modified on the result of the experiment. An example, following on the Becquerel experiment, is the series of experiments by which Rutherford and others established that radioactivity involved the breakdown of one kind of atom into another. From time to time experiments of this class assume the status of crucial experiments, deciding between two hypotheses. An example is Rutherford's α-particle scattering experiment which decided definitely in favour of a nuclear atom-model against a plausible atom-model in which electrons were embedded in a distribution of positive charge. A very famous crucial experiment in a different field was the Michelson-Morley experiment which made unreasonable the existence of a fixed aether, and another example is provided by the Geiger-Bothe experiment on the coincident discharges of counters separated by an absorbing layer which decided in favour of the particulate nature of cosmic rays and against the view usually held at the time, that the rays were high-energy γ-rays.

A further stage in the interaction of theory and experiment occurs when experiments are undertaken to test the predictions of a highly developed theory which may come to be modified as a result of the experiment. On account of experimental difficulties on the one hand and theoretical approximations on the other, such experiments are rarer than most people believe : the plausibility of most physical theories rests on their application over a wide range rather than on the success of very detailed prediction. However, a recent example of this type of experiment is the investigation of details of the structure of the hydrogen line spectra in order to check the predictions of the Dirac quantum mechanics.

An apparently rather different situation arises in applied physics, where the typical experiment is the measurement of a quantity more or less exactly defined in advance. Such experiments must be performed frequently, both as routine checks in industry and in "applied research" where they serve to provide data for design calculations and to investigate the behaviour of newly designed systems. In fact' when experiments of the "pure research" type are actually performed, they usually have to be put into the same form as the experiments of applied physics. A distinctive skill of the pure research physicist is the ability to devise experiments which take the form of straightforward measurement, but which answer as unambiguously as possible questions set by speculation.

The experiments carried out in teaching laboratories usually resemble those of industrial physics in that a definite measurement has to be performed. We have seen that the experiments of pure research are also, in fact, put into this form when they are performed. In every case an important part of the work lies in securing that the quantity measured actually corresponds to the quantity defined, whether by practical or theoretical considerations. This is one aspect of the elimination of systematic error which is discussed in Chapter 2.

It is the purpose of this book to direct attention to those branches of physics which are important in the planning and execution of experiments in physical research—to act as a text-book of physics applied to physical experiment. The main emphasis is laid on the principles of physical experiment, on the resources at present available and on the limitations of contemporary technique in certain directions. The examples used as illustrations and the tables have been chosen to be useful for reference in planning an experiment.

CHAPTER 2

ERRORS AND THE TREATMENT OF EXPERIMENTAL RESULTS

2.1 Introduction

Most experiments in physics give as their immediate result some numerical quantity, and we usually need to attach to this result some estimate of the amount by which it may be in error. This quantitative estimation of experimental uncertainty is clearly important when we compare the result of one experiment with another in which some condition is altered, and have to decide whether the observed differences are significant, or when we compare experimental results with a theoretical calculation and have to decide whether or not the experiment supports the theory. Random errors of observation can be estimated by calculation (§ 2.4 *et seq.*) though the estimate will not be very reliable unless fairly large numbers of readings are available. The effects of errors of a systematic kind can only be estimated by judgment supported by such methods of experiment as are suggested in § 2.3. Finally, we have to decide how far the quantity measured in the experiment is that to which theory or definition refers, and this, of course, lies at the core of the design of the experiment.

2.2 Types of Experimental Error

If a physical experiment is repeated by reproducing the conditions as nearly as possible, the result is not usually the same as before. Since the basic assumption of physical science is the consistent behaviour of natural phenomena (except on a small scale, see e.g. Ch. 10) this variation is held to mean that conditions have not been exactly reproduced. This is not surprising, since the system under observation is in principle influenced by every change in the world outside, and even with care and precaution it is not possible to isolate it completely. In some important cases, if the experiment is repeated many times, the variations in the results are found to be distributed according to a particular mathematical law —the normal error law treated in § 2.6. In any particular case, it is a matter of experimental fact whether the variations are in accordance with the normal law or not : there is a body of mathematical work devoted to tests for accordance with the law and to giving numerical values to the trustworthiness of observations which have errors of normal type.

A less tractable type of error arises, fundamentally, because the result of the experiment is affected in a systematic way by causes which are not recognised as operating. An elementary example is given by the heat transfer losses in determining a specific heat by the method of mixture. The heat losses always act in one direction and cannot be detected by any number of identical repetitions of the experiment. A famous example of this kind of error occurred in the Millikan oil-drop determination of the electronic charge, where an investigation made with the greatest skill and yielding highly consistent results contained a considerable error due to the use of a wrong value for the viscosity of air. These are examples of systematic error ; closely connected with them are " errors of interpretation " arising because the measurements made do not correspond to the theoretical conditions assumed to exist. An example from the history of cosmic ray investigation will illustrate the point ; it is known that the number of showers of particles which can be detected by counters under a layer of lead varies with the thickness of the lead and goes through a maximum when this is about 2 cm. This result had been explained by theory, and considerable interest was produced by the discovery of a second maximum at about 17 cm. lead. It later appeared that this maximum was due to the use of peculiarly shaped blocks of lead, which for purely geometrical reasons give a maximum of the ordinary type from their margins, when the main layer of lead was 17 cm. thick.

The elimination of errors of these types is a major problem in the design of physical experiments. A few possible lines of attack on this problem are indicated below, but the devising of experiments to investigate a particular point, to the exclusion of disturbing factors, is the most exacting task of the experimental physicist.

2.3   Systematic Errors

The possibility of a particular systematic error may be detected by thinking over the experiment in advance, and a method may be devised, (*a*) to exclude the disturbing effect physically or (*b*) to eliminate it by a proper arrangement of the experiment and treatment of the results. For example, the heat loss in the calorimeter experiment mentioned above may be excluded by having the calorimeter in an enclosure maintained always at the same temperature as itself (case *a*), or the loss of temperature may be measured and a cooling correction applied (case *b*).

It often happens that the uncontrolled conditions affecting an experiment drift more or less steadily with time, and it may then be possible to arrange the readings so that the drift does not produce a systematic error. An example is given by galvanometer readings of a sensitive bridge balance. If alternate readings are taken with the bridge current on and off (or reversed), a drift of the balance may be detected. If a drift is found, one should try to stabilise conditions, e.g. by improving the control of the temperature of the resistances. When these possibilities have been exhausted, a residual *linear* drift may be eliminated from the results by taking the readings at regular intervals and comparing each " direct " reading with the mean of the " reversed " readings on either side of it.

It is in principle possible to eliminate drifts which are not linear. If the alternate readings are a_0, b_1, a_2, b_3 . . ., a second order drift could be eliminated by comparing $\frac{1}{2}(b_1 + b_3)$ with $\frac{1}{8}(a_0 + 6a_2 + a_4)$ etc., but it is doubtful if this result is of much practical use.

In some cases an error which would appear to be systematic can be converted into a random error by arrangement of the work, and the error may then be reduced by taking the mean of a number of readings (§ 2.5). Thus the random errors of the divisions of a graduated circle give rise to an error in angular measurement which cannot be detected by repeating the measurement on the same part of the circle. If the circle is now turned and the readings repeated on another part of the circle, or if extra reading microscopes are provided, the division errors appear as random errors, and their effect may be reduced by taking the mean of a number of readings. Again, in photographic photometry (§ 8.32) where light intensities are measured by the blackening of a photographic plate, irregularities of plate manufacture and processing may cause a systematic change of sensitivity across the plate. Photometric plates bear, in general, calibration exposures and experimental exposures, e.g. of spectra, and if these are placed alternately across the plate, the errors obtained in comparing the experimental exposures with the calibrations are sometimes in one direction and sometimes in another. Furthermore, the positions of experimental exposures on the plate should be arranged in a random way with respect to any variable (e.g. concentration of absorber) whose effect is under investigation, so that a false systematic effect is not introduced. " Randomisation of errors " of this kind is very important in field trials in agricultural research, and the elaborate methods devised for this purpose may occasionally be of interest to the physicist.

Since systematic errors arise from the effect of a finite number of disturbing causes (cf. § 2.6), they may often be detected by varying conditions as widely as possible. For example, in the calorimetric experiments referred to above, it would be possible to vary the temperature range, the mass of substance used, the time taken to transfer it from heater to calorimeter. As a result of such changes it may be possible to set a definite limit to a particular systematic error, or to eliminate it by calculation ; e.g. in the heat measurement discussed above the " transfer error " could be eliminated by extrapolating the experimental relation between specific heat and transfer time to zero time.

The most radical and often the most satisfactory way of resolving doubts about the result of an experiment is to use an entirely different method to obtain the result or to support the conclusion. The long unsuspected error in the oil-drop value of the electronic charge was discovered when a value was deduced from X-ray measurements of the absolute spacing of crystal lattices, and thus of absolute atomic masses. Almost invariably the important theoretical conclusions of physics rest on a broad experimental base, and nearly all the important numerical data have been determined in more than one way.

2.4   Random Errors

We now consider the treatment of errors of the random type referred to in § 2.2.

Suppose we wish to plot on a convenient diagram a succession of results which can each be represented by an integral number ; e.g. the number of peas in the pods of a plant. We can draw a diagram of the type shown in Fig. 2.1, in which the length of each vertical line represents the number of occasions on which the observed number corresponded to the abscissa of

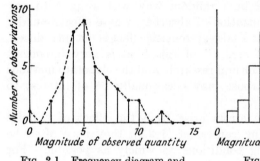 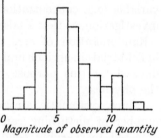

FIG. 2.1   Frequency diagram and frequency polygon   FIG. 2.2   Histogram

the line. This is called a *frequency diagram*, and if the tops of the vertical lines are joined up as in Fig. 2.1, it becomes a *frequency polygon*. A more general case is that of a continuous variable, for which the results of observations take the form of : " On y occasions the measured value of the variable lay between x_1 and x_2." An appropriate graphical representation is the *histogram* of Fig. 2.2. If the intervals of x, i.e. $(x_2 - x_1)$, etc., are all alike, it does not matter if we represent the number y by the height of the appropriate rectangle, or by the area, and the diagram takes the same form if we adopt either of these courses. If, however, we have to deal with unequal intervals of x, we obtain a more significant form for the diagram if we make the *area* of the rectangle stand for the number of observations. For consider the effect of uniting two adjacent groups of the distribution shown in the histogram, Fig. 2.2. It is clear that we produce little distortion of the shape of the histogram if we make the area included in the new group between, say, x_5 and x_7 the same as the total area previously included in groups $x_5 \ldots x_6$ and $x_6 \ldots x_7$.

This idea serves as an introduction to the general idea of a distribution function appropriate to a very large number of observations of a continuously variable quantity. This distribution function is obtained by a limit process in which the interval between x_n and x_{n+1} is made smaller and smaller. The function $D(x)$ is defined in the following way : the integral

$$\int_{x_1}^{x_2} D(x)dx$$

represents the number of occasions on which the variable x lies between x_1 and x_2.

If $N(x_0)$ is the number of observations for which $x \leqslant x_0$, we can plot $N(x_0)$ against x_0 and obtain a curve (Fig. 2.3).

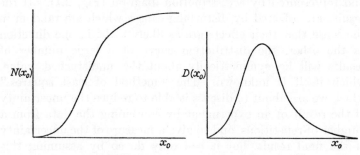

FIG. 2.3 Integral distribution curve

FIG. 2.4 Distribution function corresponding to Fig. 2.3

This is called the integral distribution curve (the ogive curve of some older statisticians), and if it is taken as representing a continuous function, it is clear that the distribution curve of Fig. 2.4 may be obtained by differentiating it with respect to x_0, for

$$N(x_0) = \int_0^{x_0} D(x)dx$$

$$D(x_0) = \frac{dN}{dx_0}$$

11

This result leads to a verbal interpretation of the distribution function $D(x_0)$; it represents the number of observations per unit range of the variable x over a very small range in the neighbourhood of x_0.* If we divide each ordinate of the curve by a suitable constant so as to make the total area under the curve unity, we obtain a "normalised" curve for which

$$y = \frac{D(x)}{\displaystyle\int_0^\infty D(x)dx}.$$

The area between ordinates at $x_1 x_2$ now represents the *fraction* of all observations which lie between x_1 and x_2 and this normalised curve is sometimes simply called the frequency curve of the observations.

2.5 The Mean

Suppose a number of observations $a_1 a_2 \ldots$, are taken and represented by a distribution diagram (Fig. 2.1). If the results are affected by disturbing causes which are random in the sense that their effects are as likely to be in one direction as the other, the distribution curve of a large number of results will lie symmetrically about the undisturbed value, which itself is unknown. The "method of least squares" which we are about to discuss is able to reduce the uncertainty of the result of an experiment by combining the data from a number of repetitions, and to give a measure of the uncertainty of the final result, but it can only do so by assuming this symmetry. One ought therefore, in principle, to examine carefully the frequency spectrum of a set of results before making any serious use of the method.

Suppose the true value of an observed quantity is a, and that N observations are taken giving results $a_1 a_2 \ldots$ The errors of the observations are of the form

$$x_1 = (a_1 - a) \text{ etc.}$$

a and the x_1's are, of course, unknown in practice.

---

* Distribution curves obtained in this way are, of course, in common use in physics—e.g. to represent the velocity spectrum of gas molecules, the energy spectrum of β particles.

The arithmetic mean of the observations is

$$M = \frac{1}{N}\Sigma a_1.$$

The error of this mean is

$$E = \frac{1}{N}(\Sigma a_1 - Na) = \frac{1}{N}\Sigma x_1.$$

Now

$$E^2 = \frac{1}{N^2}(\Sigma x_1)^2 = \frac{1}{N^2}(\Sigma x_1{}^2 - 2\Sigma x_1 x_2).$$

Now if the observations are numerous and the errors symmetrically distributed about zero, the second sum is small compared with the first and we have

$$E^2 = \frac{1}{N^2}\Sigma x_1{}^2 = \frac{1}{N^2} \cdot N\mu^2 = \frac{1}{N}\mu^2$$

where μ^2 is the mean square error of the individual observations. The error of the mean of N observations under these conditions is then $\dfrac{1}{\sqrt{N}}$ of the root-mean-square (r.m.s.) error of a single observation, and it follows that the arithmetic mean of a very large number of observations may be taken as free from random error. As yet we have no method for obtaining the average error of a single observation, but we may guess that a useful measure of this quantity could be obtained from the mean square of the differences taken between single observations and the mean of a finite, but not small, number of observations. These differences are called the residuals about the mean.

The practical calculation of the mean of a large number of observations may be lightened by the device of a false mean, best explained by a simple example :

Observations	.	27·1	27·0	26·7	26·8	27·2
		27·4	27·4	27·1	26·6	27·2

Take as a false mean 27·0, which lies among the readings and is arithmetically convenient. Tabulate the positive and negative differences from this.

+	−
0·1	0·3
0·0	0·2
0·2	0·4
0·4	—
0·4	0·9
0·1	
0·2	
1·4	
− 0·9	

10) 0·5   + 0·05   mean   27·05

Formally, if $a_1 a_2$ . . . are the observations, A the false mean, M the arithmetic mean

$$M = \frac{\Sigma a_n}{N} = \frac{AN + \Sigma(a_n - A)}{N}$$

$$= A + \frac{\Sigma a_n - A}{N}.$$

In practical calculation, an arithmetical check is required, and this may take the form of a similar calculation with residuals about a different false mean, or summation of the residuals about the mean already found, which should of course give zero.

The device of a false mean can also be used with advantage in calculating the mean square of the residuals. Let σ^2 be the mean square of the residuals about the arithmetic mean M, and S^2 the mean square of the residuals about a false mean A, chosen for convenience in calculation.

$$S^2 = \frac{\Sigma(a_n - A)^2}{N} \qquad \sigma^2 = \frac{\Sigma(a_n - M)^2}{N}.$$

Then $S^2 - \sigma^2 = \frac{1}{N}\{2(M - A)\Sigma a_n + N(A^2 - M^2)\}$

$$= \frac{1}{N}\{2(M - A)NM + N(A^2 - M^2)\}$$

$$= M^2 - 2MA + A^2.$$

So that $\sigma^2 = S^2 - (M - A)^2.$

As well as providing a convenient trick of calculation, this result contains an important general principle, for it shows that the sum of the squares of the residuals about the arithmetic mean is less than the sum of the squares of the residuals about any other mean. This property of minimising the sum of the squares of the residuals is widely accepted as the distinguishing mark of the best representation of a series of results. It has given the name " method of least squares " to a whole branch of statistical analysis. We shall refer again to the limitations of the method.

2.6   The Law of Errors

In estimating the effect of random error on a series of observations it is useful to represent the frequency distribution of errors by a formal law, and the Gaussian distribution or Normal Error Law is the most generally useful. The applicability of the law to any given case is a matter for empirical trial, but the law may be deduced *a priori* on the following lines :

Suppose the observation is affected by a number N of independent elementary errors, and that each of these may with equal likelihood take the values $+ \epsilon$, $- \epsilon$. Then the total error may assume the values $+ N\epsilon, (N - 2)\epsilon \ldots -N\epsilon$, and the probability of an error $(N - 2m)\epsilon$ can be calculated as follows.

The probability of each of the elementary errors being negative is $\frac{1}{2}$, and the probability of any particular selection of errors (say the first m) being all negative is $(\frac{1}{2})^m$. But if m errors and m only are to be negative, this probability must be multiplied by the probability of all the remaining elements being positive, which is $(\frac{1}{2})^{N-m}$. The configuration thus achieved is only one of $^N C_m$ possible configurations having the same total error, so that the probability of a total error $+ (N - 2m)\epsilon$ is

$$(\tfrac{1}{2})^m (\tfrac{1}{2})^{N-m} . \, ^N C_m$$

$$= (\tfrac{1}{2})^N \, \frac{N!}{m!(N - m)!} .$$

15

It will be seen that, with a finite number N of elementary partial errors, the histogram representing the frequency distribution of the values of total error has the heights of its sections proportional to the binomial coefficients in the expansion of

$$(1 + x)^N.$$

If the number of partial errors tends to infinity, it may be shown that the normalised histogram tends to a continuous distribution curve of the form

$$y = \frac{h}{\sqrt{\pi}} e^{-h^2 x^2}.$$

The probability of observing an error which lies between x, $x + dx$, can be shown to be proportional to $e^{-h^2 x^2} dx$ and $\dfrac{h}{\sqrt{\pi}}$ is a normalising factor which secures that the total area under the curve is unity. $\displaystyle\int_{x_1}^{x_2} y\,dx$, then, represents the fraction of all observations in which the error lies between x_1, x_2.

The form of the curve is indicated in Fig. 2.5, p. 26 and it has the following properties of present practical importance :

(a) The shape of the (normalised) curve depends on the one parameter h. If this is large, the curve is thin and tall ; if it is small, the curve is low and spreading.

(b) The mean square residual σ^2, about the mean, of all observations represented, may be calculated. For if there are N observations (N being large), then the number lying in the range between x, $x + dx$ is

$$\frac{Nh}{\sqrt{\pi}} e^{-h^2 x^2} dx$$

and their contribution to the sum of the squares of the residuals is

$$\frac{Nh}{\sqrt{\pi}} x^2 e^{-h^2 x^2} dx$$

so that

$$\sigma^2 = \frac{1}{N} \cdot \frac{h}{\sqrt{\pi}} \cdot \int_{-\infty}^{+\infty} N x^2 e^{-h^2 x^2} dx = \frac{1}{2h^2}.$$

We have therefore

$$\sigma = \frac{1}{h\sqrt{2}}\;;\quad h = \frac{1}{\sigma\sqrt{2}}.$$

(c) The proportion of all observations, forming a normal distribution, whose errors lie between $+ x_1$ and $- x_1$ is

$$\frac{h}{\sqrt{\pi}}\int_{-x_1}^{+x_1} e^{-h^2x^2}dx = \frac{2h}{\sqrt{\pi}}\int_0^{x_1} e^{-h^2x^2}dx.$$

Writing $t = hx$, this becomes

$$\frac{2}{\sqrt{\pi}}\int_0^{hx_1} e^{-t^2}dt = \text{erf}\,(hx_1)$$

where erf (x) is a tabulated function defined by

$$\text{erf}\,x = \frac{2}{\sqrt{\pi}}\int_0^x e^{-t^2}dt.$$

It is convenient to work in terms of the standard deviation or root-mean-square residual σ. The proportion of observations with residuals lying between $- r\sigma$ and $+ r\sigma$ is

$$\text{erf}\,hr\sigma = \text{erf}\,\frac{r}{\sqrt{2}}.$$

The proportion of observations, calculated from this formula, with errors lying outside certain useful limits is given in Table 2.1.

TABLE 2.1

Useful Quantities connected with the Error Integral erf x

(1) Chance that a normally distributed error lies inside or outside given multiples of the r.m.s. error or standard deviation σ.

Error E	Chance of error $< E$	Chance of error $> E$
$\pm\,\sigma$	erf $0\cdot707 = 0\cdot682$	$0\cdot318$
$\pm\,2\sigma$	erf $1\cdot41\ \ = 0\cdot954$	$0\cdot046$
$\pm\,3\sigma$	erf $2\cdot12\ \ = 0\cdot997$	$0\cdot003$
$\pm\,4\sigma$	erf $2\cdot83$	$7\cdot10^{-5}$
$\pm\,5\sigma$	erf $3\cdot54$	$6\cdot10^{-7}$

TABLE 2.1 (*contd.*)

(2) Limiting errors corresponding to given values of the probability of finding the error within the limits $\pm\, x$.

Probability = Erf x	Limiting Error x	x in terms of σ	x in terms of probable error
0·5	0·477	0·683 σ	1 × P.E.
0·99	1·82	2·6 σ	3·8 × P.E.
0·999	2·32	3·3 σ	4·9 × P.E.

The value of the error which is as likely as not to be exceeded in a series of observations is called, rather unhappily, the *probable error*, and its value is approximately 0·68 of the standard deviation. In interpreting published work it is sometimes important to note which measure of deviation has been used. It is preferable to standardise procedure in this matter by using the standard deviation (r.m.s. deviation).

We have not yet considered fully the problem of estimating the *error* of an observation from the *residuals* obtained about the arithmetic mean of a *finite* series of observations (cf. § 2.5). It can be shown that the best estimate of the r.m.s. deviation of the single observations about the true value of the observed quantity is

$$\mu = \sqrt{\frac{\Sigma v^2}{(N-1)}}$$

where N is the number of observations and Σv^2 denotes the sum of the squares of the residuals. This is larger than the r.m.s. value of the residuals about the mean

$$\sigma = \sqrt{\frac{\Sigma v^2}{N}}$$

because it contains an allowance for the fact that the arithmetic mean of N observations has itself a probable deviation from the true value which would be obtained as the mean of a very large number of observations.*

* For a proof see Yule and Kendall, 1945: in very many cases the simpler formula for the deviation about the mean may be used to give the s.d. without *significant* error.

The r.m.s. error of the arithmetic mean of N observations is then given by

$$\mu_N = \sqrt{\frac{\Sigma v^2}{N(N-1)}} \, .$$

It must be stated that the value of the r.m.s. error obtained from a small series of observations is not very accurate. With ten observations there is about a 97 % chance that the calculated r.m.s. error is within 50 % of the correct value : with fifty observations there is a 95 % chance that it is within 20 % of the correct value. It is highly desirable, when giving r.m.s. errors or standard deviations of readings, to state the *number of readings* on which the estimate is based.

With a large number of observations the numerical calculation of the squares of the residuals becomes tedious, and it is possible to use a formula based on the properties of the normal error distribution

$$\mu_m = \frac{1 \cdot 25 \, S}{\sqrt{N(N-1)}} \quad \text{(Peters's formula.)}$$

where S denotes the sum of all the residuals, taken as positive without regard to their real signs.

2.7 The Rejection of Observations

Observations which are distributed according to the normal law of errors show a very small number of large residuals. This is in spite of the fact that the error function goes only asymptotically to zero ; numerical values of the probabilities are obtainable from Table 2.1. There has been considerable controversy about what should be done with observations whose residuals are too large to appear with reasonable probability, and several criteria have been devised for their rejection, see e.g. Chauvenet's criterion in Worthing and Geffner 1943. None of these appears to be in general use, but the following simple rule has been recommended : Reject observations for which the residual about the mean is greater than 5 times the probable error (say 3·5 times the r.m.s. error), and examine the circumstances of observations which give residuals of more than 3·5 times the probable error (say 2·5 times the r.m.s. error). Reject these if the circumstances appear suspicious. These numbers correspond to probabilities of about 0·001, 0·02 respectively.

2.8   The Combination of Errors

The result of an experiment is usually obtained by combining arithmetically a number of observations of different quantities, and we must consider the precision of a function of several variables, each carrying an error.

If A is a linear function of the observed quantities $a_1 a_2 \ldots$ which are affected by normally distributed errors with r.m.s. values $e_1 e_2 \ldots$, and we have

$$A = c_1 a_1 + c_2 a_2 + \ldots$$

then it may be shown that the error in A also has a normal distribution with r.m.s. error E where

$$E^2 = c_1^2 e_1^2 + c_2^2 e_2^2 + \ldots$$

If the functional relation between A and $a_1 a_2 \ldots$ is not linear, the same analysis may be used to deal with small errors, for if

$$A = A(a_1 a_2 \ldots)$$

$$\delta A = \frac{\partial A}{\partial a_1} \delta a_1 + \frac{\partial A}{\partial a_2} \delta a_2 + \ldots$$

and

$$E^2 = c_1^2 e_1^2 + c_2^2 e_2^2 + \ldots$$

where

$$c_n = \frac{\partial A}{\partial a_n}.$$

Table 2.2 gives the results of applying these calculations to simple and important functions.

It is clear from the form of these equations:

(*a*) If the observations enter more or less symmetrically into the result, but have different r.m.s. errors, the largest r.m.s. error will tend to dominate the result, and particular attention should be paid to reducing it.

(*b*) If the result depends particularly on observations of one quantity, i.e. if $\dfrac{\partial A}{\partial a_1}$ is large, as, for example, when a_1

TABLE 2.2

Combination of errors in certain cases, where A is the result obtained by combining the quantities a_1 a_2 a_3 . . . which are affected by normal errors with r.m.s. values e_1 e_2 e_3 . . . E is the r.m.s. error to be assigned to A

(a) Sum

$$A = a_1 + a_2 + a_3, \ldots$$
$$E^2 = e_1{}^2 + e_2{}^2 + e_3{}^2 \ldots$$

(b) Linear combination

$$A = c_1 a_1 + c_2 a_2 \ldots$$
$$E^2 = c_1{}^2 e_1{}^2 + c_2{}^2 e_2{}^2 \ldots$$

(c) Product

$$A = a_1 \times a_2 \times a_3 \ldots$$

In this case we apply the result of § 2.8 to the logarithms and obtain

$$\frac{E^2}{A^2} = \frac{e_1{}^2}{a_1{}^2} + \frac{e_2{}^2}{a_2{}^2} + \ldots$$

which implies that the square of the *percentage* error is the sum of the squares of the percentage errors of the factors.

(d) Sum of Powers

$$A = a_1{}^p + a_2{}^q \ldots$$
$$E^2 = (p_1 a_1{}^{(p_1 - 1)})^2 e_1{}^2 + \ldots$$

(a) Product of Powers

$$A = a_1{}^p a_2{}^q \ldots$$
$$\frac{E^2}{A^2} = p^2 \frac{e_1{}^2}{a_1{}^2} + q^2 \frac{e_2{}^2}{a_2{}^2} + \ldots$$

enters the final equation as a high power, the error of a_1 will tend to dominate the result, and particular attention should be paid to reducing it.

These considerations are often important in planning an experiment and in choosing apparatus. It is simply wasting effort to push one measurement, say a weighing, to a very high degree of precision if the result of the experiment is dominated by another measurement.

2.9 An Application of Least Squares—fitting a Relation to Experimental Results

The following problem often appears in working out the results of an experiment: One variable x is given a series of values in the course of the experiment and the consequent values of another variable y are measured. The values of x,

21

y or both are affected by errors of normal type, but the mathematical form of the relation between x, y is assumed to be known. What are the best values to take for the parameters in the relation ? A simple example occurs in an attempt to find the effect of barometric pressure (B) on cosmic ray intensity (I) at ground level. For ordinary barometric changes (which are small compared with the pressure) there is good reason to assume a linear relation,

$$I = I_0\{1 - \alpha(B - B_0)\}$$

but single experimental values of I are affected by serious errors of more or less normal type.

In ordinary laboratory cases of this kind of relation, the values of x, y may be plotted and the best curve drawn through them by eye. A valuable technical device in the linear case is to stretch a thread over the points and to move it until it lies evenly among them ; if a ruler is used, it obscures points on one side of the line and tends to a false balance of errors. There is a tendency, which should be guarded against, to give undue weight to the end points of the set, when aligning the thread or drawing the line.

This method of fitting a relation by curve drawing can be used when the relation between the variables is not linear, but it is preferable in such cases to plot related variables chosen to give a nearly linear plot. It may be desirable to use logarithms of one variable (in the case of a nearly logarithmic or exponential relation), or of both (in cases where a power law is a good approximation).

Logarithmic plotting is useful in any case where the variables cover a very wide range. It is then convenient to plot on semi-logarithmic or logarithmic paper in which one or both co-ordinate axes have divisions numbered according to the natural numbers but placed according to their logarithms. Such paper is obtainable with one, two or more cycles, each corresponding to a power of 10.

The " eye " method works well when there is a small number of points of fairly high precision. Each point is often the result of repeated measurement and some guidance in drawing the line can be obtained by plotting the points as crosses with arms equal to the r.m.s. error of the observations ; in other cases the arms may be drawn equal to some *a priori* estimate of the error involved.

When there are a large number of points, each of low precision, the eye method becomes uncertain, and it is better to use the method of least squares, provided that the errors are really of random type. The method used depends on the assumption that the best approximation is that which minimises the sum of the squares of the deviations between the values of the variables actually observed and those given by the functional relation adopted.

In many important cases the values of one variable (x) are known accurately, and the observations of the other (y) are subject to random errors. The method of least squares then proceeds in principle.

(*a*) Assume a functional relation $y = f(x)$ with undetermined constants $A_1 A_2 \ldots$, and calculate the values of $f(x_1), f(x_2)$, etc.

(*b*) Form the differences $y_1 - f(x_1)$ etc. which will contain $A_1, A_2 \ldots$, and calculate the sum of the squares of these differences.

(*c*) The method assumes that the best values of $A_1 A_2 \ldots$ are those which make this sum a minimum. If we differentiate the sum partially with respect to $A_1 A_2 \ldots$ and equate the partial differential coefficients to zero, we obtain equations containing $A_1 A_2 \ldots$, which may be solved for these unknowns. These are called the " normal equations ".

For the simple case where the relation between y and x is assumed linear, and the values of x are assumed accurately known, it is found that :

(*a*) the best line passes through the centre of gravity of the N points $(x_1 y_1)$ etc., i.e. through the point

$$\bar{x} = \frac{\Sigma x_n}{N} \qquad \bar{y} = \frac{\Sigma y_n}{N}$$

(*b*) the best slope is given by

$$\frac{\Sigma(x_n - \bar{x})(y_n - \bar{y})}{\Sigma(x_n - \bar{x})^2} .$$

This is equivalent to

$$\frac{\Sigma x_n y_n - N\bar{x}\bar{y}}{\Sigma x_n^2 - N\bar{x}^2}$$

—a form more convenient for calculation in most cases.

This result would be applicable to the cosmic-ray problem quoted above, where the barometric pressures are known with ample accuracy and the cosmic-ray measurements are affected by random variations.

When the relation adopted is more complicated than a linear one, the setting up and solution of the normal equations is a rather laborious matter. The practical calculation is described in the Appendix to this chapter, and it is there shown that it is sometimes possible to choose functions which can be fitted to data without the use of normal equations.

2.10   Other Applications of Least Squares

A rather different use of the principle arises when we have a number of experimentally determined relations involving unknowns fewer in number than the relations. Because of experimental errors, the equations (called conditioned equations) will be numerically inconsistent, and the problem is to find the " best " values of the unknowns. The method of least squares is greatly used by surveyors and astronomers for dealing with problems of this kind, and they form the main content of many text-books of the method.

If the set of equations is linear, we may write

$$a_{11}x_1 + a_{12}x_2 + \ldots = A_1$$
$$a_{21}x_1 + a_{22}x_2 + \ldots = A_2$$

etc.

where $x_1 \ldots$ are the unknowns, $A_1 \ldots$ are the observations. These may be re-written as a consistent set

$$a_{11}x_1 + a_{12}x_2 + \ldots - A_1 = D_1$$
$$a_{21}x_1 + a_{22}x_2 + \ldots - A_2 = D_2$$

where the $D_1 \ldots$ represent unknown adjustments which must be added to the observed quantities $A_1 \ldots$ to make the equations consistent. It is now assumed that the best values of the x's make ΣD^2 a minimum, and the normal equations are formed by differentiating ΣD^2 partially with respect to x_1, x_2, etc. These normal equations can then be solved for x_1, x_2, etc.

In the linear case, it may be shown that the first normal equation can be obtained very simply from the equations

$$a_{11}x_1 + a_{12}x_2 + \ldots - A_1 = 0, \text{ etc.}$$

by multiplying each equation by the coefficient of x_1 (a_{11}, etc.) which occurs in it and adding all together.

The second, third, normal equations are obtained similarly by multiplying by the coefficients of x_2 x_3. . . .

If the equations are not linear, the principle is the same, but the construction of the normal equations is more complicated. It may be found, e.g. in Worthing and Geffner 1943, and in any text-book of least squares. The method has been applied, notably by Birge, to find the best values of the fundamental constants of atomic physics (e, h, etc.) from the great mass of experimental results which involve combinations of these quantities. (This work is discussed briefly in Worthing and Geffner, *op. cit.*, results to 1947 given in DuMond and Cohen 1948.)

2.11 Non-Gaussian Distributions

It has been stated (§ 2.6) that the validity of the normal error law for a particular distribution is a matter to be tested by experience and not assumed *a priori*. An example will show that the Gaussian law is not always applicable. If the diameters of a number of spherical water drops follow the normal distribution, which is symmetrical about the mean value, the masses of the drops must be spread out in a distribution which is not symmetrical and cannot be Gaussian. Levy (1944) quotes some arguments of engineering interest, in which it appears that the distribution in time of failures of a compound machine is far from Gaussian, even if the failures of elementary parts follow a normal distribution. The importance of the normal law is that it is often a very good representation of small errors of the kind met in physical experiment and that the simple mathematical results to which it leads are often good approximations even if the distributions concerned are not exactly Gaussian.

2.12 The Poisson Distribution

A non-Gaussian distribution of special interest in physics is that which gives the frequency distribution, among equal time intervals, of events which occur at random in time. This is directly applicable to counting experiments in nuclear

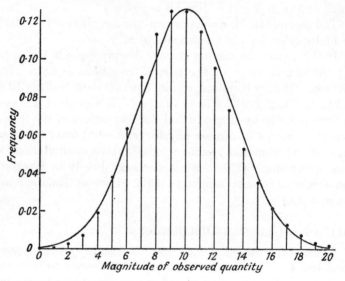

FIG. 2.5 Frequency diagram corresponding to a Poisson distribution for $Z = 10$ (shown by dots) and Gaussian distribution function centred on 10 with $\sigma = \sqrt{10}$

physics and other fields. It is shown in a note at the end of this chapter that if, taking the mean of a large number of equal intervals, Z counts occur in a certain time interval, the probability that r counts occur in this interval is

$$\frac{Z^r}{r!}e^{-z}$$

This is called the Poisson formula. The Poisson distribution is very skew for small values of Z, but for large values of

Z, the curve near the maximum closely resembles a Gaussian curve with standard deviation $\sqrt{Z}$. Fig. 2.5 shows a Poisson frequency diagram calculated for $Z = 10$ and on the same axes a normal error curve centred on $Z = 10$ and having a standard deviation $\sigma = \sqrt{10}$. The Gaussian curve is here a fair approximation to the Poisson distribution, and the approximation becomes very close indeed for larger values of Z.

If N particles are counted in an experimental period the reliability of the result is indicated by the standard deviation $\sqrt{N}$ associated with it, and in any ordinary case Table 2.1 (calculated for the normal distribution) gives sufficiently accurately the chance that in any given count the deviation from the true value exceeds $\sqrt{N}$, $2\sqrt{N}$ . . . , etc.

2.13 Mathematical Note on the Statistics of Counting. (Poisson Distribution)

Suppose the mean rate of counting is N per sec. In a time interval t, the average number of counts is $Nt = Z$. It is required to find the probability P_r that exactly r counts appear in the interval t. The time t may be divided into n equal sub-intervals; the probability of a count appearing in any particular one of these sub-intervals is $p = \dfrac{Nt}{n}$, which is small if n is large. The chance of two or three counts appearing in a sub-interval depends on higher powers of $\dfrac{Nt}{n}$, and may be made as small as we please compared with p by making n large.

The probability that any given sub-interval will contain a count is p; the probability that it will not contain a count is $(1 - p)$. Now the probability that the first sub-interval of the n will contain a count and that none of the others will contain a count is $p(1 - p)^{n-1}$, and this represents one of n equally probable ways in which one count only can appear in the whole interval.

The value of P for $r = 1$ is therefore $np(1 - p)^{n-1}$.

Similarly, the probability that (say) the first r sub-intervals contain a count and the remaining $(n - r)$ be empty is

27

$p^r(1-p)^{n-r}$, and this is one of ^nC_r equally probable ways in which r counts (only) can be distributed over the whole interval.

We have then

$$P_r = {}^nC_r p^r (1-p)^{n-r}$$

$$= \frac{n \cdot (n-1) \ldots (n-r+1)}{r!} p^r (1-p)^{n-r}$$

which becomes for $n \geqslant r$ and p small compared with unity

$$\frac{n^r}{r!} p^r (1-p)^n$$

$$= \frac{Z^r}{r!}\left(1 - np + \frac{n \cdot (n-1)}{2!} p^2 - \ldots\right)$$

$$= \frac{Z^r}{r!} e^{-Z}$$

since n is very large and $Z = np$.

This is the "Bateman" formula giving the probability of actually making r counts in an interval in which the expected (average) number is Z.

The mean square deviation of the values of r, obtained in a large number of trials from the mean Z, is

$$\sum_{r=0}^{r=\infty} \frac{Z^r}{r!} e^{-Z} (Z-r)^2 = \sum \frac{Z^r}{r!} e^{-Z} (Z^2 - 2Zr + r^2)$$

$$= Z^2 e^{-Z} \sum \frac{Z^r}{r!} - 2Z e^{-Z} \sum \frac{rZ^r}{r!} + e^{-Z} \sum \frac{r^2 Z^r}{r!}$$

$$= Z^2 - 2Z^2 + e^{-Z}\left(Z + \frac{4Z^2}{2!} + \ldots \frac{r^2 Z^r}{r!} + \ldots\right)$$

$$= -Z^2 + e^{-Z}Z\left(1 + \frac{2Z}{1!} + \ldots \frac{rZ^{r-1}}{(r-1)!} + \ldots\right)$$

$$= -Z^2 + e^{-Z}Ze^Z + e^{-Z}Z^2\left(1 + Z + \ldots \frac{Z^{r-2}}{(r-2)!} + \ldots\right)$$

$$= Z.$$

The r.m.s. deviation of the values of r from Z is then $\sqrt{Z}$.

APPENDIX

These notes are intended to provide a guide to and illustration of some of the simpler calculations suggested by Chapter II. Though not meant to be exhaustive, they are supplemented by reference to texts which, together, contain all the information necessary for calculations likely to arise in experimental physics.

2.14 General Principles

Numerical calculations should be planned in detail, with the object of reducing as far as possible the number of individual operations and of presenting the results in a convenient tabular form. Not only does this save time, but it can do a great deal to reduce the frequency of accidental errors. The latter are especially prone to occur in reading from tables and in writing down the results of intermediate operations.

The following suggestions may not be out of place. It is convenient to use paper ruled in $\frac{1}{4}$ in. squares, so that the ruling of columns is made unnecessary and the positions of decimal points more easily ascertained. Long columns of figures are much more accurately handled if they are broken up into blocks of four or five numbers. The familiar confusion between the written characters 1 and 7 for the digits one and seven may be avoided by the use of the continental seven ($\bar{7}$).

The best methods of calculation are self-checking, in the sense that accidental errors prolong the process but do not affect the accuracy of the result. The " relaxation " method for the solution of linear differential equations is a typical example (Southwell 1941). If such a method is not available, it is wise to devise some artificial check other than a mere repetition of the calculation.

Often a column of numbers obtained by calculation shows unexpected irregular variation between one number and the next. This variation is more apparent on tabulating the differences between neighbours in the column, and is due to the presence of gross errors of calculation. The technique may be extended, by the use of finite differences of higher orders, to discover relatively small errors (Whittaker and Robinson 1944, Ch. VI ; Milne 1949, Ch. VI).

A clear idea of the number of significant figures that must be retained at each stage of a calculation must be formed. Especially when using a machine it is tempting to carry as many figures as possible. Not only does this consume time, but it adds to the danger of making mistakes. It should be remembered that the number of significant figures in a number y, and one derived from it, say e^y, are not always the same. Thus if $y = 1 \cdot 32 \times 10^{-2}$ (3 significant figures) $e^y = 1 \cdot 1034$ (five significant figures).

The representation of numbers by a certain finite number of digits—" rounding-off "—can lead to a small error in calculation. Thus if $x = 1 \cdot 7305 \ldots$ and $y = 7 \cdot 3625 \ldots$, these are rounded off to four significant figures by taking x equal to $1 \cdot 731$ and $y = 7 \cdot 363$. The sum $x + y$ is now calculated as $9 \cdot 094$, which differs from the rounded-off value of the true sum—$9 \cdot 093$—by $0 \cdot 001$. On account of this rounding-off error, it is customary to carry one extra digit in a calculation.

Particular care should be taken to recognise the existence of cumulative errors inherent in a calculation and usually arising in the subtraction of roughly equal numbers. A succession of such operations can considerably reduce the significance of a result, and should suggest the possibility of modifying the procedure so that the difficulty is avoided.

The common aids to numerical calculation differ considerably in scope, accuracy and convenience ; their merits are briefly compared below.

2.15 Logarithm Tables

Tables of $\log_{10} x$ to four and seven figures are commonly available. They should never be used for multiplication and division when a calculating machine is available, because of the great danger of misreading them and the excessive expenditure of time involved. Interpolation in 7-figure tables is especially tedious.

The rounding-off of figures in a table of logarithms may result in appreciable error in the result of a calculation where several logarithms are combined. Thus in calculating

10·95 × 14·75 with 4-figure tables, the result 160·4 differs from the true product by 0·1. The error varies with the part of the table used.

2.16 Other Mathematical Tables

A great number of other functions have been tabulated. On occasion it is possible to simplify a calculation by the use of a relatively unknown table of an unusual function. To cite an almost trivial example, values of $\sin x$ and $\cos x$ for values of x which are specified in radians may be especially suitable for some purposes. Barlow's tables of powers of x are invaluable. A comprehensive index to published tables of functions is available (Fletcher, Miller and Rosenhead, 1946).

2.17 Slide Rules

Ten-inch rules are cheap, quick and portable, but only able to deal with numbers of three significant figures. More accurate instruments of circular or helical form and equivalent to 100 or 1000 inches of rule can deal with numbers of four and five figures respectively. They are, however, slow and expensive.

2.18 Calculating Machines

The following comments concern the practical use of ordinary desk calculating machines; no mention is made of those designed for special purposes (e.g. harmonic analysis, solution of simultaneous equations). It is well to remember that the manufacturer's handbook supplied with each machine provides an invaluable appraisal of that machine's performance. Machines differ considerably in their fitness for a specified purpose. The following considerations are relevant.

(i) *Keyboard and Setting*

The ease with which a number may be accurately placed on the keyboard and so transferred to the machine is important because this process can lead to accidental error. Many hand-operated machines are unsatisfactory in this respect; that type of keyboard upon which the number is typed out, digit by digit, is probably the most accurate.

(ii) *Scope*

The simplest type of machine is designed to perform the addition or subtraction of two or more numbers ; multiplication of a number by a small integer is also rapidly accomplished. Such adding machines have the advantage of cheapness and speed in operation.

Other machines are capable of multiplication and division as well as the processes of adding machines. They are able to form the sum of a long series of products directly. Division is always a slow process, so that if a series of quotients has to be obtained with the *same* divisor, it is good practice to form the reciprocal of this divisor and to multiply this into the dividend to give each quotient.

That type of machine in which the result of each operation is printed, on a roll of paper, offers several advantages. Accidental errors in recording results are eliminated, the results are presented in a form which allows them to be checked conveniently, and a permanent record is provided.

(iii) *Computers*

Workers in many laboratories now have access to electronic computers of great power and considerable versatility. These machines should be used if possible for any extensive calculating routine, and in some types of experiment it is possible to record the experimental results automatically in a form which can be assimilated directly by an electronic computer, e.g. punched teleprinter tape, pulse-coded magnetic tape.

2.19 Curve Fitting

Let there be N pairs of observations of two related experimental quantities y and x with results y_n and x_n ($n = 1, 2, 3 \ldots N$). The least-squares procedure described in § 2.9 makes it possible to determine the parameters in any function $y = f(x)$ so that this represents most closely the relation between the experimental quantities.

The need to do this may arise in two different ways. Either the form of $f(x)$ may be suggested by theoretical arguments and the data used to discover the values of the parameters, or it may be necessary to represent the data by a mathematical function in order that they may be handled conveniently. In the latter case the choice of $f(x)$ is to some extent arbitrary and must be decided with regard to any theoretical or intuitive ideas that may be available.

It should be remembered that, even though the polynomial function

$$f(x) = a_0 + a_1x + \ldots a_mx^m \qquad . \qquad . \quad (1)$$

can fit any set of data over a restricted range of x by taking m to be sufficiently large, other functions (e.g. e^{ax^2}, e^{ax}, $a \log x$, x^a) may be more appropriate. These can often be reduced to simpler linear or quadratic forms.

The most important forms of $f(x)$ are those in which the unknown parameters are involved linearly and in such cases the problem may be reduced to the solution of a set of linear simultaneous equations. These contain as many unknowns as there are undetermined parameters in the function, and are called the *normal equations*.

The following calculations illustrate the application of this method to certain common forms of $f(x)$. The reliability of the procedure is discussed in § 2.23 below.

2.20 Polynomial Form

If $f(x)$ has the form indicated in equation (1) and the degree m is specified, the normal equations by which the parameters $a_0, a_1, a_2 \ldots a_m$ are determined become

$$s_0a_0 + s_1a_1 + \ldots + s_ma_m = t_0$$
$$s_1a_0 + s_2a_1 + \ldots + s_{m+1}a_m = t_1$$
$$\cdot \quad \cdot \quad \cdot \quad \cdot \quad \cdot \quad \cdot \quad \cdot$$
$$\cdot \quad \cdot \quad \cdot \quad \cdot \quad \cdot \quad \cdot \quad \cdot$$
$$s_ma_0 + s_{m+1}a_1 + \ldots + s_{2m}a_m = t_m$$

Here the abbreviations

$$s_k = \sum_{n=1}^{N} x_n{}^k$$
$$t_k = \sum x_n{}^k y_n$$

have been used.

Table 2.3 shows how a fourth-degree polynomial may be fitted to the data of Barschall, Bockelman, Peterson and Adair (*Phys. Rev.*, **76**, 1146, 1949) concerning the total cross-section (y) for the interaction between neutrons and lead nuclei at different neutron energies (x). The first and second columns display the results of 27 pairs of measurements of y and x.

To avoid the occurrence of large numbers, it is convenient to refer the measured values of x to an origin near the centre of the range of x at 520 keV., i.e. to put $X = (x - 520)10^{-2}$. The values of X obtained in this manner are shown in Col. 3 of Table 2.3. The fourth, fifth and sixth columns contain the squares, cubes and fourth powers of the entries in Col. 3. The co-efficients s_0, s_1, . . . s_4 are obtained from these by adding up the respective columns; the others, s_5, s_6, . . . s_8 and t_0, t_1 . . . t_4, are also obtained from these columns. Thus s_8 results by adding together the squares of the numbers contained in Col. 6.

A check on the accuracy of the calculation is provided by verifying that relations like

$$\sum_{n=1}^{N} (1 + X_n^2)^4 = s_8 + 4s_6 + 6s_4 + 4s_2 + N \qquad . \quad (2)$$

are satisfied by the values computed for s_1, s_2, . . . , etc. Equation 2 depends on the identity

$$(1 + X_n^2)^4 = X_n^8 + 4X_n^6 + 6X_n^4 + 4X_n^2 + 1$$

The left-hand side of (2) has been evaluated in Table 2.3 by computing the values of $(1 + X_n^2)^4$ and adding the results. Other relations of this type may be used for checking purposes.

A solution of the normal equations is shown in Table 2.5. The resulting polynomial may be found in the last line of Table 2.3—the significance of each parameter is discussed in § 2.23 below.

It is necessary to remember that each of the quantities x and y is subject to random errors of measurement. In this present set of data, the observed values of y, y_n, are estimated to be normally distributed about their (unknown) true value with standard error 0·25 barns.

TABLE 2.3

1	2	3	4	5	6	7	8
$y \times 10^{-1}$ (barns)	x (keV.)	$X =$ $(x - 520) \times 10^{-2}$	X^2	X^3	X^4	$f(X_n)$	$y_n - f(X_n)$
5·40	450	− 0·70	0·490	− 0·343	0·240	4·69	+ 0·71
4·70	457	− 0·63	0·396	− 0·250	0·157	4·56	+ 0·14
4·80	463	− 0·57	0·324	− 0·185	0·105	4·51	+ 0·29
4·90	470	− 0·50	0·250	− 0·125	0·062	4·50	+ 0·40
4·60	475	− 0·45	0·202	− 0·091	0·041	4·53	+ 0·07
4·20	482	− 0·38	0·144	− 0·054	0·020	4·59	− 0·39
3·80	488	− 0·32	0·102	− 0·032	0·010	4·66	− 0·86
3·40	495	− 0·25	0·062	− 0·015	0·003	4·76	− 1·36
3·40	502	− 0·18	0·032	− 0·005	0·001	4·87	− 1·47
3·40	508	− 0·12	0·014	− 0·001	—	4·96	− 1·52
3·80	513	− 0·07	0·004	—	—	5·04	− 1·24
4·60	515	− 0·05	0·002	—	—	5·07	− 0·47
4·50	519	− 0·01	—	—	—	5·13	− 0·63
5·80	522	+ 0·02	—	—	—	5·17	+ 0·63
7·80	524	+ 0·04	0·002	—	—	5·19	+ 2·61
8·40	527	+ 0·07	0·005	—	—	5·23	+ 3·17
7·20	530	+ 0·10	0·010	+ 0·001	—	5·27	+ 1·93
5·90	533	+ 0·13	0·016	+ 0·002	—	5·30	+ 0·60
5·40	538	+ 0·18	0·032	+ 0·005	—	5·35	+ 0·05
5·50	540	+ 0·20	0·040	+ 0·008	0·001	5·37	+ 0·13
4·80	546	+ 0·26	0·067	+ 0·017	0·004	5·43	− 0·63
9·70	530	+ 0·30	0·090	+ 0·027	0·008	5·46	− 0·76
4·70	553	+ 0·33	0·108	+ 0·035	0·012	5·49	− 0·79
5·20	559	+ 0·39	0·152	+ 0·059	0·023	5·54	− 0·34
5·90	565	+ 0·45	0·202	+ 0·091	0·041	5·59	+ 0·31
5·30	571	+ 0·51	0·260	+ 0·132	0·067	5·65	− 0·35
5·50	580	+ 0·60	0·360	+ 0·216	0·129	5·77	+ 0·27

$$S_1 = - 0·6500 \qquad S_5 = - 0·2418$$
$$S_2 = + 3·3753 \qquad S_6 = + 0·3213$$
$$S_3 = - 0·5086 \qquad S_7 = - 0·2807$$
$$S_4 = + 0·9322 \qquad S_8 = + 0·1236$$

$$t_0 = + 137·60 \qquad t_1 = + 0·2500$$
$$t_2 = + 16·851 \qquad t_3 = - 2·1673$$
$$t_4 = + 4·7499$$

From Table 2.5 the resulting polynomial is
$$y \cdot 10^{-1} = 5·14 + 1·37X - 0·96X^2 - 0·94X^3 + 2·72X^4$$

2.21 Trigonometric Approximation

In some circumstances it is natural to expect that y is a periodic function of the quantity x and that this is revealed by the experimental observations y_n and x_n. Then, with a period of length $2L$, it is necessary to use a function $y = f(x)$ of the form

$$f(x) = a_0 + a_1 \cos \frac{\pi x}{L} + \ldots + a_p \cos \frac{p\pi x}{L}$$
$$+ b_1 \sin \frac{\pi x}{L} + \ldots + b_p \sin \frac{p\pi x}{L} \quad (3)$$

consisting of a finite number of terms of a Fourier series with unknown co-efficients a_i and b_i. Most often the data represent the variation of the quantity y with *time;* thus the variation of geophysical quantities with time is often found to be of this form, with a period equal to the length of a solar day. (Atomic scattering experiments provide data in which x is the angle of deflection.)

If the values x_n have been chosen arbitrarily, the normal equations are so difficult to obtain that they are of no practical use. Uniformly spaced abscissae, on the other hand, lead to equations which are especially simple and which form the basis of practical *harmonic analysis*. Suppose that the N observations x_n lie between 0 and $2L$ in such a way that they take the values $0, \dfrac{L}{m}, \dfrac{2L}{m}, \ldots L, (m+1)\dfrac{L}{m}, \ldots (2m-1)\dfrac{L}{m}$. ($N$ is even and $N = 2m$.) Then the co-efficients a_k and b_k are determined, by least squares, to be

$$a_0 = \frac{1}{m} \sum_{n=1}^{N} y_n$$

$$a_k = \frac{1}{2m} \sum_{n=1}^{N} y_n \cos \frac{k\pi x_n}{L}; \quad k = 1, 2, \ldots p \quad (4)$$

$$b_k = \frac{1}{2m} \sum_{n=1}^{N} y_n \sin \frac{k\pi x_n}{L}; \quad k = 1, 2, \ldots q$$

Data which extend over several periods (and which are uniformly spaced) may be handled by taking as y_n the mean of all values of y corresponding to the abscissae x_n, $x_n + L$, $x_n + 2L$, . . . etc.   In this way the data of Table 2.4, representing the variation of cosmic ray intensity with time of day,

TABLE 2.4

Harmonic analysis of percentage deviation of cosmic ray intensity from the daily mean. Data due to Dr. H. Elliott. Col. 2 are the cosmic ray intensities at the times shown in Col. 1.   The last row of the table contains the numerical values of the four constants a_1, a_2, b_1, b_2.   The estimated standard error of each observation of y is 0·020

1	2	3	4	5	6	7	8	9
Time t	y	θ (deg.) $= \dfrac{\pi x}{L} \cdot \dfrac{360}{2\pi}$	$\sin\theta$	$\sin 2\theta$	$\cos\theta$	$\cos 2\theta$	$f(\theta)$	$y - f(\theta)$
0·00	− 0·164	0	0·000	0·000	1·000	1·000	− 0·163	− 0·001
2·00	− 0·121	30	0·500	0·866	0·866	0·500	− 0·117	− 0·004
4·00	− 0·089	60	0·866	0·866	0·500	− 0·500	− 0·090	+ 0·002
6·00	− 0·086	90	1·000	0·000	0·000	− 1·000	− 0·108	+ 0·022
8·00	− 0·145	120	0·866	− 0·866	− 0·800	− 0·500	− 0·140	− 0·005
10·00	− 0·026	150	0·500	− 0·866	− 0·866	0·500	− 0·041	+ 0·015
12·00	+ 0·106	180	0·000	0·000	− 1·000	1·000	+ 0·113	− 0·007
14·00	+ 0·275	210	− 0·500	0·866	− 0·866	0·500	+ 0·255	+ 0·020
16·00	+ 0·255	240	− 0·866	0·866	− 0·500	− 0·500	+ 0·278	− 0·023
18·00	+ 0·159	270	− 1·000	0·000	0·000	− 1·000	+ 0·154	+ 0·005
20·00	− 0·009	300	− 0·866	− 0·866	0·500	− 0·500	− 0·022	+ 0·013
22·00	− 0·153	330	− 0·500	− 0·866	0·866	0·500	− 0·147	− 0·006
			b_1	b_2	a_1	a_2		
			− 0·133	+ 0·094	− 0·138	− 0·205		

were compiled from a whole year's observation of cosmic ray intensity at 2-hourly intervals by averaging over the year the intensity at each of the 12 hours concerned.   Equations (4) are applied directly to concentrated data of this kind.

The procedure becomes especially simple when N takes one of the values 6, 8, 12, 24, . . . etc., for in those cases many of the numerical values of $\cos\dfrac{k\pi x_n}{L}$ and $\sin\dfrac{k\pi x_n}{L}$ occur repeatedly.

C   37

A calculation of this kind is shown in Table 2.4.   Col. 2 contains the percentage deviation from the daily mean of the cosmic ray intensity at each of the times indicated in Col. 1. (These have been compiled from a whole year's observations in the manner explained above.)   There are grounds for expecting that the intensity will fluctuate with periods of 24 and 12 hours, i.e. that the co-efficients a_1, b_1, a_2 and b_2 of (4) will provide a satisfactory representation of the data.*

Col. 3 contains values of $\dfrac{\pi x_n}{L}$ and the next four columns contain values of $\sin \dfrac{k\pi x_n}{L}$ and $\cos \dfrac{k\pi x_n}{L}$ for $k = 1$ and 2.   The co-efficients have been computed directly, on a calculating machine, from formulae (4).   Thus a_2 has been obtained by adding together (taking account of sign) the products of corresponding elements in Cols. 2 and 3.

Formulae (4) are closely related to those for the Fourier co-efficients A, B, of a continuous function $g(x)$ with period $2L$: viz.

$$A_k = \frac{1}{2L} \int_0^{2L} g(x) \cos \frac{k\pi x}{L} dx, \text{ etc. .} \qquad . \qquad . \quad (5)$$

In fact, A and B are determined by the condition that the integral of the squared deviation

$$\left\{ g(x) - \left(A_0 + A_1 \cos \frac{\pi x}{L} + \ldots + B_1 \sin \frac{\pi x}{L} + \ldots \right) \right\}^2$$

shall be minimum.   If

$$I = \int_0^{2L} \left(g(x) - A_0 - A_1 \cos \frac{\pi x}{L} - B_1 \sin \frac{\pi x}{L} - \ldots \right)^2 dx$$

$$= \int_0^{2L} g^2(x) dx - 2 \sum_{k=0}^{\infty} A_k \int_0^{2L} g(x) \cos \frac{k\pi x}{L} dx$$

$$- 2 \sum_{k=1}^{\infty} B_k \int_0^{2L} g(x) \sin \frac{k\pi x}{L} dx$$

$$+ \sum_{k=0}^{\infty} A_k^2 \int_0^{2L} \cos^2 \frac{k\pi x}{L} dx + \sum_{k=1}^{\infty} B_k^2 \int_0^{2L} \sin^2 \frac{k\pi x}{L} dx$$

* In this example a_0 vanishes because the data are deviations from the mean value.

its minimum is determined by $\dfrac{\partial I}{\partial A_k} = \dfrac{\partial I}{\partial B_k} = 0$, i.e. by

$$- 2 \int_0^{2L} g(x) \cos \frac{k\pi x}{L} dx + 2A_k \int_0^{2L} \cos \frac{k\pi x}{L} dx = 0$$

with a similar condition involving B_k. These lead directly to equations (5).

Often the time-fluctuation of y may be the result of two or more causes each of which, alone, would produce a variation of characteristic period unrelated to that of the others. Thus the height of the tide at a fixed place depends upon the position of the moon and, to a lesser extent, upon that of the sun. These are both periodic functions of the time with approximate periods of 25 and 24 hours respectively. Thus it is necessary to fit a set of tidal data with a function of the form

$$f(t) = A + a \cos \frac{2\pi t}{25} + b \sin \frac{2\pi t}{25} + c \cos \frac{2\pi t}{24} + d \sin \frac{2\pi t}{24}$$

($t =$ time in hours).

Other terms are added if they are necessary. The normal equations have to be determined and solved in the usual way, and are often complicated.

The time-variation of experimental quantities is often too complicated to be analysed by these simple methods. Thus this data may represent the superposition of periodic and aperiodic (" trend ") effects, or relatively slow random fluctuations of Brownian type may be evident. Sometimes the characteristic periods themselves are unknown, and have to be determined from the data before these can be analysed. For a discussion of these matters the reader is referred to one of the comprehensive texts on statistics (Kendall 1946, Vol. II, p. 29).

2.22   Other Forms of $f(x)$

Other forms of $f(x)$ are convenient for special purposes. Thus a linear combination of Legendre polynomials may be used with advantage in the analysis of scattering data and, occasionally, in connection with tidal observations. The Gram-Charlier approximation, depending on the Gaussian function $e^{-x^2/2}$ and its derivatives, is convenient if $f(x)$ is required to approach zero quickly as n becomes large. Details of these methods may be found in specialised texts.

The discerning reader will have recognised that the procedure of harmonic analysis (§ 2.21) is considerably simpler than that of § 2.20, in that the parameters are directly expressed in algebraic form and do not have to be obtained by the numerical solution of normal equations. It has the further advantage that additional parameters may be introduced into $f(x)$ without changing the " best " values of previously determined parameters. This depends on the fact that $\cos \dfrac{j\pi x}{L}$ and $\cos \dfrac{k\pi x}{L}$ are " orthogonal ", or that

$$\sum_{n=1}^{N} \cos \frac{j\pi x_n}{L} \cos \frac{k\pi x_n}{L} = 0 \quad \text{if} \quad k \neq j : k, j < \frac{N}{2}$$

An infinite set of polynomials which has this same property with respect to any set of points x_n (not necessarily uniformly spaced) may be constructed. If $f(x)$ is chosen to be a linear combination of such polynomials, many of the advantages of harmonic analysis obtain ; such a choice is entirely equivalent to the original method of § 2.20 (Kendall, 1946, Ch. 29 ; Milne, 1949, p. 265).

2.23   The Significance of Least-Squares Calculations

The result of any calculation of this kind has to be qualified by forming an idea of the significance, or the degree of reliability, of the numerical values assigned to parameters. It may be, for example, that the data are not sufficiently numerous to predict, with any worthwhile degree of certainty, values of the higher parameters in the function $f(x)$. It is necessary to have a method of deciding on the number of parameters * that can be properly used in $f(x)$, and on the uncertainty which is inherent in each of them.

Three practical procedures are described below ; each of them depends on the calculation of the residuals (or deviations) $f(x_n) - y_n$ (see for example, Col. 8 of Table 2.3). It will be assumed that each measurement of y, say y_n, is subject to random errors of standard deviation σ_y, and that errors in the

---

* Clearly this must be less than the number of pairs of observations available as data.

measurement of x may be neglected. These conditions are often satisfied.

The methods of this section are related to the calculation of regression co-efficients (Kendall 1944, Vol. II). In fact, when the errors in y are very large it is not possible to do more than assign a value to that parameter which implies a *linear* relation between x and y—the linear regression co-efficient.

Clearly there is nothing to be gained by using so many parameters that the residuals are consistently *smaller* than the standard deviation σ_y. On the other hand, if the residuals are consistently larger than σ_y, it is to be expected that another parameter could be introduced into $f(x)$ and given some meaning by a least-squares procedure. Thus a qualitative estimate of the reliability of such a calculation may be obtained by comparing the size of the residuals with σ_y.

For example, consider the residuals shown in Col. 8 of Table 2.3. Most of these are much larger than the estimated standard deviation. Thus it is safe to say that a fourth-degree polynomial does not represent the data very well, and that a sixth- or seventh-degree function would be more appropriate.*

This argument may be given quantitative form by the use of Karl Pearson's " chi-square " test. It can be demonstrated (Kendall 1945, Vol. I, p. 305) that, if z_n are the (unknown) true values of which y_n are erroneous estimates, the quantity

$$\chi^2 = \frac{1}{\sigma_y{}^2} \sum_{n=1}^{N} (y_n - z_n)^2$$

has a most probable value N (the number of pairs of observations) and in most cases may be considered to be normally distributed about this value with standard deviation $\sqrt{2N}$. Now the values of $f(x_n)$ given by a least-squares function are intended to be, in the ideal case, equal to the true values z_n. Therefore, in that case, the value of

$$\chi_0{}^2 = \frac{1}{\sigma_y{}^2} \sum_{n=1}^{N} (y_n - f(x_n))^2$$

---

* The data of this example are not well suited to calculation with polynomials—the Gram-Charlier would probably give a better representation with less effort.

has the same behaviour as χ^2, i.e. its most probable value is N, its standard deviation about this $\sqrt{2N}$.

The following statements are now valid. If $\chi_0{}^2$ is found to lie between $N + \sqrt{2N}$ and $N - \sqrt{2N}$, $f(x)$ is a good representation of the data. If $\chi_0{}^2$ is greater than $N + \sqrt{2N}$, another parameter could have been included in $f(x)$. If $\chi_0{}^2$ is less than $N - \sqrt{2N}$, *too many* parameters * have been employed.

The results of the calculation of Table 2.4 may be analysed in this way. From the last column of Table 2.4 and the estimated standard error $(0\cdot014)$ χ^2 is calculated to be $10\cdot01$. This lies between the limits $12 + \sqrt{12}$ and $12 - \sqrt{12}$; it is concluded that the calculation of § 2.21 has included the correct number of parameters.

For small values of N it is necessary to take account of the fact that the distribution of χ^2 is not normal. Tables are available for each value of N less than 30 of the probability $P(\chi^2)$ that χ^2 should exceed certain values on the assumption that its fluctuations are entirely due to random errors. The same information is also available in graphical form (Kendall, 1945, Vol. I, p. 444.1 ; Deming and Birge, 1934).

In the case of the calculation of § 2.21, for example, the tabulated probability that χ^2 is greater than $10\cdot3$ is $0\cdot54$; that it should be less than $10\cdot3$ is $0\cdot46$. Clearly the observed value of χ^2 is very nearly equal to that which would be expected on the assumption that its fluctuations are entirely due to random errors of observation.

For many purposes it is not sufficient to know that the curve fitting process has been stopped at the correct stage ; it may be necessary to have some numerical estimate of the uncertainty, or error, of each parameter a_n. If, for example, $f(x)$ is to be differentiated, it is desirable to have a method of estimating the uncertainty in the derivative caused by the use of calculated values of a_n.

This situation is analogous to that of § 2.5, where it is shown that a good estimate of an unknown quantity is provided by the mean of a number of experimental observations, and

---

* It must be emphasised that small values of $\chi_0{}^2$ are just as undesirable as large ones. They indicate that some of the parameters which have been determined have very little significance.

that the accuracy of this estimate is measured by $\sigma/\sqrt{N}$ (see
p. 13), the " standard error of the mean ". In the present
case the " unknown " is the " true " value, say $a_n{}^0$,of a parameter, and there is available a single estimate of this—the
value a_n obtained by least-squares calculation. The standard
error of a_n may also be calculated from the data if it is assumed
that the calculated values a_n are normally distributed about
the true values $a_n{}^0$ (Kendall, Vol. II, Ch. 18).

Let

$$\omega^2 = \sum_{n=1}^{N} (y_n - f(y_n))^2$$

and h be the number of parameters included in $f(x)$. The
standard error of a will be denoted by σ_a. Two cases arise.

(1) If $f(x)$ is the polynomial of § 2.20 ($h = m + 1$)

$$\sigma_{a_j} = \frac{\omega}{\sqrt{N(N-h)}}\sqrt{\frac{\Delta_{jj}}{\Delta}}$$

where Δ is the determinant,

$$\begin{vmatrix} s_0 & s_1 & \cdots & s_m \\ s_1 & s_2 & \cdots & s_{m+1} \\ & & & \\ s_m & & \cdots & s_{2m} \end{vmatrix}$$ (see p. 33).

and Δ_{jj} that obtained from it by omitting the jth row and the
jth column.

In practice, these determinants may be obtained as by-
products of the numerical solution of the normal equations (c).

(2) If $f(x)$ is a trigonometric function (see § 2.21 ;
$h = p + q + 1$) the standard errors of all co-efficients are the
same, and equal to $N\dfrac{\omega}{\sqrt{2/N - h}}$.

2.24 The Solution of Simultaneous Linear Equations

In this section are described two methods for the numerical
solution of simultaneous equations which are useful in two
different sets of circumstances. Briefly, it may be said that
it is often necessary to supplement the first (" Elimination ",

§ 2.25) by the second (" Relaxation ", § 2.26) ; the necessity for this is described in § 2.27.

That familiar method of the algebra text-books, in which solutions are obtained as the ratio of two determinants, should not be used for numerical calculation when the number of unknowns is greater than two ; for the only satisfactory methods of evaluating determinants involve, in effect, the direct solution of equations.

It is necessary to beware of the occurrence of large inherent errors, which may, in certain rare but unpredictable circumstances, render the results of *any* method of calculation illusory. These are discussed in § 2.27.

Linear equations which arise in vibrational problems (and many other important situations) take the form of the following examples :

$$(l_{11} - \lambda)x_1 + l_{12}x_2 = 0$$
$$l_{21}x_1 + (l_{22} - \lambda)x_2 = 0$$

They are homogeneous, but contain a parameter λ (the " eigenvalue ") which has to be determined in order that the equations be satisfied.* Such equations are not often dealt with by either of the methods described in this section, though Fox has used the relaxation method for this purpose. More suitable and specialised techniques are available (Aitken, 1939 ; Duncan, Frazer and Collar, 1946 ; Morris and Head, 1944).

2.25 Systematic Elimination

This is probably the most convenient method of solving linear equations if there is no approximate estimate of the unknowns (see § 2.26). Consider, as an illustration, three equations for the unknowns x_1, x_2 and x_3

$$l_{11}x_1 + l_{12}x_2 + l_{13}x_3 = l_{14} \qquad . \qquad . \qquad \text{(i)}$$
$$l_{21}x_1 + l_{22}x_2 + l_{23}x_3 = l_{24} \qquad . \qquad . \qquad \text{(ii)}$$
$$l_{31}x_1 + l_{32}x_2 + l_{33}x_3 = l_{34} \qquad . \qquad . \qquad \text{(iii)}$$

The first is divided by l_{11} and used to eliminate x_1 from (ii) and (iii), giving

$$x_1 + m_{12}x_2 + m_{13}x_3 = m_{14} \qquad . \qquad . \qquad \text{(iv)}$$
$$m_{22}x_2 + m_{23}x_3 = m_{24} \qquad . \qquad . \qquad \text{(v)}$$
$$m_{32}x_2 + m_{33}x_3 = m_{34} \qquad . \qquad . \qquad \text{(vi)}$$

* In vibrational problems, λ is proportional to the square of the frequency.

where $\qquad m_{12} = \dfrac{l_{12}}{l_{11}}, \quad m_{13} = \dfrac{l_{13}}{l_{11}}, \quad m_{14} = \dfrac{l_{14}}{l_{11}}$

and the other co-efficients are given by

$$m_{jk} = l_{jk} - \sum_i \frac{l_{ji}l_{ik}}{l_{11}}.$$

Equation (v) is now used to eliminate x_2 from (vi), and the set of equations becomes

$$x_1 + m_{12}x_2 + m_{13}x_3 = m_{14} \quad . \quad . \quad \text{(vii)}$$

$$x_2 + n_{23}x_3 = n_{24} \quad . \quad . \quad \text{(viii)}$$

$$n_{33}x_3 = n_{34} \quad . \quad . \quad \text{(ix)}$$

where the co-efficients n_{jk} have been calculated from the m_{jk}.

The solutions may now be obtained directly. Equation (ix) gives $x_3 = n_{34}/n_{33}$; this value is substituted in (viii) to give x_2 and both values give, with equation (vii), the value of x_1.

In practice some method of tabulating the calculation is necessary; the most familiar is that due to Doolittle, but a more convenient one has been given by Milne (Milne 1946, Ch. 1).

The array Y is written down

$$\left. \begin{array}{ccccc} l_{11} & l_{12} & l_{13} & l_{14} & l_{15} \\ l_{21} & l_{22} & l_{23} & l_{24} & l_{25} \\ l_{31} & l_{32} & l_{33} & l_{34} & l_{35} \end{array} \right\} \quad . \quad . \quad (Y)$$

The first four columns contain the co-efficients of the original equations. The fifth column contains numbers which are the sums of the co-efficients in the same row

$$(\text{e.g. } l_{25} = l_{21} + l_{22} + l_{23} + l_{24}),$$

and is used as a check on the accuracy of the computation in a manner that is explained later.

From Y is calculated another array (Z) in six stages, the order of computation being indicated by the numerals $1, 2 \ldots 6$.

c*

$$
\left.
\begin{array}{ccccc}
\lambda_{11} & \lambda_{12} & \lambda_{13} & \lambda_{14} & \lambda_{15} \quad (2)\\
\lambda_{21} & \lambda_{22} & \lambda_{23} & \lambda_{24} & \lambda_{25} \quad (4)\\
\lambda_{31} & \lambda_{32} & \lambda_{33} & \lambda_{34} & \chi_{35} \quad (6)\\
(1) & (3) & (5) &&
\end{array}
\right\} \ (Z)
$$

(1) This column is the same as the first column of Y, i.e. $\lambda_{j1} = l_{j1}$.

(2) These numbers are obtained by dividing the numbers in the first row of Y by λ_{11}, i.e. $\lambda_{1k} = l_{1k}/l_{11}$.

(3) λ_{22} and λ_{32} are computed from
$$\lambda_{j2} = l_{j2} - \lambda_{j1}\lambda_{12}$$

(4) λ_{23}, λ_{24} and λ_{25} from $\lambda_{2k} = \lambda_{22}^{-1}(l_{2k} - \lambda_{21}\lambda_{1k})$.

(5) λ_{33} from $\lambda_{33} = l_{33} - \lambda_{32}\lambda_{23} - \lambda_{31}\lambda_{13}$.

(6) λ_{34} and λ_{35} from
$$\lambda_{3k} = \lambda_{33}^{-1}(l_{3k} - \lambda_{32}\lambda_{2k} - \lambda_{31}\lambda_{1k}).$$

(7) The unknowns x_1, x_2 and x_3 are now calculated from
$$x_3 = \lambda_{34}; \quad x_2 = \lambda_{24} - \lambda_{23}x_3$$
$$x_1 = \lambda_{14} - \lambda_{13}x_3 - \lambda_{12}x_2.$$

Each of these steps is performed directly on a calculating machine. The form of tabulation may be extended to deal with equations containing more than three unknowns. Thus the numbers on and to the left of the principal diagonal (the line through λ_{11}, λ_{22}, etc.) are obtained from

$$\lambda_{jk} = l_{jk} - \lambda_{j,\,k-1}\,\lambda_{k-1,\,k} - \lambda_{j,\,k-2}\,\lambda_{k-2,\,k} - \ldots - \lambda_{j1}\lambda_{1k}$$

and the others from

$$\lambda_{jk} = \lambda_{jj}^{-1}(l_{jk} - \lambda_{j,\,j-1}\,\lambda_{j-1,\,k} - \ldots - \lambda_{j1}\lambda_{1k}).$$

The solutions are given by

$$x_j = \lambda_{j,\,l+1} - \lambda_{jl}x_l - \lambda_{j,\,l-1}\,x_{l-1} - \ldots - \lambda_{j,\,j+1}x_{j+1}$$

where l is the number of unknowns (and equations) in the general case.

The fifth column of Z provides a check on the computation in the following way (Milne 1946, p. 24). It can be shown, accidental errors apart, that each number in this column is equal to one greater than the sum of the other numbers in the same row which *lie to the right of* the principal diagonal, i.e.

$$\lambda_{j5} = \left\{ \begin{array}{c} \text{sum of numbers in } j\text{th row which} \\ \text{lie to right of diagonal} \end{array} \right\} + 1.$$

Thus the completion of any row of Z should be followed by a comparison of the sum of the numbers to the right of the principal diagonal (excluding the last) with the last number. If these do not differ by $1 \cdot 0 \ldots$, the two preceding stages in the calculation must be repeated.

A final step is to verify that the original equations are indeed solved by the numerical values which are calculated. In this connection, it should be noted that the elimination of a large number of unknowns can lead to quite considerable rounding-off errors, which make it appear that the equations are not well-satisfied. But this danger is rarely great, and can usually be avoided by carrying an extra digit in the computation.

This procedure is illustrated by Table 2.5, which is concerned with the normal equations that arise in the calculation of Table 2.3. The five unknowns (a_0, a_1, a_2, a_3 and a_4) are the co-efficients of a fourth-degree polynomial determined by the least-squares condition.

In that table, the first six columns contain the co-efficients of the normal equations (taken from Table 2.3). Col. 7 (in both Y and Z) is the check column. Array Z has been calculated from Y by the rules given above—the solutions of the equations are shown in the last row of the table.

The numbers in italics above the elements of the principal diagonal of Z are the reciprocals of those elements used in the computation of elements to the right of the diagonal. The four digits after each of the numbers in the check column (in Z) are the digits after the decimal point in the sum of the numbers to the right of the principal diagonal. The small discrepancy in the fourth decimal place is due to rounding-off errors. The last column in Y shows the values taken by the

TABLE 2.5

		1	2	3	4	5	6	7	8
		a_4	a_3	a_2	a_1	a_0			
Y	1	0·1236	− 0·2807	+ 0·3213	− 0·2418	+ 0·9322	+ 4·7499	+ 5·6045	+ 4·7499
	2	− 0·2807	+ 0·3213	− 0·2418	+ 0·9322	− 0·5086	− 2·1673	− 1·9449	− 2·1668
	3	+ 0·3213	− 0·2418	+ 0·9322	− 0·5086	+ 3·3753	+ 16·8510	+ 20·7294	+ 16·8510
	4	− 0·2418	+ 0·9322	− 0·5086	+ 3·3753	− 0·6500	+ 0·2500	+ 2·1571	+ 0·2505
	5	+ 0·9322	− 0·5086	+ 3·3753	− 0·6500	+ 27·000	+ 137·600	+ 167·749	+ 137·597
Z	6	*8·0906* + 0·1236	− 2·2710	+ 2·5995	− 1·9563	+ 7·5421	+ 38·4295	+ 45·3438	(1135)
	7	− 0·2807	*3·1636* − 0·3161	− 1·5435	− 1·2119	− 5·0883	− 27·2698	− 34·1134	
	8	+ 0·3213	− 0·4879	*1·1763* + 0·8501	+ 0·8367	+ 4·0401	− 20·9482	+ 26·8248	(8250)
	9	− 0·2418	+ 0·3831	+ 0·7113	*0·3608* + 2·7714	+ 0·0899	+ 1·8361	+ 2·9259	(9260)
	10	+ 0·9322	+ 1·6084	+ 3·4346	+ 0·2492	*+ 0·07015* + 14·2547	+ 5·1371	+ 6·1371	
	11	+ 2·7221	− 0·9409	− 0·9561	+ 1·3743	+ 5·1371			

left-hand side of each equation when the calculated values of the unknowns are substituted.

A calculation of this complexity should take about one hour's work if a good desk calculating machine can be used.*

2.26 The Relaxation Method

This method has developed from a technique used extensively for the solution of differential equations by Southwell and others (Southwell, 1941). Its main features are that much of the arithmetic may be performed mentally, and that computational errors do not affect the accuracy of the results, but merely prolong the calculation—its chief advantages, that it may be used to find accurate solutions when approximate solutions are known, and that the process may be halted when the solutions have attained any desired degree of accuracy.

TABLE 2.6

	x_1'	x_2'	R_1	R_2
1	1	1	2	5
2	-1		-1	1
3		$+0\cdot2$	$-0\cdot2$	$1\cdot6$
4	$-0\cdot2$		$-0\cdot8$	$0\cdot8$
5	$-0\cdot8$	$+0\cdot8$	0	0
6	$-1\cdot0$	$+2\cdot0$	0	0

Speedy use of the relaxation method demands a certain amount of practice. For this reason it is recommended that it should only be applied to improve the accuracy of a solution obtained by some other method, or to find accurate solutions when approximate values are already known.

As an example, consider the following set of two equations.

$$3x_1 + 4x_2 = 5$$
$$4x_1 + 3x_2 = 2.$$

* With a programme already available for a modern electronic computer, the data for the computation could be fed into the machine in about a minute and the computation completed in a few seconds.

If x_1' and x_2' are any two numbers, not necessarily the solutions of the equations, the numbers

$$R_1 = 3x_1' + 4x_2' - 5$$

and

$$R_2 = 4x_1' + 3x_2' - 2$$

are called the *residuals*. The procedure of the relaxation method is to choose arbitrary values x_1' and x_2' for x_1 and x_2, and to vary these systematically so that R_1 and R_2 are reduced to zero.

The rows of Table 2.6 (numbered 1, 2 . . . 6) correspond to the following operations :

1. Values $x_1' = 1$ and $x_2' = 1$ are chosen, and entered in the first two columns. The residuals are calculated and entered in Cols. 3 and 4.

2. In order to reduce the size of the largest residual $(R_2 = 5)$ x_1' is decreased by one unit (a change of -1), the change in the residuals calculated and the actual values of the residuals corresponding to the new values of x_1' and x_2' determined. The *alteration* in the unknown is entered in Col. 1—the *actual value* of the residuals in Cols. 3 and 4.

3, 4, 5. Similar steps are carried out. Their object is to reduce the size of the largest residual. Row 5 corresponds to a simultaneous change of both unknowns, and reduces both residuals to zero.

6. The contents of Cols. 1 and 2 are added together, and yield -1.0 and $+2.0$ respectively. In order to eliminate the possibility of accidental error the residuals are recalculated for these values, and are found to agree with the values in 5.

From this it is concluded that the solutions of the equations are

$$x_1 = -1.0, \quad x_2 = +2.0.$$

In this simple example, of course, these solutions could have been obtained more quickly by other means.

More usually the co-efficients of the equations contain several digits, and the solutions are required to a comparable accuracy. Then it is best to proceed in different stages of approximation. Thus the equations

$$3 \cdot 1x_1 + 4 \cdot 4x_2 = 4 \cdot 9$$

and $\qquad 3 \cdot 7x_1 + 2 \cdot 7x_2 = 2 \cdot 1$

are simplified by rounding-off the co-efficients to the nearest integer. This results in the set of equations already dealt with in Table 2.6, and the solutions obtained there are taken as the starting point of another stage of relaxation, the process being continued until the residuals are smaller than $0 \cdot 1$.

In order to operate with numbers which are roughly integral, it is convenient to consider the co-efficients on the right-hand side of the equations to be multiplied by ten, i.e. to solve the equation

$$3 \cdot 1x_1 + 4 \cdot 4x_2 = 49 \cdot 0$$

$$3 \cdot 7x_1 + 2 \cdot 7x_2 = 21 \cdot 0.$$

Approximate solutions are now $x_1 = -10 \cdot 0$, $x_2 = +20 \cdot 0$. This stage of the calculation is shown in Table 2.7.

TABLE 2.7

− 10	+ 20	+ 8	− 4
+ 4	− 4	+ 2·8	0
+ 1	− 1	+ 1·5	+ 1·0
	− 0·25	+ 0·4	+ 0·275
	− 0·1	− 0·04	+ 0·05
− 5·0	+ 14·65		

Even if it is desired to obtain more accurate solutions than those shown in Table 2.7, it is wise to halt the process at that stage, to check the residuals by recalculation and to continue the relaxation process after multiplying the right-hand side of the equations by a power of ten.

2.27 The Accuracy of Solutions

If the co-efficients of a set of equations are not known exactly, either because they are experimental quantities or because they are rounded-off to a certain decimal place, the accuracy of the solutions obtained by *any* computational process is limited. It must be emphasised that this limitation is inherent in the set of co-efficients, and that it cannot be estimated without solving the equations.

Suppose that the co-efficients of the equations

$$l_{11}x_1 + l_{12}x_2 = l_{13}$$

$$l_{21}x_1 + l_{22}x_2 = l_{23}$$

have been rounded-off to the first decimal place,* i.e. each co-efficient is uncertain by 0·05. If x_1' and x_2' are approximate solutions, the uncertainties in the residuals, δR_1 and δR_2, are both approximately 0·05 $(|x_1'| + |x_2'| + 1)$. There is no object in finding, by any process, more accurate values of x_1 and x_2 so the size of the residuals is less than this quantity.†

If, for example, the co-efficients of the equations discussed in Table 2.7 were obtained by rounding-off to the first decimal, the approximate solutions obtained in Table 2.7 yield

$$\delta R_1, \ \delta R_2 = 0·05 \ (0·5 + 1·47 + 1) = 0·15.$$

This means that all sets of values for x_1 and x_2 which give residuals less than 0·15 are equally consistent with the equations. It will be seen that the relaxation method has accomplished this in the third row of Table 2.7, and that the solutions obtained at that stage ($x_1 = -0·5$, $x_2 = +1·5$) are as satisfactory as those obtained at the end of the table.

In terms of the probable uncertainty, $\delta R = 0·15$. This stage is reached at the end of Table 2.7.

The following results of this discussion are important. More accurate estimates of the uncertainties may be made in specialised ways (Milne 1946, p. 32).

---

* This brief discussion is easily extended to the case of uncertainties due to experimental error.

† The estimate of δR_1 and δR_2 given here is the greatest possible uncertainty. Strictly speaking, it is more desirable to work in terms of the *probable uncertainty*. This is calculated on the assumption that the *mean* uncertainty in each co-efficient is 0·025, leading to the estimate

$$\frac{0·025}{\sqrt{3}} \ (|x_1'| + |x_2'| + 1).$$

1. An indication of the point beyond which it is unnecessary to continue the relaxation method is provided in the manner discussed above.

2. Occasionally it is found that relatively large variations in x_1 and x_2 do not carry the residuals outside the limit δR. For example, the equations

$$1 \cdot 1 x_1 + 1 \cdot 2 x_2 = 1$$

and

$$0 \cdot 9 x_1 + 0 \cdot 8 x_2 = 1$$

(with exact solutions $x_1 = +2$, $x_2 = -1$) have $\delta R = 0 \cdot 2$ if it is assumed that the co-efficients are rounded-off to the first place. But changes $+1$ and -1 in x_1 and x_2 respectively yield residuals $-0 \cdot 1$ and $+0 \cdot 1$ for the two equations. These values are both less than δR, so that the solutions $x_1 = 3$, $x_2 = 2$ are as satisfactory as the exact values.

Equations showing this behaviour are said to be ill-conditioned (Morris 1946).

3. In contrast to this, the equations may be such that very small changes in the unknowns produce large changes in the residuals. In such circumstances, it may be possible to determine solutions of great accuracy (i.e. a large number of figures may be significant) when the uncertainty in the coefficients is relatively large. This can conveniently be done by relaxation.

It will be recognised, since the nature of any given set of equations can only be determined when approximate solutions are known, that the accuracy of solutions obtained by elimination or similar methods may be assessed by performing one stage of a relaxation calculation.

2.28 Numerical Integration

Definite integrals of the form $\int_a^b y\,dx$ may require numerical evaluation for one of two reasons. The integrand, y, may be given as an explicit function of x which no mathematical procedure can integrate directly.* Alternatively, the integrand

---

* In such cases the use of asymptotic expansions may avoid numerical integration.

may only be specified at a number of points inside the range of integration. Thus it is often the case that experimental values of this integrand $y_1, y_2 \ldots y_N$ have been determined at the points $x_1, x_2 \ldots x_N$.

The most familiar and generally useful methods depend on the use of quadrature formulae which are described in § 2.29. The accuracy of these processes and the complications introduced by experimental errors in observed values y_1, y_2, etc., are discussed in § 2.30.

2.29   The Use of Quadrature Formulae

It will be assumed that N values, $y_1, y_2 \ldots y_N$, of the integrand are specified inside the range of integration $x = a$ to $x = b$—these will either have been obtained experimentally or will have been calculated from the intractable integrand.

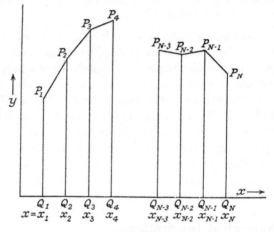

FIG. 2.6

Also that the intervals between successive values x_n and x_{n+1} are all equal, and that $x_1 = a$, $x_N = b$. This restriction is not, in principle, necessary but formulae obtained under other conditions are so complicated that they are of little use for computation. When the values $x_1, x_2 \ldots x_N$ are not equally spaced, other methods should be sought.

The points P_1, P_2, . . . P_N in Fig. 2.6 represent the points defined by the pairs of co-ordinates (x_1, y_1), (x_2, y_2) . . . (x_N, y_N) respectively. The integral $\int_{x_1}^{x_N} y\,dx$ is equal to the area under *some* unknown or unspecified curve which passes through these points.

To obtain a first approximation to the value of the definite integral, the unknown curve connecting the points P_1, P_2 . . . P_N is assumed to be that obtained by joining successive points by straight lines in the manner of Fig. 2.6. The area under this curve is the sum of the areas of all the trapeziums $P_1P_2Q_2Q_1$, $P_2P_3Q_3Q_2$, etc. Assuming that the intervals $x_2 - x_1$, $x_3 - x_2$, etc., are all equal to h, the area of a typical trapezium is $\frac{h}{2}(y_n + y_{n+1})$. Thus a first approximation to the value of the integral is given by the *Trapezoidal Rule*

$$\int_{x_1}^{x_N} y\,dx = \tfrac{1}{2}h[y_1 + 2y_2 + 2y_3 + \ldots 2y_{N-1} + y_N].$$

It is to be expected that a more accurate expression for the integral would be obtained by representing the unknown curve by a series of parabolas (polynomials of the second degree) passing through the sets of three consecutive points $P_1P_2P_3$, $P_2P_3P_4$, etc. This leads, if the number of intervals is assumed to be even, to *Simpson's Rule*

$$\int_{x_1}^{x_N} y\,dx = \frac{h}{3}\left[y_1 + 4y_2 + 2y_3 + \ldots + 2y_{N-2} + 4y_{N-1} + y_N\right].$$

These, and other more complicated formulae obtained by representing successive portions of the unknown curve by cubics, quartics, etc., may be obtained by the following method, which is applied here to the proof of Simpson's Rule.

Consider the integral $\int_{x_1}^{x_3} y\,dx$, and assume that if y is any curve of the second or of a lower degree which passes through P_1P_2 and P_3, then the integral is given *exactly* by

$$\int_{x_1}^{x_3} y\,dx = ay_1 + by_2 + cy_3$$

where a, b and c are undetermined constants.

These constants may be determined by choosing three particular forms for $y(x)$, and equating, in each case, the values of the integral which are calculated directly to the values given by the above expression.

1. Put $y(x) \equiv 1$. i.e $y_1 = y_2 = y_3 = 1$

$$\int_{x_1}^{x_3} ydx = 2h = a + b + c$$

2. Put $y(x) \equiv (x - x_2)$ i.e. $y_2 = 0$, $y_1 = -y_3 = -h$.

$$\int_{x_1}^{x_3} ydx = 0 = -ah + ch.$$

3. Put $y(x) \equiv (x - x_2)^2$ i.e. $y_1 = y_3 = h^2$. $y_2 = 0$

$$\int_{x_1}^{x_3} ydx = \tfrac{2}{3}h^3 = ah^2 + ch^2.$$

The three simultaneous equations

$$a + b + c = 2h$$

$$-a \quad\quad + c = 0$$

$$a \quad\quad + c = \frac{2h}{3}$$

are now solved to give $a = c = \dfrac{h}{3}$; $b = \dfrac{4h}{3}$, and it is concluded that

$$\int_{x_1}^{x_3} ydx = \tfrac{1}{3}h[y_1 + 4y_2 + y_3].$$

Simpson's Rule is now obtained by adding-up similar expressions for each of the intervals (x_1, x_3), (x_3, x_5). . . .

The relation

$$\int_{x_1}^{x_4} ydx = \frac{3h}{8}[y_1 + 3y_2 + 3y_3 + y_4]$$

is exact for integrands which are of the third or of a lower degree, and can be proved by the method illustrated above. Called the *Newton Three-Eighths Rule*, it is comparable in accuracy with Simpson's Rule, and is often used instead of this when the number of intervals is not even.

There is a large number of formulae which differ from those described above at the ends of the range (at a and b) and which have greater accuracy ; some of them are especially suitable for the integration of differential equations (Milne 1946, Ch. III and IV ; Whittaker and Robinson 1944, Ch. III).

These formulae may be applied to the data of Table 2.4, to evaluate, for example, $\displaystyle\int_0^{x_N} ydx$.   It will be assumed that x is measured in hours, i.e. that it is given by Col. 1 of Table 2.4. With these units, $h = 2$. Table 2.8 shows the results obtained by the use of the Trapezoidal Rule and Simpson's Rule. The

TABLE 2.8

$\int_0^{x_N} y\,dx$ obtained by different methods

Trapezoidal Rule	Simpson's Rule	6th Order Polynomial	Least-Squares Function
$- 0\cdot992$	$- 0\cdot972$	$- 0\cdot912$	$- 1\cdot016$

value of the integral obtained for the most complicated quadrature formula, which is exact for polynomials of sixth or lower degree, is shown in Col. 3 of that table. Col. 4 contains the result obtained by integrating over the appropriate interval the least-squares trigonometric function obtained in § 2.21.*

2.30 The Accuracy of Numerical Integration

The errors that occur in numerical integration are of two kinds, which are best discussed separately. The first are inherent in the use of quadrature formulae, and are present when the ordinates y_1, y_2 . . . y_N are known exactly ; when, for example, they have been computed from an explicit mathematical function which cannot be integrated analytically. The second arise when the ordinates are subject to random errors of observation.

1. *Errors of Quadrature Formulae*

It has been explained that these formulae depend on the fact that the unknown function, $f(x)$, has been regarded as a polynomial of finite degree over consecutive portions of its range. Since this may not be exactly true, results obtained

---

* The only term of $f(x)$ which gives a non-vanishing contribution to $\int f(x)dx$ is a_0, i.e. $- 1\cdot016$.

by using the formulae will be in error. Suppose that the function has been represented as a polynomial of degree k between the points P_1, P_2, . . . P_{k+1}. By the use of Taylor's Theorem, the inaccuracy of any quadrature formula can be expressed in terms of the $(k + 1)$th derivative at some arbitrary point between x_1 and x_{k+1} (Milne 1949, p. 111 ; Whittaker and Robinson 1944, Ch. III). In practice, the value of the derivative at this point is replaced by its largest value in the range P_1 . . . P_{k+1}.

For example, when $k = 1$ (Trapezoidal Rule) it can be shown that

$$\int_{x_1}^{x_2} ydx = \frac{h}{2}(y_1 + y_2) - \frac{y''(z)h^3}{12}$$

where $y''(z)$ is the value of $\dfrac{d^2y}{dx^2}$ at some point z which lies between x_1 and x_2. The error, E, is given by the last term of the expression and it may be said that

$$|\epsilon| \leqslant \frac{h^3}{12} |y_+''^{(12)}|$$

where $y_+''^{(12)}$ is the largest value of y'' between x_1 and x_2. By adding up formulae of this kind for each of the ranges P_1P_2, P_2P_k, there is obtained the familiar expression for the trapezoidal rule. The error, E, is given by

$$|E| \leqslant \frac{h^3}{12}\{|y_+''^{(12)}| + |y_+''^{(23)}| + . . . + |y_+''^{(N-1, N)}|\}$$

which may be simplified to

$$|E| \leqslant \frac{h^3}{12}(N - 1)|y_+''|$$

when each maximum value of y'' for the ranges (x_1, x_2) . . . etc., is replaced by y_+'', the maximum value of y'' anywhere between x_1 and x_N.

Table 2.9 summarises the expressions for the error obtained for those quadrature formulae that have been described above. The second row gives the values of $|\epsilon|$ which arise from each elementary range of integration (specified in the first row) while the error involved in applying these to an extended range, E, is shown in the third row of Table 2.9.

The row labelled σ_y is referred to on p. 60.

TABLE 2.9

	Trapezoidal Rule	Simpson's Rule	Newton's Rule
Elementary Range	$x_1 \to x_2$	$x_1 \to x_3$	$x_1 \to x_4$
$\lvert \epsilon \rvert$	$\dfrac{h^3}{12}\lvert y_+'' \rvert$	$\dfrac{h^5}{90}\lvert y_+'''' \rvert$	$\dfrac{h^5}{80}\lvert y_+'''' \rvert$
$\lvert E \rvert$	$\dfrac{h^3}{12}(N-1)\lvert y_+'' \rvert$	$\dfrac{h^5}{90}\left(\dfrac{N-1}{2}\right)\lvert y_+'''' \rvert$	$\dfrac{3h^5}{80}\left(\dfrac{N-1}{3}\right)\lvert y_+'''' \rvert$
σ_y	$\dfrac{h\sigma}{2}\sqrt{4N-6}$	$\dfrac{h\sigma}{3}\sqrt{10N-12}$	$\dfrac{3h\sigma}{8}\sqrt{\dfrac{22N-28}{3}}$

If the ordinates $y_1, \ldots y_N$ have not been obtained from some explicit function of x, but are, for example, experimental values, it is clear that no certain estimate of the $(k+1)$th derivitive if y can be formed, and that no certain estimate of the error of the quadrature process is possible. But data of this kind are often subject to random errors of observation, which lead to uncertainties in the integral which are usually greater than those discussed above.

2. *The Error due to inaccurate Ordinates*

Suppose that the ordinates $y_1, y_2 \ldots y_N$ are subject to random errors of observation, and that the standard error of each about its unknown true value is σ. The value given by any quadrature formula may be regarded as an approximation to some unknown true value, and the accuracy of the formula may be measured by the standard error of this approximation.

This standard error may be obtained in the following way. If $Y = ay_1 + by_2$ where y_1 and y_2 have standard error σ, then the standard error σ_y of y is given* by $\sigma_y = \sqrt{a^2 + b^2} \cdot \sigma$. and if

$$Y = a_1 y_1 + \ldots + a_N y_N$$

$$\sigma_y = \sqrt{a_1^2 + a_2^2 + \ldots a_N^2} \cdot \sigma$$

This result has been applied to the three integration formulae of Table 2.9 to give the results shown in the fourth row (σ_y).

In a sense, the true values y_1^0, y_2^0, . . . etc., are not completely unknown. For it has been shown in § 2.2 that curves which are fitted to the ordinates by least-squares calculation may be used, with a definite degree of certainty, to predict y_1^0, y_2^0, . . . etc. The value obtained by integrating directly a function which has been fitted to the data is more accurate than that given by any other method. (For this purpose, the function *must* contain the correct number of parameters ; neither too many or too few.) Unfortunately, the work involved in least-squares calculations often makes this refinement impossible.

---

* Let $E\{Y\}$ $E\{Y^2\}$ etc., mean the "expectation", or probable value of Y and Y^2 etc., respectively. Then

$$\sigma^2 = E\{(y_1 - y_1^0)^2\}, \quad \sigma_y^2 = E\{(Y - Y_0)^2\}$$

where $Y_0 = a y_1^0 + b y_2^0$.

But $E\{(Y - Y_0)^2\} = E\{(a y_1 - y_1^0)^2 + b(y_2 - y_2^0)^2\}$

$$= a^2 E\{(y_1 - y_1^0)^2\} + 2ab\, E\{(y_1 - y_1^0)(y_2 - y_2^0)\} + b^2\{(y_2 - y_2^0)^2\}$$

$$= a^2\sigma^2 + b^2\sigma^2 = (a^2 + b^2)\sigma^2$$

i.e. $\sigma_y = \sqrt{a^2 + b^2} \cdot \sigma$.

CHAPTER 3

MECHANICAL DESIGN

3.1 Introduction

This chapter deals with the design of scientific apparatus from the mechanical standpoint; the principles developed here can be applied to improvised apparatus as well as to that designed for deliberate construction in the laboratory workshop, or for commercial production.

In all mechanical designs the requirements to be met are:

(a) Kinematical or geometrical: the form of the parts must ensure the required positional relation between them, and moving parts must be constrained to move only in the required way.

(b) Statical: forces between parts must act to the best advantage, the parts must not fail under stress, and their deformation under stress must not interfere with their function.

(c) Dynamical: the stresses due to the acceleration of moving parts must not produce disturbing effects. In particular, certain balancing conditions for rotating parts may be important.

3.2 Kinematics

In domestic life, and in engineering practice, connections between different parts of a structure are often made by " brute force " methods, e.g. by multiple nailing, screwing or bolting. It is easy to see that with such connections it is not possible to reproduce exactly a given position of the parts if they are dismantled and reassembled, for since the constraints may conflict, some tolerance for inaccuracy of manufacture must be given, e.g. the bolt holes must be slightly oversize. Furthermore, internal strains must be produced in the parts on assembly, since the tightening up of any connection must deflect the part from the position which it had taken up under the previous constraints. In certain parts of scientific apparatus it is worth while to design the mating surfaces so that they impose only those constraints which are necessary and sufficient for the occasion. This idea was stated by Maxwell in 1876, and it has been taken into increasing use in the design of scientific instruments for commercial production during this century.

3.3   Kinematic Design

The position of one rigid body relative to another may be defined by six co-ordinates, and it is therefore said to have six degrees of freedom. A useful set of co-ordinates (not the only possible ones) for defining displacements of the body is composed of the changes (δx, δy, δz) in the Cartesian co-ordinates of one point in the body, and the angles through

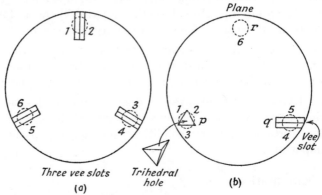

FIG. 3.1 (*a*) and (*b*)   Two alternative kinematic arrangements for the relative location of two parts. Balls are attached to piece A, slots etc. formed in piece B. Numbers indicate position of the six constraints

which the body turns about the three axes. Any small displacement of the body may be represented by combinations of these. Contact of a point in the body with a surface in the outside world removes one degree of freedom, since no relative motion is possible in a direction normal to the surface so long as point and surface remain in contact. Small displacements which do not require motion in the normal direction are not inconsistent with the constraint.

If one piece of apparatus A (supposed for the moment rigid) is to be located in a fixed position relative to another piece B, the kinematic design for the connection between A and B must involve contact at six points properly chosen. Fig. 3.1 shows two well-known methods for securing this result. The arrangement of three vee slots shown in Fig. 3.1(*a*) is symmetrical and easily constructed (e.g. by a shaping or milling machine); it is shown in Fig. 3.2 forming the locating elements of a set of laboratory stands which can be piled to any height as long as the feet of each remain in contact with the vees. The arrangement of 3.1(*b*) has the advantage that the part A may be rocked about the line *pq* by turning a levelling screw

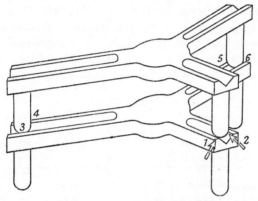

FIG. 3.2   Laboratory stands with kinematic location

which carries the ball or similar mating surface at *r*. Imperfections of the screw, e.g. bad centring, drunkenness of thread, or shake, do not affect the position of A to the first order of accuracy. The hole at *p*, which provides three constraints, must in principle be trihedral, and may be formed in some materials (e.g. brass) by punching. A very good set of constraints is provided by a nest of three steel balls soldered to a plate, preferably in a cylindrical well.

These two constructions illustrate several main features characteristic of so-called kinematic design.

(*a*) The parts may be separated and replaced in the same position whenever required; the relative location of the parts is exact although precise dimensional construction is not called for. In a perfectly rigid material, high finish would not be required, and in fact the stands of Fig. 3.2 work well for many purposes as roughly dressed castings. It is easy to see, however, that chance projections at the contact surfaces (which are heavily loaded, see below) may readily be deformed when the parts are removed and reassembled. In precise applications, therefore, the mating surfaces should be hard and highly finished. Steel balls (commercial bearing balls) are particularly suitable for these surfaces. They may be soft-soldered into place in the components or pressed tightly into undersized holes.

Quantitative information on the loading of ball-plane contacts has been given by Pollard (1937), who found that the load P which gave a small permanent deformation of the plane ($\frac{1}{2}$ wavelength of green light) was connected with the diameter D of the ball by the relation $P = SD^2$. Values of S are given in Table 3.1, abridged from Pollard's paper.

TABLE 3.1

Material of plane	S lb./in.^{2}	S kg./mm.^{2}
0·9 % carbon steel, hard . . .	348	0·245
superhardened .	1040	0·731
Ball-bearing steel (chrome carbon) max. value obtained by tempering at 315° C. (spring temper)	730	0·513
Brass	6	0·004
Phosphor-bronze	17	0·012
Cast iron	16	0·011

(b) Wear of the mating surfaces does not introduce " play " : the parts settle down to a new, but well-defined, relation. It is often possible to provide simple adjustments to remove the displacements due to wear.

(c) The contacts which form the kinematic constraints are in theory points, and in fact small areas heavily loaded. This fact limits the application of strict kinematic design when the parts are heavy. It may then be necessary to expand the constraints into finite areas which must now, in principle, be correctly shaped and fitted. Such designs are often called semi-kinematic—in them, benefit has been obtained by the use of the kinematic idea in deciding how many bearing surfaces are required and how they should be arranged.

(d) The principle of kinematic constraint assumes that the mating points will remain in contact. The provision of forces to hold them so, whether by using the weight of the parts, by springs, or otherwise, has to be considered in addition to the kinematic constraints themselves. It is in neglecting to provide these forces in a satisfactory manner that many ill-considered kinematic designs fail. On the other hand,

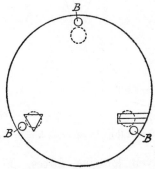

FIG. 3.3 Location arrangement of Fig. 3.1 secured by bolts at *BBB*

kinematic constraints do not themselves introduce indeterminate stresses in the parts. Such stresses are introduced when there are redundant constraints (constraints beyond the minimum kinematic number) which are forced into mating; a simple example occurs when the fourth leg of a table is forced into contact with an uneven floor. It may be useful to employ kinematic principles even in the design of parts which are bolted together; for example, the stands of Fig. 3.1(a) could be bolted as shown in Fig. 3.3. They would then be firmly connected and the indeterminate stresses due to the bolting would be confined to the immediate neighbourhood of the constraints; the main body of the stand would be free from clamping stresses.

(e) Although there are no critically defined positions for the constraints, the ordinary principles of statics should be used to secure that the forces at the mating surfaces act in advantageous directions.   There are some positions in which the system is degenerate and will not work.   In Fig. 3.4(*a*), the three slots are placed so that they lie tangentially to a circle, and they do not effectively constrain rotation about the axis of this circle.   In Fig. 3.4(*b*) the hole lies on the normal to the slot, with similar results.   It is clear that any close approximation to these conditions will lead to inefficient

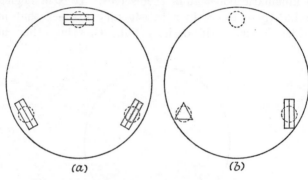

(*a*)   (*b*)

Fɪɢ. 3.4 (*a*) and (*b*)   Degenerate kinematic location

location under given locating forces.   For most effective location each surface which constrains movement should be normal to the movement which could take place at that point without infringing the remaining constraints if the surface were removed.

3.4   One Degree of Translation—the Kinematic Slide

We may now consider the important application of kinematic principles to give one degree of translational freedom :— the kinematic slide with five-point constraint.   Fig. 3.5(*a*) represents a slide which is nearly truly kinematic and which is suitable for light loadings ;   Fig. 3.5(*b*) shows a slide in which the point contacts are expanded into more or less linear regions giving a semi-kinematic design.   By contrast Fig. 3.5(*c*) shows a dovetail slide of conventional form.   It is clear that such a slide, if undeformed, can only make contact at a few random points.   The more accurate the construction, the less deformation is required to increase the number and size of the areas in contact. In fact, slides of this type are used with a lubricating film which distributes the load evenly over them. They are thus suitable for transmitting large forces and are always used in the slides of machine tools. In measuring instruments where the loadings are comparatively light, however, the kinematic designs give superior accuracy of location with much less expense of workmanship.

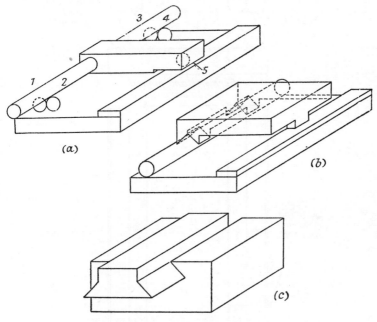

FIG. 3.5   Designs for sliding motion

(a) Kinematic   (b) Semi-Kinematic   (c) Dovetail

In order that the motion in Fig. 3.5 shall be accurately limited to pure translation, it is necessary that the guiding surfaces should be exactly straight and parallel. The straightness condition is fulfilled by turning, grinding or lapping the bars (the processes are in increasing order of precision and cost); the parallelism condition requires precise construction or adjustment. In some designs it may be achieved economically by making the guides from accurate cylinders and clamping

them against a machined plane surface. This is illustrated
in Fig. 3.6 which also shows how the kinematic design of
Fig. 3.5 may be modified to replace sliding by the rolling
movement of steel balls. On account of the high quality of
commercial steel balls, the permissible loadings are fairly

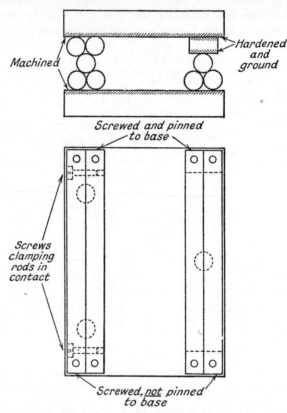

FIG. 3.6   Construction of a kinematic ball-bearing slide

heavy. Ball slide designs are very suitable for slides in
instruments of the highest precision ; they have been applied
(e.g. by Leitz) in the fine adjustment slides of microscopes.

In order to carry heavy loads, a number of steel balls may
be used in the slides. The design then ceases to be kinematic,
but since the balls may be obtained very exactly equal and

spherical, a good distribution of load can be obtained with very little deformation, provided that the grooves are accurately straight.

3.5 One Degree of Freedom—Rotation

There are a number of kinematically-designed systems of constraints which allow rotation about an axis; Fig. 3.8(a) shows designs suitable for laboratory-built apparatus, and

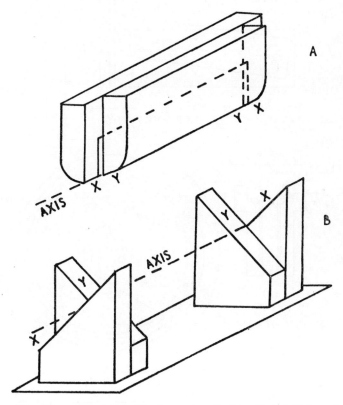

Fig. 3.7. Kinematic pivot. The two pairs of edges X and Y formed on element A are collinear and work on the corresponding planes of element B

Fig. 3.8(b) and (c) show axis designs used in Hilger instruments. (Pollard 1929.) The kinematic hinge shown in Fig. 3.7 was adopted for the Cambridge Instrument Company's

D   69

" rocking microtome " in 1885 and remains unchanged in principle in current models; furthermore instruments using it have retained accuracy of function after sixty years' use.

In this field of simple rotation, however, kinematic designs have been used less than in slides. This is not because of the shortcomings of kinematic design, but because traditional

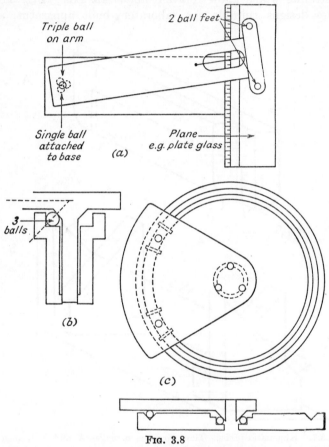

Fig. 3.8

(a) Simple kinematic design for rotation (after G. F. C. Searle's goniometer)
(b) Semi-kinematic design used in Hilger spectrometer. The measured rotation of the axis is given by a micrometer screw whose axis is in the same horizontal plane as the intersection of the normals to the cone through the balls
(c) Another axis design used by Hilger

" fitted " designs are here at their best. The usual construction for the vertical axis of a spectroscope or theodolite consists of mating cones of angle 3°-5°, which may be relieved so that they make contact only at the top and bottom of the mating

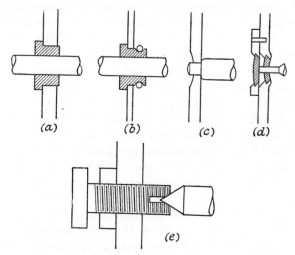

FIG. 3.9 Normal engineering design for bearings

(*a*) Bronze bush pressed into position
(*b*) Bush fitted to thin support with small clearance and retained by spring clip, allowing self-alignment
(*c*) Clock pivot—note sink to retain oil
(*d*) Watch pivot running in jewel bearing with end-stone
(*e*) Conical pivot running in centres

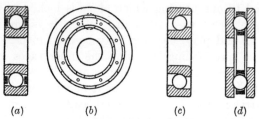

FIG. 3.10 Ball-bearings

(*a*), (*b*) Deep-groove ball-bearing with cage. This bearing will take end thrust as well as journal load
(*c*) Angular contact bearing—to be used in pairs. In the version shown (magneto bearing), the inner race and the balls may be removed from the bearing
(*d*) Pure thrust bearing

71

surfaces. It is usual to take most of the load by adjustable collars or ball-bearings, leaving the lightly loaded cones to enforce accurately concentric motion. In a few theodolite designs, ground and lapped cylindrical surfaces have been used as centring elements with ball races to take end thrust. It may be noted, however, that even very accurately made centres of this type have been improved by converting them into semi-kinematic designs like Fig. 3.8(*b*).

The horizontal bearings of these instruments commonly consist of turned (or ground) cylindrical trunnions resting on open Y's—this is an example of semi-kinematic design.

Fig. 3.9 shows some of the classical bearing systems which may be used in physical apparatus. Ordinary ball-bearings (Fig. 3.10) are over-constrained, not kinematic, designs—they consist of dimensionally fitted parts in which high dimensional accuracy is achieved by using very special mass production methods. High quality steel is used and the distribution of load depends on small and carefully controlled deformations of the balls and races. It is therefore important not to distort the races in assembling them to the rest of the instrument or machine, and the makers issue precise instructions on this point. Where there is a heavy end thrust, this may be taken by pure thrust bearings, independent of the radial (journal) bearings. More frequently in instrument practice, " deep groove " bearings may be used to take both radial and axial loads. In ordinary practice the end location of a shaft is entrusted to one bearing which alone is locked in position ; the others are left as a push fit. When it is important to eliminate all end play, bearings may be used in pairs with an elastic force (pre-loading) pressing the inner races apart and the outer races against locating stops. Selected bearings mounted in this way have been used in very precise applications (Harrison 1938). Commercial ball bearings probably deserve to be used more freely than they have been in measuring instruments.

3.6 Summary of the Uses of Kinematic Designs

It may now be pointed out that strict, or nearly strict, kinematic design is of value (*a*) In the design of *ad hoc* laboratory apparatus where precision of function may be secured without dimensional accuracy of construction.

(*b*) In the design of workshop constructed or commercial instruments where much may be saved by the elimination of close dimensional tolerances. Machine tools are intrinsically well adapted to produce true forms (e.g. flat surfaces or true cylinders) but the production of particular dimensions depends greatly on the skill and care of the operator.

(*c*) In applications of the highest precision, e.g. in metrological apparatus, where the best workmanship can hardly give enough precision of function in a " fitted " design, and where the effects of minute amounts of wear are important.

On the other hand, the " traditional " type of bearing or slide with large lubricated surfaces worked to a fit may be required if large forces are to be transmitted. It is often useful in designing such bearings to consider them as extended semi-kinematic arrangements.

We shall now consider some special points which arise in the design of measuring instruments.

3.7 Motional Hysteresis—the Use of Spring Constraints

If we have a measuring instrument, say a travelling microscope, in which there is " play " (" backlash " or " lost motion") between the parts, then the position of the measuring element at a given reading of the index will depend on the direction from which the reading is approached, and if we plot the position against the reading, we obtain a hysteresis curve. This curve will be closed if we take a cyclic set of readings unless there is some other varying factor. Also, in all the arrangements for sliding and rotating motion described above, there is some friction, which changes its direction with the direction of motion. The forces in the system are therefore not reversible, and in precise work the deformation of the parts under the frictional forces may be appreciable, so that friction will contribute to the motional hysteresis. We have seen that backlash should be absent from a kinematically constrained system, but frictional hysteresis still occurs in such a system.

It is common practice in using such instruments as measuring microscopes to make the final setting always from one direction, so as to secure consistent readings free from hysteresis.

If we connect two parts of an instrument by properly placed springs, we may obtain a constraint which allows translational (Fig. 3.11(a)) or rotational (Fig. 3.11(b)) movement without friction (except for the very small internal

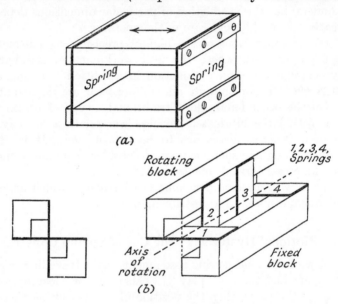

Fig. 3.11   Spring constraints
(a) Flat springs allowing parallel motion
(b) Crossed springs allowing rotation about an axis

friction of the springs). We can now only move one part with respect to the other by applying and maintaining a definite force, but in many instruments, and especially in accurate metrology, this is less objectionable than frictional hysteresis (see *Dictionary Applied Physics*. Description of measuring machine in Vol. III, article " Gauges ", for an excellent example). Spring constraints have considerable practical merit, especially in portable equipment, for the parts are permanently connected and the constraints are not easily damaged by vibration or impulsive overloads due to falls or shocks.

Spring systems giving more accurately rectilinear motion than 3.11(a) have been described (Jones 1951, 1955, 1956).* These allow a precision of motion which it would be difficult to obtain by other means.

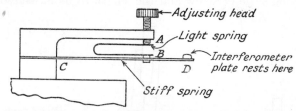

FIG. 3.12 Spring fine adjustment e.g. for interferometer plate

Spring constraints may be used in a very elegant way to provide very fine adjustments of position, e.g. in interferometers. Fig. 3.12 shows an adjustment of this kind—tightening the screw at A bends the part AB and applies bending forces to the relatively stiff portion BC; the motion of the point D is therefore controlled very finely. It is clear that the method is limited to small displacements.

3.8 Sine and Cosine Errors in Measuring Instruments

In measuring microscopes and some other instruments, errors arise because the guiding surfaces depart from exact straightness, and the size of these errors depends markedly on the design of the instrument. Consider the instrument shown schematically in Fig. 3.13. Since the ways are not straight, the angle between the axis of the screw and the optic axis of the microscope changes as the instrument is traversed. If the sighting plane of the microscope contains the axis of the screw, the errors introduced depend on $(1 - \cos \theta)$ and are second-order small quantities. If the object plane is displaced from the screw axis through a distance l, measured in the direction of sighting, the errors introduced by tilt θ depend on $l \sin \theta$, and are of the first order in θ. The distinction between errors of sine and cosine type is

* See also *Notes on Applied Science* No. 15, produced by N.P.L. and published by H.M.S.O., London 1956.

important in all instruments which use a sliding motion to measure length—sine errors appear, for example, in the ordinary vernier caliper, but not in the ordinary micrometer. If possible these instruments should be designed so that the measuring scale or screw and the length to be measured lie in

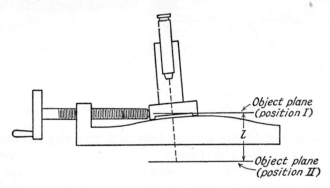

FIG. 3.13 To illustrate sine and cosine errors in measuring instruments (§ 3.8)

the same straight line—only cosine errors can then be present. In measuring microscopes for photographic plates (an important class of instruments) it is usually easiest to secure this result by allowing the screw to move the plate carriage under a fixed microscope.

3.9   The Control of Translational Motion

The traditional method for the accurate control of translation is the micrometer screw and nut. The most accurate screws are produced singly by lapping a well-made screw with a long nut, so that errors are removed by distributing them uniformly. The local errors of a screw made in this way may be reduced to a few Angstrom units. Commercial screws are necessarily made less laboriously, and good ones have an accuracy of about 1μ. If this accuracy is to be effectively used, the mounting of the nut and the end thrust arrangements for the screw must be most carefully considered, and excellent workmanship is required for them. One arrangement for the end thrust is to work the hardened end to an accurate sphere and to press it by a spring against a polished plate of hardened steel or sapphire ; it is preferable to have the convex surface fixed, to have the plane surface on the screw, and to verify by optical methods that it is normal to the axis of rotation.

The connection between the measuring screw or nut and the travelling carriage must be such as to constrain only the lengthwise motion of the carriage, leaving the latter free to be guided by its own ways.   Fig. 3.14 shows some arrangements which have been used for this purpose.   Fig. 3.14(*b*) shows a beautiful device originally designed by Sir Horace Darwin

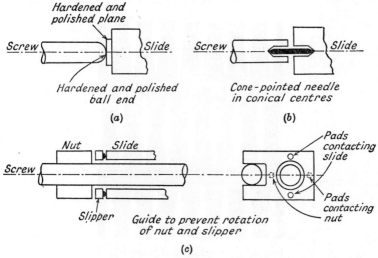

FIG. 3.14   Arrangements for connecting a screw or nut to a travelling carriage

for the Cambridge Instrument Company.   The parts are connected by a blunt-ended needle held by spring pressure between hard hollow cones on the two moving elements.   The principle can be widely applied and is strongly recommended.

Short micrometer screws (1 in.) mounted in nuts with graduated thimbles are available commercially at moderate prices from the makers of engineers' micrometers.   They are very valuable for producing accurately controlled movements. The best of them read directly to 2μ.   The thimble may be clamped in a suitable hole and the translational movement of the screw transferred to a slide by the device of Fig. 3.14(*a*) or (*b*).

Since long accurate screws are expensive, difficult to obtain, and difficult to mount, it is often economical to measure considerable displacements optically, using a low power microscope (provided with an eyepiece graticule or micrometer) to observe an accurate, finely divided scale on glass or metal.

During the past ten years, a method of measuring linear displacements has been developed (mainly by the National Physical Laboratory) which depends on the moiré fringes obtained when light passes through two superposed ruled gratings. These fringes move when the two gratings are moved

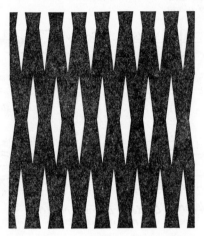

Fig. 3.15. Formation of Moiré fringes

relative to one another, and the movement of the fringes may be made large compared with that of the gratings. If the gratings are coarse compared with the wavelength of light, and if they are maintained at a very small separation, the fringes may be understood as a purely geometrical effect, as illustrated by Fig. 3.15.

When the gratings move relatively by one grating space, the fringes move by one fringe period, an obviously larger distance if the angle between the ruling directions is small. When the gratings are finer, the fringes are roughly similar in appearance, but the distribution and direction of the light must be obtained from diffraction calculations (Guild 1956,

1960). Moiré fringes are well suited to counting and interpolation by the use of photoelectric elements, and they are
being applied to such purposes as automatically-recording
measuring-microscopes and the operation of the slides of a
machine tool under the control of a digital computer. A
similar technique, using radial-line rulings, can be used for
measuring rotation.

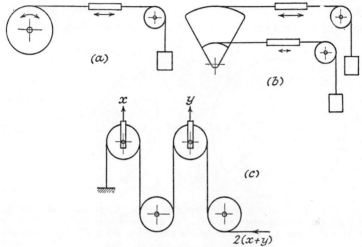

FIG. 3.16   Use of steel band in transmitting movement
(a) Conversion of translation to rotation
(b) Production of two proportional translations
(c) Addition of two translations

A mechanical element which is capable of very good
accuracy in controlling translational motion is a thin (0·002 in.)
stretched steel band, moving, where necessary, over pulleys and
wheels of large radius (Fig. 3.16). It may be used, for example,
to connect two translational motions, to transform translation
into rotation, and to perform elementary computing operations.

3.10 Centring Errors—the Measurement of Rotation

It is often required to measure the rotation of a shaft by
means of a divided circle. If the circle is read by a single
pointer, vernier, or microscope, the accuracy will usually be

limited by the accuracy with which the centre of rotation can be made to coincide with the centre of the divided circle, i.e. the centre about which it was rotated when the divisions were cut. Fig. 3.17 shows that the error in reading a rotation may be greatest when the rotation is 180° (rotation from 90° to 270° in Fig. 3.17), and that the error is then $2d/r$ where d is the centring error and r the radius of the circle. For a 5 in. diameter circle and the very moderate accuracy of 1 minute of arc, the centring error permissible is only 0·0003 in., and its attainment is a rather difficult workshop operation.

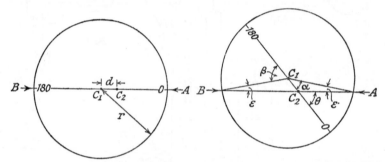

FIG. 3.17   To illustrate centring error (§ 3.10). C_1 is centre of division, and rotation θ takes place about C_2. α, β are rotations read from pointers A, B.   We have $\alpha = \theta - \epsilon$, $\beta = \theta + \epsilon$ where $\epsilon = d \sin \theta/r$ approximately.

This error is eliminated by obtaining the rotation as the mean of the values given by two verniers or microscopes at opposite ends of a diameter. Opposite indicators must be provided and read in any precise measurement of angles.   The averaging of opposite readings has the additional advantage of reducing the effect of random errors in the graduation of the circle, and removing certain periodic errors of graduation.   Further pairs of microscopes spaced round the circle are provided in some instruments (e.g. astronomical transits) for these purposes.

3.11   The Size of Physical Apparatus—General Considerations

When apparatus is planned for a physical experiment, one of the first things to consider is the general scale on which it is to be constructed.

The size of an instrument may sometimes be decided by its primary function and by the scale of the natural phenomenon with which it deals. Thus the diameter of a telescope objective may be set by the wavelength of light and the angular resolving power required, or by the light-collecting power required to see stars of a certain magnitude. The size of a cloud chamber used to investigate α-particles may be set by the range of the particles, and the diameter of a cyclotron is fixed by the momentum of the fastest particles to be produced and the strength of the magnetic field. The latter is rather narrowly limited by the properties of magnetic materials, so that high energy cyclotrons have to be machines of heroic proportions.

In other cases the scale of an instrument is not dictated so closely by the primary function and must be decided on a balance of advantages. It may in practice be set by some standard or existing equipment which is to be incorporated ; by pure convenience in use ; or by considerations of construction. The size of the ordinary microscope is apparently determined very largely by the scale of the human body, since the adjustments and the object on the stage must be manipulated while the seated observer is looking down the instrument. Instruments for geophysical survey depend for their usefulness on portability, and the economics of using them may depend markedly on the number of men needed to carry them.

The size of an instrument may be influenced by the ease of making it, and this is specially apparent when the best size from the point of view of function alone is very small. Small size usually requires increased accuracy of dimensions, and the accuracy of machined metal parts is fairly definitely limited by the resources of the workshop in equipment and skill.* It may, besides, be difficult to hold small parts during manufacture, and to apply cutting forces without distorting them— such parts may be much more heavily stressed during construction than in their working lives. New and unorthodox methods of construction have often been developed by experimenters themselves or by specialist technicians in order to

* 0·001 in. is a normal workshop tolerance for good machining. 0·0001 in. is a precision tolerance involving special workshop methods.

avoid the difficulties of making very small parts by normal workshop methods. The introduction of quartz fibres (Boys 1895) was a landmark in this sort of development, and it is further exemplified in the construction of small thermopiles (cf. Strong 1938).

On the whole, there has been a tendency for commercial instruments to be made smaller as the precision of workshop methods has increased and as the penetration of design has improved. For example, accurately constructed theodolites with circles about 5 in. in diameter have replaced 36 in. instruments used at the beginning of the nineteenth century ; the typical precise balance of the modern chemical laboratory is a short-beam instrument with optical magnification of its deflections. The same tendency appears in electrometers and galvanometers. At the same time, the proportions of the instruments have been altered to produce greatly increased stiffness, which makes the instruments easier to handle and read, since they deflect less with the touch. The reduction in overall size has allowed the sectional areas of the parts to be increased relatively without making the whole instrument unreasonably heavy.

3.12 Example—Rotating Wheels

Very often it is possible to find the direction in which to develop the size of an instrument by a simple calculation. For example, there are a number of physical experiments in which rapidly rotating bodies are required. If we consider geometrically similar bodies, the strength and density of the material set a limit to the *linear peripheral speed*, above which the body will fail under centrifugal forces. (For a proof of this and discussion of the best shape for a spinning disc see Stodola.)

We have for similar bodies

$$r^2\omega^2 \propto E/\rho$$

where r, ω are the radius, angular velocity for the limiting case, E is the tensile strength, ρ the density.

If the purpose of the experiment requires the *greatest linear velocity* from a wheel of given material (e.g. measurement of the Doppler effect of radiation scattered from the wheel, some forms of velocity sorter for molecules), then strength considerations give no definite indication of size.

If the requirement is the *highest accelerational field* as in a centrifuge, then since the acceleration is $\omega^2 r \propto \dfrac{1}{r} \cdot \dfrac{E}{\rho}$ the rotor should be made as small as possible, and this is also true if the *angular velocity* is to be made large as in an apparatus for determining the velocity of light on Foucault's principle. In all these cases the material for the wheel should be chosen to have the highest possible value for E/ρ, and the choice lies between a high-tensile steel and a light, strong, magnesium or aluminium alloy.

In another type of work, the maximum gyroscopic effect (moment of momentum $I\omega$) may be required from the wheel. For geometrically similar bodies, I is proportional to ρr^5 and we have

$$I\omega \propto \rho r^5 \omega \propto \rho r^4 \sqrt{\frac{E}{\rho}}$$

so that it is now advantageous to use a *large* wheel of a material having a maximum value of the product $E\rho$. A dense tungsten alloy has occasionally been used in the wheels of small gyroscopes.

3.13   The Size of Instruments—Other Examples

A celebrated analysis of the optimum size for an instrument was made by C. V. Boys (1895) for the Cavendish gravitation experiment. If the time of swing is to be kept constant the effect of altering all the dimensions of the suspended system and of the attracting masses in the same ratio is to keep the sensitivity unaltered. The moment of inertia of the suspended system is increased in the ratio x^5, where x is the ratio of the linear dimensions. The time of swing condition then requires the torsional stiffness of the suspension to be increased in the ratio x^5, while the gravitational attraction between the spheres increases in the ratio x^4 and the deflecting couple in the ratio x^5, so that the angular deflection remains unchanged. But a reduction in size made it possible greatly to reduce disturbances due to temperature inequalities, and also made it convenient to increase the size of the attracting masses relative to the rest of the apparatus. The construction of a small suspended system with a fairly long time of swing was made practical by Boys' introduction of the quartz fibre suspension, and the sensitivity of the apparatus was increased considerably compared with that of Cavendish's large apparatus. A similar analysis of the moving coil galvanometer (§ 6.6) shows that for a given time of swing, the sensitivity is highest when the moving system is made as small as possible.

There are other ways in which the properties of small suspended systems may be turned to account—the air damping of a small system is much larger than that of a bigger system of similar configuration and the same periodic time. In portable instruments it is sometimes possible to increase the robustness of the suspended system against the inertia forces which arise when the instrument is handled or dropped. If all the dimensions of a galvanometer are reduced, keeping the periodic time constant, it can be shown that the robustness measured by the loading of unit area of the suspension is slightly reduced, but we have seen that the sensitivity is considerably increased by this change, and the designer may choose to forego some of this increase in sensitivity, and instead to reduce the periodic time, at the same time reducing the intensity of loading in the suspension and making the instrument more robust.

3.14 The Size of Physical Apparatus—Thermal Considerations

(a) In calorimetric experiments in which quantities of heat are measured, the quantity of heat involved depends on x^3 and the rate of heat loss from surfaces depends on x^2 where x is a measure of the linear dimensions. There is therefore an advantage in performing calorimetric experiments on a large scale, provided that the experiment can be designed so that the time taken to attain thermal equilibrium is not much lengthened by the increase in size.

(b) The time required for temperature differences in a mass of material of given shape to decay by thermal conduction depends on the square of the linear dimensions and inversely on the diffusivity h (h = Thermal conductivity k / specific heat per unit volume). The simplest case to consider is that of an infinite slab, for which the heat conduction equation has the form

$$h \frac{\partial^2 \theta}{\partial z^2} = \frac{\partial \theta}{\partial t}.$$

If the faces are initially at the temperature of the surroundings, and the temperature excess at a point inside the slab is a sinusoidal function of the distance from a face, the equation has a simple solution

$$\theta = \theta_0 e^{-t/\tau} \sin \pi z/a$$

where

$$\tau = a^2/\pi^2 h, \; a = \text{thickness of slab.}$$

This indicates that the temperature excess subsides exponentially without change of form and with time constant given by τ.* τ gives the order of magnitude of the relaxation time for any body of dimensions similar to the thickness of the slab. As an example, the relaxation time for a 2 cm. aluminium slab ($k = 0.5$ cal. cm.$^{-1}$ sec.$^{-1}$ °C^{-1}; sp. ht. = 0.21 cal. gm.$^{-1}$ °C^{-1}, density = 2.7 gm. cm.$^{-3}$, $h = 0.88$ cm.^{2} sec.$^{-1}$) is approximately $\frac{1}{2}$ sec., and that for a 2 cm. sphere or cube, calculated from the three-dimensional equation, is about $\frac{1}{8}$ sec.

(c) Temperature differences may in several ways disturb physical measurements. Thermal distortion of optical surfaces, thermoelectric e.m.f.'s and the effects of convection currents (Boys 1895) may all be important. It is clear from (b) above that these temperature differences will decay more rapidly in a small apparatus than in a large. In order to allow these temperature differences to decay, and to shield against temperature differences introduced from outside, the sensitive element may be surrounded as closely as possible with a medium of high diffusivity, and this in turn with

---

* If the initial distribution is more complicated, it may be expressed by a Fourier series and the terms of higher order decay more rapidly than the simple sinusoid. The latter therefore represents the distribution of temperature in the latter stage of the decay and τ is the most significant time constant.

several layers possessing alternately low conductivity and high diffusivity. In rather extreme cases the outermost layer may be a stirred liquid bath in which mechanical motion replaces conduction as the mechanism of heat transfer. It is clearly easier to apply these precautions to a small system than to a large one.

3.15 The Balancing of Instruments

In the moving parts of instruments it is often necessary to arrange that the masses are balanced about an axis of rotation, i.e. that the centre of gravity of the moving parts lies in the axis of rotation as defined by the bearings. This condition secures that gravitational couples remain balanced

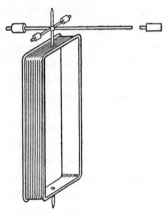

FIG. 3.18   Balance weights on a moving coil meter

whatever the orientation of the instrument, and that inertia couples are balanced if the instrument is subject to acceleration. It is clearly important, e.g. in an ammeter which may be used with its dial horizontal or vertical, or in an aircraft instrument which may be used in peculiar acceleration fields. This condition is called " static balance " ; and mathematically, if OZ is the axis of rotation, it requires

$$\Sigma mx = \Sigma my = 0$$

where xy are the co-ordinates of the elementary mass m. It is in general necessary to provide two adjustments to allow this condition to be met, and Fig. 3.18 shows how two adjustable masses may be used to balance the moving system of a pivoted moving-coil instrument. In unambitious instruments it is common to provide a weight to balance the pointer and to bend its stem to enable the double condition to be fulfilled.

3.16 Dynamic Balance

Sometimes another type of balance condition becomes important. Consider a shaft rotating in bearings and carrying statically balanced masses as shown in Fig. 3.19. On

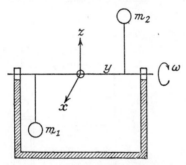

FIG. 3.19. To illustrate dynamic unbalance

rotation " centrifugal " forces are required to keep the masses in their circular paths. In the instantaneous position shown, these forces are of magnitudes $m_1z_1\omega^2$, $m_2z_2\omega^2$, and they produce a couple about the x axis

$$(m_1y_1z_1 + m_2y_2z_2)\omega^2.$$

This couple must be balanced by the reaction of the bearings on the shaft, and the plane containing the resultant couple rotates with the shaft. The result is that alternating forces act on the frame carrying the bearings, and the argument can clearly be extended to any number of masses. If the rotating system is, e.g., the rotor of an electric machine, disturbing vibrations will be set up in the surroundings. If the mass is distributed so that these couples do not arise, the system is said to be dynamically balanced. Dynamic balance for rotation about the axis OY requires the two conditions

$$\Sigma myz = 0 \quad \Sigma mxy = 0.$$

This is equivalent to saying that the axis of rotation must coincide with a principal axis of inertia. In engineering practice dynamic balance is aimed at by making rotating parts as symmetrical as possible. In rapidly rotating elements such as gyroscope wheels, final dynamic balance is secured by adjustment—the wheel is run in a flexibly mounted bearing frame and mass is removed by drilling holes in the proper places until vibrationless running is obtained.

In a delicately suspended measuring system dynamic balance is required for another reason—if the condition is not fulfilled, there is dynamic coupling between the rotation of

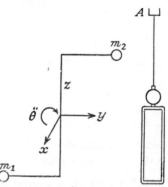

FIG. 3.20 Effect of dynamic unbalance on the vibration of a suspended system

the system about the suspension axis and rotational movements about a horizontal axis. Consider the dynamically unbalanced system of Fig. 3.20 subjected to an angular acceleration $\ddot{\theta}$ about the y axis. The inertia forces $m_1 z_1 \ddot{\theta}$ $m_2 z_2 \ddot{\theta}$ will produce a couple

$$m_1 y_1 z_1 \ddot{\theta} + m_2 y_2 z_2 \ddot{\theta}$$

about the z axis which will only disappear if $\Sigma myz = 0$. This we have seen is one of the conditions for dynamic balance.

It is now clear that if we consider, say, the galvanometer suspension of Fig. 3.20, and if the point A is subject to horizontal vibrations, pendulum vibrations will be forced into the suspended system, and that in the absence of dynamic balance these will give rise to disturbances in the deflections measured about the vertical axis of suspension.

3.17   Mechanical Disturbances—Anti-Vibration Supports

Many instruments are seriously disturbed by mechanical vibrations, and require to be isolated from them, even in ordinary laboratory situations. The need becomes more pressing when an instrument is used in certain industrial

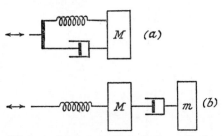

Fig. 3.21   Simplified mechanical equivalents to anti-vibration mountings
(a) with damping between suspended mass and " earth "
(b) with " internal " damping

conditions, and is very acute indeed in aircraft. The first line of defence against vibrational disturbance lies in the design of the instrument itself—for example, the microphonic vibrations of thermionic valves may be reduced by improving the support of the electrodes, and several makers supply valves in which well-supported electrodes are a feature of the construction. The effect of vibration on suspended instruments such as galvanometers depends greatly on the state of dynamic balance of the moving system (§ 3.16).

An instrument can be isolated, more or less effectively, from vibration by supporting it on an anti-vibration mounting, which consists in principle of a mass connected to its mountings by a system of elastic springs. If we consider one co-ordinate, it may be shown that the attenuation factor (amplitude of vibration/amplitude of imposed disturbance) for a harmonic vibration of frequency p is

$$\beta = \text{mod.} \left\{ 1 \middle/ \left(1 - \frac{p^2}{n^2} \right) \right\}$$

where n is the natural vibration frequency of the system. It appears from this that there is great attenuation if the natural period of vibration is much longer than the period of the disturbance, and that there is no attenuation for disturbances of very low frequency ($p/n < 1$). For moderately low frequencies of disturbance the anti-vibration device is worse than useless, and at $p = n$ the amplitude of vibration becomes infinite in the absence of damping.

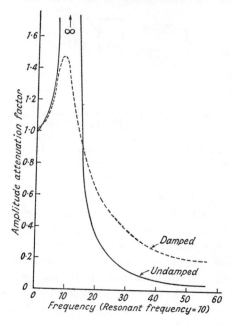

FIG. 3.22 Attenuation of vibration for a system consisting of a mass suspended on a spring—with and without damping in parallel with the spring

If damping is added in parallel with the spring support (Fig. 3.21), the effect is to reduce the amplitude of vibration around resonance, but as shown in Fig. 3.22, the attenuation of disturbances over the frequency range where the anti-vibration device is useful is less than in the undamped case. The basic reason for this result is that the damper offers a path for vibrations to pass to the suspended mass. A better result is obtained by using damping *internal* to the vibrating mass. Such a damping system is shown schematically in

Fig. 3.21(*b*) and a form of it, using a vibrating mass of oil, is discussed below.

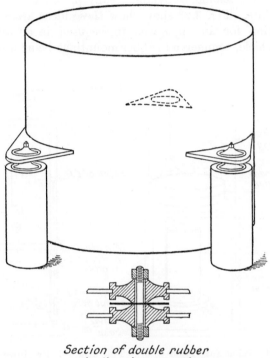

*Section of double rubber
anti-vibration mounting*

FIG. 3.23   Use of rubber anti-vibration mountings.   The centre of gravity of the suspended mass should lie in the plane of the mountings

3.18   Practical Forms of the Anti-Vibration Support

In constructing practical anti-vibration supports, we must take into account the following principles :

(*a*) The connection between the supported mass and the surroundings must have as long a period as possible compared with that of the expected disturbances.

(*b*) Translational vibrations transmitted to the supported mass must not be converted into rotational vibrations, for the latter are usually more detrimental than the former.   To this end, the centre of gravity of the suspended mass should be in the plane containing the points where the suspensions are attached, and should be symmetrically placed with respect to these points.   Fig. 3.23 shows how these ideas are applied to a mounting for an apparatus to be used in an aircraft or motor vehicle, commercial rubber mountings being used as the

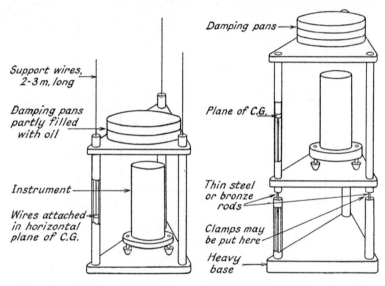

Support wires, 2-3 m, long

Damping pans partly filled with oil

Instrument

Wires attached in horizontal plane of C.G.

Damping pans

Plane of C.G.

Thin steel or bronze rods

Clamps may be put here

Heavy base

FIG. 3.24   Julius suspension— with internal oil damping

FIG. 3.25   Müller (Inverted elastic pendulum) anti-vibration suspension

elastic elements.   In this arrangement vibrations in all directions are treated more or less equally, but suspended instruments, which are particularly important in laboratory practice, are nearly insensitive to vertical vibrations, and it is therefore advantageous to design a support which has a long period for horizontal motion, even if it possesses considerable vertical stiffness.   One such support is the Julius suspension shown in Fig. 3.24.   The wires are long enough to give a pendulum period of the order 2-3 sec., and the points of attachment of the wires to the instrument cage lie in a plane with the centre of gravity of the loaded cage.   Julius used as damping pads of cotton wool between " ground " and the points of attachment of the wires to the cage, but it is found that the fluid damping system described below is more efficient.

The main disadvantage of the support is its size, which makes it difficult to instal in an ordinary room and to shield from draughts—this shielding from draughts is an important factor. An alternative to the Julius support is an inverted elastic pendulum as devised and discussed by Müller, who also introduced a form of internal damping by the friction of liquid (light oil) in shallow cylindrical chambers (Fig. 3.25).

APPENDIX 1

In this appendix are collected hints on certain elementary points which arise in the design of physical apparatus ; and a few warnings against design faults which, according to experience, are commonly committed by physicists without engineering training.

It is often possible, by careful design, to facilitate the making of a piece of apparatus without any detriment to function. The designer can often choose between using a casting and a built-up structure. Casting is advantageous if several copies are required, or if the alternative involves much waste cutting or a number of joints. Castings should be designed so that the pattern is easily drawn from the mould : cire-perdue casting is a useful special method for awkward shapes ; it is described by Strong. The stiffness of castings is usually good and can readily be improved by incorporating strengthening ribs, but the ultimate strength of many cast materials is rather low. Sometimes a casting, an instrument base for example, need be machined only locally where other components are attached. In such cases machining is made easier if pads are formed to stand above the general level of the face. Turning is the easiest and most accurate machining operation, and should be used wherever possible: it is often useful to design on a casting projections which serve to attach the piece to a machine table or chuck and serve no other purpose. They may very materially help in machining and may be left on the finished piece if they are harmless, cut off if they are detrimental to function or appearance.

Screws or bolts,* used to connect two pieces, should not be considered as providing accurate location of one part relative to the other, and the holes through which they pass should not be a close fit. The location can be effected by proper kinematic elements (§ 3.3), the screws supplying the closing forces, and this method is desirable if the pieces must be reassembled frequently and the location must be accurate. In normal instruments it is usual to rely upon dowel pins (Fig. 3.26). When the pieces have been adjusted to position and clamped, the holes for the dowel pins are drilled and taper

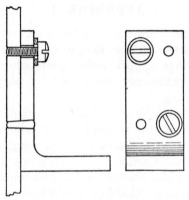

FIG. 3.26   Use of dowel pins

reamered. In certain cases it is important that one part be exactly centred on another, but minute relative rotations are of no consequence. It is then very good practice to turn on one part a cylindrical spigot which mates with a female element on the other, and it is usually sufficient to rely on the bolts for angular location.

A rotating shaft is normally provided with two bearings, which must be accurately in line if they are of appreciable length. It saves difficulty if the bearings are self-aligning ball bearings, and Fig. 3.9(b) shows a simple form of self-aligning sleeve bearing which has proved useful. In instrument work it is never necessary or desirable to support a shaft in three or more

---

* " Fitted bolts " with unthreaded cylindrical locating surfaces are occasionally used. They are less convenient in instrument construction than dowel pins.

bearings. If two shafts, nominally in line, are to be connected this must be done by a flexible coupling (see Fig. 3.27).

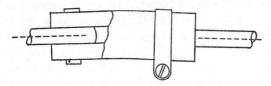

Thick-wall rubber tubing with clamps or wire binding

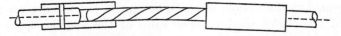

Flexible steel shaft (dental drive) as universal joint

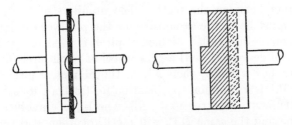

Flexible disc coupling   *Oldham coupling*

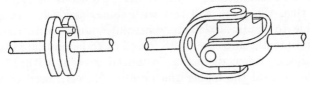

Simple pin-slot coupling   *Hooke's joint*

FIG. 3.27   Forms of universal coupling

It is very undesirable to design a mechanism which depends on a cam or a lever forcing a part into a position defined by a stop, e.g. a valve should not be closed against its seat by a cam. The condition could be met by very accurate workmanship, but it is then at the mercy of wear. It is slightly better to provide an adjustment by which the condition can be set up when necessary, but a better solution is to introduce a springy element at the correct place—the fundamental idea is to take up reasonable tolerances without producing unreasonably large elastic forces. In many cases (e.g. valves) only one position is necessarily defined by a stop and the moving part should be held against the stop by spring pressure and lifted off by the cam. Two spring devices can clearly be combined where both ends of the travel have to be definite.

Toothed gearing is frequently used to connect shafts which are to revolve at related, possibly different, speeds. Instrument gearing is of cycloidal (clock) tooth form or of involute form, but the details of tooth design do not usually concern the laboratory worker. The ratio of the angular speeds of two wheels is given inversely by the ratio of the diameters of two circles called the pitch circles, in which lie the points of contact between the teeth. The numbers of teeth in the wheels must be in the same ratio as the pitch-circle diameters and a convention called diametral pitch is used to specify the fineness of gear teeth. If a gear wheel of pitch circle diameter d inches has n teeth, then n/d is the diametral pitch (D.P.). " 40 D.P." is a common specification for (rather robust) wheels in instrument construction. All wheels (of involute tooth form) having the same D.P. will mesh together, and the theoretical distance between gear centres is half the sum of the pitch-circle diameters ; if the centre distance is rather greater than this, the gears will run with some backlash. It is not possible to obtain satisfactory involute pinions with less than about 10 teeth, since the tooth form has to be mutilated to give clearances. Some distortion is indeed present with 12 teeth and in general the higher the number of teeth used in a pair of gears the smoother will the wheels run. On the other hand coarse teeth are stronger than fine, and their meshing is less affected by a given departure from the correct centre distance.

Worm gearing is more compact than spur gearing for large velocity ratios, but the mechanical efficiency of instrument worm gearing is always low. This is not always a serious disadvantage. It must be remembered that the end thrust of a worm must be properly taken, and that friction in the thrust bearing has a serious effect on the overall efficiency. A ball thrust bearing is usually well justified.

APPENDIX 2

It is convenient to quote here a few standard engineering formulae which may be useful in the design of experimental apparatus. In many cases very rough design methods suffice for the greater part of an apparatus, and the simple formulae given here may be used. Particular parts of the apparatus may, however, need to approach in some way the limits of possible performance, and in such cases more sophisticated studies will be required.

TABLE 3.2

Useful Data on Loaded Beams

	Light beam clamped at one end, loaded at the other. Deflection . . . $Fl^3/3EI$ Maximum stress . . . Flh/I
	Light beam supported at both ends, loaded at centre. Deflection . . . . $Fl^3/48EI$ Maximum stress . . . $Flh/4I$
	Light beam clamped (encastré) at both ends, loaded at centre. Deflection . . . . $Fl^3/192EI$ Maximum stress . . . $Flh/8I$
	Uniformly loaded beam—clamped at one end. Deflection . . . . $fl^4/8EI$ Maximum stress . . . $fl^2h/2I$
	Uniformly loaded beam—supported at both ends. Deflection . . . . $5fl^4/384EI$ Maximum stress . . . $fl^2h/8I$
	Uniformly loaded beam, clamped at both ends. Deflection . . . . $fl^4/384EI$ Maximum stress . . . $fl^2h/12I$

F = force (concentrated).
f = force per unit length (distributed). E = Young's modulus.
I = second moment of cross section, often called Moment of Inertia.
I is given for some important sections below in Table 3.3.
h = maximum distance of a fibre from neutral axis.

TABLE 3.3

Second Moments (about axes indicated)

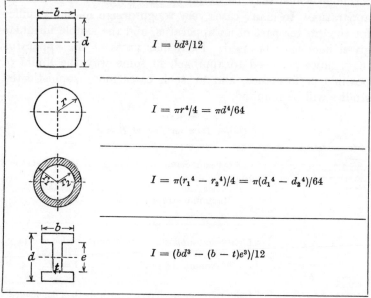

$I = bd^3/12$	
$I = \pi r^4/4 = \pi d^4/64$	
$I = \pi(r_1{}^4 - r_2{}^4)/4 = \pi(d_1{}^4 - d_2{}^4)/64$	
$I = (bd^3 - (b - t)e^3)/12$	

Some other shapes may be considered as sums or differences of these sections—the sections 3 and 4 above have obviously been derived in this way.

TABLE 3.4

Data on Thin, Centrally Loaded Struts in Compression

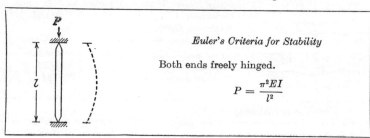

Euler's Criteria for Stability

Both ends freely hinged.

$$P = \frac{\pi^2 EI}{l^2}$$

I is second moment of cross-section as given above.

TABLE 3.4 *(cont.)*

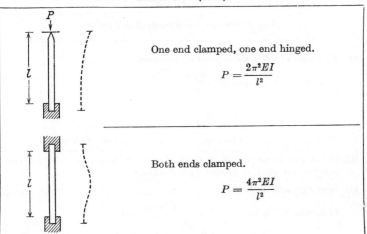

One end clamped, one end hinged.

$$P = \frac{2\pi^2 EI}{l^2}$$

Both ends clamped.

$$P = \frac{4\pi^2 EI}{l^2}$$

I is second moment of cross-section as given above.

TABLE 3.5

Data on Behaviour of Circular Shafts

(a) Twist/unit length $= \dfrac{M}{GI_p}$ radians/unit length

(b) Maximum shear stress $= \dfrac{Md}{2I_p}$

where $M =$ couple transmitted, d maximum diameter.

$G =$ shear modulus of elasticity.

$I_p =$ second polar moment about axis $= \iint r^2 dx dy$.

$I_p = \dfrac{\pi}{32} d^4$ for a solid circular shaft; diameter d.

$I_p = \dfrac{\pi}{32}(d_1{}^4 - d_2{}^4)$ for a hollow shaft; d_1, d_2 external and internal diameters.

Note that maximum allowed shear stress $= \frac{1}{2}$ maximum tensile stress for a given material.

(c) Lowest whirling speed of a shaft, supported in bearings which do not constrain its direction.

$$\frac{\pi}{2l^2}\sqrt{\frac{EI}{W}}$$

where

$l =$ length between bearings; $W =$ mass/unit length;

$E =$ Young's modulus, in *dynes/cm.*^{2} or *poundals/in.*^{2};

$I =$ second moment of cross-section about a meridian plane (Table 3.3).

TABLE 3.6

Wall Stresses in Vessels subject to Pressure

(*a*) Thin curved walls under internal pressure.

Tensile stress in cylinder $= \dfrac{pr}{t}$

in sphere $= \dfrac{pr}{2t}$

where $p =$ internal pressure, $r =$ radius, $t =$ wall thickness.

(*b*) Disk under pressure, e.g. flat end of cylinder, under conditions where deflection is small compared with thickness.

(**1**) Disk *supported* at edge

Deflection at centre $= \dfrac{3}{16} \dfrac{(1 - \sigma)(5 + \sigma)}{Et^3} \cdot pa^4.$

Maximum tensile stress (centre)

$$\frac{3}{8} \frac{a^2}{t^2}(3 + \sigma)p.$$

(**2**) Disk *clamped* at edge

Deflection at centre $\quad \dfrac{3}{16} \dfrac{(1 - \sigma)^2}{Et^3} pa^4.$

Maximum tensile stress (edge) $= \dfrac{3}{4} \cdot \dfrac{a^2}{t^2} \cdot p.$

$a =$ radius of disk ; $t =$ thickness ; $E =$ Young's modulus ;

$\sigma =$ Poisson's Ratio ; $p =$ pressure.

CHAPTER 4

MATERIALS OF CONSTRUCTION

4.1 Introduction

In the physical laboratory it is often necessary to design apparatus according to ordinary engineering rules, using materials which have become traditional. Some information is given here on the properties and uses of these materials; further data and formulae are to be found in engineering textbooks and handbooks. There are, however, some materials in common laboratory use which are little used in general engineering. Even more important, experimental methods may depend on the use of certain materials whose properties are outstanding in particular directions, e.g. the elastic properties of fused quartz fibres, the high melting-point of tungsten, the magnetic permeability of certain nickel-iron alloys. To an increasing extent these " extreme " substances are used in industry because their usually high cost is more than counterbalanced by the advantages to be gained from their use, but in experimental work they are particularly important, because the properties of a substance may control the whole performance of an instrument, and a better choice of some critical material may open a new region of investigation.

4.2 Metals—Mechanical Properties

Metals are, of course, used freely in constructing apparatus, and Fig. 4.1 gives an idea of the ways in which metal parts of instruments and machines can be made. Usually only processes of the last two groups shown are carried on in the laboratory workshop, but small forgings and castings and the making of patterns may also be done there.

The following terms are used in defining the strength of materials; the parameters chosen usually refer to simple tension.

E 101

(*a*) Elasticity (Young's modulus).

(*b*) Ultimate tensile strength: this is the highest stress reached in a tensile test carried to breakage. It is usual and

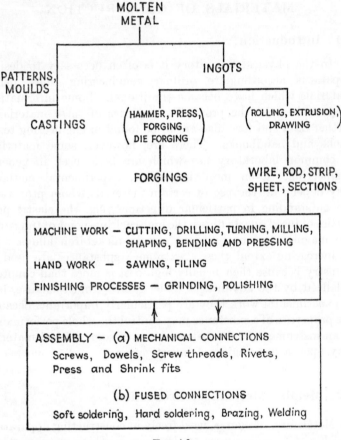

FIG. 4.1

convenient to calculate the stress as the force per unit area of the initial specimen. The fractional elongation at breakage is also recorded.

(*c*) The limit of proportionality: the lowest stress at which the material departs visibly from a linear stress-strain relation. This is less definite than (*d*) The 0·1 % (0·2 % etc.) proof stress, which is the stress required to produce a permanent elongation of 0·1 % (0·2 % etc.) of the original length.

(*e*) The yield point, which is shown only by certain materials, and which is the stress at which the material elongates without further increase of load. When yield has taken place, there is usually a further fairly regular increase of elongation with stress.

All the above quantities are usually given in British and American engineering work in tons/sq. in. or lb./sq. in.* In using these quantities in design, it is necessary to apply " safety factors " which allow for variations of the material, for temporary increases of stress due, e.g. to inertia forces (shock loading), and for elastic fatigue. In a few cases where personal hazards are involved (e.g. boilers, lifting tackle) these factors are specified by law ; in general, they are left to the experience of the designer. In a typical case, the working stress may be two-thirds of the 0·1 % proof stress, provided that conditions are rather definitely known. More conservative practice would be to make the working stress half the proof stress.

The properties of metals are profoundly affected by heat treatment and by mechanical deformation. In most pure metals and in some alloys, the main effect of treatment at high temperature is to develop a crystalline structure. This structure becomes coarser as the heat treatment is prolonged, and this is usually undesirable. The material annealed by proper heat treatment is soft and has relatively low strength, but it will withstand considerable deformation without fracture.†

When the material is cold-worked by stretching, bending, drawing, or hammering, the uniform crystalline structure is broken up and a fibrous structure appears. The material becomes harder and stronger, but also more brittle ; it often shows marked anisotropy due to the fibrous structure. For example, cold-rolled brass has a higher strength along the

---

* 1 Ton/sq. in. = 2240 lb./sq. in. = 157 kg./sq. cm. = 1·57 kg./sq. mm. = 1·55. 10^8 dynes/sq.cm. 1 American ton = 2000 lb.

† Some metals (tantalum, lead) are soft but do not withstand deformation well because they do not harden at all with cold working. Some degree of work-hardening acts as an automatic distributor of stress during working.

direction of rolling than across it, and while it can be bent across the direction of rolling, it cracks readily if the fold lies in the rolling direction.

The effect of heat treatment on alloys is often complicated by changes in the phase structure of the material—e.g. the separation, from a homogeneous mass, of crystals of a different composition. This phenomenon is particularly important in the iron-carbon alloys (steels) and in those alloys like duralumin and beryllium copper which show precipitation hardening.

4.3   Steels—Iron Alloys containing Carbon *

Table 4.1 gives a general classification of the plain iron-carbon steels. Mild and medium steels are not, in general, heat-treated in the workshop, though they may sometimes be worked hot or softened between cold working processes by

TABLE 4.1

Plain Carbon Steels

Mild steel . . .	0·06-0·25 % C.	Lowest carbon content used for rivets. Normal plates and angles lie in range 0·15-0·25 % C. These steels do not harden significantly by heat treatment.
Medium carbon steel .	0·25-0·6 % C.	Rails, bright drawn bar.
High carbon steel .	0·6-0·8 % C.	Springs, tools without cutting edges.
Tool steel (small bars sold as "silver steel")	0·8-1·5 % C.	Cutting tools. Steel with 1·1-1·5 % C used for light tools to take a keen cutting edge.

annealing at 550°-650° C. The ultimate tensile strength obtainable with mild and medium carbon steels varies with the specification of the steel from about 20 tons/sq. in. (with 28 % elongation) to 35-45 tons/sq. in. (with 12-15% elongation). The strength can be greatly raised by cold-drawing into wire ; mild

* A valuable guide to the properties of steels is given in B.S. 971/1950.

steel wire may have a U.T.S. of 40-60 tons/sq in., and for high-quality cold-drawn wire the U.T.S. may exceed 100 tons/sq. in.*

Carbon tool steels owe their usefulness to the way in which their hardness can be controlled by heat treatment. If these steels are heated to a temperature about 800° C. (bright red heat) and quenched in water, they become extremely hard and brittle.† This fully hardened (martensitic) steel is only useful for special purposes ; it is made tougher and less hard by the re-heating process called tempering. In this process the martensite, which is a hard, nearly homogeneous dispersion of carbon and iron, decomposes into a mixture with a fine granular structure, and the properties of the steel can be closely controlled by varying the temperature and duration of the tempering process. In good industrial practice, the process is controlled by thermometer, but in small workshops it is usually controlled by the traditional method of " temper colours " ; the piece is cleaned bright with emery and heated, e.g. on an iron plate. The oxide films which form show interference colours, first pale yellow, changing ultimately to blue. When the appropriate colour appears, the piece is removed and quenched. After tempering the steel is still too hard to be machined, but it may be finished to exact dimensions or

PRODUCTION OF A COMPONENT IN HARDENED STEEL (∼ 1 % C)

Annealing—Heat treatment at 750°—800° C and slow cooling.
|
(Steel normally bought in this condition)
|
Working by hand and machine tools, forging at red heat.
|
Hardening—heat to ca. 800° C and quench in water.
|
Tempering—heat to temperature in range 200°-300° C and quench.
|
Finish by grinding.

FIG. 4.2.

* It is possible to exploit the high strength of drawn wire by winding it tightly on a pressure vessel which is designed so that it can yield safely to an extent sufficient to transfer the tensile force to the wire.

† There are alloy tool steels which can be fully quenched at a much lower rate of cooling ; these steels are quenched in oil or in an air blast. This is an advantage, since warping or cracking may occur in violent quenching.

worked to a cutting edge by grinding.   During this process it must not be allowed to get hot enough to affect the tempering. Fig. 4.2 presents these facts graphically.   Table 4.2 gives a list of the film colours used as a guide in tempering.

TABLE 4.2

Tempering of Tool Steel

Temper colours	Temperature °C.	Uses
Pale yellow . .	225	Light turning tools, surgical cutting instruments, razors.
Light straw . .	235	Lathe tools, milling cutters.
Deep straw . .	240	Drills, small knives.
Brown . . .	255	Reamers, taps and dies, knives.
Purple . . .	275	Drills.
Dark blue . .	290	Wood saws.
Medium blue . .	305	Fine saws.
Light blue . .	315	Wood drills, cold chisels.

4.4   Alloy Steels

In industry, and especially in making motor-car parts, steels containing alloying elements (such as Ni, Cr, V, W, Mo) in addition to carbon are now freely used.   Alloy steels are not very likely to be used in the laboratory workshop except under special advice, but it must be remembered that they can provide considerably higher tensile strength than plain carbon steels.   For example, a steel with 3·5% nickel and 0·4% carbon, properly heat-treated, has a U.T.S. of about 110 tons/ sq. in.   High-tensile steel bolts are commercially available, and are sometimes valuable in saving space, since their diameter can be much less than that of mild steel parts of the same strength.

Steels containing chromium (12-18%) and carbon (0·3-0·7 %) are fairly hard, and show high resistance to corrosion (stainless cutlery steels) ; and steels containing tungsten, with chromium, carbon, and perhaps vanadium, retain hardness at temperatures up to red heat and are used for heavily loaded cutting tools (high speed steels).

Certain alloy steels with little carbon preserve at ordinary temperatures the crystalline form (face-centred γ-iron) characteristic of iron at high temperatures. These " austenitic " alloys are paramagnetic, not ferromagnetic : they harden by cold-work, but not by heat treatment. Austenitic steels containing 10 % manganese are used industrially to withstand heavy crushing loads by virtue of exceptional work-hardening under small deformation. The austenitic stainless steels (particularly the 18 % Cr, 8 % Ni steel marketed in this country as Staybrite) are strong (e.g. 45 tons U.T.S., further increased by cold rolling), tough, and particularly resistant to corrosion. This alloy is easily manipulated as sheet, strip, and rod, and may be machined, though it is too tough to machine very freely. These steels are described in British Standards as En 58. Special variations provide for deep drawing or for free machining.

4.5   Invar and Elinvar

The thermal expansion of the iron-nickel alloys varies with composition in the peculiar way shown in Fig. 4.3, and shows a minimum at about 36 % Ni. The alloy of this composition (the commercial product contains a little manganese and a minimum amount of carbon) is called Invar, and it is useful for the construction of parts of apparatus (e.g. interferometer spacers, clock pendulums) whose dimensions should not vary with changes in room temperature. The low coefficient of expansion is only obtained over a short temperature range. The actual value depends on the heat and mechanical treatments, and may be nearly zero for some specimens. The alloy is valuable for working standards of length, particularly surveyors' tapes, which do not then need accurate temperature control. Its dimensional stability over a long period is not, however, beyond suspicion (see e.g. Rolt 1929).

The thermal conductivity of 36 % nickel iron is very low (0·026 cal./cm. sec.) and the alloy may be used when a mechanical and electrical connection (resistivity 90 $\mu\Omega$-cm.) is required to conduct as little heat as possible, as in low-temperature apparatus or in certain supports inside vacuum tubes. An adjusted alloy containing nickel and iron with another element, usually chromium, has the property that Young's modulus does not vary with temperature. It is called "Elinvar". It has been used for making tuning forks, and, extensively, for the balance-springs of watches.

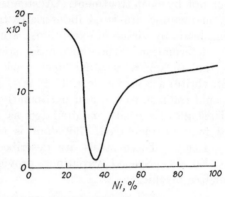

FIG. 4.3   The thermal expansion of iron-nickel alloys.
(Temperature range 0—100° C.)

4.6   Copper and its Alloys

Copper is important mainly because of its electrical properties (§ 4.14) ; its high thermal conductivity is sometimes important, and the metal is used for pipes because of the ease with which it can be soldered and cold-worked. Between bouts of cold-working, copper is annealed by heating at about 600° C. (red heat), and it may be quenched from this temperature. The machining of copper is rather difficult because the soft, tough metal clings to the tool. For the important applications of copper in vacuum technology, the special O.F.H.C. grade should be used. See p. 183.

4.7   Copper-Zinc Alloys—Brasses

The zinc brasses are cheaper, stronger, and more easily machined than copper ; the electrical and thermal conductivities are, however, much lower. Brass is bought as rod, tube, sheet, or strip, and the hardness and strength of the material is that due to cold-working in manufacture. If it is necessary to anneal brass during manipulation it is heated to 500°-600° C. for a short time. Brass is still one of the most useful metals in laboratory constructional work because of the ease with which it is worked. It can very easily be soft-soldered or silver-soldered. Since brazing alloys are themselves brasses with melting-points not very different from that of constructional brass, brazing is not easily possible. Brass castings are made in large numbers, and can be used for many purposes, but they are not reliably leak-tight.

4.8 Copper-Tin Alloys—Bronze and Gun Metal

Alloys containing tin are much more costly than brasses, and they are therefore only used for the sake of their special properties.

Gun-metal makes good clean castings which are much less likely to be porous than brass castings. It should therefore be used for all sorts of leak-tight vessels.

Phosphor bronze (containing phosphorus only as a minor constituent) is used for heavily loaded bearing bushes (which are machined from material bought as chill-cast rods), and for springy parts, which are cut from cold-worked sheet or wire. The worked material can be bought in different degrees of cold-working ; the fully work-hardened alloy is one of the strongest non-ferrous materials. Rolled phosphor bronze sheet is markedly anisotropic, and springy parts must be cut with attention to the " grain " or direction of rolling.

4.9 Copper-Nickel Alloys

These alloys are tough, strong and particularly resistant to corrosion ; they go under various names, e.g. German silver. The alloy Constantan is one of the most important materials for electrical resistances (§ 4.14) ; it may also be used for electrodes and other structures inside vacuum tubes. A further special use of the nickel-copper alloys is in certain thermal apparatus where pipe connections are required to have a very low heat transmission. Invar (§ 4.5) and some of the austenitic chrome steels have still lower thermal conductivities.

4.10   Copper-Beryllium

An alloy containing about 2 % beryllium in copper has very special properties which make it valuable for springs and highly stressed parts. Properly treated, it is probably the strongest non-ferrous material available. The material is bought as sheet, wire, etc., and it can be supplied with different degrees of hardness obtained by cold-working. After cutting and bending to shape it can be hardened by heat treatment only ; this property gives it an important advantage over alloys such as phosphor bronze which can only be hardened by cold work. A typical heat treatment, for material initially " half-hard ", consists in heating to 300° C. for $1\frac{1}{2}$ hr.* The process which takes place is called precipitation hardening ; it is due to the separation of a network of hard crystals from a solid supersaturated solution. The fully heat-treated material has a U.T.S. of 75-100 tons/sq. in., with a 0·1 % proof stress of 60-70 tons/sq. in. Beryllium copper can be silver-soldered before the heat treatment or soft soldered after heat hardening without affecting its final properties.

4.11   Aluminium and Light Alloys

These materials have densities in the region 2·7-2·8 ; at present they are considerably cheaper than brass when compared on the basis of volume or strength. Alloys are available for casting or forging and a wide variety of drawn and extruded sections are made. Most of the alloys machine very well, and some have strength comparable with that of mild steel. Light alloys are therefore of great and increasing use in the construction of physical apparatus. Their outstanding disadvantage is that they cannot be jointed satisfactorily by soft soldering and although welding is used in industry, it requires special skill and is not always available in laboratories. In ordinary practice, therefore, mechanical connections must be used. There is scope for certain plastic bonds for making or sealing joints in aluminium (§ 4.13).

* The operation can very conveniently be carried out on small components by boiling them in benzyl benzoate (B.P. 324° C.) in the bottom of a long wide tube heated by a small flame so that the liquid refluxes continuously.

Commercially pure aluminium can be cold worked and annealed when required at about 350° C.; it is useful for sheet metal work, as constructing chassis for electronic equipment, but its tensile strength is low (*ca.* 5 tons/sq. in. U.T.S., rising somewhat with cold work). There is a very great variety of aluminium alloys, covered by a series of British Standards (B.S. 1470-1477 and B.S. 1490). Comprehensive information is obtainable in England from the Aluminium Development Association. Alloys containing silicon (e.g. LM6, corresponding to the former L33) are particularly suitable for instrument castings: but there are casting alloys which develop considerable strength (e.g. 20 tons/sq. in. U.T.S. after heat treatment).

Some of the wrought alloys of aluminium can be worked cold without special precautions, but the stronger alloys, and particularly the important duralumin group (Al, Cu, Mg, some Mn) do not withstand much cold work. They show the phenomenon of precipitation hardening (cf. § 4.10) at room temperatures : duralumin is softened by heating to 480°-500° C. (solution treatment) and quenching in water. Precipitation hardening (ageing) begins at once, and is nearly complete in four or five days at ordinary temperatures. Cold working of any severity should be complete in an hour or two after quenching. In industrial practice, the heat treatment is carried out in a salt bath (usually a fused mixture of sodium nitrite and nitrate) or in a closed furnace.

Magnesium and alloys based upon it are the lightest commercial constructional metals. They have densities around 1·75-1·85, and some alloys have U.T.S. values up to about 16 tons/sq. in. (wrought). Magnesium alloys machine particularly well. It is sometimes possible, by using magnesium alloys, to reduce considerably the weight and inertia of moving parts of instruments.

4.12 The Jointing of Metals—Soldering

As indicated in Fig. 4·1, metal parts can be joined by mechanical or fusion methods. The latter are considered here in more detail. In the soldering processes, a solder is used whose melting-point is below that of the metals to be joined, and the latter are heated, at least momentarily above the melting-point of the solder.   The solder then wets the metals, and alloys with them superficially.   If the joint is torn asunder the failure occurs in the solder rather than at its junction with the other metal.   For this union to take place the surfaces must be clean, and it is usually necessary to use a chemical flux, e.g. zinc chloride solution, which dissolves oxide films. The flux must be removed when the joint is finished by washing with hot water.   For the special case of soft solder applied to clean surfaces as in making electrical connections, resin is used as a flux and its function is to protect the metal from oxidation rather than actively to dissolve oxides.   It is not corrosive.   Solder wire provided with a core of resin flux is

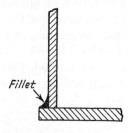

FIG. 4.4   Fillet formed on a soldered joint

very largely used in wiring electric circuits.   In soft-soldering the work is heated by a flame or by a hot copper bit, and it is *essential* that it reach the melting-point of the solder, which will not stick to cold metal.   In using the soldering bit, the liquid solder is manipulated so that it helps the thermal contact between bit and work and the bit is drawn slowly along the line of the joint.   When cored solder is used, the metals must be cleaned, and preferably tinned, in advance, and the solder and soldering bit must be applied simultaneously to the joint.   It is not good to melt the solder on the bit and then to apply the bit to the work.   In soldering electrical connections the iron must be so hot that the connecting point is heated to the soldering temperature without a prolonged use of the bit which overheats adjacent parts.   It is often possible to protect delicate electrical components from the heat of soldering operations by applying a mass of good conductor (" thermal shunt ") to the connection between the

component and the joint which is being made. Pliers, used to
hold a component, may often be employed as thermal shunts.

TABLE 4.3

Solders

	Composition	m.p.	Notes
Wood's metal	Bi 50 Cd 12·5 Pb25 Sn 12·5	61° *a*	Special low temperature soldering. Fusible safety devices.
Rose metal .	Bi 50 Pb 25 Sn 25	94° *a*	
Hard low m.p. solder	Pb 40 Sn 40 Bi 20	150°	Recommended for instrument springs.
Soft solder .	Pb 67 Sn 33	240° *a*	Low tin content gives cheaper and harder solders which go through a pasty stage on solidification.
	Pb 50 Sn 50	188° *a*	
	Pb 36 Sn 64	181° *a*	Eutectic—suitable for electric connections.
Silver solder	Ag 45 Cu 30 Zn 25	720° *b*	Ag–Cu Eutectic. Recommend for high vacuum work ; no volatile constituents.
	Ag 72 Cu 28	778° *c*	
	Ag 50 Cu15·5 Zn16·5 Cd 18	630° *b*	
	Ag	962° *c*	
	Cu	1084° *c*	
Brazing brass	Cu 54 Zn 46	875° *b*	

a = Zinc-chloride flux ; *b* = Borax flux ; *c* = Best used in vacuum without flux.

A common cause of failure in soldering is relative movement of the parts, just as the solder is setting. In constructional work it is often good to " tin " the parts with solder, assemble them, and heat the whole until the solder flows (" sweating "). A thin film of soft solder used to seal and lock a mechanical joint (e.g. a male and female screw coated with solder and screwed together hot) makes an extremely strong and gastight joint. In a more frequently used type of joint, the solder forms a " fillet "—(Fig. 4.4). It is well to form the fillet on the hot joint by leading the solder into place with a wire dipped in flux, and to clean up the joint with a wire dipped in clean water before allowing it to cool. Any soldered joint made with a corrosive flux should be well washed with hot water after completion.

Hard solders are much stronger than soft solders, and used with a flux they flow very freely into narrow spaces. The heating is nearly always done with a blowpipe flame, concentrated in the case of larger work by a simple hearth of firebrick. Brazing alloys are soft brasses which are used like hard solders, mainly for joining copper and steel parts. Pure silver and copper may be used as jointing metals, by a method described in § 5.8.

In welding the pieces to be joined are locally melted, and the additional jointing material, if any, is more or less similar in composition to the pieces. In flame welding an oxyacetylene flame is usually used, and metal is melted in from a rod held in the flame. In an ordinary workshop this process is most often applied to mild steel, but copper, aluminium, and other metals can be flame welded. The strength of the welds and their freedom from leakage depend markedly on the skill and conscientiousness of the operator. Electric arc welding requires more elaborate apparatus than flame welding, but is much used in industry: in a comparatively new and very advantageous method the arc is struck between the work and a tungsten electrode and the arc region is flooded by a stream of inert gas (for economic reasons argon is used in Britain and helium is common in the United States). The process requires special equipment to control and maintain the arc; the weld metal is fed in as usual from a rod. This method is eminently applicable to aluminium and its alloys, magnesium alloys, and stainless steel. Very good welds can be made, since the inert gas prevents the formation of oxides which might contaminate the weld. Vacuum vessels are now often fabricated in this way.

Spot-welding is very much used for making electrodes for vacuum tubes, and is discussed in Chapter 5, Appendix 2; it may be used for light general construction, but laboratory spot-welders are not usually powerful enough for materials more than a millimetre or so thick.

4.13 Plastic Cements for Metals

Very recently, some thermosetting plastics have been introduced which stick well to metals and which can be used for making and sealing joints in laboratory practice. They are particularly valuable for use with aluminium, which cannot be soldered effectively. The substance sold as " Araldite " melts to a free-flowing liquid at about 100° C., and polymerises at about 200° C. to a solid which is an effective general adhesive.* Cold setting resins of the same type are available. They are mixed with a " hardener " just before application. These substances are further discussed on p. 135.

4.14 Metals for Electrical Purposes

For ordinary electrical conductors, copper is in practice unrivalled. Aluminium has occasionally been used for coil windings, more frequently for heavy current busbars, where its large surface for a given mass or given conductivity leads to good heat dissipation. Silver is important as a conductor in thin films in condensers and as a plating on high-frequency conductors ; it is not often economically possible to use it as a massive conductor. The conductivity of copper depends greatly on its purity and the figure given refers to an international standard of commercially pure, worked and annealed copper. A slightly higher conductivity is sometimes obtained. Data for iron, platinum and tungsten are given in Table 4.4 because of their importance for special purposes. The elec-

---

* Epoxy resins such as Araldite, once polymerised, are unaffected by most ordinary chemicals. If coatings are to be removed or joints broken, the best reagent appears to be dimethylformamide. (Brit. Pat. 818331.)

trical resistances of all pure metals vary very roughly in proportion to the absolute temperature.*

TABLE 4.4
Commercially Pure Metals for Electrical Purposes

	Density g./cc.	Sp. resist. at 20° C. microhm. cm.	Temp. coefficient resistance at 0° C.	m.p. °C.
Copper	8·9	1·7	4 . 10^{-3}	1083
Silver	10·5	1·63	4 . 10^{-3}	961
Aluminium	2·7	2·8	4 . 10^{-3}	658
Iron	7·8	9·6	5 . 10^{-3}	1530
Platinum	21·4	10·6	4 . 10^{-3}	1771
Tungsten (wire)	19·0	5·5	5 . 10^{-3}	3400

4.15   Alloys for Electrical Purposes

Cadmium is one of the metals which has the least effect on the conductivity of copper, and 1-2 % cadmium copper is a useful alloy where a metal of high conductivity is required to be stronger and harder than pure copper.

Electrical resistances are conveniently made of alloys whose resistivity, high compared with that of pure metals, varies much less with temperature than theirs. Some important alloys are given in Table 4.5. Table 4.6 gives approximate data for some metals and alloys which are useful in constructing thermocouples. Thermocouples for radiation measurement are discussed in § 9.8.

4.16   Magnetic Materials (Soft) (see Chapter 6)

The magnetic materials used in laboratory practice fall into two groups : " soft " magnetic materials with high per-

---

* This relation is useful for estimating the working temperature of a copper winding from its measured resistance compared with the resistance at room temperature. A more accurate value of the temperature coefficient of resistance for copper is 0·00428 per °C. calculated on the resistance at 0° C., so that the resistance is proportional to Centigrade temperature + 234°.

TABLE 4.5

Alloys with Important Electrical Properties

	Sp. resist. microhm. cm.	
Cadmium copper . 1-2 % Cd.	*ca.* 1·8	Higher strength than copper, combined with high electrical conductivity (95-90 % compared with pure copper). *Uses:* stressed wires and special windings, electrodes for spot-welders, switch contacts.
Constantan (Eureka, Advance) about 55 Cu, 45 Ni	*ca.* 50	Low temperature coefficient of resistance. High thermo-E.M.F. against copper (*ca.* 40 microvolt/C). *Uses:* resistances for measurement and current control, low-temperature heaters up to 400° C.
Manganin . .	*ca.* 44	Low temperature coefficient of resistance. Low thermo - E.M.F. against copper. *Use:* measurement resistances where the high thermo-E.M.F. of constantan against copper cannot be tolerated. The alloy must be hard-soldered, and should be annealed after winding. It is then a very stable resistance material.
Nickel chromium . 80-20 (e.g. Nichrome V, Chromel A)	103	Resists oxidation at high temperatures. *Uses:* electric heaters and furnace windings operating in air up to 1100° C.
Nickel chromium with iron and manganese (e.g. Nichrome, Chromel C)	109	More ductile than above, but maximum temperature about 950° C. *Uses:* electric heaters and regulating resistances.

A proprietary alloy called Kanthal, of undisclosed composition, is available for heater and furnace windings operating in air up to 1350° C.

meability and small retentive power, and " hard " magnetic materials with high retentivity and coercivity.*

TABLE 4.6

Thermocouples

(See B.S. 1041/1943. *Temperature Measurement*)

($V =$ approximate thermo-E.M.F. in μV/°C. at working temperature)

	V
(a) *Special Alloys for Highest Sensitivity* (See Strong 1939, and refs. quoted there) Bismuth v Bi/5 °/$_0$ Sn Bismuth v Antimony The E.M.F. of these couples depend on crystal orientation	$\sim$ 120 75-150
(b) *Laboratory Measurements at Low Temperatures* Copper v Constantan—400° C. Constantan v. (Ni Cr 90/10 "Chromel P")—750° C.	40 70
(c) " *Base Metal* " *Couples for Furnaces*, at moderate temperatures up to 1000° C. and intermittent use at higher temperatures up to 1200° C. Chromel P v Alumel (Ni/Al 94/2 with Si, Mn) Wires are obtainable from makers with approximate batch calibrations, giving accuracy of a few degrees	40
(d) " *Platinum* " *Thermocouple Alloys* Platinum v Pt/10 °/$_0$ Rh Useful up to 1300° C. (1500° for short periods) Accurate batch calibrations are available from makers and with proper precautions, accuracy of 1°-2° is attainable at 1000° C.	10

Table 4.7 gives the characteristics of some " soft " magnetic materials. Soft iron is used where a steady, high induction is required, as in electromagnet cores. Wherever an electromagnet is to be designed to give the highest possible

---

* Both types are described very fully in Bozorth 1951.

field in the air gap, the saturation induction in the iron is decisive. If the field required is higher than the saturation induction, the poles of the magnet must be coned down (see p. 216), and it may be worth while to make the pole tips of the relatively expensive 50/50 cobalt iron, for which B at saturation is about 10 % higher than for the best commercial iron. Apart from cobalt, all additions to pure iron reduce B_{sat}, and the purest iron available is used for electromagnet poles, though low-carbon steel, thoroughly annealed, is not much inferior.

Silicon iron (usually about 4 % Si, e.g. Stalloy) is of great engineering importance because it has a small hysteresis loss when taken round magnetisation cycles of amplitude about $B_{max} = 13,000$ gauss. It has an electrical resistance several times that of pure iron, and this acts to reduce eddy-current loss in electrical machinery. Silicon iron is the normal material for transformer cores ; a new material now being introduced is 3 % silicon steel which has been subject to drastic cold rolling producing an oriented structure. This material shows improved magnetic behaviour compared with normal silicon steel if the direction of magnetisation in use is the same as the direction of rolling. It is of course necessary to design the magnetic circuit of a transformer specially to take advantage of this property: the core may be made by winding a continuous strip, or more conveniently by clamping together strips in the form of a C.

The materials of Table 4.7B are distinguished by very high permeability in low magnetic fields. Their hysteresis loops are very narrow, but the induction at saturation is not particularly high. One of their most interesting uses is in the cores of audio-frequency transformers. They have revolutionised the performance of these devices, since even with cores of comparatively small area, the core flux can be made very large compared with the magnetic leakage. The cores must not be exposed to appreciable d.c. magnetisation, since they saturate even in fairly weak fields and lose their characteristic high permeability. Similarly, these alloys make excellent magnetic shields, e.g. for transformers and galvanometers, provided that the disturbing fields are small enough.

TABLE 4.7

Soft Magnetic Materials

Materials for use at high B

	$4\pi I_{max}$
Softest iron . . .	21,500
3·7% Silicon steel .	19,500
Cobalt iron (40-50% Co)	23,000

Note.—The *permeability* of iron is very sensitive to impurity. For a "dynamo steel" a representative value is about 5000 at $B = 8000$. The *alternating hysteresis loss* for 4% silicon steel is about 0·6 of that for "dynamo steel" when B_{max} lies between 10,000-13,000.

B.   *Materials for highest permeability in low fields*

	$\mu_{initial}$	μ_{max}	Effective saturation
Mumetal, Permalloy C .	$3 \cdot 10^4$	$\sim 10^5$ at $H = 0.05$	$B = 8000$ at $H = 0.5$
Supermalloy, Super-mumetal . . .	$\sim 10^5$	$\sim 10^6$ at $H = 0.003$	$B = 8000$ at $H = 0.05$

C.   *Materials with intermediate permeability characteristics*

	$\mu_{initial}$	μ_{max}	Effective saturation
Radiometal, Permalloy B	2000	2.10^4 at $H = 0.3$	15,000 at $H = 3$
Rhometal, Permalloy D	1500	8000 at $H = 0.5$	11,000 at $H = 5$

D.   *Materials for temperature compensation—(low Curie point)*

30/70 Ni/Fe	Permeability 100 → 20 over temperature range 0° — 50° C.
70/30 Ni/Cu	,, 25 → 6 ,, ,, ,, 0° — 60° C.

This table is indicative of the properties of available materials—for fuller information (Mond 1949) or the makers' publications must be consulted.

They must usually be shielded themselves by an iron outer shield. The property of saturation in a small field has been applied in a number of devices for detecting small magnetic fields (see p. 221).

The characteristic properties of the high permeability alloys appear only after careful annealing (e.g. $\frac{1}{2}$ hr. at 1000° C. in a hydrogen atmosphere) ; they are very sensitive to cold work, and the material must be re-annealed after any but very small deformations. Any cutting or drilling after annealing must be done with specially sharp tools to avoid work-hardening and consequent worsening of the magnetic properties.

The properties of the materials in Table 4.7, group C, are similar to those of group B, but less extreme ; their permeabilities, initially lower than those of group B, are maintained in higher fields. Their principal use is in transformer cores for audio and low radio frequencies.

The materials of Table 4.7, group D, have Curie points at relatively low temperatures, and their useful characteristic is that their permeability falls rapidly with increasing temperature at ordinary temperatures. They can be used for compensating electrical instruments against temperature effects on permanent magnetism and coil resistance, since a magnetic shunt of one of these alloys by-passes a decreasing fraction of the available magnetic flux as the temperature increases.

4.17 Magnetic Materials (Hard)

The alloys available for permanent magnets have also been greatly improved in recent years. The usual duty of a permanent magnet is to maintain a magnetic field in an air gap (e.g. moving coil meters, magnetrons) or to maintain a magnetic moment (e.g. compass needles, magnetometers). In each case, the magnetic material is exposed to a demagnetising field which can be calculated. The permanent magnetic material must therefore possess coercivity (see Fig. 4.5) and in use it will be working under conditions represented by the quadrant of the magnetisation curve shown in the figure. In the magnetic circuit of, p. 217, calculation shows that the magnetic material is used most economically when the dimensions are chosen so that BH has the maximum value for the material.   Permanent magnet materials can be compared (volume for volume) on the basis of the maximum value of BH which each can attain.   Table 4.8 shows that $(BH)_{max}$ is much higher for some of the new materials than for the older magnet steels, so that a much less volume of the material is required for a given duty.   On account of the high value of the coercive force corresponding to $(BH)_{m\;x}$, the new materials are often

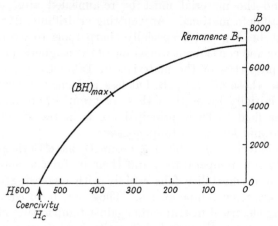

Fig. 4.5   Demagnetisation curve for a permanent magnet alloy.   (Data approximately correct for Alnico)

best employed in the form of relatively short blocks provided with soft iron pole pieces, and this construction fits well with their mechanical properties.   They are too hard and brittle to be machined ; they must be cast to shape and finished by grinding.   Quite recently, magnets have been made from these alloys by the methods of powder metallurgy.   Pieces can be pressed to accurate dimensions, and soft iron extensions can be incorporated.   The maximum magnetic properties are a little inferior to those of the cast metals.

The anisotropic alloys of Table 4.8 acquire their optimum properties if they are annealed after manufacture and cooled in a magnetic field.   They must then be magnetised and used with the magnetisation in the same direction as obtained during cooling, and the design of the magnetic circuit must be appropriate to this condition.

The magnetisation of these alloys is considerably less affected by temperature than that of magnet steels (the change in magnetisation between 0° and 100° C. is of the order of 1 % for Alnico, and 10 % for tungsten steel) ; the alloys are also more resistant than steel to demagnetisation by alternating

TABLE 4.8

Representative Permanent Magnetic Materials

	$B_{remanent}$ gauss	$H_{coercive}$ oersted	$(BH)_{max}$	B, H for $(BH)_{max}$	
Anisotropic alloys . e.g. Alcomax III Alnico V(U.S.A.) Ticonal G Columax	12,500-13,500	600-750	$4 \cdot 5 - 7 \cdot 5 \times 10^6$	9500	500
Alnico alloys . .	7500	550	$1 \cdot 7 \times 10^6$	5000	350
Alni alloys . .	5800	550	$1 \cdot 25 \times 10^6$	3500	350
35 % Cobalt steel .	9000	250	$0 \cdot 95 \times 10^6$	6000	16
3 % Cobalt steel .	7200	130	$0 \cdot 35 \times 10^6$	4250	83
6 % Tungsten steel .	10,500	65	$0 \cdot 3 \times 10^6$	7000	43
Vicalloy . . . (Ductile)	9000	300	1×10^6	5500	180
" Hard " Ferrites e.g. Caslox, Vectalite Magnadur	2000	1750 1600	$0 \cdot 95 \times 10^6$	950	1000

This table is indicative of the properties of available materials.   For fuller information see Tyrrell 1950, or the makers' publications, in particular those of the Permanent Magnet Association, Sheffield.

fields.   The performance of magnets can be stabilised by artificially demagnetising them slightly from the working conditions assumed in Fig. 4.5 ; any small changes of magnetisation due to applied fields then take place on a subsidiary hysteresis curve which has considerably less slope than the normal magnetisation curve.

The properties of the new magnet alloys allow permanent magnets to be used in ways formerly reserved for electromagnets ; they can, for example, be seriously considered for mass spectrographs, and for α and β-ray spectrographs, where their inherent constancy is an obvious advantage in long exposures.

4.18 Ferrites

At present, there are many important applications of the magnetic materials called ferrites, which are substances in which other elements replace part of the iron in ferrous ferrite (magnetite) $Fe(Fe_2O_4)$. Properly chosen ferrites can behave as "soft" or "hard" magnetic materials and they can exhibit interesting and useful behaviour at high frequencies and in respect to the shapes of their hysteresis loops (Ferrites 1957). Their magnetic properties are combined with electrical resistivity characteristic of moderate insulators (up to about 10^7 ohm-cm.) so that they can be used without lamination up to the highest frequencies. Mechanically they may be compared with ceramics: they are microcrystalline powders, which are prepared by moulding under pressure and sintering at a high temperature. Typical " soft " ferrite materials have initial permeability in the region 100-800, maximum permeability up to a few thousand, and saturation flux density up to about 3000. They are therefore less advantageous than metallic ferromagnetic alloys for power and similar frequencies. They have, however, been used for transformer and inductor cores at audio frequencies, and very effectively for cores at radio intermediate frequencies of hundreds of kilocycles and at telephone carrier frequencies; the Q factors of the coils at such frequencies are high and stable. At broadcast radio frequencies, ferrite rods with coils wound upon them find application as directional radio aerials. " Hard " ferrites are mentioned in Table 4.8. They are characterised by high coercivity, low permeability and moderate maximum BH product, and therefore show to advantage where magnetisation must be maintained in a coercive field: certain focusing magnets for cathode-ray tubes are typical. By proper choice and treatment of ferrites, magnetic cores can be made with nearly rectangular hysteresis diagrams, and these are used extensively as two-state memory elements in computer technology. The elements usually take the form of small rings; the two circumferential directions of magnetisation represent the digits 0 and 1, and the state is reversed by passing current through windings on the rings. The passage of a ring from one state to the other is detected by the voltage induced in another winding. Two- or three-dimensional arrays of toroids with appropriate circuits form stores for computers, including various special-purpose data-handling systems. Finally, ferrites are used for certain special purposes at microwave frequencies, since they exhibit strong Faraday effect (rotation of the plane of polarisation of waves in the presence of a magnetic field). In conjunction with properly shaped waveguides and cavities, they form elements which allow propagation in one direction only, or which perform more complicated, non-reciprocal routeing operations in microwave propagation.

4.19 Non-Magnetic Materials

There is no difficulty in obtaining materials which are sufficiently non-magnetic (i.e. free from ferromagnetism) for ordinary purposes. In this connection it is sometimes useful to remember that austenitic steels (§ 4.4) are paramagnetic but not ferromagnetic.

It is comparatively difficult to find metallic materials which are sufficiently free from ferromagnetic impurities for use in sensitive magnetometers and similar instruments. In critical applications it is necessary to test specimens with a sensitive magnetometer before use (Johnson and Steiner 1937), and it must be noted that a substance which shows an apparently correct paramagnetic or diamagnetic permeability may still show a remanent magnetisation due to ferromagnetic impurity. The effect may be detected by testing with a sensitive magnetometer after exposure to a strong magnetic field.

Magnetic impurity, presumably iron, may be introduced in casting, and some manufacturers are prepared to supply brasses and bronzes in non-magnetic qualities. Chapman and

Bartels (1940) give directions for casting non-magnetic copper alloys. It has been found that copper can be made non-magnetic by heat treatment in hydrogen (2 hr. at 850° C.) ; the impurity apparently dissolves in the copper lattice under this treatment. (Constant *et al.* 1943 ; see also B.S.I.R.A. 1924). A special non-magnetic alloy is described by Pugh (1958).

Some commercial light-alloy specimens are satisfactory in this connection, and Perspex is excellent where applicable.

It is not certain whether important amounts of ferro-magnetic impurity are picked up from clean steel tools in ordinary machining, but it is a reasonable precaution to use carbide-tipped tools and to observe a high standard of cleanliness.

4.20   Insulating Materials

Electrical insulating materials can conveniently be divided into classes :

(*a*) High temperature insulators, available above, say, 200° C. Table 4.9.

(*b*) General purpose insulators, including textiles and plastics. Tables 4.10, 4.12.

(*c*) Wire coverings.

(*d*) Insulating varnishes—used largely to impregnate textiles and windings.

(*e*) Insulating oil—used to immerse electrical apparatus to improve its behaviour at high voltages or to help in cooling.

(*f*) Insulators good enough for electrostatic work.   Table 4.11.

4.21   Plastics

A number of organic resinoid materials have come into industrial use in recent years. Their moulding properties cannot usually be exploited in the laboratory workshop, and unless ready-made mouldings can be used, plastics have to be worked and machined like metals.   In most of their laboratory

TABLE 4.9

Insulating Materials for High Temperatures

Material	Density g./cc.	Dielectric constant	Power factor	Electric strength	Notes
Mica	2·75-3	6-7	2-8.10⁻⁴ at 50 c/s 2.10⁻⁴ at 1 Mc/s	10-20 kV for 0·1 mm.	Thin flexible plates, useful up to 500° C. (certain kinds to 900° C.). Amber phlogopite electrically inferior to ruby muscovite, but withstands higher temperatures. Uses include washers and separators loaded in compression, heating elements and furnace winding insulation, condenser dielectric.
Hard porcelain	2·3-2·5	6	~ 2.10⁻² at 50 c/s — 1 Mc/s	30 kV for 1 mm. 90 kV for 5 mm.	Useful up to 1400° C. Not readily worked after manufacture. Uses include furnace tubes and beads for insulating wires at high temperatures.
Special ceramics for high frequencies (1)	2·7	6	10⁻³ at 50 c/s 3.10⁻⁴ at 1-50 Mc/s		Used for coil formers and condenser dielectrics at high frequency. Types (2) and (3) can be used as condenser dielectrics and combined to give temperature-compensated combinations of condensers.
(2)		80 Neg. temp. coefft.	3.10⁻⁴ at 1-50 Mc/s		
(3)		20 Pos. or zero temp. coefft.	3.10⁻⁴ at 1-50 Mc/s		

TABLE 4.9—(*cont.*)

Materials	Density g./cc.	Dielectric constant	Power factor	Electric strength	Notes
Steatite . Pyrophyllite .	2·6–2·8	5·5–6·5	2.10^{-3} at 50 Mc/s	5–10 kV for 1 mm. 800 V for 5 mm. at 900° C.	Can be worked readily before baking at about 1000° C. Baked material softens about 1500° C. Insulation good at 600° C. and useful at higher temperatures. Uses include vacuum tube parts, machined components.
Alumina .	3·0–3·9	Up to 9·9 (sintered)		800 V for 5 mm. at 1200° C.	Tubes and rods available commercially. Cannot be worked readily after manufacture. Uses include furnace cores and other parts, for temperatures up to 1900° C.
Zirconia Magnesia Thoria Beryllia	Special insulators for high temperatures				
Glass (Pyrex type) .	2·25	4·5	$\sim 3.10^{-3}$ at 30 kc/s; increases with temperature	19 kV for 1 mm.	Conducts by electrolysis at temperatures well below melting-point. Pyrex and similar high silica glasses electrically better than soft soda glasses.

TABLE 4.9—(cont.)

Materials	Density g./cc.	Dielectric constant	Power factor	Electric strength	Notes
Fused silica	2·0-2·2	3·5-3·7	∼ 3.10⁻⁴ up to 50 Mc/s	20-40 kV for 1 mm.	Uses include furnace tubes, insulators for thermocouples, resistance thermometers and general purposes to 1000° C. Higher temperatures for short periods.
Asbestos				2 kV for ¼ mm.	Available as paper, board, woven fabric, cord. Electrical properties poor. Wire insulation to 150° C. continuously and to 250° C. intermittently. Attacks metals at higher temperatures.
Asbestos cement board	1·5			3 kV for 6 mm.	Rather brittle and shatters at high temperatures; not suitable for use as primary insulation, but used for fireproof insulating casings, arc barriers in switches, etc.

TABLE 4.10

General Purpose Insulators

	Dielectric constant	Power factor	Approximate electric strength (puncture or breakdown)	
Rubber .	2·5		90 kV/3mm.	Unvulcanised or lightly vulcanised. Inflammable, subject to oxidation. Temperatures below 90° C.
Hard rubber .	2·5-4	0·01-0·04 (R.F.)		Properties depend on loading materials.
Dry paper . Pressboard .			30 kV/3 mm.	Serviceable under oil.
Vulcanised fibre			7 kV/3 mm.	Mechanically strong. Not suitable for primary insulation.
Phenol-formaldehyde paper board			25 kV/3 mm. (B.S. 113) Special products may be better	Very wide uses, especially for mounting components in electric equipment. B.S. 113 requires 1000 MΩ insulation between terminals spaced 32 mm. "Tracking" properties poor. Similar products available as tubes.
Insulating tape to B.S. 1078 .			1 kV	
Polyvinyl Chloride .	6—9		25-30 kV/2 mm.	Wire covering and sleeving.

TABLE 4.10—(cont.)

	Dielectric constant	Power factor	Approximate electric strength (puncture or breakdown)	
Nylon . .	4	0·02	25 kV/2 mm.	
Polystyrene .	2·5	2.10^{-4}	62 kV/1½ mm.	H.F. uses, electrostatic insulator.
Polyethylene .	2·3	2.10^{-4}	62 kV/1½ mm.	H.F. cables, electrostatic insulator.
PTFE . .	2	10^{-4}	30 kV/1½ mm.	H.F. uses, electrostatic insulator.

TABLE 4.11

Insulators for Electrometer Circuits

(a) *Ebonite.* Affected by light and oxidation—not normally used now for electrometer work.

(b) *Sulphur.* Formerly used as beads for electroscope insulation ; should be carefully cast at low temperature and protected from light.

(c) *Hard Paraffin Wax.* Very good insulator, suitable for temporary work, not hygroscopic.

(d) *Amber, Pressed Reconstituted Amber.* Machine readily, good insulators.

(e) *Fused Quartz.* Can be cleaned with strong acid and blowpipe flame, mechanically strong but difficult to work. Surface slightly hygroscopic.

(f) *Methacrylate Resin (Perspex).* Moderately good insulator, surface hygroscopic.

(g) *Polystyrene Resin.* Outstandingly good insulator, practically non-hygroscopic ; machines readily.

(h) *Polyethylene Resin.* Soft and flexible, not hygroscopic.

(i) *Polytetrafluorethylene.* Outstandingly good insulator, may be used to 250° C. May be cleaned with strong acid.

TABLE 4.12

Notes on Insulating Materials for Electrical Windings, etc.

(1) Temperature Classes (International Electrotech. Commission, 1935)
(see also B.S. 171)

Class	Description	Hottest spot (A.I.E.E.)	Temp. rise (a)	Max. Temp. (b)
O	Cotton, silk, paper . . Not impregnated or immersed	90° C.		
A	Cotton, silk, paper . . Impregnated or immersed Moulded and laminated plastics. Varnishes, enamels, on conductors	105° C.	55° C. (Natural cooling) 75° C. (Forced cooling)	110° C.
B	Mica, asbestos, glass fibre with binding cement .	130° C.	75° C. (Dry)	145° C.
C	Mica, glass, porcelain, etc. (inorganic materials)			

(a) The temperature rises are deduced from resistance measurements of windings (B.S. 171). The maximum ambient temperature is 40° C.

(b) These are maximum normal temperatures for heavily loaded motor windings (B.S. 178) as deduced from resistance measurements.

(2) *Wire Insulation* in windings performs an important mechanical function in "cushioning" the turns and layers, and enamelled wire wound solid is not very satisfactory in this respect. Enamelled S.C.C. wire may be used for winding or the layers may be interleaved with paper. Enamelled wires may now be obtained coated with vinyl resins. They resist crushing and abrasion better than resin-enamelled wires.

Minimum Breakdown Voltages between Turns

Resin enamel wire ; bare dia. 0·001-0·002   150 V. r.m.s. for 1 min.
(B.S. 156)   0·005   350 V.
                         0·018   1000-1200 V.

D.C.C. wire, dipped once in impregnating varnish should have a breakdown voltage of about 1000 V. between turns.

Wire insulated with glass fibre is useful for windings which must be heavily loaded. If organic materials are used for binding, they limit the permissible temperatures, but silicone materials have recently been introduced for this purpose. The mechanical properties of glass insulation are not very good.

(3) *Transformer Oil* (B.S. 148/1951), should have a minimum breakdown voltage of 40 kV. r.m.s. for a 4 mm. gap between 13 mm. spheres. This can only be achieved with thoroughly dry oil.

TABLE 4.13

Plastics

Designation	Density g./cc.	Approximate U.T.S. lb./sq. in.	Softening temp. or highest useful temp. °C.	Uses
A. Thermo-setting resins				
(a) Phenol-formaldehyde				
Unfilled casting resin	1·33	2000-5000	120	Moulded insulators and mechanical parts.
Resin with filler (more or less isotropic)	1·3-2	6000-8000	120-150	Insulators. Table 4.10.
Laminated products containing paper or textile	1·3-1·5	8000-15,000 Special products to 45,500	120-150 according to filling	Mechanical parts including gearwheels. See § 4.21.
(b) Urea formaldehyde (filled)	1·45-1·55	∼ 6000	75	Non-tracking insulators.
(c) Melamine formaldehyde (filled)	1·5-2	6000-12,000	110-180 according to filling	Non-tracking insulators.
(d) Alkyd, or polyester resins (glycerol-phthalic, etc.)				Lacquers.
(e) Special cold-setting resins used with accelerators Polyesters and epoxy resins				Adhesives. Hermetic embedding of electrical components.
(f) Araldite				See § 4.13.

TABLE 4.13—(*cont.*)

Designation	Density g./cc.	Approximate U.T.S. lb./sq. in.	Softening temp. or highest useful temp. °C.	Uses
B. Thermoplastics				
(a) Nitrocellulose (celluloid)	1·35-1·4	3000-10,000	60	Lacquers and adhesives. Films.
(b) Cellulose acetate	~1·3	4000-8000	50-100	Thin films prepared by evaporating solutions on glass, water, mercury.
(c) Nylon	1·15	9000 (maximum solid) 45,000-55,000 filament	150	Strong fibres and films.
(d) Polyvinyl esters (especially chloride P.V.C.)	1·2-1·4	1500-2600	100	Wire coverings and other flexible, water resistant wrappings.
(e) Methyl methacrylate (Perspex, etc.)	1·2	~7000	80	Transparent covers and instrument parts.
(f) Polystyrene	1·05	7000	~80	Outstanding electrical properties. Transparent covers and instrument parts.
(g) Polyethylene	0·9	1800	100	Outstanding electrical properties. Very low water absorption. Flexible wrappers, etc.
(h) Polytetrafluorethylene PTFE Fluon, Teflon	2·2	about 2000 moulded 10,100-15,000 cold rolled	270	Outstanding electrical properties. Inert to chemicals. Self-lubricating properties. Co-efficient of friction between two PTFE surfaces is about 0·04

Materials not considered in detail above include casein, natural and synthetic rubbers, hard rubber.

applications they are used as electrical insulators which are easily worked and fairly strong. They are also useful in mechanical construction where lightness is important and stresses are not large.

The plastics are usually divided into thermo-setting and thermo-plastic materials ; the former undergo an irreversible change when they are first moulded under heat, and are then rigid and infusible at temperatures up to that at which they char : the latter may be softened repeatedly by heat.

Table 4.13 summarises the properties of some of the most important groups of plastics which may find laboratory applications.

4.22   Note on the Materials of Table 4.13 and some other Plastics.

The Bakelite (Phenol-formaldehyde) plastics are not ordinarily used without an inert filler, though a product called " Catalin ", which can be polymerised by heat in simple open moulds has been used in making models for optical stress analysis and might have other laboratory applications. The fabric-reinforced materials have good mechanical properties ; they are used, e.g., for quiet-running gearwheels to mesh with steel pinions, but their electrical applications are confined to low voltage work. Some of the paper-reinforced materials have the best electrical properties of the group (see Table 4.10) and are largely used for mounting components in electrical equipment. We have occasionally met unsatisfactory insulation resistance, and it is well to test the material before using it for high-voltage small-current work. Many of these substances machine fairly well, though it is necessary to take care to avoid separation of the laminations in the reinforced materials (in particular, when they are drilled, they should be closely backed with a material into which the drill penetrates) ; and they blunt tools rapidly.

Satisfactory mouldings can only be produced from most thermo-setting plastics in highly finished moulds under considerable pressure. The epoxy resins and polyester resins, which include the adhesives of § 4.13, have, however, the property that the change from liquid to solid polymer after the addition of an appropriate catalyst takes place without evolution of a gas or vapour and without a large change in volume. They can therefore be moulded without applied pressure in simple moulds. It is possible to " pot " electrical components in the liquid resin which sets to a protective block: elaborate circuit assemblies can be treated in this way. The main limitations arise because of the contraction on setting (about 1·5 % for a typical epoxy-resin) and the large thermal expansion of the solid (about three times that of copper for an epoxy-resin). The curing contraction and thermal expansion of polyester resins are about twice as great: epoxy-resins, which are much more expensive, are therefore preferable to polyesters for potting. The effects can be reduced by mixing the resin with an inert filler such as finely powdered quartz, and in some cases like transformer windings, by cushioning the structure with cotton or p.v.c.

It is possible to build up strong and light laminated shells on simple moulds by impregnating layers of glass fibre or synthetic fabric with liquid resin (usually polyester), and allowing it to set. Boats and motor-car bodies are made in this way and the techniques might be valuable for laboratory equipment.

Methacrylate resin (Perspex) is very transparent to visible light ; the ordinary material cuts off the ultraviolet beyond 3000 A. U. It has been used to a small extent for optical purposes (a special quality is available for this work) and we have made cylindrical condenser lenses from ordinary Perspex by turning and polishing. Perspex is very convenient for transparent instrument covers ; covering calibrated paper scales, etc. It is a very good insulator (not so good as polystyrene and polyethylene) and electrostatic charges may be very troublesome if it is used near delicate moving systems. Perspex machines excellently ; it is soft enough to bend or mould to shape at 110°-130° C., but simple bending can be done under hot water.

Polystyrene (Distrene) is also a clear thermo-plastic material ; it is not hygroscopic and it is comparable with the best insulators for electrostatic purposes. It has a very low power-factor at radio frequencies ; it is very easily machined and becomes workably plastic at about 80° C.

Polyethylene (Polythene, Alkathene) is an extremely good insulator for steady and radio-frequency currents. It is a tough flexible material and it has made possible the manufacture of flexible radio frequency cables whose losses are small at 200 Mc/s and not prohibitive at 3000 Mc/s.

Polytetrafluorethylene (Fluon, Teflon, PTFE) is an extremely good insulator for steady and radio-frequency currents. It is highly immune from chemical attack, and is hard and chemically stable up to rather high temperatures. It can be used up to 250°-300° C., but when heated to higher temperatures decomposes with the production of highly toxic fumes. There is therefore some danger of poisoning if smoking tobacco is contaminated with PTFE dust and precautions should be taken against this. The moulding of PTFE requires special techniques but machining is quite easy. In laboratory practice insulators would be machined from the solid, and they could then be drastically cleaned, e.g. by boiling in strong nitric acid, before assembly. This is an important advantage of the material over other plastics. PTFE has the useful property that it does not stick easily to other substances. Also the friction between the substance and itself, or other materials, is very low, and it may be used for sliding bearings or bushes which are to run reliably without lubrication. A sintered bearing metal containing PTFE is made commercially and is a very convenient low-friction material.

4.23 Glass

The transparency, easy (though peculiar) working and chemical resistance of glass have given it a unique importance in the history of laboratory technique. All ordinary glasses are homogeneous mixtures of silicates and borosilicates which have cooled from the molten state without crystallising. They are supercooled liquids and on heating they become continuously less viscous (Fig. 4.6). There is no definite melting-point, and the glasses are characterised by the temperatures at which the viscosity has certain values. Glassblowing processes depend on exploiting these viscosity changes. On the other hand, glass at ordinary temperatures behaves as a brittle solid with good elastic properties and the technique of the optical workshop depends on working it in this condition. (For optical workshop methods see Strong 1938, Twyman 1952.)

4.24 Glass as a Mechanical Material

Glass is very strong in compression, but its strength in tension is subject to large fluctuations from sample to sample, and is very sensitive to small surface flaws. Where strength is required in tension or bending, as when a flat window is used in a pressure or vacuum vessel, it is often advantageous to use " toughened " or " armourplate " glass which is heat

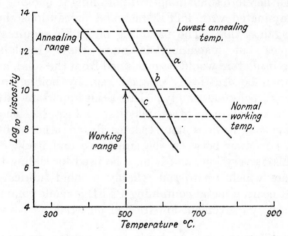

FIG. 4.6   Viscosity temperature relation for representative glasses
(a) Chance GHA (borosilicate)
(b) Chance GSA (soda-lime)
(c) Chance GSB (lead)

treated in such a way that the surface is pre-loaded in compression, and considerable forces must be applied before the surface stress is reversed. This glass must be obtained from the makers, worked to size and complete with any holes, for it cannot be cut or scratched after the heat treatment.*

* Attention must be called to the danger to life and limb which arises when an evacuated glass vessel of any size is broken. Pieces may be projected with great violence and a cathode ray tube, for example, ought to be handled with care and viewed in normal use through a protective screen of toughened glass.

138

Ordinary glass is bought as sheet (drawn from molten material) and plate (cast and polished). Plate glass has surfaces flat enough for rough optical work, and small pieces with a better standard of flatness can be obtained by selection. There is a special product called " twin ground " glass whose faces are much more nearly parallel than ordinary plate. Sheet and plate glass are cut with a diamond, a hard steel wheel, or a tool of tungsten carbide. Accurate cuts in thick glass are best made with a thin steel wheel impregnated with diamond powder and used as a saw. Holes may be ground through glass with a copper tube used in a drilling machine and fed with carborundum powder and water, but recently, hard three-cornered drills of tungsten carbide have been introduced which drill glass freely. With both these methods, special care is required to prevent the drill breaking through violently at the end of a cut, and it is safest to wax a piece of scrap glass on to the back of the workpiece before drilling. Glass boxes to withstand all ordinary solvents may be jointed with Araldite (§ 4.13), using simple jigs to hold the plates while the cement is polymerised in an oven.

4.25 Glassblowing

In laboratory glassblowing the glass is brought to the working viscosity by a blowpipe flame. The main types of glass used for laboratory apparatus are soft soda glass, and borosilicate glasses like Pyrex and Chance GHA ; the other glasses of Table 4.14 are used for special purposes. Soft glass is worked in the air-coal-gas blowpipe, hard glass in a oxy-gas blowpipe or in an air-gas blowpipe with oxygen enrichment. The most important working characteristic of the hard glass is its resistance to thermal shock, i.e. to cracking by sudden or local changes in temperature. This property is due to its low coefficient of expansion, combined with good mechanical strength. In any but the simplest blown glass work, one part of the piece may cool below the annealing temperature while other parts are being worked, and cracks due to this cause are a major plague of the unprofessional glassblower working in soft glass.* Hard glass is much more accommodating in

* Cracks cannot appear in hot glass above the annealing temperature.

TABLE 4.14

Properties of Glasses

A.   *Glasses for Lampworking*

Designation	Density gm./cc.	Annealing Temperature ° C.	Coeff. expansion 10^{-6}	Uses
Soda-lime . .	2·5	510	8·7	Lamp bulbs, chemical apparatus.
Lead-soda-potash	3·0	390	8·6-9·1	Pinch seals. Better electrical resistance than soda-lime glass.
Borosilicate (Pyrex type) .	2·25	560	3·3	Laboratory apparatus Vacuum apparatus
Borosilicate sealing glasses (range of glasses) . .	From 2·23 to 2·30	From 570 to 450	From 3·8 to 5·0	Seals with W, Mo, Fe-Ni-Co alloys. See Chap. V, Appendix.
Fused silica .	2·0-2·2	1050	0·6	See § 4.25.

Note.—The annealing temperature corresponds approximately to a viscosity of 10^{13} c.g.s.u. At this temperature strains disappear with a time constant of a few minutes, and an evacuated bulb will collapse. The working temperature in glassblowing is 150°-200° higher.

The coefficient of expansion given is that at ordinary temperatures. The expansion is not strictly linear, and increases markedly in the neighbourhood of the annealing temperature.

B.   *Sheet and Plate Glasses.*—*Soda-Lime Type*

Density *ca.* 2·5 gm./cc.	Expansion *ca.* 8·0 . 10^{-6}.

C.   *Optical Glasses.   See Chapter 8, Appendix p. 363.*

D.   *Special Glasses*

Vacuum sealing	See Chapter V, Appendix.
Iron sealing	Sealing to iron, e.g. windows for machinery.
Intermediate	Joining dissimilar glasses by graded seal, joining fused silica to glass.
Solder glasses	Joining glass parts by relatively low temperature process.
Lindemann (Lithium) glass	For X-ray tube windows and specimen tubes transparent to X-rays.
Alkali-metal-resistant	Sodium vapour lamps.
High-conductivity	Glass electrodes for pH determination.
Thermometer glasses	Mercury thermometers with high zero stability.
Combustion glasses (e.g. Jena Supremax)	Chemical apparatus for high temperature.

this respect, but internal strains must be relieved by annealing at the end of the glass-blowing operation. Some operations, such as bending, are more difficult to carry out in hard glass than in soft (mostly because of the limitations of laboratory burners) and hard glass joints often contain pinholes, which are nearly unknown in soft glass.

Only a few general principles can be given to guide the actual manipulation of glass before the blowpipe ; the manual dexterity must be obtained by practice. The main difficulty lies in completely co-ordinating the movements of the hands when they are holding two pieces of tube connected by a mass of thoroughly softened glass. The skilled glassblower achieves this co-ordination and can work with the connecting mass very soft ; the unskilled worker is tempted to soften only part of the tube and thus to preserve some degree of rigid connection. It is permissible to make some use of this makeshift and in working large tube it is inevitable, but it is always necessary to fuse the pieces thoroughly together when making a joint, i.e. every part must at some time be brought to a thoroughly fluid condition and furthermore, at the end of the operation, the whole piece must be made soft enough to relieve internal stresses. For large and complicated pieces this may be done by oven annealing, but in ordinary laboratory work it is often done before the blowpipe, using a large flame. This annealing secures the absence of permanent strain when the whole work has attained a uniform temperature, but it is still possible to crack the glass during the cooling process if different parts of the structure cool at different rates. The hot glass is therefore cooled in the oven or in a large smoky flame without air or oxygen, and similarly when a piece of glass is first heated, this is done in a large cool flame with constant turning until the glass is so hot that the danger of cracking is past. These precautions are needed especially with high-expansion soft glass.

It is necessary to have the walls of a glass piece of nearly uniform thickness so as to avoid strains caused by non-uniform heating or cooling. In the case of the ordinary laboratory worker this consideration takes precedence over the external symmetry of the work. If a piece in work is blown into immediately on removing it from the flame, the thinnest walls will be further blown out, and this fact is used when one wants to blow a hole in a glass tube (e.g. for a side tube). If, however, the operator waits a few seconds before blowing, the thinner parts will have cooled to a lower temperature than the thicker, and the latter are blown out preferentially. This method is used to equalise the wall thickness of a piece of work.

4.26 Fused Quartz

Pure silica fuses to form a typical glass which has important uses. It is made commercially as a clear transparent glass and also as a white translucent mass which is opaque because of tiny bubbles. The latter, which is much cheaper than the transparent silica, is useful for furnace tubes, etc. When it is used for vacuum purposes it should have its surface glazed by fusion, and tubes can be bought in this condition. The clear material can be blown like glass in an oxy-hydrogen blowpipe (an oxy-gas flame suffices for very small work).* The working range of temperature is short, and cooling by radiation is rapid at the working temperature, so that much of the blowing must be done while the work is still in the flame, in contrast to normal glassworking practice. The low expansion of the material gives it a resistance to thermal shock so great that ordinary-sized pieces never crack by sudden changes of temperature.

The outstanding properties of silica glass are :

(*a*) Thermal behaviour. The thermal expansion is very small, and the return to size after heating and cooling is very perfect. The material may be held for a long time at 1000° C., and for short periods at higher temperatures, but if it is kept for a long time at a high temperature, the metastable glass gradually crystallises.

(*b*) Optical properties. The glass is very transparent throughout the visible spectrum, the ultraviolet to about 2000 A. U., and the infra-red to about 3·5 μ. It is therefore used for discharge lamps and photocells for the ultraviolet.

(*c*) Electrical properties. The glass is one of the best " electrostatic " insulators, and has the advantage that

---

* It is necessary to wear dark glasses when working silica at the blowpipe.

insulators made of it can be drastically cleaned (e.g. with strong nitric acid) and finally heated in a blowpipe flame. It has also a low loss angle in high-frequency fields (4.10^{-4} up to 50 Mc/s).

(*d*) Mechanical properties. The glass has very remarkable mechanical properties, especially when drawn into fibres.

4.27 Quartz Fibres

The breaking stress and elastic constants vary considerably with the diameter of the fibre, and the breaking strength of a fine fibre (5 μ) is greater than that of steel or tungsten of the same diameter. The material behaves elastically up to its breaking point.

Table 4.15 gives some figures derived from data given by Reinkober, who found that the breaking load varied greatly from fibre to fibre and deduced from his experiments that breaking occurs at local faults. The values in Table 4.15 are obtained from his average values for " old " fibres. The elastic properties are more consistent than the breaking stress but show variations of the order 10 %.

TABLE 4.15

Torsion Constants and Tensile Strengths of Quartz Fibres

(Torsion values in 10^{-5} dyne cm. for 1 radian twist, on 1 cm. length)

Diameter in μ	Torsion constant	Probable breaking load in g.
1	0·8	
2	11	1·2
3	50	2·0
5	325	3·5
10	4,100	8·0
20	55,000	17·0
30	254,000	30·0

Note.—Fused Quartz shows the unusual property of an increasing elasticity with rise in temperature. The shear (torsion) modulus changes by about $0·013°/_0$ per °C.

Fused silica has exceptionally perfect elastic properties. Torsion fibres made of it return accurately to their initial form after deflection, and a torsion pendulum has a very low decrement.* Quartz fibres are used for torsion suspensions in a variety of instruments, and silica spiral springs and Bourdon tubes have also been used. Fused quartz torsion fibres were introduced by C. V. Boys (1923), who drew them by means of a straw arrow shot from a crossbow. One end of a piece of silica rod is attached by wax to the arrow, the other is held in a clamp, the silica is melted by hand blowpipe and the bow released.

A simple method which can be used to produce fibres between 2 μ and 30 μ diameter is to draw them horizontally by the pull of a stretched rubber cord. A piece of silica rod is fastened to the end of a length of $\frac{1}{4}$ in. square catapult elastic,

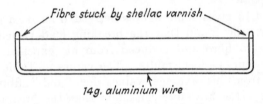

Fibre stuck by shellac varnish

14g, aluminium wire

FIG. 4.7   Storage jig for quartz fibres

which is then pulled out to 10-15 % more than its natural length. The silica rod is fused to the end of a fixed piece of silica and drawn out to a thickness determined by trial. It is then heated by a hand oxy-hydrogen blowpipe with the tension on the rubber. A buffer is arranged to catch the end of the rubber as it flies back, and a fibre is formed which usually remains attached at both ends to the pieces of silica. The diameter of the fibre is controlled by the initial diameter of the drawn-out piece of silica and by the size and temperature of the flame.

Fibres of greater diameter than 30 μ can be drawn by hand, and fibres of less diameter than 2 μ may be drawn in a suitable oxy-hydrogen flame by the drag of the flame gases. A long quiet flame burning from a nozzle about 1 mm. in diameter is directed nearly vertically upwards, and a piece of black velvet is stretched on a frame above it. The operator takes a

---

* Heyl (1930) claims that drawn tungsten is equal to quartz in its torsional properties, and that it is less subject to sudden failure in tension.

piece of silica rod in each hand, and touches them together and pulls them apart in the flame. The fibres blown away from the molten silica collect on the velvet, where they appear as cobwebs when the velvet is examined in a good light. They can be transferred with good forceps to wire storage jigs (Fig. 4.7).

Much information about the drawing and use of quartz is given by H. V. Neher in Strong (1939).

APPENDIX

Small Laboratory Furnaces

This subject is treated in Strong (1939), and particularly thoroughly in Surugue (1947) ; see also Walden (1939). It is, however, convenient to give here some notes on the construction of simple furnaces using materials discussed in Chapter IV.

Small tube furnaces are often used in the baking of glass vacuum tubes, charcoal traps, etc., to temperatures not exceeding 500° C. They are best made by bending two layers of mica sheets over steel or copper tubing, and winding with nickel-chrome wire which is in turn covered with mica sheets and two layers of asbestos cord. The nickel-chrome wire is secured at the ends by wrapping several turns in contact and passing the free end under some of the end turns. The free end should be twisted double to avoid local heating by the current, and the latter is brought in through a brass barrel connector.

Hot nichrome should not be in contact with asbestos or with fireclay cements, which attack it. Alumina (Alundum) cement may be used.

The tube furnaces described above have rather large heat losses : furnaces with higher efficiencies for higher temperatures may be made by winding nichrome wire or ribbon on tubes of (translucent) fused quartz, or high temperature ceramic, embedding the winding in alumina cement and packing the whole thing in a sheet iron or asbestos board case with a thick layer of kieselguhr thermal insulation.

Baking ovens for larger vacuum tubes are made by lining sheet-iron boxes with about 1 cm. of soft asbestos board (*not* asbestos-cement sheet) and using as heaters commercial electric fire elements. The connections are conveniently made with pure nickel wire which does not corrode at this temperature. The hot windings of the elements should not come into contact with the asbestos-board ; distance pieces are best made of steatite or unglazed porcelain.

Box-shaped furnaces for temperatures up to 1200°-1300° C. are made with an inner lining of special refractory bricks with Nichrome or Kanthal windings resting in shaped grooves in the internal walls. The outer layers are made of insulating bricks. Furnaces of this kind are available as small pottery kilns as well as specialised laboratory equipment and the component parts are also available for assembly. Laboratory furnaces for temperatures above 1300° C. require rather special materials; tubes of recrystallised alumina are available, and the refractory oxides of magnesium, zirconium, and beryllium can be used for packing and insulation. Kanthal windings can be operated up to 1350° C. in an oxidising or neutral atmosphere, platinum can be used up to a rather higher temperature, and although it is very costly most of the value can be recovered after failure. Molybdenum can be used at much higher temperatures but requires a reducing atmosphere, usually obtained by circulating pure hydrogen over the windings. It is also possible to use a molybdenum winding entirely contained in a good vacuum, the charge of the furnace being supported or suspended within it and heated entirely by radiation.

There are also ceramic resistance rods made of silicon carbide, which can be operated in oxidising atmospheres at 1400° C., and molybdenum disilicide which goes up to 1500° C. The resistance of these substances falls rapidly with increasing temperature, so that a high voltage must be provided for rapid heating from cold, and the current must be stabilised by external means when the elements reach a high temperature.

Graphite tubes, embedded in carbon black as a thermal insulator, the whole bathed in an inert gas, can be used to attain 3000° C.

CHAPTER 5

VACUUM TECHNIQUE

5.1 Introduction

Vacuum technique is used in the physical laboratory for two main purposes—to secure for atomic and molecular particles paths relatively free from collision, and to preserve surfaces relatively free from contamination.

The pressure required for the first purpose can be estimated from the mean free paths of gas atoms at normal pressure (Table 5.1). The free paths at low pressures are inversely

TABLE 5.1

Molecular Quantities useful in Vacuum Calculations

Number of molecules in one gram-molecule of gas at 0° C. and 760 mm.	$6 \cdot 06 \cdot 10^{23}$
Number of molecules in 1 cc. of gas at 0° C. and 760 mm.	$2 \cdot 71 \cdot 10^{19}$
r.m.s. velocity of molecules, molecular weight M ($O_2 = 32$) at $T°$ K. (cm./sec.) . . .	$1 \cdot 58 \cdot 10^4 \sqrt{\dfrac{T}{M}}$
Arithmetical average velocity of molecules (cm./sec.) .	$1 \cdot 46 \cdot 10^4 \sqrt{\dfrac{T}{M}}$
Mean free paths λ of gas molecules at 300° K and 10^{-3} mm. mercury	cm.
$\quad\quad\quad\quad\quad\quad\quad\quad H_2$	9·4
$\quad\quad\quad\quad\quad\quad\quad\quad$He	14·9
$\quad\quad\quad\quad\quad\quad\quad\quad O_2$	5·5
$\quad\quad\quad\quad\quad\quad\quad\quad N_2$	5·1
$\quad\quad\quad\quad\quad\quad\quad\quad$A	5·4
$\quad\quad\quad\quad\quad\quad\quad\quad H_2O$	3·4
$\quad\quad\quad\quad\quad\quad\quad\quad$Hg	2·7

Note.—The mean free path is variously defined. The values given in Table 5.1 follow Chapman (Chapman and Cowling 1939); the values given in I.C.T. and in Kaye and Laby follow an older treatment and are about 50% higher. The difference is not very important in calculation of orders of magnitude.

The unit 1 torr. = 1 mm. Hg is increasingly used in this country.

proportional to the pressure, and the probability of a collision occurring in the course of the path x is x/λ (when x/λ is small).

Thus, if less than 1 % of mercury atoms are to make collisions in traversing a path of 10 cm. in the vapour, the pressure must be less than $\dfrac{2 \cdot 7 \cdot 10^{-3}}{10.100} \simeq 2 \cdot 7 \cdot 10^{-6}$ mm. Hg.

The second purpose requires only moderate vacua if surfaces are to be kept free from gross chemical contamination, but becomes very onerous if a surface cleaned, e.g. by heating, is to be kept free from molecular films for an appreciable time.

The number of collisions made in 1 sec. with unit area of a surface exposed to a gas is given by $\frac{1}{4}nv_a$

where n is the number of molecules per unit volume

$\quad\quad v_a$ is the arithmetical average velocity.

If we require that a surface accumulate a mono-molecular film of oxygen (say, 10^{15} molecules/cm.²) in not less than 1000 sec., and if we assume that all oxygen molecules which strike the surface remain there, then if p is the partial pressure of oxygen in mm. Hg, we have

$$\frac{10^{15}}{1000} = \frac{1}{4} \cdot \frac{p}{760} \cdot 2 \cdot 7 \cdot 10^{19} \, 1 \cdot 46 \cdot 10^4 \sqrt{\frac{300}{32}}$$

so that the pressure required is about $2 \cdot 5 \cdot 10^{-9}$ mm. of mercury.

5.2 Pumping Speeds

At the pressure ruling in high-vacuum systems, the flow of gases is " molecular "—collisions between gas molecules and the walls of the apparatus are much more important than collisions between molecules. This will be true if the free path calculated from Table 5.1 is large compared with the dimensions of the apparatus.

If we have gas at pressure p in an enclosure of volume V, and make an opening of area A into a perfectly evacuated space, all the molecules which strike the opening are lost to the enclosure for ever, and the pressure in the enclosure follows the equation

$$\frac{1}{p}\frac{dp}{dt} = \frac{1}{N}\frac{dN}{dt} = -\frac{1}{nV} \cdot \frac{1}{4}nv_a A$$

where N is the total number of molecules, so that

$$p = p_0 \exp\left(-\frac{v_a A t}{4V}\right) = p_0 \exp\left(-\frac{St}{V}\right).$$

The quantity S, which has the dimensions of volume/time, may be called the pumping speed of the opening. It is most conveniently measured in litres per second. For air at 300° K. the pumping speed of unit area is 11·7 l./sec. and for other gases and temperatures this figure must be multiplied by $\sqrt{\left(\dfrac{29T}{300M}\right)}$, where T = absolute temperature, M = molecular wt. The speed of any pumping system can be defined in the same way; it must, of course, always be less than the "hole" speed of the orifice presented to the vacuum chamber. The pressure in a volume V exhausted by a pumping system of speed S falls ideally in the ratio $1 : 1/e$ in the time V/S.* If a pumping system of speed S is working continuously at a pressure p atmospheres, the volume of gas pumped, measured at normal pressure P, is Sp/P l./sec., and it is this quantity which remains constant for a number of pumps connected in cascade. It must therefore be used in calculating the speed requirements of the successive stages of such a cascade. It is common to measure gas flows in vacuum systems, and especially leakage rates, in "lusecs", this unit being equivalent to 1 litre of gas per second measured at a pressure of 1μ (10^{-3} mm.) of mercury.

Under conditions of molecular flow the resistance offered by a tubular connection is due to the following mechanism: any molecule which strikes the wall rebounds in a direction which does not depend on its initial direction but which is given statistically by the cosine law. Only a part of the incident gas therefore passes in the pumping direction, and the pumping speed of the tube is reduced, compared with that of an orifice of the same diameter.

Since the net flow down a tube under these conditions (as well as in ordinary viscous flow) is proportional to the pressure difference between its ends, pumping down a tube follows the

---

* In practice, the effects of absorption or emission of gas by the walls may be important.

same exponential law as pumping through a hole, and we may define the pumping speed of a tubular connection as above. If several tubes, or tubes and a pump, are connected in series, the pressure difference is divided between them, and we can show that

$$\frac{1}{S} = \frac{1}{S_1} + \frac{1}{S_2} + \dots$$

where S is the final speed and $S_1 S_2 \dots$ are the speeds of the component parts.

For air at 300° K, the speed of a tubular connection of length l cm. and diameter d cm. is

$$\frac{12 \cdot 3 \, d^3}{(l + \frac{4}{3}d)} \text{ l./sec.}$$

and the speed for another gas and temperature may be obtained by multiplying this figure by

$$\sqrt{\left(\frac{29 \, T}{300 \, M} \right)}.$$

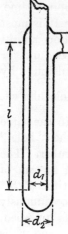

FIG. 5.1

TABLE 5.2

Pumping Speeds of Connections—Molecular Flow

	l./sec.
(a) Hole 1 sq. cm. area in thin wall	11·7
(b) Tube 2 cm. diameter, 20 cm. long . . .	4·5
(c) Liquid air trap, concentric portion only. Internal tube dia. 2 cm., external tube dia. 3·2 cm., length of concentric portion 15 cm. (Fig. 5.1). Speed is reduced to about 2 l./sec. at temperature of liquid air	3·2
(d) Seal-off constriction, length 1 cm., diameter 5 mm.	1·0
(e) Tube 10 cm. diameter, 50 cm. long . . .	195

Notes.—(b), (c) and (d) are typical elements of " static " vacuum systems, (e) is a typical element of a " kinetic " system, (c) is calculated from a formula given by Dushman (1949), who states that the best ratio between the inside diameters of the inner and outer tubes is 1·6, the wall thickness of the inner tube being neglected. The speed of the concentric portion of the trap is then given by

$$1 \cdot 45 \frac{d^3}{l} \text{ l./sec.}$$

where d is the diameter of the outer tube.

5.3 The Principles of Vacuum Pumps

The pumps used to produce moderately low pressures work on the displacement principle—a portion of gas at the low pressure is isolated by a moving piston and compressed until it reaches a high enough pressure to be discharged into another stage of the pump or into the atmosphere. The mechanical

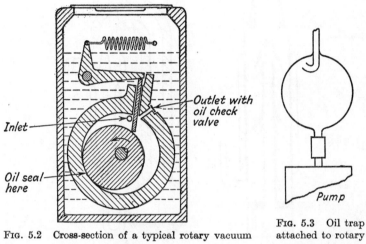

FIG. 5.2   Cross-section of a typical rotary vacuum pump

FIG. 5.3   Oil trap attached to rotary vacuum pump

backing pumps which are currently used in vacuum work are rotary pumps on this principle, which run immersed in oil. The oil fills the dead spaces and so allows a high compression ratio to be obtained ; it seals the moving piston against leaks, besides lubricating and cooling the pump * (Fig. 5.2).

* Note on the Use of Mechanical Vacuum Pumps.

Most of these pumps allow oil to rise into the vacuum system if the rotation is stopped without breaking the vacuum. Cleaning the system after such a catastrophe is a most time-consuming job. The pump should therefore not be stopped until the vacuum has been let down. It is desirable to arrange a trap (Fig. 5.3) to cope with any accidental failures of the pump drive. In static vacuum systems which are left unattended it is very safe and convenient to exhaust a sizeable reservoir with the backing pump and then to cut off the pump with a tap. The high vacuum pump will pump into the reservoir for a long time without difficulty. Where a number of pumping systems are used, their reservoirs may be exhausted in turn by a single backing pump, and an accident on one system need not affect the others.

The speed of these pumps is low at low pressures (compared with that of molecular pumps)—the final vacuum is in practice chiefly limited by the dissolved gases and vapours which contaminate the oil. It is particularly difficult to deal with vapours which condense in the later stage of the compression cycle. Many manufacturers now provide in their pumps the " gas

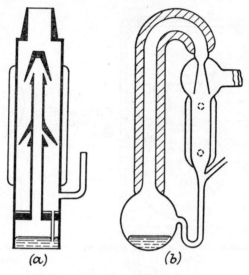

(a)   *(b)*

FIG. 5.4   Representative diffusion pumps

(a) Two stage umbrella pump in metal
(b) Single stage glass pump with long divergent nozzle

ballasting " invented by Gaede (1947). A small flow of air is allowed from the atmosphere into the compression region of a rotary pump through a passage near the outlet valve. At each cycle a considerable amount of this air is passed through the outlet, even when the gas taken in from the high vacuum side makes only a small contribution. This air carries out vapour, continuously purging the oil. Some of the ballast air inevitably leaks to the high vacuum side through the rotor seal, so that it is advantageous to make the ballast flow controllable and to dispense with it when the oil has been purged and no considerable quantity of vapour is being pumped.

When the pressure has been reduced so that the mean free path of a molecule is a millimetre or so, it is possible to use pumps which depend directly on the kinetic behaviour of molecules. Pumps have been constructed by Gaede, Holweck, and Siegbahn (Dushman 1949, p. 151 *et seq.*) in which the molecules are speeded in the desired direction by collision with a rapidly moving disk or drum, and these pumps are still used in some European laboratories. The important high vacuum pumps in general use are " diffusion pumps " in which molecules entering the pumping region are swept away by a stream of vapour.

The essential points of such pumps are :

(*a*) The gas molecules must have free access to the pumping region.

(*b*) The vapour jet must be favourably formed to have maximum forward sweeping effect combined with minimum back streaming of vapour into the space to be evacuated.

(*c*) The vapour must be such that the molecules which do stream back can be removed by condensation, leaving only a very small vapour pressure.

Fig. 5.4 shows representative designs of diffusion pump. The point (*b*) requires empirical analysis, for the conditions in the vapour nozzle and in the pumping region lie in the theoretically awkward borderland between hydrodynamic and molecular flow ; several analyses have been made (Copley *et al.* 1935 ; Alexander 1946) and the results show that for greatest efficiency the nozzle should be long and divergent, and that the opening to the backing pump should be covered by a high density bombardment of vapour molecules extending right up to the cooled walls. The pumping speed observed in different pumps lies between 0·1 and 0·5 of the ideal value of 11·7 l./sec./sq. cm. of gas admission area. The speed of a pump depends markedly on the boiler pressure and goes through a maximum for a certain value of heat input to the boiler. In using a pump the best heat input must therefore be found by experiment or ascertained from the maker.

The point (*c*) was met until 1928 by the use of mercury vapour, a liquid-air-cooled trap being interposed between the pump and the vessel under exhaustion. The trap is designed so that any molecule passing back from the pump must collide with a cooled surface. Mercury pumps are still useful in much vacuum work, but in high speed pumping systems they have been very largely replaced by pumps using liquids

TABLE 5.3

Diffusion Pump Fluids

Ultimate vacua (experimental values) given in 10^{-6} mm. Hg.

Designation	Maximum backing pressure mm.		Ultimate vacuum	
	Single boiler pump	Fraction- ating pump	Single boiler pump	Fraction- ating pump
Apiezon A			10(a) 45(b)	19(b)
Apiezon B			11(a) 17(b)	9(b)
An Apiezon C oil with a lower vapour pressure than B has recently been introduced.				
Litton oil			14(b)	6(b)
Butyl phthalate . . .			40(a) 225(b)	
Butyl sebacate . . .	0·1	0·15	25(c)	10(c)
Amyl sebacate (Amoil S) . .	0·1	0·17	10(c)	2(c)
2-ethyl hexyl phthalate (Octoil) .	0·1	0·25	5(c)	0·25(c)
2-ethyl hexyl sebacate (Octoil S)	0·1	0·2	6(b) 1(c)	3(b) 0·05(c)
Silicone Fluid (D.C. 702, 703) .			10(a)	

(a) Sullivan 1948 (type of pump not specified); (b) Blears 1947; (c) Hickman 1940.

The values given by different workers are clearly not comparable—those given by Blears were taken using a high-speed gauge and are probably the most realistic. They refer, however, to equivalent pressures on an ionisation gauge calibrated with nitrogen and are probably higher than those attained with the actual vapours.

which have a much lower vapour pressure than mercury at room temperature and which allow the liquid-air trap to be omitted in many applications. A pumping liquid must allow boiling at a suitable pressure to give the vapour jet; the boiler pressure usually lies between 5-25 mm. Hg. A number of liquids which have been used are listed Table 5.3; the petroleum distillates (e.g. Apiezon oils) have been used largely in this country (Burch 1929), while the esters have been developed and extensively used in America (Hickman 1936). There is still some dispute over the relative merits of these products. The silicones have been more recently introduced (Brown 1945, Sullivan 1948) ; they appear to have advantages, particularly on the score of resistance to oxidation if air is accidentally admitted to the hot pump.

These pump liquids differ from mercury in that they dissolve significant quantities of volatile impurities which may come from the vacuum system external to the pump, or from the decomposition (cracking) or oxidation of the pump oil. The elimination of these substances by distillation into the backing line is very slow, and until it is complete, the pump will not give its full final vacuum. This problem is dealt with in a way which has been developed mainly by Hickman (Hickman 1940) ; the pump is designed so that the oil is continuously fractionated, and the fluid which provides the vapour jet for the high vacuum stage has had its volatile constituents boiled off in the boilers supplying the high pressure stages. Fig. 5.5 shows how this principle has been applied to a horizontal jet pump and to an " umbrella " pump ; it has been shown by direct measurement that the fractionating system improves the final vacuum produced by a pump, even when the oil is not abnormally contaminated.

The following precautions must be taken in the design and use of oil diffusion pumps.

(a) The boiler must be designed to avoid superheating of the vapour, and the passage which conveys vapour from boiler to jet must be short, wide, and well insulated thermally, so that the boiler temperature does not have to be unduly high to produce a proper jet stream. It has been reported that the decomposition of the oils goes on faster in the presence of certain metals, and that unplated copper or brass should be avoided in the boilers and jet parts of pumps.

(b) The hot pumping fluid should not be exposed to air or oxygen at anything like atmospheric pressure ; the boiler of a pump should be cooled down before air is admitted to the system.

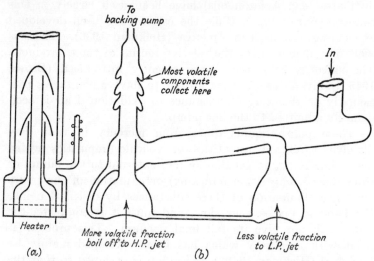

FIG. 5.5   Application of the fractionating principle to oil diffusion pump

(a) Two stage umbrella pump with fractionating baffles in boiler

(b) Two-stage glass fractionating pump (based on Hickman's design as made by Distillation Products, Inc.)

(c) Water must be carefully excluded from the vacuum system as it is eliminated with great difficulty from the pumps, and there is usually no trap in the system cold enough to condense it completely.

(d) The effectiveness of oil diffusion pumps is very markedly affected by "backstreaming" of vapour molecules, which in turn depends on the detailed design of the high vacuum end of the pump (Power and Crawley 1957).   When the pump has been designed with the proper precautions it must still be provided with baffles to prevent direct molecular backstreaming.   In large modern pumps it is common to cool these baffles with a small refrigerating plant.

5.4 The Measurement of Low Pressures—Vacuum Gauges

A number of physical principles can be applied in the measurement of low pressures but not all of these are of much practical use (Table 5.4). It is not often important to know the absolute gas pressure in a vacuum system ; much more frequently a gauge is used to indicate changes in vacuum conditions and its (relative) readings are compared with the satisfactory or unsatisfactory behaviour of the system under investigation. In many experiments on thermionic emission and on surface conditions, the phenomenon under investigation is itself a sensitive indication of pressure. Gauges are, however, important in following and in controlling the outgassing of a vacuum system (§ 5.9) or as an aid in detecting leaks (§ 5.11).

Even in this restricted field, gauge readings must be interpreted with care at very low pressures, for many gauges either evolve or absorb gases during their operation, and the pressure in the significant part of the vacuum system may be very different from that in the gauge unless the two are joined by a connection of very high speed (§ 5.2) (Blears 1944).

In practice, the simple discharge tube is very valuable in the initial setting up of a vacuum system for detecting gross leaks. Beyond this, the most useful gauges are probably a Pirani or thermocouple gauge for higher pressures (as on the backing vacuum line of a diffusion pump) and the ionisation or Penning gauge for low pressures. The Pirani gauge consists of a wire (tungsten, platinum, or nickel) suspended in a tube connected to the vacuum system and connected in a Wheatstone bridge circuit. The wire of the gauge and the other resistances in the circuit are chosen so that, while the gauge wire is at 100°-200° C., the other resistances are not heated enough to affect their resistance values. The changes in temperature of the gauge wire brought about by changes in the thermal flow across the vacuum either produce a measurable unbalance in the bridge, or are compensated by altering the potential applied to the bridge by a measured amount. An ordinary tungsten filament lamp has sometimes been used as a Pirani gauge, but it is better to use a construction in

TABLE 5.4

Vacuum Gauges

Gauge	Pressure range mm. Hg	Principle	Notes
Discharge tube	$10-10^{-3}$		Rough indication of pressure, e.g. in backing systems.
McLeod .	$1-10^{-4}$ mm.	Compression to directly measurable pressure. Boyle's law.	Absolute readings possible. Does not read pressures of vapours. Lower limit set by uncertain behaviour of adsorbed films.
Radiometer .	$10^{-2}-10^{-7}$	Momentum of molecules rebounding from heated surface	Absolute readings possible. Technique difficult; gauge sensitive to vibration, etc.
Viscosity .	$1-10^{-4}$	Viscosity of gas measured by drag or by damping of vibration	Slow in use and affected by vibration. Applicable to special researches in sealed-off tubes, vapour pressures.
Hot-Wire (Pirani)	$1-10^{-4}$	Thermal conductivity of gas	Simple and useful over restricted range. Sensitivity low at lower pressures.
Thermocouple	$1-10^{-4}$	do.	Technical variant on above.
Ionisation (hot cathode)	$10^{-3}-10^{-8}$; Special forms to 10^{-10} or lower	Production of $+$ ions by collision of electrons with atoms	Much used at low pressures. Hot cathode may be damaged by admission of gas to high pressure or by poisoning. May affect gas pressure by chemical or electrical clean-up.
Penning (cold cathode)	$10^{-3}-10^{-7}$	Electric discharge in magnetic field	Most convenient for relative measurement of low pressures.

which the filament is firmly fixed to its supports to avoid uncertainties in thermal contact (Fig. 5.6). The thermocouple gauge is shown in Fig. 5.7. The filament is here heated by a separate circuit and the temperature is measured by a thermocouple and galvanometer. The circuit arrangements are simpler than those of the Pirani, and the heater can be operated from A.C. Both these gauges become insensitive

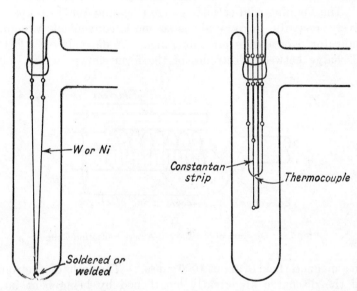

FIG. 5.6 Pirani gauge (cf. Ellett and Zabel, 1931)

FIG. 5.7 Thermocouple gauge

when the pressure is so low that heat losses to the supports are larger than conduction through the gas.

The ionisation gauge consists of a three electrode system which may be similar to that of a triode valve. Electrons from the filament are accelerated by a positively charged grid until they produce ionisation by collision. The positive ions are collected by a negatively charged electrode, and the ratio of ion current to electron current is taken as a measure of the gas pressure. It has been shown that most ionisation gauges read high on the lowest pressures because of the photoelectrons ejected from the ion collector by soft X-rays, and gauges have been designed in which this effect is suppressed by using a collector of very small area (Bayard and Alpert 1950).

It is very convenient to use with an ionisation gauge a feedback regulator which controls the cathode heating to give a predetermined electron current. Commercial regulators, containing also various protection devices, are available. A circuit typical of recent practice is described on p. 289.

The Penning cold-cathode gauge (Penning 1937), comparatively recently introduced, is a most convenient vacuum indicator over a wide pressure range. It depends on a D.C. discharge between electrodes of the form shown in Fig. 5.9,

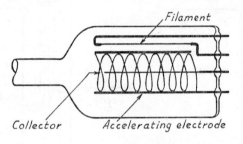

FIG. 5.8.   Diagram of the Bayard-Alpert Ionisation Gauge

in a magnetic field of about 1000 gauss.*   The paths of electrons in the discharge are greatly lengthened by being bent into helical form by the field, and by oscillation of the electrons about the ring anode, so that a measurable ionisation current is produced even at low pressures. This discharge current is very nearly proportional to the pressure. In practice the magnetic field is provided by a permanent magnet and the driving potential of about 2000 V is provided by a small rectifier. If accurate measures of pressure are required, the gauge must be calibrated with the appropriate gas, but for most purposes (see above), it is sufficiently accurate to use the calibration of Fig. 5.9(*b*) with the gauge dimensions given there.

* For the data of Fig. 5.9 I am indebted to Prof. F. A. Vick.

The calibration of thermal conductivity gauges depends on the molecular weight of the gas (the higher the molecular weight, the less the conductivity), and the calibration of

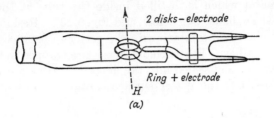

2 disks – electrode

Ring + electrode

H

(a)

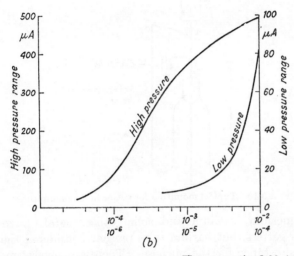

(b)

Fig. 5.9 (a) Sketch of Penning gauge. The magnetic field is applied perpendicular to the electrode system. The two nickel disks and the inside of the ring are 2 cm. diameter, the separation of the disks is 1 cm. The nickel ring is made of 1 mm. diameter wire and lies symmetrically between the disks

(b) Typical calibration for above gauge. Applied voltage 2 kV ; series resistance 2 megohms

ionisation and Penning gauges depends on the gas composition in a complicated way. It has, however, been pointed out that gauges are used, in practice, usually to observe changes in vacuum conditions and that the actual sensitivities are not often required.

5.5 Getters

In sealed-off vacuum tubes, the vacuum can be improved and maintained by the use of a " getter "—usually a chemically active metal which is distilled inside the tube at the proper stage of the exhaust (see below, and Fig. 5.10).   Residual gas in the tube may then combine with the getter to form compounds of low volatility.   Furthermore, gases are trapped in the fresh getter surface and sealed into the deposit.   After the tube has been sealed off, the getter surface continues to absorb gases.

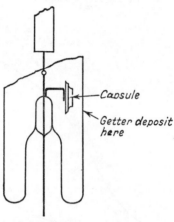

Fig. 5.10   Typical mounting for getter in a vacuum tube

Magnesium, calcium and some other metals have been used as getters, but barium is at present considered the most useful substance for the purpose.   There are several methods for liberating the barium in the right place at the correct moment.   Alloys are available commercially (e.g. Ba-Mg, Ba-Al), which are fairly stable in air ; a small pellet of the alloy is put into a little tack-welded nickel capsule, which is mounted in such a plane that it can be heated by eddy currents independently of the other electrodes.   In commercial valve making the getter is sometimes fastened to the anode, and " fired " by raising the temperature at the end of the outgassing process.*

* The 50/50 Ba/Al alloy is most generally used in present-day valve manufacture.

The temperature required to give a suitable vapour pressure of barium is about 700°-800° C. The temperature of the getter capsule is therefore raised gradually so that the getter is first outgassed and then volatilised. A very convenient form of getter consists of barium or a barium alloy contained in a tubular sheath of copper, nickel or iron; a nickel sheath of the a form shown in Fig. 5.11 is specially advantageous. The getter may be welded to a plate and volatilised as described above, or arranged with leads so that it can be heated by passing a current. The main difficulty introduced by the use of getters is the risk of spoiling the insulation inside the tube by a film of

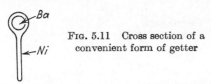

Fig. 5.11 Cross section of a convenient form of getter

deposited metal. It is necessary to design the tube so that the getter does not deposit on insulating parts; and in industrial practice, getters are not used in tubes in which insulation is particularly important, e.g. high-tension valves and electrometer valves. A very high vacuum may be obtained in laboratory work by a two-stage gettering process. The getter is arranged in a side tube, and it is outgassed and partly volatilised before the tube is sealed from the pump. After seal-off the remainder of the getter is volatilised, the side tube with the getter film being plunged into liquid air during and after this process.

Closely allied to gettering is the clean-up of gases by hot tungsten (and other metals) which results in a considerable improvement in the vacuum during the operation of sealed-off tubes containing hot filaments.*

Tantalum (see Appendix 3), which may be outgassed at a high temperature, absorbs many gases energetically at a low

---

* Oxygen, nitrogen, and hydrogen are cleaned up by hot tungsten. Water vapour, or hydrogen in the presence of oxygen, however, attack tungsten filaments badly, even at low pressures, without being effectively cleaned up ; atomic hydrogen and tungsten oxide are formed at the filament and these substances react on the bulb walls, forming a black tungsten deposit and re-forming water vapour. This cycle goes on indefinitely.

red heat. An anode made of this material, operating at a suitable temperature, can therefore exert a gettering action on a tube. Pieces of tantalum may be attached to an electrode for this purpose, and titanium, zirconium and thorium are also used in this way.

5.6   Static and Kinetic Vacuum Systems

The vacuum systems in current use may be divided rather sharply into static and kinetic types. Typical static systems

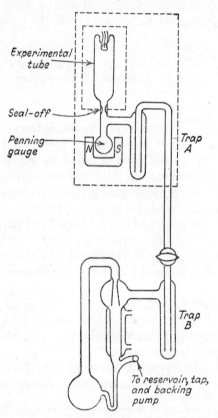

FIG. 5.12   Typical example of a " static " vacuum system

are made of glass, and elaborate precautions are taken to prevent the evolution of gas in the enclosure. These systems include those where a vessel (e.g. a thermionic valve) is sealed off from a pumping system, and then used without further pumping. In kinetic systems, which are typically large and enclosed in metal, some evolution of gas is accepted, and the design is such that the gas is pumped away without interfering with the function of the system. Cyclotrons, apparatus for coating surfaces by evaporation, and continuously pumped X-ray tubes are examples of kinetic systems.

5.7 Static Vacuum Systems—Arrangement

Fig. 5.12 shows a typical vacuum system for evacuating, e.g. a tube for experiments in thermionic emission. It is normal to use mercury diffusion pumps made in glass for such purposes. The pumping speed required (0·5-5 l./sec.) can be obtained with such pumps even through liquid-air traps, and it is obviously convenient to have fused glass joints throughout. Mercury pumps are not so easily contaminated as diffusion pumps using organic fluids, either by vapours or by oxidation products formed if air is admitted to the hot pump. Cooled traps are in any case required to obtain the lowest possible pressures. For less stringent vacuum requirements it is probable that pumps operating with organic liquid could be used without liquid air.* The pumps should then be designed on the fractionating principle so that the high-vacuum jet is supplied with vapour freed from the more volatile components.

The connections should be designed so that the pumping speed is not unduly reduced from the limit given by the pump available (except possibly by the constriction required for sealing off).

5.8 Static Vacuum Systems—Construction

We deal here expressly with systems for producing very high vacua ; many laboratory experiments require what are really low speed kinetic vacuum systems in which the " static " construction is generally followed but many of the precautions are relaxed.

---

* Organic vapour pumps have been much used in valve manufacture, but mercury is preferred by some manufacturers for pumping high-quality small valves.

Static vacuum systems must contain only materials which can be freed from gas by heating.* Organic substances such as waxes and greases, volatile metals such as zinc and brass which contains zinc, and fusible metals such as soft solder, must therefore be excluded. The most important materials of construction are glass and certain metals ; these are indicated in Appendix 3. Metal parts for vacuum tubes can often be bent or pressed from sheet metal and joined mechanically by folding over, or by spot welding. Small steel bolts

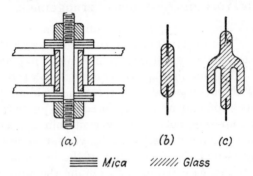

(a) (b) (c)

≡ *Mica*   ////// *Glass*

Fig. 5.13   Insulators for use in vacuum tubes
(a) Assembly of glass tubes and mica washers
(b) Glass bead
(c) Glass bead with petticoat

may be used, and metal parts can also be joined by flame-welding, silver soldering or brazing. These processes can be used for metal parts too heavy for spot-welding. The silver-solder should preferably be silver-copper alloy free from zinc ; very good brazed joints are made by clamping a thin sheet of pure silver or copper between the steel or nickel parts to be joined, and heating the assembly to the melting-point of the brazing metal in high vacuum or in hydrogen. In industrial practice a mixture of nitrogen and hydrogen ("forming gas"). is often used in this and similar operations.

There is some difficulty in finding easily worked insulating materials for use in high vacuum systems. Glass and fused quartz can be used (Fig. 5.13). Mica is often used in radio

* A monomolecular gas film on 1 sq. cm. will give a gas pressure of the order 1/50 mm. if evaporated into 1 cc.

receiving valves, to support the electrodes and to centre them in the bulb. It is not, however, very easy to outgas, and at a temperature between 550° and 800° C. (depending on its composition), it loses water and becomes electrically and mechanically weak. Ceramic materials are often used industrially, but are not conveniently worked or made to shape on a laboratory scale. Steatite (soapstone, talc) is a soft mineral which can be worked with ordinary tools and made into a hard insulating material by heating in air to 800°-1300° C. Only small shrinkage takes place in this operation.

5.9 Static Vacuum Systems—Procedure

It has been emphasised that the production of good vacua in " static " systems depends on treating all the parts exposed to the vacuum so that they do not evolve gas, and this procedure begins before the system is assembled. Metal parts can be freed from gas by heat treatment in a vacuum furnace.* Since the gas in the interior of the metal reaches the surface by diffusion, the temperature should be as high as possible ; a nichrome-wound quartz tube furnace may be used for nickel, iron, and copper. High-frequency eddy currents can also be used ; the outer tube then remains cool and refractory metals can be outgassed at very high temperatures. Instead of using vacuum, the metal parts may be furnaced in a slow stream of dry hydrogen. This method is even more effective, probably because oxygen compounds are energetically reduced, but it must not be used for copper and tantalum which become brittle under hydrogen treatment. After outgassing, the metals may be exposed to air, though they must be kept free from grease and not touched with bare hands. The thin surface films which they pick up under these conditions are readily removed during the final treatment on the pumps. Glass also gives up a good deal of its gas by pre-heating but this process is not so generally used, probably because it is difficult to avoid wetting the glass again during the operations of sealing up the vacuum system. When the vacuum tube has been assembled and sealed to the pumping system, the

---

* Nickel which has been treated in this way is commercially obtainable.

outgassing follows a schedule like that of Table 5.5 ; this table refers specially to a very high vacuum tube containing a tungsten cathode, and modifications of it apply to most high-vacuum experiments. In many experiments which require the very highest vacua, the tube is sealed off from the pumps and the residual gases are cleared up by " getter " action by the electrodes or by a special getter.

TABLE 5.5

Typical Evacuation Schedule for Hard-Glass Apparatus
(Refer to Fig. 5.12)

(1)	Bake in oven at 450° C., including trap A and gauge in baking zone. Liquid air on trap B. Baking time—1 hr.
(2)	Remove oven, run filaments to highest safe temperature, heat other metal parts by current, eddy current or bombardment.
(3)	Put liquid air on both traps, bake tube in oven at 300°-350° C. until gauge shows that no more gas is evolved.
(4)	Heat metal parts until gauge shows no more gas is evolved. Flash filaments.
(5)	Fire getter (first stage).
(6)	Seal off.
(7)	Fire getter, second stage—tube or side tube immersed in liquid air.

Notes on Table 5.5

(*a*) Two liquid air traps provided only when very good vacuum required ; in other cases only trap B is present.

(*b*) Stages (5) and (6) apply to tubes which are sealed from the pumping system.

(*c*) Stage (7) is a rather special technique for obtaining the highest vacua.

(*d*) If oxide-coated cathodes are present, they are usually activated immediately before stage (5).

5.10   Kinetic Vacuum Systems (see Fig. 5.14)

These systems have become important in the last fifteen years or so ; they are now used on a considerable scale in industry, and an engineering technique of " vacuum plumbing " is becoming established (Sullivan 1948 ; Kurie 1948).   The characteristic feature of these systems is the use of very fast pumps. These are usually oil diffusion pumps, but in some large systems with stringent vacuum requirements [e.g. the ion accelerators developed very successfully by the High Voltage Corporation] mercury pumps with liquid air traps are preferred.

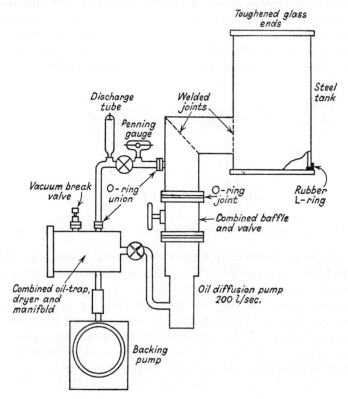

FIG. 5.14   A typical " kinetic " vacuum system—evaporation plant for vacuum coating

With oil pumps cooled baffles are used to prevent backstreaming of oil molecules from pump to vacuum system, and it is increasingly common to cool the baffles by means of a small refrigerating plant. It is useful to put at strategic points re-entrant thimbles cooled with liquid air (cold fingers). The backing pumps must be fast enough to maintain the backing vacuum with the

diffusion pump operating at full speed, and it is usually economical to use a "booster pump"—a suitably designed jet
pump—between the main diffusion pump and the mechanical
pump, rather than to use a very large mechanical pump.

The outer walls of these systems are made of metal, and
although a high standard of cleanliness should be maintained
in assembling, outgassing by heat is not usually attempted.*
The apparatus should be made from rolled or drawn brass or
steel; castings are usually too porous for this work, and if
used may have to be tinned completely internally.

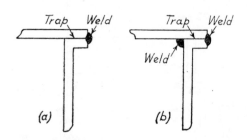

Fig. 5.15.   Bad vacuum practice—formation of traps at welded joints

Joints in vacuum apparatus are welded, brazed, or made
with hard (silver) or soft solder.   Argon arc welding in aluminium or stainless steel is very satisfactory: brazing and hard
soldering are done best by induction heating in a suitable
atmosphere (cf. p. 166).   Soft solder joints are not very strong
and preclude any but the mildest heating when the apparatus
is in use, nevertheless soft soldered joints are satisfactory in
many applications and are easy to make free from leakage.
They should be designed so that their strength is obtained
mechanically and the solder acts as a mechanical lock and a
vacuum seal.   It is important to design the joints in a vacuum
system so that there is no possibility of gas or dirt being trapped
in narrow cavities and slowly escaping into the vacuum
(Fig. 5.15).

In some kinetic vacuum systems rubber gasket joints are
freely used, (Fig 5.16) and one of the most successful of these is

---

* The surfaces should be cleaned with acetone on clean rags, and then
kept free from finger marks and other grease.

the seamless toroidal ring (O ring). The ring should be trapped in a joint so that it cannot be sucked out of place: the makers

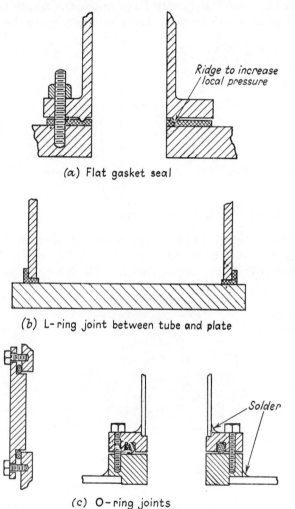

(*a*) Flat gasket seal

(*b*) L-ring joint between tube and plate

(*c*) O-ring joints

FIG. 5.16   Rubber gasket joints for vacuum system

of rings supply dimensions and tolerances to which the grooves should be machined. Non-circular gaskets of the same sections can be made up out of rubber cord, but it is highly desirable to use circular gaskets since the grooves can be formed with ease and accuracy by a simple lathe operation. It may be worthwhile, particularly with large apparatus, to use two concentric gaskets with access through suitable ports to the " guard

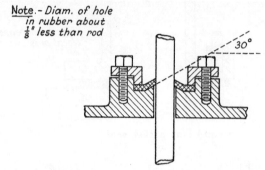

Note.- Diam. of hole in rubber about $\frac{1}{8}''$ less than rod

30°

FIG. 5.17   " Wilson " seal allowing translation and rotation

ring " space between them. This space can then be tested for leakage and left evacuated to reduce possible leaks. Alternative forms of rubber joint are shown in Fig. 5.16; all these joints

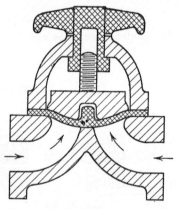

FIG. 5.18   " Saunders " diaphragm valve. Shown closed

are easily opened and are particularly valuable for vacuum evaporation plants which must be opened up during each cycle of operations. The gaskets may be used dry or very lightly coated with low-vapour-pressure grease. Rubber diaphragms

have been used ("Wilson" seal, see Fig. 5.17), for allowing
mechanical motion to be transmitted into the vacuum space
of a kinetic system; it is also possible to use conical greased
ground joints for this purpose. It is usually necessary to
provide couplings to allow the internal parts to rotate free from
jamming or strain imposed by the ground joint.

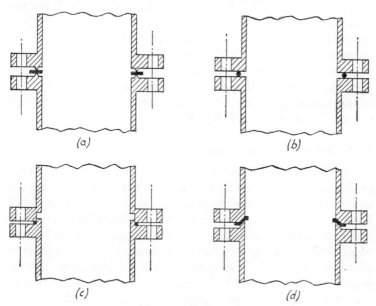

FIG. 5.19.   Metallic gasket seals for high vacuum
(*a*) Flat gasket between pressure faces
(*b*) Soft metal ring between flat faces
(*c*) Soft ring in stepped seal
(*d*) " Shear " seal—flat gasket deformed between conical faces

Valves are sometimes used to isolate the pump from the
rest of the vacuum system, so that the latter may be opened
to air without admitting air to the pump; the valve in the
main pumping line is necessarily very large, and may with
advantage be combined with the oil-baffle. Several suitable
arrangements have been described, and some are made
commercially (Hickman 1940; Edwards). Smaller valves
for by-pass and backing-pump connections may be of the
" Saunders " diaphragm construction (Fig. 5.18).

G*   173

Rubber gaskets emit some vapour into the vacuum, and cannot be heated; silicone elastomers will withstand rather higher temperatures. It is possible to use soft metal gaskets between faces designed to produce high local pressures (Fig. 5.19(a)), and joints of this kind can be made using pressure-faces of glass and ceramics, as well as metal. Softened copper is a suitable material for the gaskets; joints which require lower interfacial pressures can be made using indium. Quite recently Messrs. Edwards's laboratories have reported work (Holden *et al.* 1959, 1960) on the use of aluminium wire gaskets which after baking adhere strongly to well-finished joint faces, so that they no longer depend on the maintenance of mechanical pressure. They will then remain tight through several baking cycles (cf. Fig. 5.19(b)).

5.11 Ultra-high Vacuum

At present there is being evolved a technique for the regular production of pressures lower then 10^{-8} mm. Hg. Using the new methods it is, for example, possible to deposit evaporated films at pressures several decades lower than those attained in conventional evaporation plant. This possibility may be very valuable in scientific work on the nature of films as well as in preparing technically useful films. On a larger scale, the experiments on controllable thermonuclear reactions require very low concentrations of impurity atoms, and many of the largest installations are for this purpose.

The characteristic features of the ultra-high vacuum technique are the use of fully bakeable vessels, usually of stainless steel, metal bakeable demountable joints, and sometimes bakeable valves. The actual pumping may be done with diffusion pumps using oil or mercury but provided with very efficient cooled traps.* It is also possible to make use of the fact that a considerable quantity of gas is taken up in the operation of an ionisation gauge, and to combine this effect with the gettering action of hot zirconium or titanium.

---

* Alpert introduced traps containing large surfaces of folded, degassed copper foil. It is found that such surfaces are effective in stopping back-streaming of oil vapours even at room temperatures; they would usually be cooled in ultra-high-vacuum applications.

Small ionisation gauges of the Alpert design are made with zirconium electrodes, and for these it is claimed that they give a pumping speed of a few tenths of a litre per second and an ultimate pressure of about 10^{-11} mm. Hg (Mullard 1960a). A rather larger pump depends on the Penning gauge principle of a discharge in a magnetic field, and pumps under development seek to combine ionisation of the residual gas by an electron discharge and gettering by continually evaporating metal. The pumps, at least the smaller ones, are used to produce very high vacua in small, baked systems after sealing off from a conventional pumping system by glass blowing or by a valve which can withstand degassing at high temperature. There are a number of variant designs of bakeable valve, stemming from a design by Alpert: these all combine a seating hole and a nose either much harder or much softer, which is forced into the aperture by a screw mechanism acting through a flexible bellows or diaphragm. A recent discussion is given by Thorness and Nier (1961.) An ingenious laboratory method for obtaining ultra high vacuum in the upper part of a tall bell-jar depends on isolating this region by a cooled trap part-way up the jar, and using a titanium getter to remove gas (Turner *et al* 1962).

5.12 Leaks

The detection of small leaks in vacuum apparatus can be difficult. It is often impossible to use taps to subdivide a system and so localise a leak. One should therefore take advantage of stages in the building up of the apparatus to check various sections for leakage, and should be prepared to remove portions as required for this purpose. In a glass system pin-holes can be found with a discharge from an induction coil or a small Tesla transformer if the pressure in the apparatus is reduced to a suitable value (1 — 0·1 mm.). One terminal of the induction coil is connected to an electrode in the apparatus (this is unnecessary with a Tesla, since stray capacities serve as an earth connection) and the other is moved over the surface of the system. A spark passes as the electrode passes over a pin-hole. The method is not, however, sensitive to very small leaks, and it cannot be used near an electrode seal. The other "classical" method consists in watching the readings of a suitable gauge, while the system is painted over with a soap solution. The gauge reading falls when a leak is masked by the solution.

More modern and more useful methods depend on the selective response of certain gauges to particular vapours.

A primitive illustration of this principle is the applcation of a volatile organic substance (e.g. ether) to suspected leaks in a glass apparatus while maintaining a discharge within it. The rosy colour of the air (nitrogen) discharge changes to grey when the organic vapour enters the apparatus. This is an insensitive method because it requires a high gas pressure (say 1/10 mm. Hg) to maintain the discharge, and more sensitive applications of the principle are available. Oxygen will reduce the emission from the tungsten filament of an ionisation gauge: helium replacing air at a leak will produce a considerable reduction in the positive ion ratio in an ionisation gauge. A particularly useful leak detector is a Penning gauge used with butane (commercial bottled gas) as an exploring substance. (Blears and Leck 1951, which discusses carefully the best conditions of use.) A jet of the gas is played on the suspected region and the replacement of air by the gas produces a considerable increase in the gauge current. If a small leak is under investigation, it is best to build up a plasticine dam on the outside of the apparatus, so that the gas concentration may be economically maintained over the suspected leak for some time.

The principle of a selective gauge has been used in three recently developed and apparently very effective methods—the ionisation gauge connected through a palladium tube which is very sensitive to hydrogen (Nelson 1945); the production of positive ions at a heated platinum filament exposed to halogen vapours (White and Hickey 1948).* The most elaborate and most sensitive method is to connect a small mass spectrometer to the system in order to detect a suitable probe gas (Worcester and Doughty 1946, Thomas *et al.* 1946, Dushman 1949, p. 377). Several instruments on this plan are made

---

* This device is usually used to detect outward leaks from a system containing, e.g. Freon under pressure.

commercially. Helium is most often used as the probe gas since it is not easily confused with probable impurities, and its light ions are easily resolved in a simple spectrometer. It is claimed for a recent helical-focussing instrument that it can be used under certain precautions with hydrogen as a probe (Cossulta and Steckelmacher 1960).

All the gauge methods are applicable to metal vacuum systems, and the mass-spectrometer was developed for finding leaks in very large kinetic systems. Before a metal vacuum system is assembled, it is desirable to test its parts by applying a positive excess pressure to the inside, plunging the container into water and looking for bubbles. A rather less satisfactory alternative to the water tank is painting with soap solution.

APPENDIX 1

Seals between Metal and Glass (for a full treatment see Partridge, 1949)

These seals, whether in the form of wires sealed through glass, or annular seals between glass and metal tubes, play an important part in vacuum technique. They are made using two main alternative principles :

(a) The metal may be chosen so that the coefficient of expansion matches that of the glass between the annealing temperature of the latter and the temperature of use. This matching must be so close that the stresses produced in the glass during cooling, or temperature changes in use, do not crack the glass.

(b) The seal may be so designed that the metal can yield by plastic deformation before dangerous stresses are produced in the glass.

In either case the glass must " wet " the metal, and to secure this the metal is oxidised (and, in the case of copper, covered with a film of borax). At the temperature of sealing the oxide dissolves in the glass to form a thin layer of an intermediate glass which is firmly attached to the metal. The colour and appearance of this intermediate film is usually a

177

good test for a satisfactory seal. (For an account of the design of seals, see Scott 1946.)

Tungsten wire forms seals of class (a) with hard borosilicate glass ; Fig. 5.20 indicates the run of the expansion of tungsten compared with two glasses (from Chance's list). GHA is known to make satisfactory wire seals under laboratory conditions up to 1 mm. diameter, and GSD (usually used as an

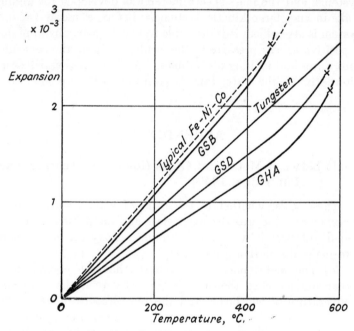

FIG. 5.20   Matching of sealing glasses to tungsten and Fe-Ni-Co alloy

intermediate glass) may be used up to larger diameters than this.* In making the seals the tungsten rod, which should be free from longitudinal cracks and drawing marks, is cleaned by heating to a red heat and stroking with a stick of sodium nitrite which attacks it vigorously. It is then washed in water and oxidised by heating in an air-gas flame. A sheath of the

* Corning G 702 P Nonex is a lead borosilicate glass which is used as an intermediate glass in American 'practice. The British B.T.H. and G.E.C. companies make several kinds of tungsten sealing glass.

appropriate glass is then slipped over it and melted down on to the wire with an oxy-gas flame, starting at the middle of the piece and working to the ends. After cooling, the seal should show a continuous golden to brown film of the intermediate glass.

Ternary alloys of iron, nickel and cobalt (Fernico and Kovar made in U.S.A., Nicosel, Nilo, and Telcoseal alloys made in this country) will form wire, ring, and disc seals of class (a) with suitable borosilicate glasses (e.g. Corning G 705 A,

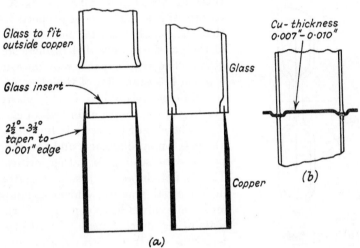

FIG. 5.21   Copper-glass seals: (a) Tubular; (b) Disk

Chance GSB, B.T.H." C 40 ", G.E.C. " F.C.N."), having expansion coefficients of the order $4 \cdot 8. 10^{-6}$ per °C. Additional intermediate glasses are required between these glasses and the most usual laboratory glasses. The ternary alloys are particularly suitable for making seal-in insulators for taking leads through metal containers. The metal parts of all these seals should be very smooth and may be cleaned if necessary by pickling in a dilute mixture of nitric and hydrochloric acid. They should then be degassed by heating to 950°-1000° in wet hydrogen. During the sealing process some oxidation should take place, but over-oxidation, indicated by a black colour in the finished seal, may lead to porosity.

Platinum wire forms seals of class (a) with soda-lime glasses (lead glasses are often used as intermediates). Platinum seals are not now used industrially, but they are easy to make and sometimes useful in the laboratory. A number of ferrous alloys, particularly chromium iron with 25-30 % Cr, are also available for sealing through soft glass ; chrome iron can be used to make ring seals to glass tubes in which the metal is up to 1 mm. thick, and such seals have been largely developed by the firm of Philips for the construction of X-ray tubes.

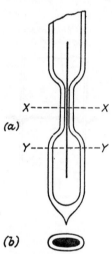

(a)

(b)

FIG. 5.22 Molybdenum ribbon seal through quartz

Wire of nickel iron alloy (42 % Ni), coated with a thickness of copper such that the radial expansion matches that of the glass, can be sealed through soft glass. The *axial* expansion of the wire is much less than that of the glass, and the difference is taken up by plastic yielding of the copper as in seals of class (*b*). The size of the seals is limited to about 0·8 mm. diameter, and the temperature of sealing is rather critical. This is not, however, a serious matter in industrial practice, and most lamps and some valves have copper-clad wire seals in a " pinch " made of lead glass which is sealed bodily to a soda-lime-glass bulb. These pinches can be bought from lamp makers for use in laboratory vacuum tubes.

The copper ring and disc seals (Fig. 5.21) (details of construction in Martin and Hill 1947, Appendix) depend entirely on plastic deformation, and the mechanical design is important. The copper for the ring seal is formed with a feather edge, lightly oxidised, dipped into borax solution and heated until it becomes covered with a borate glass film. The actual making of the joint is done in a glass lathe or in a hand jig.

Quartz-Metal Seals

There is considerable difficulty in sealing electrodes through silica glass because of the small expansion coefficient ($0·6 . 10^{-6}$)

of the glass, and invar electrodes have been fitted by grinding and by plugging with melted lead.

More recently, molybdenum strip, 15μ thick and feather-edged, has been used to make satisfactory seals of class (b) (Fig. 5.22). These seals have been developed industrially for mercury-vapour lamps. The silica is melted down on the metal in vacuum or in an inert gas. A strip 4 mm. wide will carry up to 10 A (Martin and Hill 1947, Appendix ; Espe and Knoll 1936, p. 349).

APPENDIX 2

Spot-Welding

This process is most valuable for joining thin sheet metal in making electrodes, etc., for vacuum tubes. The pieces to be joined are pressed together between blunt-pointed electrodes

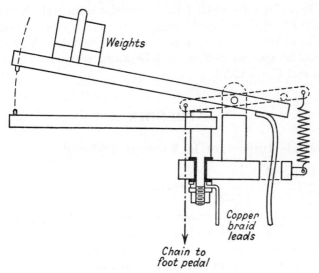

FIG. 5.23   One form of laboratory spot welder

and fused very locally by passing a momentary heavy current (100-1000 A) from a low voltage (1-4 V) transformer. It is convenient to arrange that the welder jaws are brought together under a set pressure by a weight or spring when the operator presses a pedal (see Fig. 5.23). The current is then turned on by further pressure or (in my opinion, preferably) by another pedal switch. In industrial practice the duration of the current is automatically controlled, and certain difficult materials can be welded fairly easily by a thyratron-controlled welder giving accurate control of very short current pulses. A laboratory spot-welder may be improvised using a car battery or a group of large condensers as a current source.

The ease and certainty with which metals are spot-welded depends on their electrical and thermal conductivities, their melting-points, and on the absence of strong insulating oxide films.

Nickel, constantan, iron and steel can be welded easily using copper electrodes in a laboratory spot welder. Molybdenum presents little difficulty but it is best welded under alcohol or in an envelope of reducing gas.

Copper can be welded using molybdenum rod electrodes, the heat being developed mainly in the electrodes. Tungsten can be welded to nickel, thence to other metals. Aluminium cannot be spot-welded under laboratory conditions (see also Espe and Knoll 1936).

APPENDIX 3

Materials Important in Vacuum Technique

(a) General

(1) *Glasses* (see § 4.23)

Soft soda-lime glass used for commercial sealed-off vacuum devices—most lamps and some valves. Lead glass used as sealing glass in these cases. Hard borosilicate glass (Pyrex, Chance GHA) usually used for laboratory vacuum systems, with tungsten seals. Intermediate sealing glasses (G 702 P Nonex, Chance GSD) may be used in these seals, especially in industrial production. Other borosilicate glasses with rather high expansion used industrially for sealing to molybdenum and Fe Ni Co alloy.

(2) *Nickel*

Normally used for electrodes, etc., since it is readily cleaned and outgassed.

Density 8·8-8·9 g./cm.^{3} M.P. 1452° C.

Thermal expansion 15 . 10^{-6} (0-500° C.).

Magnetic below *ca.* 350° C., initial permeability may be *ca.* 500.

(3) *Copper*

Occasionally used for non-magnetic electrodes, etc.

Used for annular seals to glass, where difference in expansion is taken up by plastic deformation of metal.

Density 8·9 g./cm.^{3} M.P. 1083° C.

Thermal expansion 18 . 10^{-6} (0-500° C.).

For vacuum applications it is very desirable to use " oxygen free high conductivity " (O.F.H.C.) copper. This is a recognised grade of metal (B.S. 1861) which contains more than 99·95 % of copper and has been melted and cast under special conditions.*

(4) *Constantan*

Nearly non-magnetic and rather stronger than nickel.

(5) *Iron*

Specially pure iron sometimes used for electrodes, etc.

Austenitic stainless steel (18%, Cr 8%, Ni) is strong and practically non-magnetic.

(b) Specially Refractory Metals

(1) *Molybdenum*

Electrodes, etc., for very high temperatures. Seals to suitable hard glasses.

Density about 10·0 g/cm.^{3} M.P. 2630° C.

Thermal expansion 5·8 . 10^{-6} per ° C.

Fairly easily worked—can be welded under precautions.

Available as wire, rod, strip, sheet, etc.

---

* Brasses and other alloys containing zinc should not be used in high vacuum apparatus, since zinc is volatile at moderate temperatures.

(2) *Tungsten*

Electrodes, particularly filaments, for very high temperatures. Anti-cathodes for X-ray tubes. Seals to suitable hard glasses.

Density 19-19·4 g./cm.^{3} (drawn wire). M.P. 3400° C.

Thermal expansion 4·4-5·5 . 10^{-6} (20°-1000° C.).

Difficult to work—may be bent and forged at dull red heat.

Available as wire, rod, strip ; other forms have been made commercially.

(3) *Tantalum*

Electrodes for high temperatures—valuable because it absorbs many gases freely, especially around 600° C., though it is outgassed easily at higher temperatures.

Density *ca.* 17 g./cm.^{3} M.P. *ca.* 2900° C.

Thermal expansion 6·5 . 10^{-6} (0°-500° C.).

Fairly easily worked ; must not be heated in air or hydrogen.

Available as sheet or wire.

(c) Sealing Metals

(1) Platinum (Thermal expansion 9·2 . 10^{-6}) seals through soda or lead glass.

(2) Fe-Cr alloys, e.g. Fe 75, Cr 25 (Thermal expansion 6-10.10^{-6}) seal through soda-lime glass.

(3) Composite wire with Fe-Ni core and copper coat (copper-clad, Dumet), seals through soda or lead glass.

(4) Tungsten seals through hard borosilicate glass (Pyrex, GHA) with or without intermediate glass (Nonex, GSD).

(5) Molybdenum seals through special borosilicate glass (Corning 704, 705. Chance GSB).

(6) Fe-Ni-Co alloys (Fernico, Kovar, Nilo, Nicosel, Telcoseal) (Thermal expansion 4·7 . 10^{-6} below 450° with a sharp rise above this temperature) seal through glasses generally similar to those used with molybdenum, but preferably chosen to allow for the kink in the expansion curve.

Very elaborate information on all these substances is to be found in Espe and Knoll (1936). Lists of glasses and sealing metals are given in Partridge (1949.)

CHAPTER 6

ELECTRICAL MEASUREMENTS AND MAGNETIC FIELDS

6.1 Electrical Measurements

The very great importance of electrical measurements in the physical laboratory arises partly from the fact that a large and increasing number of other quantities, e.g. temperature, mechanical movement, gas pressure, pH, are turned into electrical changes for the purpose of measurement. This chapter discusses some common problems of electrical measurement largely because information on them is not easily available in compact form.

6.2 Deflection Instruments for Direct Current

The direct currents met in ordinary laboratory practice range from a few thousand amperes to 10^{-14} A or less, and it is often convenient to measure them with a direct reading instrument. This is usually possible if the accuracy required is not much better than, say, 1 %. Down to about 10^{-9} A, the moving coil galvanometer in some form is the normal measuring instrument, and currents smaller than this usually require an electrostatic method. Moving coil galvanometers may take the following forms :

(1) Double-pivoted instruments with shunts or series resistances—the normal ammeters and voltmeters—read by pointer and scale. They are available down to about 1 mA full scale deflection ; more sensitive instruments are in common use, but tend to be fragile.

(2) Pointer instruments with suspended coils or " unipivot " construction—available down to a few microamps f.s.d. With them may be classed a few portable reflecting instruments with self-contained lamp and scale.

(3) Suspended-coil reflecting galvanometers—normal laboratory types with sensitivity around 10^{-9} A/mm. at 1 m. scale distance for a resistance of the order 100 ohms.

(4) Suspended-coil galvanometers with special refinements.

6.3   Ammeters and Voltmeters

Instruments of class (1) above are nearly always calibrated to read directly. A very good guide to their accuracy is a British Standard specification, B.S. 89 (1954) from which the data of Table 6·1 are taken. This British Standard contains also specified limits for the effects of temperature and external magnetic fields, information on the choice of meters and a code of identifying marks for different types of instrument. It is

TABLE 6.1

Accuracy of Electrical Instruments selected from BS. 89 (1954)

Precision Grade (Pr)	%
Permanent magnet moving coil ammeters and voltmeters	0·3 (0·03 0·06)
Permanent magnet moving coil multi-range ammeters	0·5
Other instruments	0·5
Industrial instruments (In) Portable instruments with 5 in. scale	
Permanent magnet moving coil	0·75(0·10 0·15)
Moving iron, Electrodynamic; A.C. Induction	1·0 (0·1 0·2)
Electrostatic voltmeter	1·5 (0·05)
Thermocouple	2·0 (0·3)
Rectifier	2·0 (0·25)

The permissible errors are expressed as a percentage of full scale. Lower standards of accuracy are prescribed for smaller portable industrial instruments and for panel-mounting instruments.

The figures in brackets represent the allowed temperature coefficients expressed as a percentage of the reading for 1° C. temperature change. When two figures are given the higher coefficient is for low-reading voltmeters and high-reading milliammeters and ammeters.

necessary to check meters from time to time against a laboratory standard if the accuracy of Table 6.1 is required over a period of years, and the standard must be an instrument of good quality which is carefully handled and used only for reference. Certain parts of instruments, particularly the pivots, are easily damaged by mechanical shock, and pivot friction is then a major cause of inconsistent readings. Electrical overload may produce permanent changes in calibration by overheating the control springs. The sensitivity of a moving coil instrument depends upon the magnet, the control springs, and the electrical resistance of the coil, series resistance and shunt. These factors may vary through ageing or in response to temperature changes. In practice the effect of temperature on the magnet is small, the increase of sensitivity due to the weakening of the springs with increase of temperature is larger. In voltmeters the resistance of the copper-wound moving coil is thoroughly swamped by a series resistance wound with an alloy of low resistance-temperature coefficient. In low reading millivoltmeters this is not possible and a higher temperature coefficient is to be expected, though some commercial instruments are considerably better than the limits allowed in B.S. 89. Ammeters are essentially millivoltmeters connected across a shunt which always has a low temperature coefficient, so that the temperature error of the ammeter is effectively that of the millivoltmeter. Ammeter shunts are usually made to give a potential difference of 75 mV at full rated current.

Although moving coil instruments are not extremely sensitive to magnetic fields, it is quite possible to influence their readings appreciably by the stray fields from magnets, etc., or by mounting them on a steel panel. Some instruments are provided with an internal magnetic shield, to reduce these effects. In any doubtful case the effect should be tested, e.g. by switching the disturbing field on and off, or by altering the position or orientation of the instrument.

Instruments of class (2) are very useful as low-reading milliammeters and are more reliable than double-pivoted instruments of high sensitivity. The latter are very much at the mercy of pivot friction, since the deflecting torque is low ; they therefore become unreliable after moderately rough handling. Class (2) instruments are normally provided with arrangements for clamping the moving system for transport, and rough handling is more likely to break the suspension than to produce " stickiness ". The instruments have to be used with the axis of the movement roughly vertical, and their calibration is probably not quite so consistent as that of double-pivoted instruments.

6.4 Recording Instruments

It is of course possible to record the deflections of a mirror galvanometer by allowing the spot to fall on a photographic film or paper traversed by a driving motor or clock: it is convenient to use the image of a slit or a linear lamp filament and to concentrate it by a cylindrical lens placed very near the paper. The technique has recently been extended by the introduction of recording emulsions which " print out " without development if an intense source of ultraviolet light is used, and which are rather insensitive to ordinary illumination. The record can then be read as it is made. Electric meters which produce a record by ink writing on a paper chart are now in common use. In the simplest instruments a recording pen is attached to a large moving coil instrument movement. The instruments are made with sensitivity extending to 1 mA. full scale deflection. As might be expected, the friction of the recording pen leads to a standard of accuracy markedly below that of indicating instruments; the frictional errors may be reduced in laboratory work by giving the instrument a very small mechanical vibration (e.g. by mounting on it a small motor with an unbalanced rotating mass) or injecting into the moving coil a very small alternating current.

The friction is removed and a higher sensitivity made available in instruments using the " dotting " or " thread recorder " principle. A pointer attached to a moving coil galvanometer swings freely over a chart; an inked thread or ribbon lies between the pointer and chart, and at regular intervals a pivoted bar descends and presses the pointer and thread onto the chart. These instruments are in practice limited to rather slow rates of data recording, commonly one point in thirty seconds.

A more complicated and more versatile device is the self-balancing or potentiometric recorder. In its modern forms the recording pen is moved by a servo-mechanism which simultaneously adjusts a potentiometer, bridge, or other balanced measuring system. The accuracy of recording does not depend on pen friction or on the mechanical properties of the recorder, provided that the amplification is high enough to give a large restoring force for a small departure from the balanced condition. The servo system used in these recorders usually depends on a chopper (§ 6.17) and A.C. amplifier, followed by a two-phase motor which acts as a phase-sensitive integrating detector.*

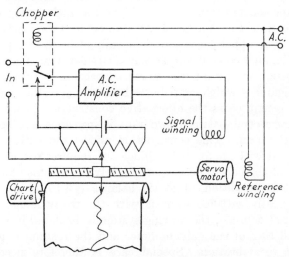

FIG. 6.1. Schematic diagram of a self-balancing recorder. In the servo system shown, the servo motor develops a torque proportional to the product of the currents in signal phase and reference phase windings, so that it acts as a phase-sensitive rectifier.

Fig. 6.1 shows the general principle of a self-balancing recorder; commercial instruments can record minimum disturbances of a few microvolts and produce full scale deflections in 1 sec. An obvious modification, sometimes useful, allows one of these instruments to record the ratio of two varying e.m.f.s, one applied to the potentiometer wire and the other to the balancing circuit. It is, for example, possible to measure optical absorption directly in this way, using two photocells. Some of the commercial instruments have special provision for use as ratio meters.

* Certain commercial instruments use galvanometers with photoelectric cells to detect their movements and control the servo: there is a French instrument which will follow and record the movements of an ordinary galvanometer spot.

6.5 Moving Coil Galvanometers

In the familiar instruments of class (3) the moving coil may rotate over an iron core, or may be long, thin and coreless. The object of the former construction is to give a radial field, and hence a linear relation between current and deflection ; the latter construction gives the highest sensitivity for a given periodic time (see Mather 1890, quoted in Gray 1921 ; and § 6.8). The upper suspension is usually of bronze strip, which gives a smaller control torque than a circular wire of equal area and tension strength ; the lower suspension is often a thin coiled ligament which contributes little to the restoring couple. But in recent years the alternative construction in which the coil is stretched between two taut suspensions has been increasingly used. This construction allows the galvanometer to be used without exact levelling, but requires the centre of gravity of the coil to lie very accurately in the axis of suspension : this condition of static balance (§ 3.15) is no longer automatically satisfied as it is with the freely hanging coil. If it is not fulfilled, the moving system is displaced in rotation by small tilts of the galvanometer and the reading is greatly affected by vibration. Special care is therefore needed in replacing a broken suspension in a taut-suspension instrument.

In low resistance galvanometer circuits, parasitic thermoelectric e.m.f.s are an important source of disturbance and galvanometers are made in which the suspension strips, as well as the coil, terminals, and internal connections, are made entirely of copper to avoid the production of thermal e.m.f.s. In using an ordinary galvanometer in a low resistance circuit, it is often desirable to shield the instrument and its connections (e.g. by an outer metal box and cotton wool lagging) against differences of temperature. Particular attention should be paid to places (e.g. terminals) where dissimilar metals come into contact.

6.6 The Practical Use of Moving Coil Galvanometers (Class (3) above)

Galvanometers of this type are generally used with lamp and scale, the latter at a distance of about 1 m. Representative sensitivity values are given in Table 6.2, and the optical system for the lamp and scale is discussed in § 8.5. The size of the mirror, like most features of a galvanometer of this class, is a compromise ; the competing factors are here light-collecting power, increase in the moment of inertia of the

TABLE 6.2

Representative Galvanometer Sensitivities

(These galvanometers, selected from catalogues, do not necessarily represent extreme types made by the various firms.)

Designation	Time of swing sec.	Internal resistance ohms	Critical damping resistance ohms	Current sensitivity mm./μA
d'Arsonval	2	20	150	120
(Cambridge)	2	450	1100	1100
Short period	4	600	25,000	4500
(Cambridge)	1·8	25	70	300
Zernicke	1·3	7	50·0	140-40
(Kipp and Zonen)	7	55	3000-200	6600-2000
Type R	6	500	7000	2000
(Leeds-Northrup)	5	12	50	125
Paschen	6	12	—	14,000
(Cambridge)				

system, and the cost of making a very light mirror of satisfactory optical quality. A concave mirror is sometimes used, but it is usually more convenient to use a plane one, which can more readily be made optically satisfactory, and to put immediately in front of it a lens of focal length roughly equal to the scale distance.

If the galvanometer is to be used for accurate work by deflection methods, the relative position of galvanometer and scale should be fixed, and the scale should be calibrated for current, since accurate linearity of deflection cannot be assured with any of the ordinary galvanometer constructions. In some instruments the shape of the calibration curve may change with the levelling of the instrument. The calibration may be made against a good ammeter or voltmeter, using the circuits of Fig. 6.2. Both in calibration and in the use of the galvanometer, it is necessary for accurate work to intersperse deflection readings with zero readings and to compare the deflections with an interpolated zero.

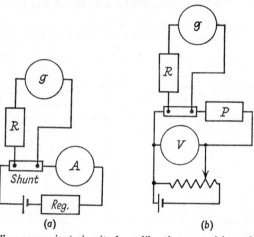

FIG. 6.2   Two convenient circuits for calibrating a sensitive galvanometer
(*a*) Using an ammeter as standard   (*b*) Using a voltmeter as standard

It is desirable to use a galvanometer with damping nearly critical ; a very slight overshoot is usually regarded as the best behaviour. If the galvanometer is used in a high impedance circuit, there is no difficulty in obtaining this degree of damping by the use of a shunt which is normally so high that it does not much alter the sensitivity. The Ayrton-Mather universal shunt is convenient. If the best sensitivity is required, combined with critical damping in a low resistance circuit, the galvanometer must be designed accordingly (see § 6.7).

6.7   Galvanometers of High Performance

Moving magnet galvanometers (especially the Paschen design) were at one time in considerable use where the highest sensitivity was required, as in the survey of an infra-red spectrum with a thermopile detector. Modern materials for the magnet system and for magnetic shielding would permit a considerable improvement in the performance of these galvanometers ; but they have, in fact, become obsolete. The systematic study and consequent improvement of the moving coil galvanometer (§ 6.8), the invention of deflection amplifiers (§ 6.9), the discovery that the useful sensitivity of a galvanometer is limited by the thermal fluctuations in the circuit (§ 10.4) have combined to make the moving coil instrument the only galvanometer of contemporary importance.

6.8 Theory of Moving Coil Galvanometers

The equation of motion of the coil is

$$I\ddot{\theta} + \left(\beta + \frac{n^2 A^2 H^2}{R}\right)\dot{\theta} + c\theta = nAHi$$

where I is the moment of inertia ; c the restoring couple per unit angular deflection ; β is the damping due to all causes other than currents induced in the coil circuit ; n is the number of turns on the coil circuit ; A the area of a turn ; H the magnetic field ; R is the total resistance of the coil circuit. The current sensitivity δ_i is then $\dfrac{nAH}{c}$, and the time of swing of the undamped motion is $2\pi\sqrt{\dfrac{I}{c}}$. If the non-electrical damping is negligible the system is critically damped when

$$\left(\frac{n^2 A^2 H^2}{R}\right)^2 = 4Ic$$

$$R = \frac{n^2 A^2 H^2}{2\sqrt{Ic}}.$$

If the coil resistance is r, and the external resistance in circuit is r', the deflection per unit e.m.f. is

$$\delta_v = \frac{nAH}{c}\Big/(r + r').$$

If we consider a coil of given size, in which the cross-section of the winding is S and the average length of a turn is l ; having n turns of conductor cross-section s, we have

$$r = \frac{nl\rho}{s} = \frac{n^2 l\rho}{S}$$

where ρ is the resistivity of the conductor and the space occupied by insulation is neglected.

$$\delta_v = \frac{nAH}{c} \bigg/ \left(\frac{n^2 l\rho}{S} + r'\right).$$

If n be varied, δ_v is a maximum for $n^2 l\rho / S = r = r'$, so that with the assumptions made here, the resistance of a galvanometer should match that of the external circuit for greatest sensitivity to an e.m.f. occurring in a circuit of given resistance. Under these conditions, the power dissipated in the galvanometer is equal to that dissipated in the external resistance.

If we wished to compare two galvanometer constructions, it would be proper to do so by comparing the deflections obtained with a given e.m.f. in a given circuit when each galvanometer was rewound with the correct number of turns to match the circuit resistance. Now if a galvanometer has current sensitivity δ_i and resistance r it may be matched to an external resistance r' by altering the number of turns from n to n' where

$$\left(\frac{n}{n'}\right)^2 = \frac{r}{r'}.$$

The current sensitivity would be altered to

$$\delta_i \sqrt{\frac{r'}{r}}$$

The quantity $\dfrac{\delta_i}{\sqrt{r}}$ may therefore be used as a criterion of the goodness of a galvanometer construction, on the assumption that the coil can be rewound to suit the external circuit. This quantity, $\delta_i/\sqrt{r} = \delta/\sqrt{i^2 r}$, the deflection divided by the square root of the power dissipated in the coil, and may be called the power sensitivity of the galvanometer.

It should be noted that the " equal resistance " matching criterion, and the usefulness of the power sensitivity depend upon a geometrical relation between resistance and number of turns, and break down when the space occupied by insulation becomes important : this will certainly occur if a large number of turns of fine wire is used.

We shall now consider the design of a galvanometer to detect an e.m.f. in a circuit of (external) resistance r', given the time of swing and the condition that the damping be critical. We consider a rectangular coil of axial length a and width b $(a \gg b)$ wound with n turns of wire of mass m per unit length, resistivity ρ and density d.*

For this coil, the current sensitivity $\delta_i = \dfrac{nabH}{c}$

the time of swing $\qquad T = 2\pi\left(\dfrac{nmab^2}{2c}\right)^{\frac{1}{2}}$

so that $\qquad\qquad c = \dfrac{1}{2}\dfrac{nmab^2}{\tau^2}$

where $\qquad\qquad \tau = \dfrac{T}{2\pi}$

the coil resistance $\qquad r = \dfrac{2na\rho d}{m}.$

Now the voltage sensitivity of the galvanometer matched to the external circuit

$$= \frac{nabH}{2cr'} = \frac{\tau^2 nabH}{nmab^2 r'} = \frac{\tau^2 H}{mbr'}$$

and the critical damping condition gives

$$\frac{n^{\frac{3}{2}}a^{\frac{3}{2}}bH^2}{2^{\frac{1}{2}}m^{\frac{1}{2}}c^{\frac{1}{2}}} = 2r'.$$

The damping condition, in effect, limits the magnetic field H which can be employed

$$H^2 = 2r'\frac{2^{\frac{1}{2}}m^{\frac{1}{2}}}{n^{\frac{3}{2}}a^{\frac{3}{2}}b}\left(\frac{nmab^2}{2\tau^2}\right)^{\frac{1}{2}}$$

$$= 2r'\frac{m}{na\tau}.$$

* The treatment given here follows closely that of Hill (1948), who quotes examples of actual galvanometers constructed in his laboratory.

So that the sensitivity becomes

$$\delta_v = \frac{\tau^2}{mbr'}\left(\frac{2r'm}{na\tau}\right)^{\frac{1}{2}} = \left(\frac{2}{r'}\frac{\tau^2}{nmab^2}\right)^{\frac{1}{2}}.$$

This result shows that the coil should be as small as possible, wound with a few turns of fine wire. The field is then set by the critical damping condition, and the suspension constant by the required periodic time. In practice the fineness of the coil wire and of the suspension are limited by the materials which can be obtained and handled, and, furthermore, there is no point in making the inertia of the coil smaller than that of the attached mirror. These principles have been applied to the construction of galvanometers by Zernicke (1921), Moll (1921), and very thoroughly by A. V. Hill (1948) and Downing. The other point of capital importance is the design of the suspension to secure good stability of the zero. In some instruments this is done by using a quartz fibre to provide the greater part of the restoring couple, the contribution of the ligaments (usually of gold) leading the current to the coil being made as small as possible ; in others, the suspensions have been made of alloys (phosphor bronze, silicon bronze) with good elastic properties.

Traces of ferromagnetic material in the coil of a moving coil galvanometer lead to unsteadiness of the zero, since the magnetic state of the coil depends upon its previous history and is in general varied when the coil moves in the magnetic field (see B.S.I.R.A. 1924). Some makers of sensitive galvanometers treat the wound coil with acid to dissolve iron particles ; Downing found it necessary to wind and insulate the coils of his sensitive galvanometers in a country work-room remote from urban dust.

6.9   Deflection Amplifiers

The optical magnification of galvanometer deflection is limited in principle by the sharpness of the diffraction image obtainable from a small mirror and in practice often by the accuracy of figure of the mirror and the inconvenience of long optical paths. A thermo-electric " galvanometer relay " introduced by Moll (Moll and Burger 1925) is indicated in Fig. 6.3.

Whenever the light-spot leaves its symmetrical position a thermo-e.m.f. appears in the thermocouple circuit and causes deflection of a secondary galvanometer. It is not now necessary for the primary spot to be very well-defined. Practically it is fairly easy to obtain a magnification of a hundred-fold or so with this device,* using a 5 mm. mirror and a 12-W galvanometer lamp. The time constant is of the order 1 sec.

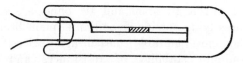

FIG. 6.3 The Moll thermo-relay. The evacuated tube contains a composite ribbon of constantan and manganin about 1μ thick.

Alternatively, an amplifier may be made with a divided barrier-layer photocell, or with a pair of emission photocells. The latter, being high-impedance devices producing essentially a definite current change for a given change of illumination, may conveniently be coupled to valve amplifying stages. In this way a deflection amplifier of very rapid response may be made. Furthermore, by feeding back a signal from the amplifier output to the initial galvanometer input circuit, it is possible to secure a system of very stable overall amplification (e.g. Preston 1946 ; Frankelhauser and Macdonald 1949),† and to modify considerably the response time and input impedance of the system.‡

6.10 D.C. Potentiometer and Bridge Measurements

These are treated fully in all text-books of electricity, and it is enough here to indicate the order of accuracy which is available. Standard cells and properly constructed resistances are very stable, and potentiometer measurements of voltages

---

* As made by Kipp and Zonen.

† For general principle of feedback, see § 7.11.

‡ Optical deflection amplifiers are not confined to use with galvanometers. R. V. Jones has described one which measures angular deflections with a sensitivity of about 10^{-10} radian.

(from a few millivolts upwards), currents (normally from a few milliamps upwards) and resistances (up to, say, 10 ohms) may be made to 1 in 1000 with apparatus of very ordinary quality. Measurements of accuracy 1 in 10,000 require calibrated resistances and systematic precautions, with rough temperature control of resistances, while an accuracy of 1 in 10^5 is possible but constitutes an experimental problem. Accuracy considerations for plain bridge measurements of resistance between 10 ohms and 10^5 ohms are very similar: for resistances lying outside these limits, plain bridges are not usually the most suitable measuring devices. Since the minute-to-minute stability of resistances and sources of electricity is high compared with their long-term stability, small and fairly rapid changes (e.g. of resistance due to an imposed temperature change) can be measured more accurately than these figures suggest. Precision electrical measurements should always be arranged to take advantage of this short term stability and to require the minimum of rearrangement of the circuits. It is, for example, relatively easy to compare two nearly identical resistances, by a rapid substitution method, to any accuracy justifiable by the stability of the resistances themselves.

6.11 A.C. Measurements

It is very difficult to get A.C. sources which are comparable in steadiness with a good battery, and the necessity for *accurate* measurements of alternating current and voltage does not (fortunately) often arise. Table 6.3 gives the types of deflection instruments ordinarily used.

TABLE 6.3

Deflection Instruments for A.C. (Ammeters and Voltmeters)

Dynamometer Ammeter Dynamometer Voltmeter	Power frequencies, e.g. 25-500 c/s as above, but frequency correction from tables above say, 150 c/s	These instruments are expensive. They can be made with accuracy to 0·1 % over a limited frequency range, and then serve as standard transfer instruments from A.C. to D.C.

TABLE 6.3 (cont.)

Moving Iron Ammeter	25-500 c/s	
Moving Iron Voltmeter	25-100 c/s (above 100 v; lower voltage ranges require frequency correction)	May be used on D.C. to same accuracy. Power required much greater than moving coil instruments.
Moving Coil Rectifier	Up to 10 kc/s	These instruments read essentially mean values, and are scaled in r.m.s. values for pure sine waves. They do *not* read r.m.s. values on non-sinusoidal wave forms.
Thermocouple (moving coil)	D.C. to radio frequencies (true r.m.s. values)	These instruments are destroyed by very moderate overloads.

For accuracy see Table 6.1 and B.S. 89. In many A.C. instruments, the lower part of the range is ineffective because of the non-linear law of the instrument.

Valve voltmeters (see § 6.13) may be used to give an accuracy of a few per cent. ; they are particularly useful at high frequencies and when high impedance instruments are required. Vibration galvanometers and a variety of thermionic valve devices may be used to detect nulls in A.C. bridge technique. An instrument which is occasionally useful for special purposes is a moving coil galvanometer with the field produced by an A.C. electromagnet. This instrument is sensitive only to currents which correspond in frequency and phase to the magnetic field. Cf. § 10.11

6.12   A.C. Bridge Measurements

A.C. bridge methods are discussed in several easily accessible books (Owen 1946 ; Hague 1943). A.C. bridges may be operated at power frequency, using preferably a tuned vibration galvanometer as balance indicator ; at audio frequencies, using a vibration galvanometer, a telephone, or a telephone

199

and amplifier ; and at radio frequencies, using some kind of heterodyne detector.   They provide by far the most convenient methods for investigating the dielectric properties of materials (except at high radio frequencies) and for measuring capacities and inductances.   In the latter use, it must be remembered that the values of the capacities and inductances being measured may change with frequency, mainly because the current redistributes itself on account of skin effects.   The change is not usually important at low audio frequencies.

All precise measurements of A.C. circuit elements are complicated by two facts:

(*a*) The circuit elements considered as resistance, inductance, capacitance, are not in general pure: resistance coils, for example, possess inductance and parallel capacitance, and the relative importance of these quantities changes with frequency. The impurities in resistances and good quality condensers are not very important at low audio frequencies, but the resistance associated with an inductance coil must usually be considered and the capacitance effects in a coil may be appreciable at audio frequencies.   At higher frequencies, the reactive components of impedance are more important.

(*b*) There are always stray admittances, normally capacitative, between parts of the circuit elements and their surroundings.   In accurate work it is necessary to introduce screens to make these admittances definite and to arrange the measuring circuits so that it is quite certain what is being measured. Usually the screens are connected to a common point ("earth"), and it may be shown that all the stray capacitances are equivalent to capacitances between each of the corners of a bridge circuit and earth.   In the circuit diagram of Fig. 6.4, the capacitances S_A, S_C do not affect the potentials at A, C, but the currents which flow to "earth" at these points return to the bridge at B, D, in a ratio which depends on the strays and upsets the balance of the bridge.

The Wagner earthing device consists of a potentiometric network of impedances connected across the sources and earthed as shown.   When these impedances, as well as the main bridge, are correctly adjusted, the excursions of A, C, about earth are such that the points B, D, remain very close to earth potential, no current flows in S_B and S_D, and the balance of the bridge is what it would be in the absence of these strays.   The Wagner arms are adjusted in practice by connecting the detector alternately in the two positions shown and adjusting the bridge

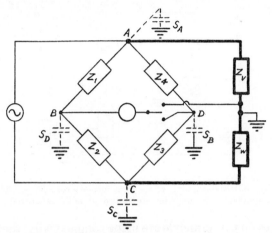

Fig. 6.4.   A.C. bridge circuit to illustrate the principle of the Wagner earth connection (which is shown in heavy line)

and Wagner arms until balance is achieved in both positions by a method of successive approximations.

An A.C. balance system which is very insensitive to stray admittances was invented by Blumlein and has been described by Clarke and Vanderlyn (1949); Golding (1961).   If the ratio arms of a bridge consist of two very closely coupled inductances (Fig. 6.5), the potentials between A,C, and the earthed tapping B are maintained very nearly in a fixed ratio irrespective of currents flowing through Z_3, Z_4 and the stray admittances. The bridge balances when the currents in Z_3, Z_4 are equal, and since D is then at earth potential, no currents flow in the stray admittances between this point and earth.   Currents flowing into the other strays have very little effect on the potentials.

It is even possible to use a bridge of this kind to measure the impedance element Z_3 when its ends are connected to earth by other circuit elements (see Fig. 6.5).   The currents flowing to earth at these points return to the bridge at the low-impedance point B without disturbing the balance conditions. This property is valuable in allowing elements to be measured *in situ* in complicated circuits and in measuring impedances connected to the bridge by long screened leads of uncertain capacity.

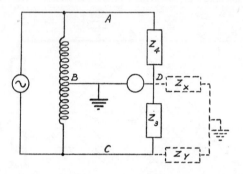

Fig. 6.5.   To show the principle of the transformer-arm bridge.   The balance is nearly unaffected by impedances connected as in the dotted parts

Bridges on this principle are made commercially, the coupled inductances being the windings of a carefully designed transformer with very small magnetic leakage.   The ratio of the bridge arms can be varied made by tappings on the transformer windings.

6.13   Valve Voltmeters

The thermionic valve is used in a number of voltmeters which have as their distinguishing features high input impedance and wide frequency range.   The stability of zero and of sensitivity is not very high, so that for accurate work the instruments have to be calibrated frequently, but the calibration can be made at low frequency and used at much higher frequencies without correction.   A number of arrangements have been devised and are described in text-books on high-frequency measurements.   One of the simplest consists of a diode rectifier controlling the grid voltage of a D.C. amplifier preferably of balanced type (§ 7.17).   If the input element is a small low-capacity diode, the instrument may be useful at frequencies up to several hundred Mc/s.   Such an instrument reads essentially peak voltage though it may be calibrated to read r.m.s. voltage on a sinusoidal wave-form.

It is more difficult to make a valve voltmeter read r.m.s. voltage directly, and the most satisfactory instrument to measure the true r.m.s. value of a non-sinusoidal voltage is probably a power amplifier of stable gain, e.g. a cathode follower, feeding a thermocouple. The thermocouple is necessarily fragile against overload, and it is in special danger in this application, since the high input impedance of the amplifier encourages electrostatic pick-up of relatively high voltages. Safety can be obtained by adjusting the resistance in the thermocouple circuit so that the couple is not destroyed by the extreme output of the amplifier ; it may then be necessary to use a sensitive galvanometer to measure the output of the couple in normal use.

6.14 The Measurement of Small Currents

Currents smaller than 10^{-10} A which are measured in the laboratory usually occur in circuits of high impedance (e.g. photocell, ionisation chamber) and are measured by the use of an electrostatic instrument—an electrometer or a thermionic valve used as an electrometer. There are three important ways in which such an instrument may be used.

(1) An insulated system is allowed to charge up and the rate of charge is measured.

(2) The charge brought to the insulated system is compensated by a measured charge induced on the system, the electrometer being used as a null instrument.

(3) The current is allowed to flow through a known high resistance, and the electrometer is used to measure the p.d. across the resistance.

The first method has usually been used to obtain the highest sensitivity. The charge sensitivity of the electrometer system must be measured, conveniently by using the circuit shown in Fig. 6.6. Here a potential V is applied to the electrode E which has a known coefficient of capacity C with respect to the insulated system S. If the change of potential of the latter is small compared with V (which is normally the case since C is small compared with the capacity of S to earth), we have

$$\text{charge induced} = VC$$

and the corresponding deflection of the electrometer may be recorded. The capacity C may be specially attached to the system for calibration purposes, or it may be possible to use, e.g. an ionisation chamber as a calibrating condenser by varying the voltage on it by a known amount. The charge sensitivity of an electrometer connected to a system of limited capacity is affected by the fact that the motion of the electrometer

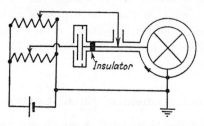

FIG. 6.6 Use of an electrometer in the Townsend compensation circuit. The upper potentiometer is used to adjust the zero of the electrometer or to measure the voltage sensitivity *via* the earthing key. The lower potentiometer is used to apply the compensating voltage to the calibrated condenser.

needle induces a charge in the insulated system which opposes the effect of the charge being measured (Cox and Grindley 1927). For this reason, an increase in the needle voltage of a quadrant electrometer which considerably increases the voltage sensitivity of the instrument may have little effect on the charge sensitivity.

If the potential V applied to the calibrating condenser is continuously varied during the measurement so as to keep the electrometer at zero the charge collected over an interval is

$$C\varDelta V$$

where $\varDelta V$ denotes the total change of the potential applied to the calibrating condenser during this interval. The method (sometimes called the Townsend compensation method) is valuable when it is required to measure a moderate current (say 10^{-12} A) with considerable accuracy (0·1 % is easily possible). The sensitivity of the electrometer and the capacity of the system need not be known ; the potentials which appear across the main insulation are only those corresponding to momentary errors of balance, and the insulation of the measuring condenser itself should be split on the " guard ring " principle, so that the insulators supporting the highly-insulated system lie only between the latter and earth (Fig. 6.6). The compensation is similar in principle to a feedback system (§ 7.11) and could be made automatic if necessary.

The third (steady deflection) method has the advantage of being direct reading, but this does not mean that it can respond rapidly to varying currents. For example, if a system has a

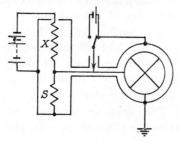

FIG. 6.7   Circuit for measuring a high resistance, using an electrometer. X is the unknown resistance, S a known resistance

capacity of 50 cm. and the measuring resistance is 10^{12} ohms, the exponential time constant is about 50 sec. The voltage calibration of the electrometer must be known and any departure from linearity must be allowed for ; the resistance must be known and stable.

A number of methods for making resistances have been described, based on liquids of low conductivity such as alcohol-xylol mixtures ; on graphite pencil lines on ground quartz rods protected by lacquer ; and on ionisation chambers with steady radioactive sources worked in unsaturated conditions. Most of these devices are not very consistent in value and parasitic internal e.m.f.s appear in them. Composition resistors are made commercially which seem to be satisfactory. The value of a resistor may very conveniently be found by the circuit indicated in Fig. 6.7 ; the electrometer deflection produced by a known high voltage in the connection shown is compared with the deflection produced by applying known potentials direct to the electrometer.

6.15   The Arrangement of Circuits for Small Current Measurements

When small currents are to be measured the insulation of the system must be very good ; it is found that electrical leaks are usually associated with parasitic e.m.f.s so that the charge on the isolated system does not remain constant even when no potential difference is apparently imposed on the insulator.   The insulating materials available are rather limited and do not include most of the substances used in ordinary electrical engineering.   Surface leakage is at least as important as conduction through the body of the substance and published resistivities do not mean very much.   Fused quartz insulators made from tube or rod are very good and have the advantage that they can be thoroughly cleaned with strong acid and the blowpipe flame.   The surfaces required to possess highly insulating properties should not be touched after cleaning. Amber, pressed reconstituted amber, and cast sulphur have been much used—the last mainly for electroscope insulators and protected from light.   Polystyrene is one of the best of the new plastic materials ; it may be readily machined and it is not hygroscopic.   The recently introduced poly-tetrafluorethylene possesses important advantages (see Table 4.11).

In dealing with really small currents the conductivity of ionised air becomes important, especially if there are sources of ionisation in the neighbourhood, and it may be necessary to evacuate the space around the insulated system, e.g. a wire may be taken along the axis of an evacuated tube, a photocell and its associated electrometer valve may be sealed up in an evacuated glass envelope.   The insulated system must also be shielded against induced charges, and fairly complete metal shielding is necessary.   This requirement is particularly stringent with electrometer valves (Hansen 1936) because the grid circuit of the valve may act as an efficient rectifier of alternating potentials induced, e.g. by high-frequency electric waves. The shielding should form a well bonded enclosure, as free as possible from holes and cracks. An " earthing key " must be provided to short circuit the electrometer, and the design of this key presents some difficulties in avoiding parasitic e.m.f.s. A well amalgamated wire dipping into a mercury cup, or a pair of platinum contacts may be used, and the switch is conveniently worked by a solenoid or by pulling a string.

It is necessary to avoid subjecting insulators to mechanical strain, which may produce parasitic charges, and as far as possible the insulators should be designed so that stray charges on their surface do not induce charges on the insulated system. This means that the surface of the insulators should not be " seen " from points on the insulated system.

6.16   The Choice of an Electrometer

A number of electrometers are well described by H. V. Neher in Strong's book (1939). The types commonly available are the Dolezalek and Compton forms of the quadrant electrometer, the Lindemann electrometer which is essentially a quadrant electrometer with a light balanced quartz needle suspended by taut quartz fibres, and the electrometer valve. A number of quartz-fibre electrometer systems have been constructed for special purposes and described in scientific papers (see Strong 1939), but they are not readily available as commercial instruments.

A simple dimensional analysis shows that for a given time of swing, the charge and voltage sensitivity of a quadrant electrometer increase with decreasing size of the instrument. The Dolezalek electrometer which is usually made with quadrants about 5 cm. across is undesirably large and the Compton electrometer is made much smaller and is preferable. The distinctive feature introduced by Compton was a vertical adjustment of one of the quadrants, which allows an adjustable electrostatic control torque to be introduced. This adjustable torque may be made to assist or oppose the fibre control, and in the latter condition very high voltage sensitivities (say 30,000 mm/V at 1 m.) may be attained. The charge sensitivity is, however, not so much increased (cf. § 6.13), the time of swing is lengthened, and the zero stability may deteriorate. The electrometer is very stable and reliable at, say, 5000 mm./V. The binant electrometer of Hoffmann, which has not been used much outside German laboratories, is an instrument for which the highest claims for ultimate charge sensitivity have been made. It is probable that the high performance of this electrometer is due less to its distinctive geometrical form than to its very careful detail design and construction. It is designed to be evacuated so as to avoid ionisation leakage and excessive damping ; it is well shielded against thermal disturbances and the effects of thermal expansion of the structure are compensated. Varying contact potentials are minimised by making or coating all the internal parts with platinum, and a properly designed calibrating condenser and earthing key are built into the instrument.

6.17 Valves as Electrometers

The thermionic valve with negative grid is essentially an electrostatic device, and it has come into increasing use as an electrometer. The difficulties which arise are of two kinds—the appearance of grid currents and the unsteadiness of the voltage zero. The classical analysis of the causes of grid current is given by Metcalf and Thompson (1930), who list the following :

(1) Conduction across insulation inside and outside the bulb.

(2) Positive ions from the ionisation of residual gas.

(3) Positive ions emitted from the cathode.

(4) Photoelectron emission due to light from the cathode.

(5) Photoelectron emission due to high-frequency radiation (soft X-rays) from the anode.

They introduced a tube (the FP.54 made by the G.E. Company of America), in which (1) was reduced by the use of quartz petticoat insulators inside the tube ; (2) was eliminated by operating the carefully evacuated tube at an anode potential (about 6 V) below the ionisation potential of the residual gas ;

(3) was eliminated by the use of a grid at a positive potential inserted between the cathode and control grid ; (4) was reduced by using a small cathode at a low temperature,* and (5) by the low anode voltage. There is a " floating potential " which the grid assumes when left isolated, and it is usually convenient to adjust the grid to this potential before isolating it. The grid resistance for small potential changes about this value (i.e. the slope of the curve connecting grid voltage and grid current) is of the order of 10^{16} ohms. A number of electrometer valve designs based on the same principles are made in various countries, and it is found that the principles may be successfully applied to the use of more normal valves as low-grid-current electrometer tubes (Nielsen, 1947).

Some receiving valves of normal construction have grid currents of the order 10^{-12} A when used with low heater and anode voltages. 10^{-15} A has been reported with selected " acorn " pentodes in which the inner grid was used to collect positive ions and the control voltage applied to the electrode normally used as screen. This is of the same order as the currents observed with the special electrometer tubes.

If a valve is used to amplify very small quasi-steady potential changes, whether under low-grid-current conditions or not, the useful sensitivity is limited by disturbances of the zero. The noise sources discussed in Chapter IX are operative ; at very low frequencies flicker noise in valves and current noise in semi-conducting resistances are particularly prominent. It is clear that wire resistances should be used in the circuits where possible.

An important possible source of zero drift is the effect of small changes of cathode temperature on the energy of the electrons leaving the cathode, i.e. on the effective potential of the cathode. For a normal oxide-coated cathode, a change of 20 % in the voltage applied to the heater may produce a 200 mV change in the effective cathode potential (Valley and Wallman 1948), so that steadiness to, say, 20μV involves maintaining the heater supply constant to 1 in 50,000. This supply may be obtained from a good accumulator using the precautions necessary in first-class potentiometer work, i.e. all

---

* The tube is of course shielded from external light.

connections must be clean and tight, the circuit must be run for some time to reach equilibrium before measurements are begun. During the life of a valve the effective cathode potential may change by several tenths of a volt but a large part of this change takes place in the first hundred hours' running.

A number of circuits have been devised to compensate drift in electrometer valves and D.C. amplifiers (Penick 1935). The most straightforward method is the use of a balanced circuit made as symmetrical as possible, and double electrometer valves are now available (e.g., Ferranti DBM4A).

The overall steadiness attained in practice seems to be fairly well established ; it is of the order of 30 μV over a 30 min. period (Bishop and Harris 1949, 1950). It is interesting to calculate that the corresponding current, assuming a 5pf. capacity, is about 10^{-19} A or about 1 electron/sec. This performance is comparable with the best claimed for the Hoffman electrometer.

It appears from the discussion above that valves used as D.C. amplifiers do not compete with good galvanometers in measuring small, quasi-steady potentials occurring in low impedance circuits, and that where the circuit resistance is high, valves and electrometers give comparable performances. The valve arrangements are then cheaper and probably easier to set up initially, but require careful attention to maintain steadiness of zero. Where comparatively large potential differences are measured (as in some ionisation chamber measurements), simple electrometers and fairly simple valve arrangements compete on level terms. Where rapid changes must be followed as well as slow ones, valve amplifiers are necessary (cf. § 10.13).

As an alternative to the amplifier with D.C. response, a number of devices have been developed to convert steady potentials into A.C. signals which can be amplified using ordinary amplifiers. The methods at present developed include rotating or vibrating commutators carefully designed to minimise contact e.m.f.s (e.g. Liston *et al.* 1946) and condensers, also designed to avoid contact e.m.f.s, whose capacity is made to vary periodically at an audio frequency, thereby inducing an alternating potential whose magnitude depends directly on the charge on the plates. The success of these devices depends on the design and construction of the commutating unit, since it is very difficult to avoid small and variable parasitic e.m.f.s.* After amplification the signal may be measured by an A.C. (e.g. rectifier) instrument, but there are special advantages in using a phase-sensitive rectifier synchronised with the chopper (see § 10.11).†

6.18 The Production and Measurement of Magnetic Fields

Many physical investigations require the use of controlled magnetic fields: they are used for deflecting and focusing beams of charged particles, for producing magnetic resonance, and for producing low temperatures by the technique of adiabatic demagnetisation. It is convenient to discuss here separately air-cored coils and iron-cored electromagnets. Coils without iron are used for producing small fields (up to say 5 oersteds) over large volumes, for producing fields up to a few hundred oersteds over moderately large volumes and for producing very large fields where the magnetisation of iron could make only a minor contribution. In most other cases it is advantageous to use iron-cored magnets.

6.19 Coreless Coils

The classical arrangement to produce axial uniformity of fields is the Helmholtz coil system shown in Fig. 6.8.—the single turns shown are of course replaced in practice by multiturn coils. Coils in this configuration are often used to neutralise the earth's magnetic field over the space occupied by an experiment.‡ More elaborate arrangements of coils can produce fields uniform over a relatively larger volume (Scott 1957).

---

* A number of electronic modulation systems are known, which control the amplitude of an A.C. output signal in accordance with an input signal, but the inherent noise and unsteadiness of these are very much worse than those of the devices we are here considering.

† For a general account with references see Kandiah and Brown, 1952.

‡ It is necessary to avoid local irregularities of the earth's field due to structural ironwork, pipes, etc.

Coils required to produce moderately large fields over considerable volumes often follow roughly the Helmholtz geometry. Rather large electric power is required and it is usually necessary to provide specially for cooling, either by forcing air over strip-wound pancake coils, by circulating oil over similar coils, or by winding the coils with copper tube through which oil or water is circulated.*

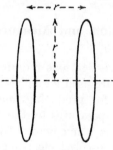

FIG. 6.8

When coils are required to produce very large fields (up to hundreds of kilogauss), the geometrical basis of the design seeks minimum electrical power for the given magnetic performance, while the actual construction is dominated by considerations of cooling and by the mechanical strength required to withstand the electromagnetic forces which tend to compress the coil axially and usually to burst it radially.

If the coils have cylindrical symmetry and uniform current density the power required (W) is related to the central field produced (H) by a formula

$$H = G\left(\frac{W\lambda}{\rho a}\right)^{\frac{1}{2}}$$

where ρ is the specific resistance of the winding material, λ is the fraction of the winding space filled with actual conductor, and a is the inner radius of the coil. G is a geometrical factor defined by the shape of the coil, and data for determining it have been published by Cockroft (1928). Its maximum value

---

* Similar coils are used for large electromagnets (§ 6.20), a very advantageous winding is of square copper section with a circular longitudinal bore.

is 0·179 for an outer radius of about $3a$ and a coil length about $4a$. A rather better performance is obtained from a coil designed by Bitter (1939) in which the current density increases towards the axis. This design, moreover, provides neatly for the circulation of cooling fluid through longitudinal holes.

It will be found from the formula that the power required in a copper coil to produce 100 kilogauss in a region of 2 cm. diameter is about 600 kw., and it is difficult to dissipate so much energy without introducing cooling passages which reduce unduly the factor λ. In one efficient coil design a spaced winding of nylon filament on square copper wire serves to separate the turns while allowing cooling water to circulate. It seems that the recent development of efficient heavy current rectifiers which operate with low voltage drop (§§ 7.2 7.26) would allow coils to be made with very heavy copper sections, and that these might be relatively easy to construct in an efficient form.

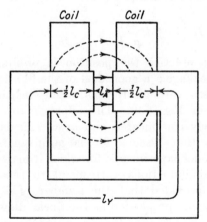

FIG. 6.9   Magnetic circuit of a laboratory magnet

6.20   Electromagnets

The iron-cored electromaget can be treated in an elementary way by using the notion of a magnetic circuit (Fig. 6.9) and applying the following analysis:

(1) The normal component of the induction B is continuous across any boundary between materials. We may therefore

write approximately that the product of B and the sectional area A is constant throughout the circuit. At any point, B and H are connected by the magnetisation curve of the material, and

$$\frac{B}{H} = \mu_{\text{effective}}.$$

(2) The line integral of H taken round any path is given by

$$\oint H dl = \frac{4\pi}{10} \times \text{ampere turns linked with the path.}$$

In Fig. 6.9, if we assume that the field in the air gap is straight across as shown, we have

$$H_a A_a = B_c A_c = B_y A_y$$
$$= \mu_c H_c A_c = \mu_y H_y A_y$$
$$\oint H dl = 1\cdot26 \times (\text{amp. turns}) = H_a l_a + H_c l_c + H_y l_y$$
$$= H_a\left(l_a + l_c \frac{A_a}{\mu_c A_c} + l_y \frac{A_a}{\mu_y H_y}\right).$$

Usually in practice the position is profoundly modified by magnetic leakage ; a good deal of the flux linked with the windings passes through regions where it cannot be used (dotted lines of Fig. 6.9). The approximate calculation of leakage is fairly complicated and exact calculation is nearly impossible so that designs for large magnets are usually checked by model experiments, for which it may be shown that the fields and inductions correspond to those in the full scale magnet provided that the number of ampere-turns is scaled in the same proportion as the linear dimensions.

Qualitatively, it is clear that the magnet design of Fig. 6.9, with the windings on short cores flanking the air gap, is better than the design of Fig. 6.10, and most modern laboratory magnets are of the type of Fig. 6.9. In a magnet of this design, stray flux passing just outside the main air gap enters the parts of the cores remote from the gap. If the magnet is used at high fields, these regions may saturate and pass into a condition where $\mu_{\text{effective}}$ is low, so that it is advantageous to make the section of the core increase away from the gap (Fig. 6.11). The exact design of pole cores is a typical case where model experiments can be used with advantage.

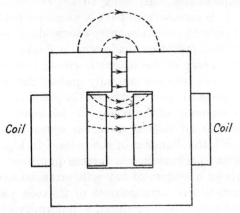

FIG. 6.10   Another design of laboratory magnet, showing considerable leakage

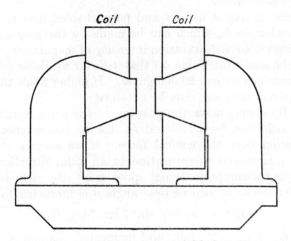

FIG. 6.11   Large laboratory electromagnet (cf. Blackett 1936).   Note coned shape of pole cores

It has been shown (Bitter 1951, 1952) that a highly efficient design is obtained by burying the windings of a magnet in a more or less cylindrical yoke and some large magnets, including the 140 kw. Uppsala magnet, have been built in this form.

215

In recent years an important application of magnets has been to nuclear magnetic resonance (Andrew 1958) and electron resonance experiments. In order to achieve high resolution in this work it is necessary to have a magnetic field with very little spatial variation over the space occupied by the specimen; the magnets used are often made with a double yoke to improve the symmetry of the magnetic circuit, and the circular pole pieces of soft iron are carefully ground flat and parallel. Annular iron shims on the outer parts of the pole faces compensate for the finite diameter of the poles: the homogeneity obtained is a few parts in 10^5 over a specimen whose dimensions are about one-tenth the diameter of the poles. In high-resolution experiments the performance is further improved by passing currents through a system of flat coils arranged over the pole faces; a sophisticated arrangement of thirteen pairs of coils described by Golay (1958) produced a uniformity of about 1 in 10^8 over a specimen whose dimensions were about one-fiftieth of the pole diameter.

If the air-gap is narrow and parallel sided, the maximum contribution to H_a which can be made by the magnetisation of the iron is $4\pi \times$ (saturation intensity of magnetisation), and it may be seen from Table 4.7 that $4\pi I_s$ for available materials does not much exceed 20,000 gauss. If higher fields than this are required, they can only be obtained :

(a) By coning down the pole faces ; the extra contribution to the field can be calculated as due to the magnetic pole distribution over the conical faces. If we assume that the iron is magnetised to saturation in an axial direction (this simplifying assumption is not quite true), the field between truncated cones of semivertical angle θ is increased to

$$4\pi I_s(1 - \cos\theta + \sin^2\theta \cos\theta \log_e D/d)$$

where D, d are the full, and truncated diameters of the poles. This indicates that the field increases only slowly with the reduction in diameter. The best value for θ in practice is about $60°$; and over a small area about 50,000 G. may be attained.

(b) By relying on the field produced directly by the windings, which is superposed on that due to the iron. In a magnet where the coils are wound on short, coned pole pieces, the windings are advantageously placed to produce fields in the gap. At very high fields,* the contribution from the coils may be large compared with that from the iron, and it may finally become economical to use a pure solenoid without iron.

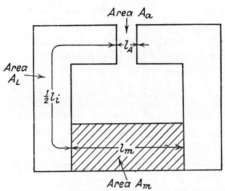

Fig. 6.12   Magnetic circuit containing a permanent magnet

The important characteristics of the materials used in an electromagnet design are, then, the value of I_{sat} for the pole tips and the values of $\mu_{effective}$ appropriate to the inductions in the remainder of the magnetic circuit. In practice the pole tips may be of specially pure iron or of cobalt-iron and the remainder of the magnet of the softest available mild steel.

It has now become possible to use permanent magnets instead of electromagnets for many purposes.

Fig. 6.12 shows a magnetic circuit containing an air-gap, pole pieces of " soft " magnetic material and an active piece of permanent magnet alloy. With the notation indicated in the figure, the fundamental conditions are :

(1) If leakage is neglected, the product of B the induction, and A the area, is constant throughout the circuit and

$$B_m A_m = H_a A_a.$$

In practice $H_a A_a$ must be multiplied by a leakage factor K, which cannot be calculated accurately.   As found by trial, its

* For magnets to produce very large fields, see Bitter 1937-39, 1952.

value may lie between 2 and 10, and the magnet designer often adopts a value from experience.

(2) The line integral of H around the circuit is zero

$$-l_m H_m = l_a H_a + l_i \frac{B_i}{\mu_i}$$

$$= l_a H_a + l_i \frac{H_a l_a}{A_i \mu_i}$$

which may conveniently be written $k l_a H_a$ where k is a factor to allow for the presence of the iron poles.

We have therefore

$$A_m = \frac{K H_a A_a}{B_m}, \qquad l_m = \frac{k H_a l_a}{H_m}$$

and the volume of the magnet alloy is

$$\frac{Kk}{B_m H_m} \times \text{volume of air-gap} \times H_a{}^2.$$

It follows from this that a magnetic material can be judged on the basis of the maximum value of BH which it will yield, and that the equations above should be used to secure that the material chosen is worked at its maximum BH value.

Another application of permanent magnet alloys is to provide a magnetic moment, as in compasses and magneto-meters. Short magnetic needles are subject to a strong demagnetising field due to their own free poles. This can be calculated approximately by assuming that the needle is a uniformly magnetised ellipsoid. It is found that the magnetic properties of the new magnetic materials, as compared with the old, allow a considerable increase in the magnetic moment per unit moment of inertia, but the mechanical properties of these alloys limit rather severely the shapes which can be used.

6.21   The Measurement of Magnetic Fields

The measurement of magnetic fields is a common laboratory requirement, and the normal method is the use of a ballistic galvanometer or a fluxmeter connected to a search coil which is suddenly withdrawn from the field or turned through 180°.

If the field collapses quickly enough (see below), the search coil may be left in place and the field switched off. In any case the change of flux through the coil must be complete in a time short compared with the time of swing of the galvanometer, and the advantage of the fluxmeter lies in the fact that this time may be quite long. The fluxmeter is a galvanometer in which the restoring force is very small compared with the electromagnetic damping forces ; the coil then moves so that the total flux embraced by the circuit containing search coil and moving coil remains constant. For theory, see Dunn (1939). In a test with a modern fluxmeter, the deflection for a given flux was found to be unaffected (to about 1 %) by increasing the circuit resistance from 0 to 100 ohms or by prolonging the time of decay of flux to 30 sec. (For precautions in accurate work, see Spilsbury and Webb 1945.)

The damping of a ballistic galvanometer used with a search coil may allowably be quite heavy, but the resistance in the galvanometer circuit must be constant during the calibration and use of the instrument.

The measuring circuit must be calibrated for anything except rough work (where the makers' calibration of a fluxmeter may be sufficiently accurate) and the most satisfactory method is to include the secondary of a mutual inductance permanently in the circuit and to calibrate when required by breaking a measured current in the primary coil of the mutual.

The deflection method described here may be made accurate to 1 % or rather better, but it is sometimes necessary to improve on this accuracy. This may be done if the search coil is withdrawn or reversed mechanically ; the primary circuit of the mutual inductance is simultaneously broken and the induced e.m.f.s are made to balance, using a ballistic galvanometer or fluxmeter of high sensitivity. The period of the indicating instrument must be much longer than the time during which the magnetic flux is changing and the different forms of the two voltage waves do not then affect the result.

The search coils used in these measurements may be wound with one or a few layers of wire on an accurate former of some mechanically stable insulating material. Careful measurements of diameter are taken over each layer and the effective area calculated from the dimensions. If a search coil of small size is required it is hardly possible to find the effective area in this way with sufficient accuracy, and it is necessary to measure the flux through the coil when it is put inside a standardising coil (a solenoid or Helmholtz pair) of known dimensions. A most elegant and accurate method is to balance the mutual inductance between the search coil and a Helmholtz pair against a mutual inductometer (cf. Nettleton and Sugden 1939).

There are several special methods for measuring magnetic fields which will only be mentioned here : see Symonds 1955.

(*a*) The change in resistance of a bismuth wire in a magnetic field is marked (e.g. 10% in 5000 G) and field measuring instruments have been made using a bismuth spiral placed in the field. The effect of temperature on the resistance and on its magnetic variation is, however, so large that the method is rather troublesome and has fallen out of use.

(*b*) The Hall effect in a semiconductor has been recently made the basis of an industrial instrument for measuring magnetic fields.

(*c*) Commercial instruments have been made in which a moving-coil movement is immersed in the field and the current required to give a standard deflection is measured on another moving-coil ammeter.

The resonance of atomic nuclei (protons) in a high-frequency magnetic field crossed with the field to be measured has been made the basis of a very accurate method of measuring magnetic fields. It is very convenient for fields between 1000 and 10,000 gauss, but the same principle is used in the free precession magnetometer for measuring the geomagnetic field. The resonant frequency is connected with the field strength by the relation $\omega = \gamma H$ where ω is the angular frequency of the H.F. field and γ is the nuclear magnetic moment per unit angular momentum. The resonance frequency is directly proportional to H and 1000 gauss corresponds to 4·25 Mc/s. (For basic theory see Bloch 1946, Pound 1952, and Andrew 1958: the Pound reference contains an account of an advantageous circuit.)

In instrumental applications of this principle, the H.F. coil is wound as closely as possible over a proton sample* which may be water or a hydrocarbon contained in a tube. The sample is contained in a probe with the H.F. field at right angles to the field to be measured, on which is superposed a small low frequency alternating field. The resonance frequency then sweeps across the fixed frequency of the oscillator. It is possible but usually less convenient to sweep the oscillator frequency. The resonance involves absorption of energy from the oscillator as the system sweeps through resonance, and is detected by an H.F. bridge circuit, or by observing changes in anode current or A.V.C. voltage in the oscillator. The arrangement is well adapted to provide a control signal to regulate a magnetic field to a predetermined value, which may be set by quartz crystal control of the oscillator frequency.

(e) A magnetometer may be based on the properties of the high permeability alloys of §4.16. A strip of Mumetal or Permalloy is magnetised by a symmetrical alternating magnetic field. If a steady field is superposed on this A.C. field, the magnetic flux cycle is distorted in such a way as to contain even harmonics of the exciting frequency : these may be picked up by properly arranged coils, filtered and amplified.

The instrument is best used as a null detector to show when the field to be measured is neutralised by a solenoid carrying a measured current. It was exploited during the war for aircraft compasses ("Fluxgate") and submarine detectors, and most descriptions of it are rather inaccessible. The theory of the device is discussed by Williams and Noble (1950), who give references.

APPENDIX

Electric Motors

D.C. Motors.—With the disappearance of D.C. public supplies in this country, D.C. motors have lost much of their importance. There is, however, no convenient substitute for

---

* Solid rubber has been used as a proton sample.

the shunt-wound D.C. motor where smooth speed control is required, and low voltage motors of this type will continue to be used in the laboratory, supplied by batteries or rectifier.

(a) *Series wound D.C. motors* have as their main characteristic the very large torque (accompanied by a heavy current drain) which they can produce at starting (or generally at low speeds). The motor-car starting motor is an extreme example. As the speed of the motor increases the torque falls off ; there

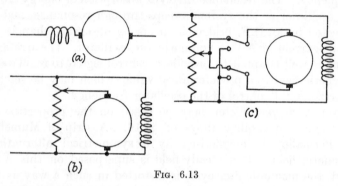

FIG. 6.13

(a) Series-wound motor
(b) Shunt-wound D.C. motor with full field excitation and potentiometer control of voltage applied to armature
(c) Circuit (b) modified to allow reversing and induced current braking. As shown, the motor is braked. If either of the switches is changed over, the motor runs in one direction or the other

is no equilibrium speed at zero load and if the motor is unloaded the speed may become dangerously high. It is clear that the use of such motors is confined to special duties ; they are occasionally useful to drive automatic mechanisms which require considerable starting torque.

(b) *Shunt-wound D.C. motors* have much less variation of torque with speed, and the unloaded motor has an equilibrium speed which is nearly proportional to the voltage applied to the armature if the magnetic field is kept constant. The circuit of Fig. 6.13(b) allows the speed of the motor to be varied smoothly from a crawl to full speed, the torque available at any speed being nearly constant. The circuit may be modified (Fig. 6.13(c)) to allow the motor to be reversed. This

222

circuit also allows the armature to be short circuited with the field fully excited : the currents induced in the armature circuit then exert a powerful braking torque.

A.C. MOTORS. Synchronous motors are usually only encountered in the form of clock motors and slightly larger motors of similar construction. These are commercially obtainable with built-in gearing and the geared motors are very convenient for driving small cyclic control mechanisms. These motors are usually designed to start themselves as induction motors, but actual clock motors are often designed to require spinning by hand at starting.

(c) *Series commutator motors* behave like rather inferior D.C. series motors, and will run on D.C. (Series motors designed for D.C. will not in general run satisfactorily on A.C.) Since most of the troubles experienced with small motors arise from the brushes and commutators, induction motors should usually be preferred to series motors, but the latter provide the only simple means of obtaining on 50 cycle A.C. mains a speed higher than the 3000 r.p.m. of a two-pole synchronous motor.

(d) *Induction motors.* 3-phase induction motors supply most of the industrial power of the country. They are cheap and simple and extremely reliable. In small sizes there are no connections to the (squirrel cage) rotor, and practically all motors used in an ordinary laboratory can be of this type, star-delta connections being used to apply an effectively reduced starting voltage to the stators of motors above 1 or 2 h.p.

The torque-speed relations of an induction motor are shown in Fig. 6.14. It will be seen that, as with the D.C. shunt motor, there is no large variation of speed with load over the working range. At normal full load the motor runs about 5% below synchronous speed ; under heavy overload, conditions become unstable and the motor stalls, draining a heavy current from the supply.

Three-phase induction motors must be connected to the mains through a protective cut out which opens all three-phase connections when an overload occurs. Fuses in the separate phases would have to be coarsely rated to cope with the large starting currents, and could not be relied upon to deal with a condition in which one phase is accidentally opened, and the motor continues to run as a single phase machine, drawing a current which is enough to overheat it but not sufficient to blow the remaining fuses.

It is not very convenient to arrange three-phase supplies to isolated or portable motors of fractional horse-power, and single phase induction motors are therefore used. They are more complicated than the three-phase machines, since

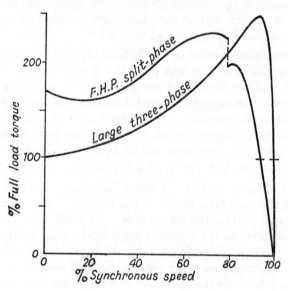

FIG. 6.14   Torque speed relations for induction motors.   Curve 1 is for a large, 3-phase motor designed for high efficiency under running conditions. Curve 2 is for a fractional horse-power split phase motor and the discontinuity corresponds to cutting out the starting winding. The efficiency is about 60 per cent. at full load

special starting arrangements are built in to produce a rotating field when the rotor is at a standstill. The currents in the starting winding are displaced in phase from those in the main winding.   The starting winding is normally only suitable for short period use, and when the motor has started, the winding is cut out by hand or more usually by a centrifugal switch.   In " capacitor " motors the starting winding is fed through a condenser, and in some rather special designs the winding remains in circuit continuously. In the shaded-pole motor the starting winding takes the form of short circuited copper loops in the stator. Small motors of this type, though not efficient, are quiet and reliable and eminently suitable for very low power laboratory applications.

CHAPTER 7

ELECTRONICS

7.1 Electronic Aids

The thermionic valve and the circuits in which it is used
are very powerful and versatile tools in experimental physics.
Recently, semiconductor electronic devices have established
themselves as equal or superior to valves in many applications.
It is only possible to discuss here a few valve and semiconductor
applications, but it is convenient to describe certain methods
and principles which are specially important in the physical
laboratory.

7.2 Power Supplies

It has become usual to provide D.C. for laboratory purposes
by transforming A.C. to a suitable voltage, rectifying and
filtering. This method is often more economical in first cost
and maintenance than the D.C. networks and battery supplies
which were common in laboratories built early this century.

For low powers it is usual to use a single-phase supply, and
the rectifiers are connected in one of the circuits shown in
Fig. 7.1, 7.2.

As rectifying elements, there are in competition :

(a) The dry plate (copper oxide or selenium film) rectifier,
which depends for its action on the properties of the contact
between a metal and a semi-conductor.

(b) The vacuum thermionic valve.

(c) The gas-filled thermionic valve. (Cold cathode and
mercury pool cathode forms are occasionally used.)

(d) Germanium and silicon junction rectifiers.

For low voltages (up to 50-100 V) the dry plate rectifier is
usually chosen, and this rectifier is also useful for low currents
at high voltages. The voltage drop across a single element is
low and the efficiency may be fairly high. The units in the
form of disks are assembled in piles and connected in series

226

and parallel groups as required. The absence of a cathode heating circuit makes for simplicity, especially in the voltage multiplying circuits, and circuits of this kind using metal rectifiers are very convenient for supplying a few milliamperes at a few kilovolts.

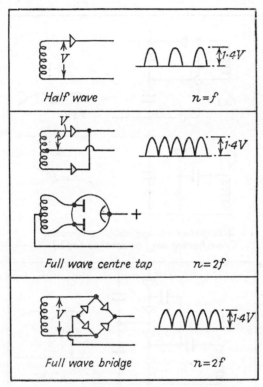

FIG. 7.1   Rectifier circuits for power supply
V = R.M.S. voltage of transformer
f = supply frequency
n = lowest ripple frequency

Silicon and germanium junction rectifiers (§ 7.26 and Table 7.2) are much more efficient than dry plate rectifiers but also much more costly. They are very small for a given rating; while this compactness is an advantage, the rectifiers have little thermal capacity and their failure under overload is sudden and catastrophic. Special precautions must therefore be taken to avoid exposing them to voltage surges and transient overloads. High vacuum rectifiers may still be preferred in some laboratory applications where efficiency is unimportant and abuse probable.

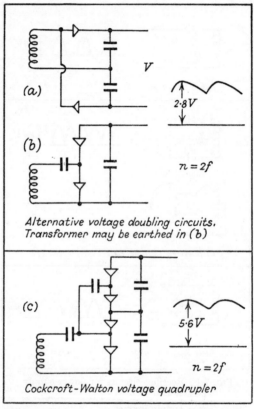

FIG. 7.2   Voltage-multiplier.   Rectifier circuits.   The transformer may be earthed in the voltage doubling circuit (b), but not in (a).   The circuit of (c) may be extended as required to give higher voltages

For moderate currents at voltages above 200 the thermionic vacuum valve is still much used; it is inefficient or impracticable at low voltages because a considerable potential must be applied to the valve to overcome the electrostatic effect of space charge.

In the gas-filled thermionic valve, the space charge is neutral-ised by positive ions rather than by the charges on the electrodes, and the efficiency can be made high even at fairly low voltages. Moreover, the cathode may be shaped to conserve radiant heat, so that the cathode efficiency (emission per unit heater power) is high in these tubes. They are often used in carefully designed and properly protected commercial equipment, but they have important disadvantages. The discharge has no inherent current limiting property, so that the current must be limited to a safe value by the external circuit. If a current overload is taken through the tube, the character of the discharge changes and the cathode may be very rapidly destroyed by positive ion bombardment. A temporary over-load on a vacuum rectifier produces no such dramatic effect. Furthermore, the sudden formation and extinction of the arc in each working cycle may give rise to high frequency disturb-ances of a troublesome sort. It is probably better not to use gas-filled rectifiers in low-power laboratory applications; their importance is in any case much diminished by the competition of junction rectifiers.

If a rectifier is used for battery charging, or to supply small D.C. motors, or relays, it may be possible to dispense with smoothing, but more often the rectifier is followed by a smooth-ing circuit in which the first element may be either a capacity or an inductance. If a condenser is used in this position, and no load current is taken, the condenser charges up to the *maximum* value of the voltage wave, and it is important to notice that on the non-conducting part of the cycle the rectifier has to withstand twice the peak value of the rectifier input voltage. When a load current is drawn the voltage across the condenser falls more or less linearly during each cycle until the charge is replenished at the next voltage peak, so that the condenser voltage has a steady component and a superposed ripple.* The calculation of these voltages is rather complicated ; their values depend to some extent on the transformer secondary resistance and leakage inductance,

---

* The condenser must be chosen to survive these conditions—certain electrolytic condensers are unsuitable though they can be used for the later stages of filtering.

and an exact estimate is seldom required for low power applications. Typical results obtained empirically are shown in Fig. 7.3. It must be noted that current is only taken to charge the condenser during a part of each half cycle. The instantaneous values of the rectifier current are therefore much larger than the D.C. load current ; and the heating of the transformer windings, which depends on the average value of the square of the current, is greater for this " peaky " wave

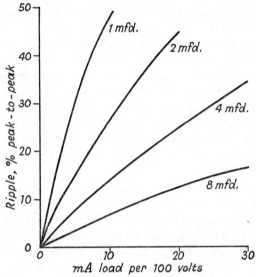

FIG. 7.3   Empirical data about voltage ripple on the first condenser of a
full wave rectifier operating at 50 c/s

than for a sinusoidal current with the same average value. The transformer must therefore be larger than one which delivers the same power in normal A.C. service. The rating of a junction rectifier must be chosen to deal with the current peaks at each cycle, and also the initial surge when the transformer is switched on with the condenser uncharged. The latter condition is often decisive in the rating of a rectifier.

If the first smoothing element is a large inductance, the current through the rectifier tends to remain constant during the cycle, for when the current falls the inductance generates an e.m.f.

which helps the failing transformer voltage. The operation is illustrated diagrammatically in Fig. 7.4. Choke-input filters make more effective use of the transformer and rectifier than condenser-input systems and they are commonly used for

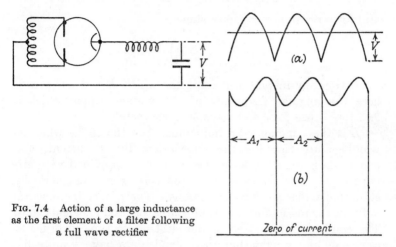

FIG. 7.4 Action of a large inductance as the first element of a filter following a full wave rectifier

(a) Shows the rectifier voltage wave and the steady voltage across the first condenser

(b) Shows the current variations in the inductance which produce the difference between these voltages. The current flows alternately to the two anodes of the rectifier

moderately large powers. It may also be shown that they give better regulation of the D.C. voltage under varying loads. Nevertheless, condenser input systems are usually cheaper than choke systems for powers up to, say, 100 W. and in laboratory power units condenser input is generally used.

In either case, the initial element is followed by a choke-capacity filter (Fig. 7.5)—occasionally by a resistance-capacity filter.

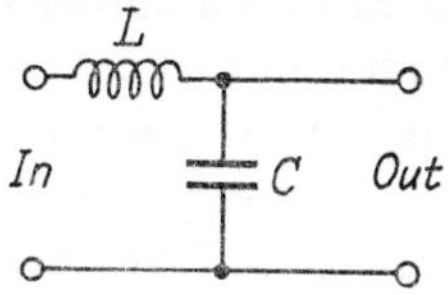

FIG. 7.5

The ratio S of the ripple voltages at the output and input terminals of a filter stage may be easily calculated if we assume that the impedance of the load is large compared with that of the condenser. This approximation is good enough in practical cases. For a choke capacity stage we have (Fig. 7.5)

$$S = \frac{1}{j\omega C} \bigg/ \left(\frac{1}{j\omega C} + j\omega L \right) = \frac{1}{1 - \omega^2 LC}$$

and for a resistance capacity stage

$$S = \frac{1}{j\omega C} \bigg/ \left(\frac{1}{j\omega C} + R \right) = \frac{1}{\omega RC}$$

approximately in practical cases for which $R > 1/\omega C$. ω is here the angular frequency of the voltage ripple which is $2\pi \cdot 100 = 628$ for a full-wave 50 cycle rectifier.

L is the "incremental inductance" of the choke when its windings are carrying the appropriate direct current, and chokes designed for this service have to be provided with air-gaps in the iron cores so that the core is not magnetically saturated under working conditions. The proper incremental value of the inductance must, of course, be used in calculations. The condensers are often of the electrolytic type in order to save cost and weight, but these condensers have a finite life and must be regarded as rather less reliable than paper dielectric condensers. In any case the condensers must be chosen to withstand the no-load voltage, which, as we have seen, is practically the peak voltage of the rectifier transformer.

(Stabilised power supplies are briefly noticed in § 11.14.)

7.3 Amplifiers

The general function of an amplifier is to produce an output signal (a voltage or current change) which is under the control of an input signal. For the present we consider cases in which the desired output is a linear copy of the input. Since very little current is collected by a valve grid held at a potential negative to the other electrodes, the valve presents a high resistance to the input circuit.[*] The output from a complete amplifier or from a single stage may be regarded as equivalent

---

[*] This is substantially true at ordinary frequencies. At high radio frequencies the input impedance may be comparatively low because of several effects in the valve. See e.g. Terman (1943), p. 310.

to that from an electric generator which gives a voltage controlled by the input voltage, and which possesses a certain internal impedance. The valve may be used to drive the grid of another valve or an electrostatic cathode ray tube, and the stage is then called a voltage amplifying stage. Alternatively the required output may be a current change in a circuit of relatively low impedance, e.g. the coil of a loud speaker, and the valve constitutes a power amplifying stage. Such a stage may operate usefully if its voltage gain is low or even less than unity.

If the input signal to an amplifier is a sine wave containing only one frequency, the output may be made very similar to the input, but no amplifier can be made to have constant gain * over an infinite frequency range ; the amplification will normally fall off at very high and very low frequencies, and there is in general a phase displacement between sinusoidal input and output signals which varies with frequency. Even if the amplifier is linear in the usual sense, these properties result in some distortion of signals, for an arbitrary disturbance may be regarded as a Fourier series or Fourier integral, and if the harmonic components are not equally amplified, and left unchanged in relative phase, the amplified signal, as calculated by reassembling the amplified components, will differ in form from the input signal.

When the input signal is a square-edged wave, the output signal can be calculated if the amplitude and phase response are known for harmonic signals of all frequencies, or it may be calculated from the circuit constants of the amplifier, using operator methods or Laplace transforms.

Fig. 7.6(*a*) is a typical characteristic for the high frequency response of an audio amplifier stage, and Fig. 7.6(*b*) shows its response to a square input wave. The general effect is to blur out the sharp edges of the pulse. In a rather qualitative way,

---

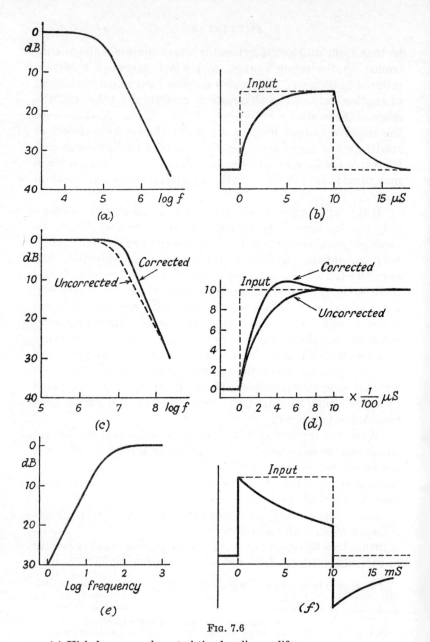

FIG. 7.6

(a) High frequency characteristic of audio amplifier
(b) Corresponding response to square wave
(c) High frequency response of video amplifier—uncorrected, and corrected by addition of inductance to anode load
(d) Corresponding response to square edge
(e) Low frequency response of amplifier
(f) Corresponding response to square wave

if the amplifier response falls off rapidly above f c/s the edges are made indefinite to the extent of about $1/f$ sec.*

In Fig. 7.6(c), the dotted line is the frequency response of an (uncorrected) video frequency stage, and the corresponding response to a square rising edge is shown in Fig. 7.6(d). If the response of the amplifier is "corrected" to give the upper curve of Fig. 7.6(c), an "overshoot" appears in the output waveform. This overshoot is connected with the variation with frequency of the phase characteristic of the amplifier, which in turn is least when the amplification falls off slowly and monotonically at the end of the pass band of frequencies.

The perfect reproduction of the flat top of a square pulse requires amplifier response down to zero frequency. If the amplification falls at low frequencies (Fig. 7.6(e)), the effect on the output will be the "droop" shown in Fig. 7.6(f). As a result of this droop the pulse is followed by an overshoot of reversed sign. This back pulse is an important feature of the behaviour of a pulse amplifier, especially when the low frequency response is drastically limited (cf. § 10.13).

It is sometimes convenient to use the response to a square wave or to a sharp pulse, as displayed on a cathode-ray tube, as a method of testing the behaviour of an amplifier. Much can be learned by simple inspection of the trace, following the guidance of Fig. 7.6. For a method of transformation of square-wave response to frequency response, see Bedford and Fredendall (1942) ; for a sophisticated arrangement for pulse testing, see Espley et al. (1946).

7.4 The Triode Voltage Amplifier—Simple Considerations

The simplest possible amplifying stage is shown in skeleton form in Fig. 7.7. The input signal is applied to the grid, and the output signal appears at the anode superposed on a steady potential. As a first approximation we may take small

---

* More accurately, the response of this simple amplifier is 3 db down at 10^5 c/s ; the rise of the pulse to half value takes about 3μs and the rise is substantially complete in 10μs.

changes in the anode current as linearly dependent on changes in anode and grid voltages

$$\delta i_a = \frac{1}{r_a}(\delta v_a + \mu \delta v_g)$$

where r_a has the dimensions of resistance (anode slope resistance) and μ is a dimensionless quantity (amplification factor) which measures the relative effect of grid and anode voltage changes on the anode current. μ depends primarily on the geometry of the valve electrodes.

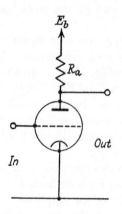

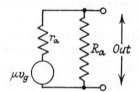

FIG. 7 8   Equivalent circuit of triode amplifier stage

FIG. 7.7   Skeleton diagram of triode voltage amplifying stage

We have also for the circuit of Fig. 7.7

$$\delta v_a = - R_a \delta i_a$$

so that

$$-\frac{\delta v_a}{R_a} = \frac{1}{r_a}(\delta v_a + \mu \delta v_g)$$

$$\delta v_a = - \frac{R_a}{R_a + r_a} \cdot \mu \cdot \delta v_g.$$

Hence the voltage gain of the stage is

$$A = - \mu \frac{R_a}{R_a + r_a}$$

and the equivalent generator circuit is shown in Fig. 7.8. The effective output impedance of the complete stage is that of R_a and r_a in parallel.

7.5 Inter-electrode Capacities and the Miller effect

Unless the voltage changes are very slow, we must consider the effect of the inter-electrode and stray capacities indicated in Fig. 7.9. The capacities C_{ak}, C_{gk} produce simple

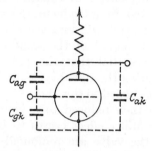

FIG. 7.9   Inter-electrode capacities in a triode

shunting effects which may be calculated in a straightforward way (§ 7.9). The capacity C_{ag}, however, has a particularly large effect, because when a potential change δv_g is applied to the grid, a potential change $-A\delta v_g$ appears at the anode, and the potential difference $(1 + A)\delta v_g$ appears across C_{ag}. The corresponding charge $C_{ag}(1 + A)\delta v_g$ has to be supplied to the grid circuit in addition to any charge necessary to charge up C_{gk} and the stray capacities. The effective capacity of the grid is therefore increased by $(1 + A)C_{ag}$ (Miller effect). This effect may be much more important than the other grid capacities. For a fairly typical high-gain triode stage, $A = 50$, $C_{ag} = 3\text{pF}$ and the Miller effect capacity is 153 pF. The impedance of this capacity may become comparable with other impedances in the circuit at quite moderate frequencies ; it is, e.g. 100kΩ at about 10,000 cycles, and we shall see that this may have an important effect on the performance of an amplifying stage.*

If the anode load of the valve is not a simple resistance the phase of the voltage changes at the anode and hence the phase of the voltage fed back across the anode-grid capacity will not be exactly opposite to that of the grid voltage changes. It may be shown that with an inductive anode load the feedback

---

* 1kΩ, 1MΩ are used as convenient notation for 1000 ohms, 10^6 ohms.

is in the direction to produce instability and the generation of oscillations.

7.6 The Screen-grid Valves—Tetrode and Pentode

The embarrassing effects of capacity between anode and grid may be removed by introducing an electrostatic screen-grid between the control grid and the anode. This screen is held at a steady potential of the same order as the anode potential. (It is essential that the potential of the screen should not vary during the signal cycle, and the circuits which supply it must be designed to this end.) The capacity between anode and grid is then reduced to a value which is usually negligible and the Miller effect ceases to be important. The characteristics of the valve are profoundly modified, for the anode potential now has practically no effect on the current in the valve over a wide range of anode voltage (see Fig. 7.12b).* The screen controls the electrostatic conditions between itself and the cathode, but it may be designed to collect much less current than the anode. The valve with a screen grid is a tetrode. It is common to introduce a third grid (suppressor) held at or near cathode potential, between the screen and the anode, in order to prevent the screen from collecting secondary electrons emitted by the anode under primary electron bombardment.

In the absence of the suppressor this collection could occur whenever the anode became negative to the screen at some part of the signal cycle, and would represent a negative contribution to the anode current. This would lead to considerable distortion of the anode current/anode voltage characteristics. The valve containing screen and suppressor grids is a pentode. A similar result may be obtained by special design and spacing of the electrodes of a tetrode, whereby the electron space charge is made to play the part of a suppressor (" beam tetrode ").

* At low anode potentials the curves connecting anode potential with anode current slope very steeply, and the grid potential has little effect on the anode current (see left-hand side of Fig. 7.12(b)). This part of the pentode characteristic (the " bottoming " region) must be avoided in linear amplifier operation, but it is valuable for certain special purposes (see e.g. §§ 7.23, 11.14).

7.7 The Properties of a Pentode—Simple Considerations

In a pentode, with the screen potential constant, the anode current is practically independent of anode voltage over a wide range, and we may write

$$\delta i_a = g_m \delta v_g$$

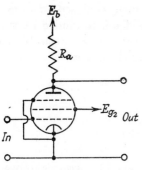

where g_m, the mutual conductance which is defined by this equation corresponds to μ / r_a of the triode equation.* There is now little point in using μ, r_a, separately.

The voltage gain of the simple resistance loaded valve of Fig. 7.10 is now

$$- R_a g_m$$

FIG. 7.10   Skeleton diagram of pentode voltage amplifying stage

since

$$\delta v_a = - R_a g_m \delta v_g.$$

The output impedance of the *stage* is practically that of the anode load resistance, the anode impedance of the *valve* being very high since a change in anode potential makes very little difference to the anode current.

It is often convenient to represent a pentode as a *constant current* generator under the control of the input (grid) voltage, and giving, as its output, current changes equal to g_m times the input voltage changes.

7.8 The Complete Amplifying Stage

In practice every valve circuit is complicated by the arrangements for maintaining the correct average potentials of the electrodes.   The anode current may be supplied direct to the anode load resistor, or through a decoupling network (R_d, C_d of Fig. 7.11). The purpose of this network is to avoid coupling between stages due to the impedance of the power supply.   It may be shown that the coupling produced

* It should be noted that the mutual conductance g_m for a given value increases and decreases quite strongly with the anode current—it is not a primarily geometrical parameter like μ.

239

in this way between a stage and the next but one is in a direction to produce instability, and since the signal multiplication between such stages is normally high, oscillations are produced by feeding back only a small fraction of the signal in the later stage. The decoupling condenser must therefore provide a shunt path where impedance is low compared with the decoupling resistance at any frequency which is amplified by the system. In really high gain amplifiers it is often desirable to use a separate anode supply for some of the stages.

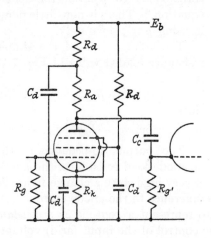

Fig. 7.11 Pentode voltage amplifying stage, showing coupling and decoupling circuits

The screen potential of a tetrode or pentode should remain constant throughout the signal cycle, and the screen must therefore be fed from a circuit whose impedance is low compared with the internal screen impedance $\left(\dfrac{\partial v_{screen}}{\partial i_{screen}}\right)$ at all frequencies to be amplified. This condition can be fulfilled by a resistance capacity network with a sufficiently large condenser (see Fig. 7.11).* If the condition is not met, the stage amplification will be reduced and the effective grid capacity will be increased by the Miller effect.

The mean voltage of the control grid may be maintained by a battery connected between the lower end of the grid leak and the cathode, but the arrangement shown in Fig. 7.11

---

* The screen may be connected direct to H.T. in certain cases. See § 7.10.

(Automatic Grid Bias) is usually preferable. In this circuit the valve cathode, which is normally heated indirectly but occasionally by a special transformer winding, is kept positive with respect to the " earth " line by the potential drop across the resistance R_k carrying the cathode current. The signal frequency variations in the cathode current give rise to negative feed back (§ 7.13) unless R_k is by-passed by a condenser. When the grid goes more positive in the course of the signal cycle, the increased cathode current flowing in R_k will introduce a voltage into the grid cathode circuit in opposition to the signal voltage. It will be shown in § 7.13 that the amplification of the stage is reduced, but is made more linear and less dependent on valve characteristics. The feedback can be removed by bypassing the cathode resistor with a condenser whose impedance is low compared with R_k at the lowest required frequency. The value of the by-pass condenser is large in typical low frequency amplifiers and electrolytic condensers are necessarily used. The automatic grid bias circuit has the desirable effect of reducing the change of amplification caused by replacing the valve by one of slightly different characteristics, for the bias is controlled by the cathode current, and it is found that two commercially identical valves behave more nearly alike at a certain cathode current than at a certain grid voltage. This property of the automatic bias circuit is important in the design of production amplifiers which must give an acceptable performance with all commercially identical replacement valves.

7.9 The Frequency Characteristics of R.C. Amplifier Stages

Fig. 7.11 shows the circuit required to transfer the amplified signal from stage to stage. If we can neglect the effect of stray capacities shunting the resistances, and if the impedance of the coupling condenser is negligible compared with the other impedances in the circuit, the amplification is essentially independent of frequency. These conditions are nearly met in practical amplifiers at moderate frequencies (e.g. 10^2-10^4 c/s). At low and at high frequencies the behaviour of real amplifiers departs from this ideal ; the complications which arise at the two ends of the frequency band are different and can be treated separately.

At low frequencies the coupling condenser (C_c) has an impedance which is not negligible compared with the grid leak resistance $R_{g'}$ of the succeeding valve. $R_{g'}$ cannot be made indefinitely large because the grid to which it is connected may in some circumstances emit electrons or collect positive ions : if $R_{g'}$ were very high this might start a cumulative process in which control of the grid potential would be lost. Safe limits are placed on $R_{g'}$ by valve manufacturers, and 1 megohm is a representative value. At a low frequency f the effect of the finite coupling condenser is to cut down the amplification in the ratio

$$\frac{R_{g'}}{\sqrt{R_{g'}^2 + \dfrac{1}{\omega^2 c_c{}^2}}} \qquad (\omega = 2\pi f)$$

and to introduce a phase displacement

$$\tan^{-1} \frac{1}{R_{g'} C_c \omega} .$$

The feedback introduced by the impedance of screen and cathode decoupling condensers leads to further reduction of the stage amplification at low frequencies. It also produces a phase displacement since the voltages which appear across the decoupling components are not in general in phase with the signal voltages. Phase distortion is important in some amplifiers because it leads to the distortion of waveforms (§ 7.3) and because it may produce instability in amplifiers provided with feedback (§ 7.15).

At *high* frequencies the ruling effect is the shunting of the anode load resistor by stray capacities between earth and the anode of the valve, the grid of the succeeding stage and the coupling components. These are all additive and we denote their sum by C_s. The effective impedance X of the anode load is then complex and given by $1/X = 1/R_a + j\omega C_s$. The voltage gain (irrespective of phase) is g_m mod $X = g_m R_a/(1 + \omega^2 R_a{}^2 C_s{}^2)^{\frac{1}{2}}$ and it is convenient to remember that the stage amplification is reduced by a factor $1/\sqrt{2}$ when $R_a =$

$1/2\pi f C_s$. Assuming a typical value 20 pf*, this occurs at 1 Mc/s for $R = 4000$ ohms, so that if an amplifier is to have nearly constant gain up to 1 Mc/s, the anode load of each stage must be quite low. A high mutual conductance g_m is then required if the stage is to have adequate voltage amplification.

The so-called gain-bandwidth product $g_m/2\pi \times$ sum of input (grid) and output (anode) capacities is a characteristic property of a valve and has the dimensions of frequency. For a simple amplifying stage and neglecting capacities external to the valves it is the product of the voltage gain and the frequency at the (upper) half power point as given by the formula above. It can be shown that this product is significant also in more complicated coupling circuits and in determining the transition time of trigger circuits. (Valley and Wallman 1948, Bruijning 1958.) In recent years it has been possible to develop valves with greatly increased gain-bandwidth product by using grids wound on a rigid frame, thus permitting very small spacing between grid and cathode. This is demonstrated in Table 7.1.

TABLE 7.1

Development of Pentodes

Valve designation	g_m	$C = C_{in} + C_{out}$	$g_m/2\pi C$ Mc/s	Notes
EF50	6·5	13·5	77	Designed for television about 1937
EF91	7·6	9	134	" Miniature " valve designed about 1943
EF95/6AK5	5·1	6·8	114	" Miniature " valve designed about 1943
E180F	16·5	11	240	Frame grid valve
E810F	50	26·5	300	Mullard Tech. Communications 1961

This table indicates the development of valve characteristics chosen from a particular maker's catalogues over twenty years. Over this period there has been also a tendency to design valves and circuits to work on rather lower voltages.

* For a pentode: normally connected triodes are obviously unsuitable for the duties discussed here.

There are a number of circuit modifications (see e.g. Valley and Wallman 1948, p. 73), which can be used to improve the gain of an amplifier at frequencies where the shunting effect of stray capacities are important. The simplest is the addition of inductance to the anode load, forming with the resistance and the stray capacities a broadly tuned resonant circuit. The effect of such a system was illustrated in Fig. 7.6.

7.10   The Design of Amplifier Stages

In designing an amplifier stage, one has to choose the type of valve, the circuit constants, the H.T. supply voltage, the static potentials of grid and screen (if any). At low frequencies the choice of triode or pentode as a voltage amplifier is rather arbitrary ; a higher voltage gain is obtainable from a pentode stage at the price of some circuit complication to provide the screen potential. At higher frequencies the Miller effect makes the triode unusable in straightforward circuits. At still higher frequencies the permissible anode load is so low that it is necessary to use a high slope pentode if we are to obtain a useful stage gain. The high mutual conductance is only obtained when the anode current is rather high (see below), so that wide band amplifiers (i.e. R.C. amplifiers possessing good amplification at high frequencies) are usually operated with standing anode currents of 10 mA or more.

The voltage gain can be calculated approximately for small signals from the formulæ

$$A = -g_m R_a \text{ (pentode)} \quad \text{or} \quad A = -\frac{\mu R_a}{R_a + r_a} \text{ (triode)}.$$

The quantities μ, R_a, g_m are not constant over any large range of electrode voltages. In particular g_m always falls if the anode current is reduced, and even at low frequencies it is not possible to increase the gain of a pentode stage beyond a certain limit by increasing R_a unless the H.T. voltage is also increased. In practice, most pentodes will give a stage gain of 100-150 with 300V H.T., provided that the anode load resistance is not restricted by the requirements of frequency response. An " ordinary " pentode is used with an anode current of the order 1 mA and an anode load resistance of 100-250 kΩ, a " high slope " pentode requires an anode current of 5-10 mA, and would be used with an anode load of 20-50 kΩ, giving a considerably better high-frequency performance. The anode load would be much lower than this in a very-wide-band amplifier, and as stated above, more complicated coupling arrangements can be used to extend the frequency response.

For the type of linear amplifier we are now considering (Class A_1),* the grid must always be so negative that no grid current flows at any point in the signal cycle. This condition decides the grid bias voltage. A lower limit to the screen potential is now set by the condition that the valve must not approach cut-off at the most negative point of the grid cycle. The best working value for the screen voltage depends markedly on the design of the valve and may be obtained from the maker's data.†

The performance of the amplifier with a trial value of anode load may now be examined by the use of a family of curves connecting i_a with v_a for various values of v_g (Fig. 7.12). A " load line " is drawn on the same diagram to show the variation of v_a with i_a, due to the voltage drop across R_a, and the intersection of the line with each of the valve curves gives i_a and v_a corresponding to a given v_g. It is now possible to examine the relation between v_a and v_g, and to adjust the value of R_a until the load line lies across the anode character-istics where they are evenly spaced. The maximum value of R_a is subject to the frequency conditions discussed above. The conditions governing the size of the coupling condenser,

---

* Class A implies that the operation of the valve is confined to a substan-tially linear part of the characteristic.

Class B amplification involves driving the valve to the point where the anode current is just zero at an extreme of the signal cycle ; in class C ampli-fication anode current is cut off for an appreciable part of the cycle. Class C amplification is, of course, far from linear, but is often admissible in radio frequency technique.   The suffix in Class A_1 indicates that grid current is excluded during the whole cycle, in Class B_2 amplifiers, for example, grid current is allowed in the positive half cycles.

† In some cases (e.g. Mazda SP41 Mullard EF50) it may be satisfactory to use the full H.T. voltage on the screen ; in others (e.g. EF36) a great part of the valve current is diverted to the screen when the screen potential is high compared with that of the anode, and bottoming occurs at unnecessarily high anode voltages if the screen potential is set too high.

the grid leak, and the components in screen and cathode circuits have already been discussed (§ 7.9).

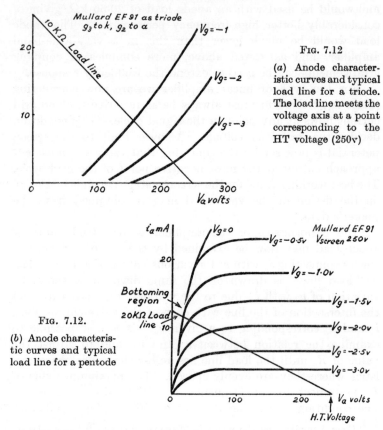

FIG. 7.12

(a) Anode characteristic curves and typical load line for a triode. The load line meets the voltage axis at a point corresponding to the HT voltage (250v)

FIG. 7.12.

(b) Anode characteristic curves and typical load line for a pentode

7.11   The Feedback Principle

There are two radically different ways of obtaining an output signal which bears a desired (typically linear) relation to an input signal.

(a) We may rely on the characteristics of a valve to generate a signal which is a replica of the input.   This method is that used in a simple resistance coupled pentode stage.   Its limitations arise from the non-linearity of the valve characteristics over the range covered by the signal.   Furthermore, the amplification is liable to serious change if a valve is replaced by one with only commercially identical characteristics, or if the supply voltages fluctuate.

(b) We may compare the input signal with a known fraction of the output signal, feeding the difference (error signal) into a high-gain amplifier which provides the output. It will be shown that the relation between input and output is nearly independent of the exact gain of the amplifier and depends essentially on the comparison circuit, which may be a passive network of unimpeachable linearity. This is the foundation of the feedback principle which is much used in modern amplifier technique.

The feedback principle is very general, and its application is not confined to electronic amplifiers. For example, a mechanical or electromechanical device might move a tool under the control of a tracing point, the movement given to the tool being a function of the " error " between the actual position of the tool and the desired position defined by the tracing point. An error controlled (feedback) system of this kind is called a servo system. A great deal of work was done on such systems for military application (e.g. gun control) during the 1939 war, and much of this work has been published (Servo Mechanism 1947 ; Porter 1951). The faithfulness and stability conditions for linear servo systems are mathematically similar to those for feedback amplifiers. There are many laboratory applications of servo principles, e.g. galvanometer deflection amplifiers, automatic temperature controls.

7.12 The Feedback Principle—Quantitative

Consider the arrangement shown in Fig. 7.13 : the input signal is v_i, the output signal is v_o. A fraction β of the output signal is fed back in opposition to the input, so that the error signal going into the amplifier is $(v_i - \beta v_o)$.

We have then

$$v_o = A(v_i - \beta v_o)$$

and the voltage gain ratio of the system with feedback is

$$A' = \frac{v_o}{v_i} = \frac{A}{(1 + A\beta)}.$$

If $A\beta$ is large compared with unity, the voltage gain with feedback $= 1/\beta$ and depends only on the properties of the attenuator. If $A\beta$ is not very large compared with unity, A' depends on A in a way which we can find by differentiating A' with respect to A

$$dA' = dA\left(\frac{1}{1 + A\beta} - \frac{A\beta}{(1 + A\beta)^2}\right) = \frac{dA}{(1 + A\beta)^2}.$$

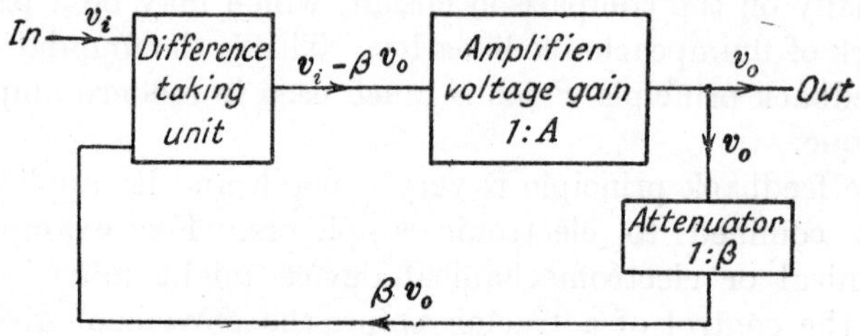

FIG. 7.13   Block diagram of feedback amplifier system

If we obtain dA', dA as fractions of A', A

$$\frac{dA'}{A'} = \frac{dA}{A}\frac{1}{(1 + A\beta)}$$

so that the fractional change of gain of the feedback system is less than the fractional change of gain in the amplifier alone in the ratio $1 : \dfrac{1}{(1 + A\beta)}$.

This means that distortion, which may be considered as a variation of A over the signal cycle, and also the effects of any change in A due to valve changes, supply variations, or limitations of frequency response, are reduced in the ratio $1 : \dfrac{1}{(1 + A\beta.)}$ This ratio is the same as that in which gain is reduced.

In comparing a feedback and a straight amplifier with equal overall gain it will be seen that more amplification must be provided if feedback is used. The signal level at the output is the same in the two cases, so that amplitude distortion is likely to be similar in the straight amplifier and in the amplifying stages of the feedback system in spite of the higher gain of the latter. The feedback then improves the distortion considerably. The uniformity of frequency response is also improved by feedback. Calculation shows that this is so where an amplifier containing two similar stages and a feedback loop is compared with a single stage without feedback, even though the two-stage amplifier without feedback has a worse frequency response than the single stage.

The effect of noise (including external electrical disturbances) in a feedback amplifier depends on the point in the loop at which the disturbance is introduced (Bode 1945, p. 34). If this is near the output end of the amplifier, the ratio of noise to signal is lower than the ratio when the same disturbance is introduced at a comparable point in a straight amplifier. If the noise is introduced early in the system, it is treated by the system similarly to the signal, and the noise-signal ratio is not affected by the feedback.

7.13   The Cathode Follower

The simplest example of a feedback amplifier is provided by the " cathode follower " (Fig. 7.14). Here the output voltage is developed across a resistance in the cathode lead of

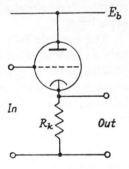

FIG. 7.14   The cathode follower

Typical values are :   cathode load = 20 k.
μ for valve, 10.
g_m = 5 ma/volt.

a triode, and the whole of this output is fed back into the input circuit.

The output voltage corresponding to an input δv_i is

$$\delta v_o = R_k \frac{\mu(\delta v_i - \delta v_o) - \delta v_o}{r_a}$$

since the change in cathode potential reduces both grid-cathode and anode-cathode voltages by δv_o.

$$\delta v_o = \delta v_i \frac{\mu R_k}{r_a + (\mu + 1)R_k} = dv_i \frac{R_k}{\dfrac{1}{g_m} + \dfrac{\mu + 1}{\mu}R_k}.$$

With practical values of the parameters, the voltage gain is nearly $\dfrac{\mu}{\mu + 1}$, and is therefore slightly less than unity.

The usefulness of the cathode follower lies in its low output impedance : if we compare the expression for the output voltage given above with the value $\dfrac{vR}{r + R}$ for the voltage developed across a resistance R by a generator of e.m.f. v and internal resistance r, we see that the effective output impedance of the cathode follower is approximately $\dfrac{1}{g_m}$. For a suitable small valve this may be of the order of 150 ohms. The cathode follower may then be used as a power amplifier. It will deal with voltage signals of considerable amplitude, since only a small fraction of the signal actually appears between grid and cathode, and it is frequently used to impress voltage changes on circuits of relatively low resistance or high capacity.*

The cathode follower has a high input impedance because only a small fraction of the signal is applied to any impedance existing between grid and cathode. The grid-anode capacity remains as a shunting input impedance in a triode cathode follower. It can be removed by using a pentode whose screen is fed by a decoupling resistance and connected by a condenser to the cathode.

The "seesaw" voltage amplifier of Fig. 7.16 has been extensively used for pulse work, and we may calculate its properties approximately by a method widely used by F. C. Williams. If the valve has very large voltage gain, the potential changes at its grid must be very small for any finite

---

* The simple cathode follower circuit has serious limitations when dealing with rapid negative-going voltage changes. See § 7.25, p. 275.

output.* If the grid potential is to be constant when a change is made in the input voltage, the changes in the currents flowing into it from the signal source and from the feedback resistor must be equal and opposite, and we have

$$\frac{\delta v_i}{R_s} = \frac{\delta v_o}{R_p}.$$

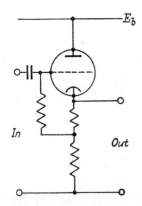

FIG. 7.15 Cathode follower showing arrangements to allow the grid bias to be adjusted independently of the cathode load

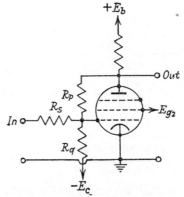

FIG. 7.16 "Seesaw" amplifier with direct voltage feedback from anode to grid

Like the cathode follower this device has a low output impedance because the feedback is derived directly from the output voltage, and the amplifier tends to maintain the output voltage constant for a given input voltage, irrespective of the shunting effect of an external load.

7.14 "Voltage" and "Current" Feedback Amplifiers

Another form of feedback with different characteristics (current feedback) appears if a voltage amplifying valve has

---

* Because the grid potential is invariant under these conditions, the grid is sometimes said to be a "virtual earth", and the property is often useful in circuit design. Cf. the "Miller integrator", p. 270.

a resistance (unbypassed by capacity) in the cathode lead (Fig. 7.17). The voltage fed back in opposition to the signal on the grid is now proportional to the changes in cathode current and is not directly the output voltage as in the cathode follower. For a pentode we may write

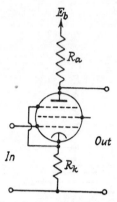

$$\delta i_a = g_m \delta v_g$$

and we have *

$$\delta v_g = \delta v_i - R_k g_m \delta v_g$$

$$\delta v_a = - R_a \delta i_a$$

$$= - R_a g_m dv_g$$

$$= - R_a g_m \frac{\delta v_i}{1 + R_k g_m}$$

Fig. 7.17 Amplifying stage with unbypassed cathode resistor, giving current feedback

$$= - \frac{R_a}{R_k} \delta v_i \text{ if } R_k g_m \gg 1.$$

A similar, slightly more complicated result is obtained for a triode.

Since the feedback signal is derived from the current through the valve, the amplifier tends to maintain a certain *current* change for a given input voltage change, irrespective of the value of the anode load. The stage therefore has a large output impedance, and may be considered as equivalent to a constant current generator.

In the systems so far considered the feedback loop (see Fig. 7.13) extends over only one valve, but it may be made to include several stages. Fig. 7.18 shows an amplifier in which there are two voltage amplifier stages giving a gain without feedback of perhaps 10,000 times (80 db), and feedback is provided by the resistor R_f in the cathode circuit of the last valve. This amplifier may be used to provide extremely stable amplification of, say, 100, set by the ratio of R_d to R_f.

---

* We have here assumed that the changes in i_a, i_k are alike equal to $g_m \delta v_g$. There is, however, a small difference due to the contribution of i_k to the screen current. This effect is small, and could be allowed for by substituting a fictitious value of R_k in the final equation.

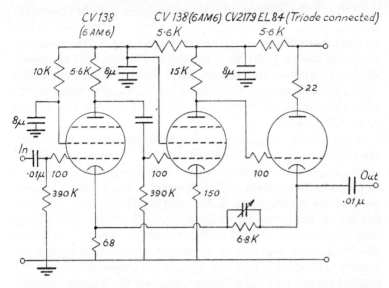

Fig. 7.18 Feedback group amplifier (ring of three) with feedback from third cathode to first cathode. Note that the second and third valves are directly coupled—this helps to reduce phase displacements in the amplifier. The small compensating condenser in the feedback path is adjusted empirically for best response to a step-shaped transient signal. All earth leads including the decoupling condensers should be taken separately to a single point to avoid couplings through the chassis. The details are taken from an actual amplifier giving amplification up to 3·5 Mc/s (3dB down)

7.15 Stability Limitation of the Feedback Principle

In feedback amplifiers of the type considered here, the feedback signal is always of such a sign as to oppose the input signal, and the role of the amplifier is to adjust these signals to balance.

If the phase of the feedback is such as to increase the output signal (positive feedback), the gain of the amplifier will be *increased* in the ratio $1/(1 - A\beta)$ and the system will become unstable if $A\beta > 1$.

We have seen (§ 7.9) that in each stage of an amplifier, signals undergo phase displacements which depend on frequency and which may change rapidly near the ends of the band of frequencies which the stage is capable of amplifying.

A feedback amplifier in which the feedback acts in the stabilising direction over a wide frequency range may yet be unstable and go into oscillation at an extreme frequency. It is necessary to design the amplifier very carefully to secure that the phase displacement does not become large until the gain has fallen off, and unless special precautions are taken, it is necessary to limit the number of stages enclosed in a feedback loop to two or possibly three.

It can be shown (Bode 1945) that in any system of circuits, the minimum phase shift obtainable at any frequency is related to the shape of the characteristic curve connecting the amplitude response of the system with frequency. The relation takes a particularly useful form if the amplitude response and frequency are expressed logarithmically. The phase shift at any frequency can be calculated by taking the slope of the logarithmic response curve at every frequency, multiplying it by a weighting function which is large near the chosen frequency and small at remote points, and integrating over the frequency range.

In a feedback amplifier, then, there is a limitation on the sharpness with which the frequency band transmitted round the feedback loop can be cut off, since the phase change must not become large enough to produce instability. A typical value for the maximum permissible slope in a heavily fed-back amplifier (expressed in logarithmic terms) is 9 db per octave ; this slope would not ordinarily be approached by the circuits associated with a single stage, but might be attained by two stages. A typical treatment for reducing the slope is to make the time-constants associated with successive stages different, so that their effects on the response are spread over a wider frequency band.

7.16 Balanced or Push-pull Amplifiers

Several important advantages can be obtained by constructing an amplifier stage with two valves connected as shown in Fig. 7.19, and arranging that the current in the two valves varies nearly symmetrically in antiphase during the signal cycle. The arrangement has long been used in high quality audio amplifiers, for it may be shown that second (and fourth, etc.) order departures from linearity in the valve characteristics produce no distortion in the combined output.

It is even possible, with suitably designed valves, to use the strongly curved lower parts of the characteristics without producing very much distortion.   The average anode current is then small in the absence of a signal and rises when a signal is applied to the grids ; a considerable economy in H.T. power can be effected in this way.   (Class B operation, see p. 245.)

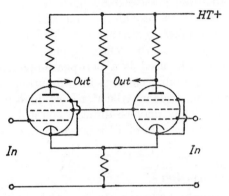

FIG. 7.19   Elementary push-pull amplifier stage.   Note that cathode and screen decoupling condensers may be omitted without producing degeneration

The push-pull principle brings other advantages which can be exploited in laboratory applications :

(1) The combined (differential) output is free from components due to ripple or other variations in the H.T. voltage.

(2) The effect of variation of cathode temperature (see § 7.17) is largely balanced out.   This is particularly important in D.C. amplifiers.

(3) If we consider the pair of valves, the currents to anodes, cathodes and screens do not vary over the signal cycle.   Decoupling is no longer necessary for these supplies ; this consideration is particularly important at low and zero frequencies. Furthermore the cathode resistance no longer has a degenerative effect and it may be shown that the ratio

$$\frac{\text{Differential voltage change at anodes}}{\text{Differential voltage change on grids}}$$

is that given by the simple formulae for a single valve.

If the common cathode resistance is large (compared with $1/g_m$), the output voltage changes at the anodes are nearly symmetrical with respect to earth even if the input voltages applied to the grids are not ; e.g. if one grid alone is driven and the other is maintained at a steady potential. This pair of valves (long-tailed pair) has several important properties in addition to those possessed by push-pull pairs in general. Its obvious use is to provide symmetrical voltage changes which can be applied to further push-pull amplifiers, or to other equipment such as the deflecting plates of a cathode ray tube. It can also be used as a non-phase-reversing amplifier or as a difference-taking element in computing and feedback systems. Since its grids may be at a fairly high potential with respect to earth, they may be directly coupled to the anodes of a preceding stage—a useful property in the design of D.C. amplifiers.

7.17 D.C. Amplifiers

It was shown in § 7.9 that the low frequency response of an amplifier depends on the coupling condensers and grid resistances. It is possible to obtain amplification down to about 1 c/s by choosing high values for these components (e.g. 2μF and 1 megohm), but if one attempts to go farther the amplifier becomes cumbersome and the protracted transient phenomena when it is switched on become intolerable. Fig. 7.20 shows how stages can be coupled directly, and amplification obtained down to zero frequency (D.C. response). Amplifiers with direct coupling are troublesome because any slow voltage drifts due to changes in power supplies or in the behaviour of valves are amplified and drive later valves of the amplifier to unfavourable parts of their characteristics. A particularly important effect is produced by changes in cathode temperature which alter the velocity distribution of electrons leaving the cathode and produce the same effect as changes in the grid-cathode voltage.*

---

* With the usual cathodes the change is about 0·1 V for a 10 % change in heater current ; spontaneous changes also occur during the life of a valve, more especially during the first 100 hours or so (see Valley and Wallman 1948).

Drift of this type can be minimised by careful stabilisation of the cathode heating current. A great improvement is obtained by designing the amplifier stages as balanced or push-pull circuits (§ 7.16). If the valves of a pair are identical and remain so, drift due to cathode changes disappears entirely. Valley and Wallman give data on how far it is reduced by using pairs of commercially identical valves or commercial twin triodes. The balanced circuits have the further advantage that large cathode resistances may be used without introducing

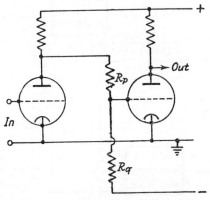

FIG. 7.20 Elementary two-stage amplifier with D.C. coupling. This form of coupling requires an additional negative voltage supply, and the signal voltage produced at an anode is attenuated between this point and the succeeding grid in the ratio $R_q/R_p + R_q$

degeneration. It is therefore possible to design a stage so that the steady cathode potential lies near the anode potential of the previous stage and direct coupling can be used simply.

Feedback may, of course, be used to stabilise the gain of a D.C. amplifier, following the principles of §§ 7.11, 12, but feedback does not reduce (relatively to the wanted signal) the voltage drifts discussed above. It may readily be shown that any voltage introduced into the first grid-cathode circuit is treated by the feedback amplifier just as if it were a signal. (For discussion of a very elaborate D.C. amplifier see Bishop and Harris 1950.)   (See also § 6.16.)

The chopper amplifier referred to on pages 210 and 211 is a drift-free D.C. amplifier but its high frequency response is seriously limited to frequencies much lower than the chopper frequency. If therefore amplification is needed at zero frequency and over a wide frequency band, it may be necessary to combine a chopper amplifier and a straight direct coupled amplifier. Fig. 7.21 indicates one way in which this can be done (Kandiah and Brown 1952). At high frequencies the chopper amplifier is inactive, gain is derived from the D.C. amplifier and is controlled by feedback to a D.C. connected

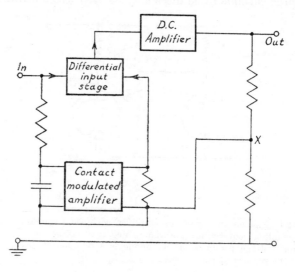

Fig. 7.21 Combined use of chopper amplifier and A.C. amplifier to give amplification from D.C. to high frequencies

differential input stage, the potential at the point X being balanced against the input signal voltage. At low frequencies the potential at point X is balanced against the input voltage by the chopper amplifier which has high gain and no drift, so that any slow drift in the D.C. amplifier or the input stage is removed.

An important application of these combination amplifiers is in analogue computers when they are used as " operational amplifiers " connected with appropriate feedback networks to give addition or integration of signal voltages.

7.18 The Valve as an Electrometer

Since the thermionic valve is a potential operated device it is in principle possible to make a D.C. amplifier which has a very high input impedance and which can be used instead of a sensitive electrometer. The combination of valve, power supplies and galvanometer may sometimes be more convenient than an electrometer of equivalent sensitivity. This use of valves is discussed in § 6.16.

7.19 Valve Oscillators

We have seen that a feedback amplifier becomes unstable if sufficient feedback is applied in the appropriate direction, and many important valve oscillators are in fact amplifiers arranged with positive feedback.

It is convenient to consider here three main types of these systems :

(1) Oscillators with tuned circuits containing inductance and capacity.

(2) Oscillators in which the feedback circuit is a network of resistances and capacities giving a phase shift of 180° at a particular frequency.

(3) Systems in which the amplifier and feedback system are sensibly aperiodic and the oscillator's behaviour is conditioned by some relaxation process (multivibrators, etc.).

7.20 Tuned Circuit Oscillators

Fig. 7.17 shows several representative tuned-circuit oscillators. In all these arrangements there is a tuned circuit containing inductance and capacity (often called the tank circuit). The frequency of free oscillation of this circuit is given approximately by $1/2\pi\sqrt{LC}$.

The valve connected to the circuit acts as a single stage amplifier, and feedback coupling in the correct sense is provided by an inductive link between grid and anode circuits. The arrangements of Fig. 7.22(a), (b), (c) are identical in principle, and the choice between them is made on practical grounds. An important practical point is the use of a circuit arrangement which allows the separation of the oscillatory circuit from the high voltage anode supply (Fig. 7.22(c)). In this arrangement the condenser, which has a low impedance at the high frequency, insulates the *LC* circuit from the steady component of the anode voltage, while the choke in the supply lead confines the high frequency energy to the tank circuit and its connections.

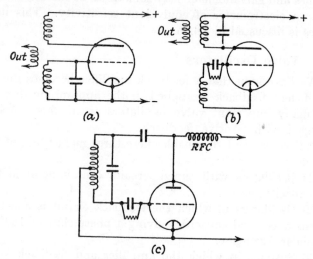

FIG. 7.22   Tuned-circuit valve oscillators

(a) Showing the tuned-grid circuit, is a simplified diagram only

(b) Showing the tuned-anode circuit, illustrates also the use of a grid leak and condenser to provide grid bias

(c) The Hartley circuit.   The figure shows also a convenient method of supplying the anode voltage while keeping the resonant circuit at a low steady potential.   *RFC* is a choke having a high impedance at the working frequency

In oscillators of this type (e.g. radio transmitters) it is usual to work the valve under class C conditions, i.e. to arrange the potentials so that anode current flows only for a small part of the signal cycle.*   The operation of the circuit is then

---

* The grid bias is conveniently obtained by inserting a condenser and high resistance leak in the grid circuit.   When the grid goes positive, grid current flows and charges this condenser.   At other times the condenser can discharge only through the leak, and the average potential of the grid therefore becomes negative to the cathode.   This negative bias increases when the amplitude increases, and stabilises the amplitude of oscillation.

analogous to that of a heavy pendulum maintained by properly timed impulses. The oscillations in the tank circuit go on with a frequency determined by the circuit constants ; and at the proper instant in each cycle, anode current is turned on to provide a maintaining impulse. It is clear that the wave-form can approximate to sinusoidal only if the oscillating energy in the circuit is large compared with the energy fed in at each impulse, and this in turn demands low damping in the tank circuit and a relatively small transfer of energy to any external load. These conditions are fairly easily met at radio frequencies ; they are most perfectly realised at high radio frequencies where the tuned circuit can take the form of a resonant transmission line. At low frequencies it is physically difficult to obtain a resonant circuit of low damping ; and in tuned-circuit audio-frequency oscillators it may be preferable to use the valve under something approaching linear conditions, giving positive feedback over the whole cycle. In an ideal linear system of this kind no limit would be set to the amplitude of the oscillations and in an actual circuit the amplitude goes on increasing until the positive feedback is reduced by the action of some non-linear element. Oscillators may be designed so that this limitation takes place with the minimum damage to the waveform. A typical device consists in decreasing the amount of feedback, e.g. by adjusting a resistance in the grid circuit by hand until oscillations only just start. As soon as grid current flows at the positive peaks of the grid cycle the additional energy loss limits the amplitude and the effect of this very small grid current on the tank circuit waveform is almost negligible.

7.21   The Resistance-Capacity Oscillator

A useful form of oscillator is obtained by providing an amplifier with a feedback network of resistances and condensers which gives at one particular frequency a phase change such that the fed-back signal assists the input. For a single valve amplifier the phase difference between anode and grid volt-ages is 180° and the feedback network produces a further 180° displacement (Fig. 7.23).

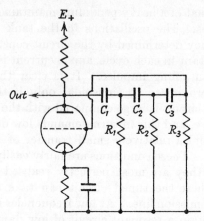

FIG. 7.23   Resistance-capacity phase-shift oscillator. For $R_1 = R_2 = R_3$; $C_1 = C_2 = C_3$, the frequency for which the phase-shift produced by the network between anode and grid is 180° is given by $n = 1/2\pi RC\sqrt{6}$. The amplitude attenuation produced by the network is 1/29, and the valve gives a voltage gain of 29 when the circuit is oscillating steadily. In an alternative network, resistances and capacities are interchanged. A three-gang variable condenser with one set of vanes connected together may then be used.

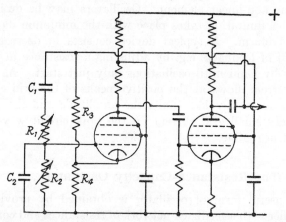

FIG. 7.24   Wien bridge oscillator. The bridge constitutes a positive feedback loop between the output and input of a two-valve amplifier. The frequency of oscillation is given by $a2\pi/\sqrt{R_1R_2C_1C_2}$ if the amplifier has no phase displacement. The mplitude of oscillation can be stabilised by giving R_3 a negative temperature coefficient (thermistor) or by giving R_4 a positive coefficient (glow-lamp)

262

For a two-valve amplifier, the feedback network is required to produce no phase change at the chosen frequency. It may take the form of a Wien bridge (Fig. 7.24).

In these oscillators also the amplitude is determined by the appearance of non-linear behaviour, and one very satisfactory way of securing steady amplitude and good waveform is the use of a non-ohmic resistance at a point where the feedback may be controlled. In Fig. 7.24 the resistance R_3 is a " thermistor " with a large negative temperature coefficient.

7.22   Aperiodic Feedback—Multivibrators

If an aperiodic feedback connection is arranged between the input and output of a two valve amplifier, a series of useful circuits may be obtained. Over a certain range of voltages any change impressed on the system is increased by the action of the amplifier and feedback, so that the change takes place at an accelerating rate and the circuits " snap over " into a new condition defined by some non-linear phenomenon.

If the couplings are made by resistances and condensers (Fig. 7.25) the circuit (multivibrator) has no permanently stable state.* Typical behaviour is illustrated by the set of waveforms in Fig. 7.26. Starting with a condition in which valve 1 is cut off by negative grid potential and valve 2 has its grid slightly positive, the grid g_1 leaks towards earth with a time constant approximately RC. As soon as anode current starts in V_1 a negative signal appears at a_1 and g_2 and begins to reduce the anode current of V_2. This results in a rise of potential of a_2 which is transferred to g_1 and starts the cumulative action. This goes on until some limiting condition is reached ; in fact V_2 cuts off, a_2 rises to a high potential, g_1 rises until it is checked by grid current with a_1 at a very low potential † and g_2 is left with a high negative potential which

---

* Some multivibrators are not self starting in the general case ; e.g. the circuit of Fig. 7.25 with the grid leaks returned to a positive potential may function as described, but there is an alternative stable régime in which both valves draw grid current and the gain round the loop is very low.

† The " overshoots " at XX in Fig. 7.26 are due to the fact that the grid cathode impedance of the valves is considerable. The grid goes therefore appreciably positive when the anode coupled to it is cut off. The overshoot produces a noticeable effect on all the waveforms of a simple multivibrator.

leaks away until the next transition is initiated. The operating cycle thus consists of rapid transitions (with ordinary triodes and circuits these may be completed in about 1 μs) linked by quasi-stable timing periods. It is clear that the repetition frequency depends on the properties of the valves (particularly on the grid voltage required for cut off) and on the voltages applied. The intrinsic frequency stability of the multivibrator is therefore poor. However, the oscillations may readily be synchronised with a periodic signal injected almost anywhere in the circuit, for if the injected signal occurs when the timing

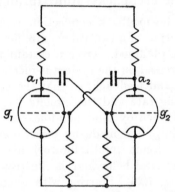

FIG. 7.25   Elementary multivibrator. In this form the circuit has no stable state and is free-running

period is nearing its end, it will be able to tip the circuit into its alternative state. This synchronisation may be adjusted to occur with the multivibrator running at 1, $\frac{1}{2}$, $\frac{1}{3}$, etc., the injection frequency. The multivibrator may therefore be used as a frequency divider.* It may also be used as a harmonic generator locked to a particular fundamental frequency, since its waveforms are very rich in overtones. Both applications are most valuable in frequency comparison and standardisation.

If one of the intervalve couplings is direct, and the other by resistances and condensers (Fig. 7.27), the circuit has one

---

* There are several frequency dividing circuits, e.g. the " Phantastron " and " Sanatron " which have better stability of division ratio than the multivibrator (see e.g. *Radiolocation* 1946).

stable state in which V_1 is cut off and V_2 is passing current. A short negative trigger pulse applied to the anode of V_1 or grid of V_2 begins the rapid cumulative change which leaves V_1 passing current and V_2 cut off by a negative grid potential

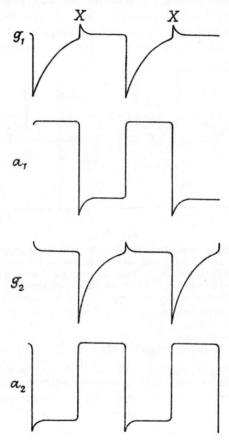

FIG. 7.26   Wave-forms from multivibrator of Fig. 7.25

which gradually leaks away. As soon as V_2 begins to conduct, the return stroke starts and the circuit snaps back to its stable condition. A circuit showing this behaviour is often called a flip-flop (univibrator, one-stroke multivibrator). It may be used to produce a pulse of fairly definite length from a very short trigger pulse. It is best to introduce the trigger pulse via a diode (Fig. 7.27(a)) which isolates the circuit from the triggering system except during the actual trigger pulse. The multivibrator of Fig. 7.25 may be used as a flip-flop if sufficient negative bias is applied to one of the valves to prevent recovery. In the circuit of Fig. 7.27(b) one of the required cross couplings is provided by a cathode resistor. V_2 is initially conducting and V_1 is cut off because its cathode potential

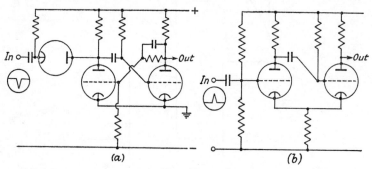

(a)   (b)

FIG. 7.27

   (a) Flip-flop or one-stroke multivibrator. This arrangement has one AC and one DC coupling, one stable state and one unstable state. Note the following feature to improve performance: (1) Triggering by negative impulses applied through diode. (2) Grid leak of V_2 returned to positive line, so that recovery of circuit is roughly linear

   (b) Flip-flop with one (AC) coupling from anode to grid, and one (DC) cathode coupling

is high. A positive trigger pulse on the grid of V_1 causes anode current to start in that valve. The grid potential of V_2 is reduced and the common cathode potential with it. This starts the cumulative action, which goes on until V_2 is cut off. Recovery takes place as in 26(a). A similar action takes place in the voltage comparator or discriminator circuit of p. 446.

If the amplifier is provided with two direct couplings suitably biased the circuit has two stable states and may be transferred from either one to the other by successive triggering impulses (Fig. 7.28). In this circuit, and in the circuit of Fig. 7.27 it is necessary to supplement the direct coupling with small coupling condensers to provide adequate transference of the fast impulses during the changeover process. These condensers are in fact essential to the completion of the transition between states, for in a system with purely resistive coupling the intermediate conditions would indeed be unstable, but the transition would go as readily backwards as forwards. The condensers between grids and opposite anodes superpose on the grids potentials which depend on the rate of change of the anode potentials and thereby preserve the direction of the

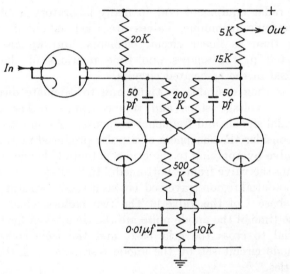

Fig. 7.28 Multivibrator with two DC couplings and two stable states. The circuit given is arranged as a scale-of-two counting stage (Higginbotham 1947). The steady potentials of input and output terminals are such that successive units of a cascade counter may be connected directly together

transition until it is completed. It is possible to see that the stray capacities between grids and the other electrodes of their own valves act in the contrary way. The grid-anode crossover condensers must therefore be made big enough to counterbalance the effect of the stray capacities.

The diode injection circuit of Fig. 7.28 ensures the isolation of the changeover circuit from the triggering circuit and also ensures that the triggering impulse is applied to the correct (more positive) grid and anode and not to the more negative grid and anode where it would oppose the changeover. This circuit is used as the characteristic element of " scale of two " counters for counting a rapid succession of impulses (e.g. from a Geiger counter in nuclear studies) since for every two negative impulses put into the circuit one negative impulse may be transferred to the next circuit through the coupling shown.

7.23 Pulse Operation of Valve Circuits *

In radar equipment and in many laboratory applications of electronic technique, valves are used as on-off switches rather than as linear circuit elements, and we are chiefly interested in the shapes and time relations of the pulses produced in the associated circuits.

It is then desirable to think and to calculate directly in terms of voltage steps and time-constants rather than of sinusoidal signals and frequency response. As an example we shall consider the sharpness of a pulse produced at the anode of a valve by applying to the grid a potential change sufficient to swing the valve from " bottomed " to " cut-off " conditions. (The potential region traversed between these two states is the " grid base " of the valve.) The two factors which control the rise time of the anode pulse are the time taken for the grid potential to cross the grid base, and the time constant of the anode circuit set by the anode resistance and the stray capacities.

If we are to have low anode capacity and a high anode current controlled by a small grid base we must use a high-slope pentode, and we shall obtain numerical data for an EF50 valve used to produce a sharp-edged square waveform from a 10 kc/s sine wave of 100 V amplitude (Fig. 7.29). By drawing a 50 kΩ load line across a set of anode characteristics it appears that the valve " bottoms " with its anode at about 20 V when the grid potential is anything above − 2·5 V and that the anode rises to over 200 V when the grid is at − 4 V. The grid base under these conditions may therefore be taken as 1·5 V. The rate of change of voltage for the 10 kc/s wave

---

* For an introductory account of the principles of pulse technique see Williams 1946, Farley 1955.

near zero is $100 . 2\pi . 10^4$ V/sec., so that the grid base is crossed in about $\frac{1}{4}$ μsec. The time constant of the anode circuit with $50\,k\Omega$ resistance and 20 pf. stray capacity is about 1 μsec., so

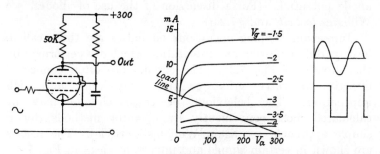

Fig. 7.29   Squaring circuit with load-line and wave-form diagrams

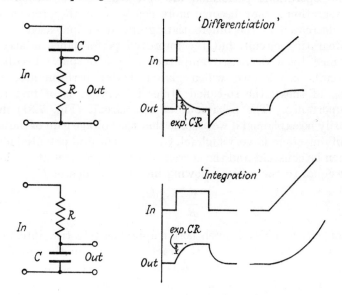

Fig. 7.30   " Differentiating " and " Integrating " circuits (so-called) with input and output wave-forms

that the steepness of the waveform is conditioned by the anode circuit. It appears that a slightly shorter rise time could be obtained by using a lower value of anode resistance, the grid base being lengthened but the anode time constant

K*   269

reduced. A much better performance could be obtained by the use of " catching " diodes connected between the anode and points of suitable steady potential to limit the excursions of anode potential. (For a discussion of the use of diodes, see Williams *loc. cit.* and § 7.24.)

Important shaping operations on pulses are those called, loosely, differentiation and integration which are performed by the circuits of Fig. 7.30. The circuits are often connected directly to valve grids, so that they work into high impedances. The behaviour of these circuits may be calculated most conveniently by operator methods (for a simple approach, see again Williams's article). The results are shown in certain simple and important cases in Fig. 7.30. The operations performed are not true differentiation and integration ; they become more nearly so as the product RC is decreased in the differentiating circuit or increased in the integrating circuit, but the improved performance is accompanied by a decreased amplitude of the output. Feedback circuits are known which give a better performance, and one of these, the so-called Miller integrator, is of first rate importance. The behaviour of this circuit (Fig. 7.31) may easily be explained if we assume that the voltage gain of the amplifying stage is very high (cf. § 7.13). The grid potential must then be constant and the current flowing in R must at all times be equal to the current flowing into the condenser C

$$-\frac{v_i}{R} = C\frac{dv_o}{dt}.$$

This circuit gives a much better approach to a true integrator than can be achieved with practical values in the circuit of Fig. 7.30. In particular if R is taken to a constant potential the change of potential at the anode is a linear function of time. With the addition of circuit elements for initiating and terminating the integrating action this circuit is a very valuable time base for cathode ray oscillographs and other purposes (see Williams and Moody 1946 ; Puckle 1951).

In the simplest applications of this kind R is taken to a positive potential v and the anode current is stopped by application of a negative voltage to the suppressor. The screen current is then large and must be limited by resistances. When the suppressor is allowed to rise to zero, anode current starts. There is a small sudden fall in anode potential which corresponds to a fall of the grid potential from its resting value near zero to a negative potential at which a little anode current flows, just sufficient to bring the anode potential to its new

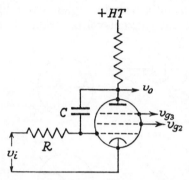

Fig. 7.31   The Miller integrator.   The valve is used as a high-gain voltage amplifier.   A high slope pentode is usually employed with an anode load about 50 kΩ

value. This is followed by the linear " run down ". During this period the current through R and the change of anode potential are connected by the equation given above. Since the grid potential changes very little during the run down, the current through R is constant and the fall in anode potential is linear. This process is terminated by the " bottoming " of the valve. It is easy to generate in this way a linear sweep of 100-200 V amplitude, and duration from microseconds to seconds depending on C, R, and v. The anode potential remains at a low value until the suppressor is again made negative : the anode then recovers with a time constant set by the anode load resistance and anode-earth capacity.

The timing circuits called the " Phantastron " and the " Sanatron " (Williams and Moody, *loc. cit.*) act in this way but provide means by which a single triggering impulse initiates the sweep, which then goes on independent of external control. They exist also in free running forms, which recover automatically and repeat the cycle indefinitely.

7.24   The Use of Diodes

Diodes are used rather freely in pulse technique to pass or reject pulses according to their polarity, and more generally to set limits to the voltage excursions of chosen points in a circuit. A small thermionic diode has a " forward resistance " of a few hundred ohms, a " backward resistance " nearly infinite, and an intermediate region extending over a volt or so in which the current-voltage characteristic is curved.

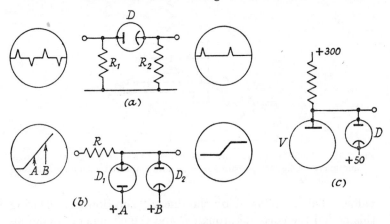

FIG. 7.32   Use of diodes

(a) Series diode used to separate positive-going pips from a mixture of positive and negative pips. The effect of the unsymmetrical current in the diode on the average potentials of the points to which it is connected must be taken into account

(b) Two parallel diodes used to select a portion of an applied wave-form between two potential levels. During the first part of the wave, diode D_1 conducts ; during the middle part both diodes are cut off ; and during the last part D_2 conducts

(c) Use of diode D to " catch " the anode of V at, e.g. 50v, when the anode current of V is cut off

Typical applications are shown in Fig. 7.32: a diode must be connected between circuit points of appropriate impedance, e.g. in Fig. 7.32(b), the resistance R must be large compared with the forward resistance of the diode, and the impedance in the circuits which supply the potentials $+A, +B$, must be small compared with R. The potentials at such points may be affected by the rectified current from a succession of pulses flowing in the impedances through which they are supplied, and such dispacements must be taken into account.

Semi-conductor diodes are now freely used in place of thermionic diodes (§ 7.26). They are very compact and require no cathode heating circuit. It is, however, necessary to take into account the limitation of backward voltage on these devices and in some applications to consider the leakage current which they allow to flow in the non-conducting direction and their properties of storing charge and liberating it as a current pulse on reversal of the voltage.

7.25   Very Rapid Pulses—Transmission Lines (Cf. § 1.14)

When rapid changes are not involved, we can regard as instantaneous the propagation of electrical changes along simple conductors, but in pulse operations the variations in voltage and current may be so rapid that transmission line theory must be used to calculate their propagation. On a simple air-spaced line, signals are propagated with the velocity of light, 10^{-9} sec. corresponds to 30 cm. distance, and these figures indicate the frequency limit at which we must abandon the approximate idea of circuits consisting of lumped elements connected by conductors in which changes are instantaneous.

A transmission line has a parameter called the "characteristic impedance" which represents the ratio of voltage to current at the entrance to a line prolonged to infinity. This impedance is resistive in the common case where the losses can be neglected. Unless a line is terminated in its characteristic impedance, reflected waves are produced at its termination and the power transfer to the terminating apparatus is less than optimum: similarly power should be fed into the line by a source of output impedance " matched " to that of the line.

The transmission lines which are used in many laboratory applications of fast pulse technique are concentric cables which for constructional and commercial reasons have characteristic impedances of the order 100 ohms. The most usual way of introducing a signal to such a cable is a cathode follower (§ 7.13) which works well if the pulse is positive-going. A simple

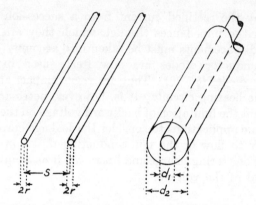

FIG. 7.33 Simple forms of transmission line

(a) Parallel-wire line.   Characteristic impedance $= 276 \log_{10} s/r$

(b) Concentric cylindrical line.   Characteristic impedance $= 138 \log_{10} d_2/d_1$.

When a line is immersed in a medium of dielectric constant k, the characteristic impedance is reduced in the ratio $1/\sqrt{k}$ and the speed of propagation of a signal is reduced in the same ratio

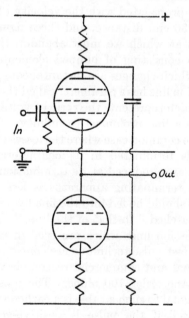

FIG. 7.34 The " White " cathode follower

274

cathode follower is not satisfactory with waveforms which contain rapid negative-going portions of considerable amplitude. The capacity connected with the cathode cannot change its charge instantaneously, so that current in the valve may be cut off if the grid goes rapidly negative. When the anode current is cut off, the cathode follower no longer acts as a low impedance: the capacity connected to the cathode can now only change charge through the cathode load resistance, with a time constant much longer than when the valve is in operation since $R_k \gg 1/g_m$. This limitation can be avoided by using more elaborate feedback circuits, such as the "White" cathode follower of Fig. 7.34. This circuit is often used to feed pulses into transmission lines; its output impedance is lower than that of a simple cathode follower and it will deal with pulses of either sign: it is not, however, immediately applicable to zero-frequency operation.

7.26 Semiconductor Electronics

In recent years electronic practice has been radically extended by the advent of semiconductor devices. Semiconductors are substances in which nearly all the electrons are made effectively immobile by their quantum properties: they inhabit a completely-filled structure of energy levels and cannot conduct electricity since they cannot change their velocities when an electric field is applied. There are, however, a few electrons thermally ionised into levels belonging to an unfilled band, and these electrons can take part in conduction (intrinsic conduction).

At present the semiconductors of greatest technical importance are the elements Germanium and Silicon in Group IV of the periodic table, and these acquire special properties if very pure crystals of the elements are "doped" with very small proportions (e.g. 1 atom in 10^8) of the elements of Group V (e.g. Sb) or Group III (e.g. In). The foreign atoms of Group V (donors) produce additional inhabited energy levels which are very easily ionised to give conduction electrons (n-type conductivity) while Group III additions provide energy levels into which electrons may easily be raised from the filled band of levels leaving mobile " positive holes " which can take part in electrical conduction (p-type conductivity).

Most of the useful semiconductor devices depend on the properties of junctions formed between p-type and n-type regions within a single semiconductor crystal. A p-n junction is shown diagramatically in Fig. 7.35.

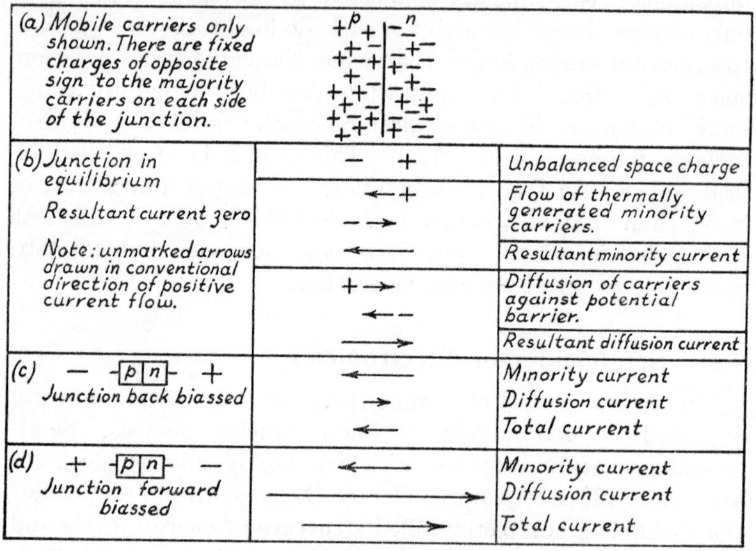

(a) Mobile carriers only shown. There are fixed charges of opposite sign to the majority carriers on each side of the junction.	+p+ | -n- + + - -+ - + -+ + - + + - +-+ + + - +-+ + -+ |+ -	
(b) Junction in equilibrium Resultant current zero Note: unmarked arrows drawn in conventional direction of positive current flow.	− +	Unbalanced space charge
	←−+ − →	Flow of thermally generated minority carriers.
	←	Resultant minority current
	+→ ←−	Diffusion of carriers against potential barrier.
	—→	Resultant diffusion current
(c) − -[p|n]- + Junction back biassed	←	Minority current
	→	Diffusion current
	←	Total current
(d) + -[p|n]- − Junction forward biassed	←	Minority current
	———→	Diffusion current
	——→	Total current

FIG. 7.35 Carrier flow in a p-n junction

The transition from p- to n-type material is supposed to be abrupt compared with the free path of the electron or hole. In the absence of an applied e.m.f. a few holes diffuse into the n region and a few electrons into p, so that the condition of electrical neutrality is upset locally and a space-charge barrier is produced which opposes further diffusion. The condition with no applied e.m.f. is one of dynamic equilibrium: carriers diffuse against the potential barrier and eventually recombine with carriers of opposite sign, and this current is balanced by a flow of minority carriers (i.e. electrons produced in p and holes in n) which are produced by intrinsic thermal ionization not involving the impurity levels. These cross the junction in a down-potential direction. If an e.m.f. is applied between the two regions in the backward direction shown in Fig. 7.35(c), there is no appreciable change in the minority flow which is controlled by the rate at which carriers are generated. The junction therefore behaves as a region of high resistance and most of the applied e.m.f. appears across it: the potential barrier is raised, and fewer of the diffusing majority carriers can cross it. There is thus a small unbalanced current, which has a saturation value equal to the minority carrier flow when the potential is enough to stop the diffusion flow. At a high reverse voltage there is a rapid increase in reverse current, due

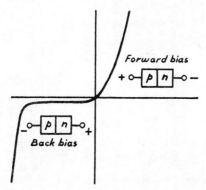

FIG. 7.36 Behaviour of a p-n junction

to other processes. For a given junction this increase is consistent and reversible: its incidence can be controlled by preparation of the p and n material and it is applied in certain voltage-controlling elements (breakdown, or so-called Zener, diodes).

If the e.m.f. is applied in the forward direction, the potential barrier at the junction is lowered, and the majority current rises rapidly with the applied e.m.f. The current-voltage characteristic of the junction is shown in Fig. 7.36, and the behaviour in the neighbourhood of zero applied voltage can be calculated quite accurately by developing quantitatively the ideas just set forth.

Diodes based on the properties of p-n junctions are used both as power rectifiers and as unidirectional conductors in

TABLE 7.2

Class of device	Name	Material	Electrical characteristics		Frequency
Power rectifiers	Junction rectifier	Ge Si	300 V peak inverse 100 V 200-600 V 200-600 V 300 V 1500 V	0.5-50 A forward current 500 A 0.5 A 3 A 100 A 0.3 A	power
	Controlled rectifier	Si p-n-p-n	400 V	3 A	
Signal diodes	Point contact diode	Ge	100 V peak inverse 25 V	30 mA forward current 30 mA	5 Mc/s 200 Mc/s
	Gold-bonded diode	Ge	100 V	100 mA	
	Microwave crystal point contact	Si	3 V	50 mA	3-30 Gc/s
	Sub-miniature junction	Si	100 V 180 V	20 mA 100 mA	10 Mc/s
Voltage reference diodes	"Zener" diodes	Si	~ 6 V	0.25 A	
Voltage regulating diodes		Si	4.75 V	Up to 75 W	
Germanium transistors	Small Signal	Ge p-n-p n-p-n	Collector 20 V Voltage	Dissipation 80 mW	Audio frequencies
	Power	Ge p-n-p	30-100 V	Up to 75 W	
	High frequency	Ge p-n-p	20-50 V	Typically 80 mW	Tpyical f_1 10 Mc/s
	H.F. Power	Ge p-n-p	30-70 V	1-5 W	f_1 up to 350 Mc/s
Silicon transistors	Small Signal	Si p-n-p Si n-p-n	15-60 V 50 V	100 mW 150 mW	Typical f_1 3 Mc/s „ 100 Mc/s
	Power	Si n-p-n	50-100 V	120 mW	„ 2 Mc/s
	Planar construction	Si n-p-n	20-90 V	250-1000 mW	f_1 up to 350 Mc/s

signal circuits: Table 7.2. based on a review article by Hibberd
(1959) and revised 1964, indicates some of the available devices.

As power rectifiers, silicon and germanium diodes are compact and have very high efficiency over a wide voltage range:
unlike vacuum valve rectifiers they are not self-protecting
against short circuit currents or surge voltages, and are rapidly
destroyed by them. Vacuum rectifiers may therefore still be
preferable for certain laboratory applications where efficiency
is unimportant and abuse probable.

7.27 Transistors

An important device, the triode transistor, consists of a
thin layer of one type of semi-conductor separating two
regions of the other type. These regions must be formed

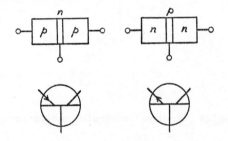

FIG. 7.37 Diagrammatic representation and conventional symbols for triode
junction transistors

within a single crystal: they are manufactured by several
different processes in germanium and in silicon in both n-p-n
and p-n-p configurations.* The arrangement and its usual
symbols are indicated in the diagram Fig. 7.37. The transistor
may be regarded as two p-n diodes back to back, separated by a
region thin compared with the free path of the carriers. The
diode formed by base and collector is biased in the reverse
direction, and passes very little current when the emitter is
open circuited. The current which flows between collector
and base with the emitter open circuited, though small,† may

---

* The p-n-p configuration, which is more easily prepared in germanium,
will be assumed in descriptive illustration below unless otherwise stated.

† It is usually denoted by I_{co}.

have important effects (cf. § 7.28). Since it is controlled by the generation of minority carriers this current is very sensitive to temperature: at a given temperature it is much smaller in silicon than in germanium transistors, since the energy gap between filled and unfilled energy bands is much greater in silicon than in germanium.

Carriers of minority sign may be passed into the base by applying an e.m.f. of appropriate sign between base and emitter, and in a normal transistor most of them reach the collector,

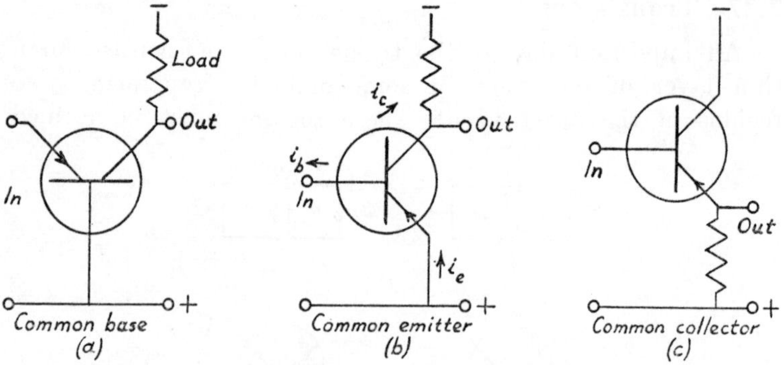

FIG. 7.38 The three fundamental transistor circuits

giving rise to a current slightly smaller than the emitter current, since a few carriers are lost by recombination. The ratio of these currents, under steady conditions, is usually denoted by α and commonly lies between 0·95 and unity. The impedance of the collector-base path is much greater than that of the emitter-base circuit, as can be inferred from the diode characteristics of Fig. 7.36, so that the arrangement of Fig. 7.38(a), called the common base transistor circuit, can act as a power amplifier in which an input current at a low voltage controls a slightly smaller current at a much higher voltage. Since this circuit gives no current gain it cannot be used in an iterative multi-stage arrangement unless step-down transformers are used between the stages to turn the power gain into current gain.

If the (current) input signal is applied to the base, and the collector current returned via a load resistance and, say, a battery to the emitter (common emitter circuit) as in Fig. 7.38(*b*), we have

$$i_e = i_b + i_c$$
$$i_c = \alpha i_e$$
$$i_c = \alpha i_b / 1 - a = a' i_b$$

Since α is not far from unity, this arrangement can give current amplification as well as the power gain which comes from the high impedance of the collector-base junction. The common emitter circuit is the foundation of many useful transistor applications: the input resistance is of the order 1000 ohms

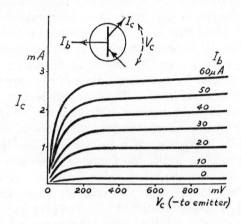

FIG. 7.39 Output characteristics for a transistor in common emitter circuit
(from makers' data for Mullard OC71)

and varies considerably with the current, so that non-linear distortion occurs unless the source impedance is high and provides an essentially current input. The output characteristics are of the general form of Fig. 7.39. It will be seen that these have some similarity to those of a pentode (Fig. 7.12(*b*)), since they show a high output impedance and " bottoming " below the knees of the curves.

The third possible arrangement is the common-collector circuit of Fig. 7.38(*c*). In this circuit the ouput voltage across the emitter load appears as negative feedback in the voltage-sensitive emitter-base path, and the arrangement has properties recalling those of a cathode follower (§ 7.13, p. 249). It is called an emitter follower. The input impedance is increased and the output impedance is low, though the input impedance depends on the output load and the output impedance on the impedance of the input source. These effects are absent or negligible in a valve circuit.

Because the behaviour of a transistor is controlled by the input current rather than the applied voltage, the circuit calculations are more complicated and the input impedance is not independent of the impedances in the output circuit. Moreover, there is interaction between the voltage of the collector and the current in the circuit in a common emitter transistor amplifier (cf. the thermionic triode). It is sometimes useful to neutralise this effect by appropriately connected feedback elements.

The high frequency behaviour of transistor circuits is frequently limited by the transit time of the carriers moving across the transistor itself. The gain obtained from a circuit is reduced at high frequencies and the phase of the signal is displaced. Several alternative quantities are in use to define the frequency limitations of a transistor. The frequency f_α is the frequency at which the common-base current factor α falls to 0·7 of its low frequency value ;* the frequency f_1 is that at which the gain of a (common emitter) stage falls to unity, and this is practically identical with f_τ the gain-bandwidth product for the stage. Much progress is being made in improving the high frequency behaviour of transistors and $f_1 = 400$ Mc/s is now easily obtainable.

7.28 Transistor Circuits—Amplifiers

A few circuits of laboratory interest will now be described qualitatively in order to introduce the special features of transistor electronics. The systematic design of many transistor circuits is discussed in Shea (1957) and elsewhere.

---

* The frequency limitation of the same transistor in a common-emitter circuit is more severe than this: the cut off frequency in common-emitter is approximately $1/a'$ times the cut off frequency for common-base operation.

Many transistor circuits contain special provision to stabilise the average values of current and potential about which the signal excursions occur. The properties of transistors are affected by rather large manufacturing tolerances; they change markedly with temperature; and as with valves, the differential parameters change when the average currents are altered. There is a special difficulty which arises in common-emitter circuits if the base circuit has a high impedance; A small leakage current due to minority carriers flows between collector and base as in any reverse biased diode: the resulting

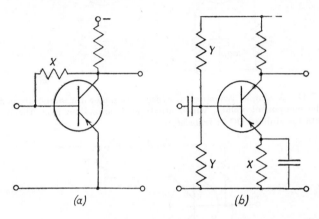

(a)   (b)

Fig. 7.40   D.C. stabilisation by feedback elements XX and potentiometer network YY

change in the potential difference between base and emitter causes an emitter current to flow which is considerably larger than the original leakage current.   If this gives rise to heating of the junction the minority current will be further increased, and the average current will be greatly disturbed from the required value.   In certain cases the increase in current may become divergent and the effects disastrous (thermal runaway).

Conditions can be stabilised by providing D.C. feedback in the proper direction (Fig. 7.40) and by supplying the base voltage from a potentiometer network of moderate impedance. Stabilising networks on these lines will be found in the circuits of Figs. 7.41, 7.43.   In common-base circuits the effects of minority currents are not cumulative and D.C. stabilisation may not be required.

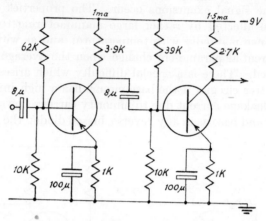

FIG. 7.41   A simple two-stage transistor amplifier for audio frequencies. The component values, which are typical, are taken from the makers' data for Mullard OC 71 transistors

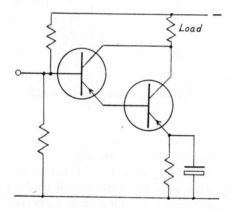

FIG. 7.42   Compound-connected common-emitter amplifying stage

Low-frequency amplification can be obtained in a resistance-coupled common-emitter circuit (Fig 7.41) which has an obvious affinity with the RC-coupled valve circuit of Fig. 7.11. The impedances throughout the circuit are much lower, since the transistor stage is essentially current-operated; the capacities of coupling and bypass condensers are larger than in the comparable valve circuit. The effective output capacitance of a transistor is fairly large and acts as a shunt to the coupling resistor (cf. § 7.9), so that the amplification is reduced at high frequencies as in a valve amplifying stage. This effect limits the stage gain for a given bandwidth, since the collector load resistance cannot be made arbitrarily large. There is also a frequency limitation peculiar to transistors, represented in order of magnitude by the common-emitter cut-off frequency: in a practical amplifier these two limitations may occur at about the same frequency. Transistors are now available which may be used for wide-band amplification up to several Mc/s; in wide-band amplifiers high-frequency compensation may be applied by using inductance in the coupling circuits.

A higher gain can be obtained from a common-emitter stage by transformer coupling, the disadvantages incurred being the cost, weight, and frequency limitations of the transformers. Step-down transformers may also be used to couple transistors operating in the common-base connection with current gain nearly unity. The transistors then act as impedance converters and the current gain of the amplifier depends almost entirely on the transformer characteristics. The gain is therefore very stable, and the arrangement is well adapted for laboratory amplifiers with well defined gain e.g. chopper amplifiers. Mullard (1960b) have published a symmetrical push-pull circuit of this kind in which the transformers carry no steady magnetic flux.

The amplifier stages so far considered deal with small signals, and the power-handling limits of the transistors are not approached: amplifiers must often be terminated in stages which handle considerable power and transfer it efficiently to external circuits. Since transistors, unlike valves, give only moderate power amplification, the driving stage preceding an output stage must often be designed for power handling. The coupling between them can be by transformer in audio-frequency applications. The directly connected arrangement of Fig. 7.42, called the compound or tandem connection, is valuable as a power handling device of particularly high input impedance and good linearity: it is used for example in the circuits of Fig. 7.45. In these circuits the output current is divided between the transistors in a rather complicated way, which varies over a signal cycle. Common base and common collector (emitter follower) versions of the compound circuit are also available. Symmetrical push-pull arrangements are often used in transistor power stages because they spread the power over two transistors and reduce distortion. Low power consumption is often sought in transistor equipment and high power efficiency is obtained (at the expense of some distortion) by biasing a push-pull pair to give "class B" operation

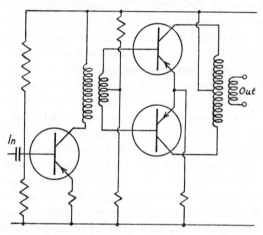

Fig. 7.43   Audio-frequency push-pull output stage using transformers

(cf. p. 245). Each transistor of the pair operates at very low current in the absence of a signal and each handles alternate half cycles of a signal: the bias voltage applied to the emitters must be such as to give a smooth transfer between the two transistors. Harmonics of any even order are cancelled by the symmetry of the arrangement. Fig. 7.43 shows a push-pull pair using a coupling transformer to produce the phase inverted inputs; resistance coupled phase-inverting networks are also possible, though it is necessary to design the couplings to take account of the relatively low input impedance of the power transistors and the fact that in class B operation the emitter-base paths of these transistors appear as diodes used over a rectifying part of the characteristics. A push-pull circuit may be designed to make use of " complementary " *p-n-p* and *n-p-n* transistors (Fig. 7.44). This kind of symmetrical circuit is of course impossible with thermionic valves. There are other applications (see Figs. 7.45, 7.46, 7.48) in which complementary transistors allow direct coupling to be used without the complications which would appear in supplying the electrode potentials to a direct-coupled series of valves (or non-complementary transistors).

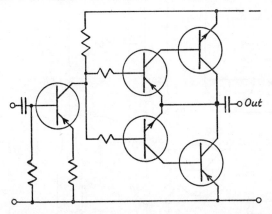

FIG. 7.44   Push-pull output system using complementary transistors, which allow the penultimate transistors to be coupled directly both to the preceding and the final stages

In output stages and other applications of high-power transistors it is important to dissipate the energy lost in the transistor without producing an undue rise in temperature. Power transistors are designed so that the semiconductors are in good thermal contact with the casing and so that the casing can be mounted to make good contact with a " heat sink ", normally a relatively large plate of well-conducting metal. The makers of transistors make recommendations in which the permissible power dissipation is related to the efficiency of the sink.

7.29   Transistor Circuits—Laboratory Control Circuits

Transistors are well adapted to the task of controlling unidirectional currents at moderate voltages.   They can be used for this purpose in power units for supplying constant voltage (or constant current) to transistor equipment or valve heaters, and on a larger scale to electromagnets. They can also be used, for example to regulate the filament current of an ionisation gauge to give constant emission. Such units consist of a power-handling stage controlled by an error amplifier in which a

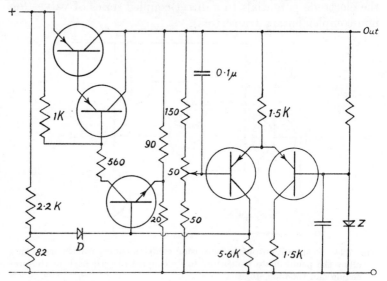

FIG. 7.45 Stabilising circuits for a power-supply unit. Note use of compound-connected power stage, complementary transistor as intermediate amplifier, and long-tailed pair as low-level amplifier. The diode Z is the voltage reference, the diode D prevents the system from going into a stable state with zero output

control system is balanced against a reference voltage provided by a battery, a discharge tube, or a semiconductor " Zener " diode.

The power stage may be a single large transistor or a group of transistors connected in parallel; a compound-connected group is often the best arrangement. The stability achieved is limited by the temperature variations of the reference element and the small-signal amplifying transistors: these elements may be enclosed in a small constant-temperature block if high performance is required. It is also advantageous to use self-compensating amplifying circuits like the "long-tailed pair" and to employ silicon transistors in the low-level stages. Sample designs for stabilising circuits are given in

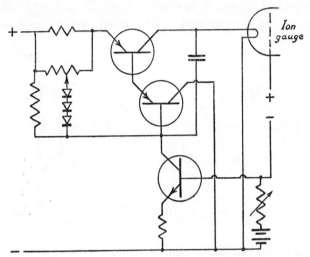

FIG. 7.46 Emission controller for filament of ionisation gauge (Holmes 1957, *Rev. Sci. Inst.* **28**, 290). The emission current is balanced against a regulable, stable current from a battery. The first amplifier uses a complementary transistor, coupled by an emitter-follower to the power transistor. A large condenser destroys the high-frequency response in the interest of stability. An additional control, derived from the main current through the diodes prevents runaway on switching on before the control derived from emission comes into operation.

Figs. 7.45, 7.46: such circuits usually contain elements to reduce the gain at high frequencies so as to avoid oscillations due to phase displacement producing positive feedback.

7.30 Transistor Circuits—Oscillators

Transistor amplifiers, like the corresponding valve circuits, can be provided with positive feedback and used to generate oscillations. The feedback can be provided by tuned L-C circuits, by frequency-sensitive R-C networks, or by aperiodic circuits giving rise to relaxation oscillations; transistors may also be used with quartz crystals as resonant elements to form oscillators of high frequency stability.

Fig. 7.47 shows types of the L-C oscillator; design manuals should be consulted for the circuit details and for modifications to improve the frequency stability, which is in the simplest circuits rather dependent on temperature and on supply voltage. The amplitude of oscillation is determined by the non-linearity

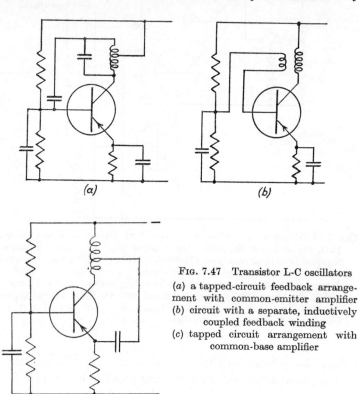

FIG. 7.47   Transistor L-C oscillators

(a) a tapped-circuit feedback arrangement with common-emitter amplifier

(b) circuit with a separate, inductively coupled feedback winding

(c) tapped circuit arrangement with common-base amplifier

of the transistor characteristics; in many oscillators the transistor " bottoms " at the extremes of the signal cycle, with a very small voltage between collector and base, but it may be preferable to adjust the electrode potentials to avoid this condition.   The most stable performance is obtained by arranging a special amplitude-control circuit as in Fig 7.48.

Fig. 7.48 shows a Wien bridge as the frequency-sensitive feedback circuit (cf. § 7.21), and as in the valve circuit of Fig. 7.24, a temperature sensitive resistor (thermistor) is used to stabilise the amplitude of oscillation.

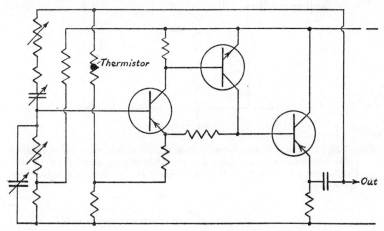

Fɪɢ. 7.48 Transistor version of Wien-bridge oscillator

7.31   Transistor Circuits—Relaxation Oscillators and Derivatives

The simple multivibrator using transistors (Fig. 7.49) is closely similar, in configuration and operation, to the valve circuit

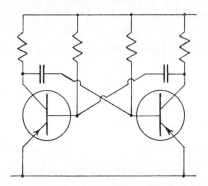

Fɪɢ. 7.49   A stable multivibrator

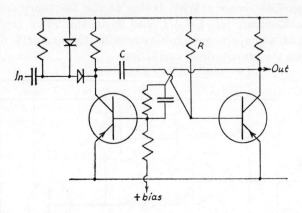

Fig. 7.50 Monostable transistor circuit which is triggered by a positive pulse and returns to its original state after a time determined by *RC*. Diodes are provided to isolate the trigger circuit from the subsequent operations

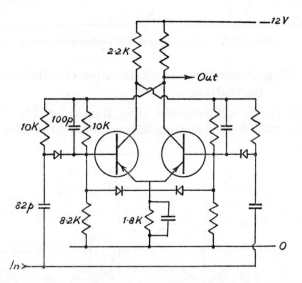

Fig. 7.51 Bistable transistor circuit arranged as scale-of-two counting element. (Details from Bradshaw, *Electronic Engineering*, **31**, 96, 1959.) The input pulses pass through " steering diodes "; the other diodes limit the base excursions in the interest of fast operation. Operation at 1 Mc/s is obtained with suitable transistors

of Fig. 7.25. If the circuit is symmetrical and the base resistors return to the supplying line as shown, a symmetrical square wave form is produced at the collectors, and the duration of one of the states is given roughly by $RC \log_e 2 = 0.7\ RC$. The duration of the transitions, which are assumed to be short-lived compared to the quasi-stationary states, depends on the transistors employed. Fig. 7.50 shows the circuit altered to give one stable and one quasi-stable state, so that it has the properties of the flip-flop described in § 7.22, Fig. 7.51 is a bistable circuit which can be used as a scale-of-two counter with resolution limited by the transistors used (a few tenths of a microsecond in 1960). As in the corresponding valve circuits the successive pulses are applied to the circuit through steering diodes.

7.32 Comparison of Transistors and Valves

In present-day laboratory practice, transistors have the following advantages over valves.

(a) The power requirements and power dissipation are much less than those of valves performing the same functions. The first consideration is specially important in portable apparatus, especially when it may be required to run for long periods on self-contained power supplies: the second becomes very important in complicated and compact apparatus such as computers.

(b) It is almost certain that transistor equipment is more reliable than valve equipment, since transistors are mechanically robust, there is no cathode deterioration, and other components benefit when less heat is dissipated in their surroundings.

(c) In some applications, e.g. the stabilisation of a magnet current, the low-voltage, low-impedance characteristics of transistors are inherently more appropriate than the high-voltage, low-current characteristics of valves. It is also true that small voltage changes and low impedances are favourable for very rapid operations in pulse technique, but advance in this direction has had to wait for the development of transistors with very fast internal response. At the moment, transistors are ahead of valves in circuits with fast pulse response, though not in circuits in which continuous oscillations are performed at very high frequency, for in such circuits capacities are tuned with inductances and the internal processes of the valves dominate the high frequency behaviour.

On the other hand, transistor circuits often contain more components than their valve equivalents, and they are harder to design because of their temperature sensitivity and internal feedback (§ 7.27). They are difficult to use effectively in conjunction with high-impedance devices like photocells or ionisation chambers, and they introduce considerably more noise into the circuits (§ 10.6). High power-handling ability and high frequency response are also antagonistic in transistor technique, and likely to remain so for some time.

APPENDIX

Relay Systems

The relays and auxiliary apparatus developed for use in telephone exchanges are extremely versatile devices which often find laboratory applications in automatic controls and simple computing systems. The basic instrument is the relay (P.O. type 3000 ; P.O. type 600 is a smaller and simpler variety) (see Cohen 1947). The relay consists of a coil, an iron magnetic circuit including a movable armature, and a great variety of alternative contact systems which can be assembled on the frame and operated by the armature. The coil can be wound with any number of turns T, normally specified by the resistance R. For the type 3000 relay, $T^2 = 250,000 \, R$ approximately. The maximum power dissipation of the type 3000 coils is 7 W, and the minimum power for reliable operation depends on the number of contacts used : it is about 1/20 W for the simplest single contact. The contact assemblies used provide for simple make, simple break, changeover, or make followed by break.

The time of operation (make of a contact) of a standard Post Office relay with full excitation is of the order 25 millisec., but there is a Siemens high speed relay with simple make and break contacts which releases within 0·5 millisec. and completes its operation in about 1·2 millisec. High-performance relays of a more elaborate sort are made for telegraphic purposes.

It is possible to delay the action of relays by placing blocks of copper (slugs) on the core; this device is used in telephone practice to allow time for one relay to operate before another. Delays up to about ½ sec. can be obtained by slugs, and by placing the slug at the proper point in the magnetic

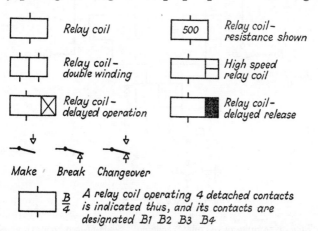

FIG. 7.52 Conventional symbols for relay circuits. For a complete list see BS. 530/1948—*Symbols for Telecommunications*.

circuit, either the operation or the release of the relay can be controlled without much effect on the other. A device which is sometimes useful in laboratory work is to delay the release of a relay by putting a large condenser, with or without a series resistance, across a (high resistance) coil.

The design of relay circuits is aided by the device of drawing them with the coils and the separate contacts in convenient parts of the diagram, the coils and contacts being connected by a numerical key. This convention is in general use (Fig. 7.52) (see B.S. 530/1948 for symbols).

One of the main circuit devices used in relay circuit design is the lock-on; a relay is operated by making an external circuit, and itself closes contacts which keep it energised until another pair of contacts is opened as a later operation.

In some of the more elaborate circuits the relay coil is provided with two separate windings. Fig. 7.53 shows how relays can be used to form a two-state system in which successive impulses transfer the system from one state to the other. Such a system can be used as a scale-of-two counter, though it does not, of course, compete in speed with the valve circuits

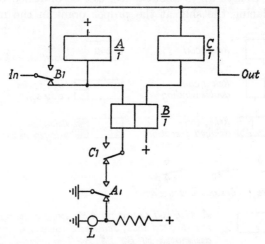

Fig. 7.53 Example of a relay scheme. Scale-of-two counting circuit, operated by applying " earth " at *IN*. All relays initially released
Sequence of operations :—

Earth ON.   *A* operates, indicator lamp *L* lights
    OFF.   *A* remains operated, *B* operates
    ON.   *C* operates, *A* releases, *B* remains operated, *L* goes out, " earth " signal to next stage at *OUT*
    OFF.   *B*, *C* release, earth removed from *OUT*

of § 11.14. The property is, however, one which is often useful in control systems. Relays are often valuable in conjunction with thermionic valves. The latter normally handle small currents in rather high impedance circuits, but they can work relays which carry heavy currents (up to 300 mA at 50 V on normal contacts, up to 1000 mA at 50 V on platinum contacts of normal design, up to 5 A at 230 V A.C. on special contacts) (see Hunt 1946).

Spark quenching circuits are required to increase the life and reliability of the contacts and to suppress high frequency disturbances. Typical circuits have a 1 μF condenser in series with a resistance (1100 ohms for platinum contacts, less for silver contacts) connected across the break. Non-linear devices such as small selenium rectifiers or composition disks whose resistance decreases with applied voltage are also valuable. The latter are available under trade names like " Thyrite ", " Metrosil ".

In addition to straightforward relays, the piece of telephone equipment called a uniselector or stepping switch has been used in laboratory work. The switch consists of a number of electrically insulated arms moving over banks of contacts, driven by an electromagnet pawl and ratchet wheel. With each electrical impulse the arms move from one set of contacts to the next (the changeover takes place on the make or break of the magnet current according to the detailed construction of the switch). The electromagnet is provided with a special contact which may be used after the manner of an electric bell, preferably with an intermediate relay to deal with the rather heavy magnet current. The switch then steps continuously from contact to contact until the circuit is interrupted. This device is useful particularly to return the switch to a home or zero contact at the end of one cycle of operations so that it may be ready for the next.

CHAPTER 8

OPTICS AND PHOTOGRAPHY

8.1 Optics and Photography

Optical systems are often required in physical experiments, and in this section we discuss the choice of systems for certain purposes. It is convenient to divide the properties of optical systems into two groups, the formation of images and the control of illumination. In some applications, e.g. condensers, searchlight projectors, illumination is of leading importance, while in other cases a more or less perfect optical image is required.

8.2 Illumination

Table 8.1 contains a selection of definitions and units required in the study of illumination. It must be remembered that the definitions of luminous quantities are based fundamentally on visual comparison of illuminations, and that measurements of radiation made in other ways must be compared with them on the basis of the visual sensations of an agreed observer (see § 8.9). The results obtained in §§ 8.3, 8.4 are, however, essentially geometrical, and could be discussed in terms of energy flux, or energy flux weighted in accordance with some spectral distribution, just as well as luminous quantities.

8.3 Brightness of an Object

The brightness of an element of surface, as appreciated by the eye, might be expected to depend on the illumination of the retinal image of the element. If the surface brightness of the source as defined in Table 8.1 is B, the flux into the eye from element dS is

$BdS \cdot \dfrac{a}{r^2}$ where a is the area of the pupil and r the distance from the source to eye. This flux is spread over an area of retina proportional to $\dfrac{ds}{r^2}$ the solid angle subtended by the element at the eye. The area a depends on the condition of the eye and the brightness of the visual field, but we may

TABLE 8.1

Quantity	Unit	Definition
Luminous intensity	Candle	Measures the illuminating power of a light source in a particular direction. Defined by comparison (fundamentally visual) of illuminating power with that of a standard, using a distance great compared with the dimensions of the source.
Brightness (of a source)	Candle per sq. cm. (Stilb)	Brightness of a source in a given direction is the candle power per unit area projected normal to that direction. This is constant if surface follows the cosine law, § 8.3. See note for definition of " lambert ".
Luminous flux	Lumen	Light emitted per unit solid angle by a source which has an intensity of 1 candle in the appropriate direction. A source of 1 candle radiating uniformly in all directions emits 4π lumens.
Illumination	Foot-candle Metre-candle (lux) Cm.-candle (phot)	Illumination of a surface on which light falls normally from a source of intensity 1 candle, 1 foot (metre, centimetre) away. An equivalent quantity is the luminous flux (lumens) which falls on 1 sq. ft. (metre, centimetre) of a surface.
		Note that if the light is incident at an angle θ, the illumination from a given source at a given distance is reduced in the ratio: $\cos\theta$; this is a purely geometrical result since the luminous flux is spread over an area bigger in the ratio $\cos\theta : 1$.

A surface of unit brightness, which emits according to the cosine law, emits 4π lumens per sq. cm. (in all directions).

A perfect diffuse reflector exposed to an illumination of 1 lumen/sq. cm. has a brightness of $1/\pi$ candles/sq. cm. (1 lambert) (§ 8.3).

One watt, completely converted into light of wavelength 5500 A.U. (at the maximum sensitivity of the normal eye), corresponds to a flux of 680 lumens.

use as a measure of brightness for comparative purposes *the light received per unit area of pupil per unit solid angle subtended by the source.*

In the case considered, this quantity is simply B, and it is independent of the distance between source and eye. This is in accordance with the observation that a brightness match between two luminous surfaces is unaffected by altering their distances from the eye.

It is found that many self-luminous surfaces appear equally bright when seen from any angle.* The light emitted per unit angle per unit area of *projected* surface is therefore independent of angle, and the light emitted per unit solid angle per unit area of actual surface is proportional to $\cos \theta$ (Fig. 8.1). It must be noted that this cosine law is an experimental characteristic of particular surfaces, and not a geometrical relation like the cosine law of illumination (Table 8.1). Many " matt " surfaces illuminated by a beam of light follow the cosine law approximately, and a perfectly diffuse reflector may be defined as one which follows it accurately, and which absorbs none of the light which falls on it. It follows that if a perfectly diffuse reflector † is illuminated with E lumens per sq. cm., and the resulting brightness is B candles/sq. cm., of projected area, the flux emitted in the normal direction is B lumens per sq. cm. per unit solid angle and the total flux emitted is

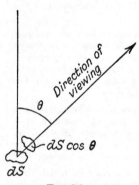

FIG. 8.1

$$\int_0^{\pi/2} 2\pi \, B \cos \theta \sin \theta d\theta = \pi B = E,$$

so that B for such a surface is E/π candles/sq. cm. (E lamberts).

---

* This result is a consequence of thermodynamic argument in the case of a *black* body—in other cases it must be tested by experiment. A red hot metal sphere appears as a uniform disk but the brightness of the edge of the sun's disk is much less than that of the central part (limb darkening).

† A surface coated with magnesium oxide by smoking over burning magnesium ribbon is the best experimentally realisable diffuse reflector.

8.4 Brightness of an Image

If an optical system is used to form an image of a luminous object two different aspects of the brightness of the image may be important according to circumstances.*

(a) If the image is received on a photographic plate or on a diffusely reflecting screen, the important quantity is the luminous flux falling on unit area of the image.

If the brightness of the object is B (candles/cm.²) and it radiates according to the cosine law, then an element of area ds_1 radiates to the lens (Fig. 8.2).

$$\int_0^{\alpha_1} B2\pi ds_1 \cos \alpha \sin \alpha \, d\alpha = \pi B ds \sin^2 \alpha_1.$$

If the transmission losses of the lens are neglected all this light is received by an image of area ds_2, so that the illumination of the image is

$$\pi B ds_1 \sin^2 \alpha_1 / ds_2$$

If the optical system fulfils the sine condition

$$n_1 h_1 \sin \alpha_1 = n_2 h_1 \sin \alpha_2$$

we have for the case where $n_1 = n_2$

$$h_1 \sin \alpha_1 = h_2 \sin \alpha_2, \quad ds_1 \sin^2 \alpha_1 = ds_2 \sin^2 \alpha_2$$

so that the illumination is

$$\pi B \sin^2 \alpha_2$$

A simple and important application of this result is to a photographic lens. In the common case where the object distance is large and the image is formed near the focal plane, the illumination of the plate is approximately proportional to $\dfrac{D^2}{f^2} = \dfrac{1}{F^2}$ where D is the diameter of the exit pupil of the lens and f is its focal length. F is the "f number" or "stop number" of the lens.† It is convenient to speak of a lens as "faster" or "slower" if it has a greater or less value of $\dfrac{D}{f}$.

---

* In systems which employ photoelectric detectors, a third quantity—the total energy in the beam—may be the significant parameter.

† It should be noted that in photographing relatively near objects the magnification, as well as the aperture of the lens, affects the intensity of the image.

(*b*) If the image is viewed by an eye placed behind it, the important quantity in determining its brightness is the light transmitted per unit solid angle through unit area of the image, for this quantity is equal to the amount of light received by unit area of the eye from unit solid angle of the image seen. This is in line with the definition of brightness in Table 8.1 and with the treatment of § 8.3.

It may be shown, under rather general assumptions, that the image radiates according to the cosine law and has a brightness equal to that of the original object, reduced by the absorption and reflection losses in the optical system.* This

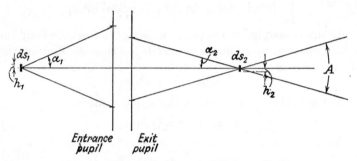

FIG. 8.2 Brightness of the image formed by an optical system. An eye placed within the cone A, and completely filled by the rays of this cone, sees the image element ds_2, less transmission losses

brightness is only effective within the cone of rays diverging through a point of the image, and can only be observed by an eye whose pupil is completely filled by this cone. The eye must clearly lie within the region A of Fig. 8.2. In optical instruments (see e.g. § 8.14) the exit pupil of the instrument is sometimes smaller than the pupil of the eye, and the brightness seen through the instrument is then cut down in the ratio

area of exit pupil/area of eye pupil,

as compared with that seen on looking directly at the object.

The illumination of a surface placed within the cone to the right of the image can be calculated from the brightness, size and position of the image, which acts as a source of light.

* For a discussion see Martin 1930-32, Vol. II.

If another optical system is placed to the right of the image in Fig. 8.2, the brightness of the final image may be calculated just as if the first image were a source of the same *brightness* as the original object. If the rays coming from the first system do not fill the entrance pupil of the second, the effective entrance and exit pupils of the latter will be reduced. This will reduce the illumination in the final image and may reduce the brightness as seen by an eye applied to the composite instrument by failing to fill the pupil.

It appears from the account above that an eye placed just to the right of the image in Fig. 8.2 will see the exit pupil of the optical system filled (flashed) with the brightness of the

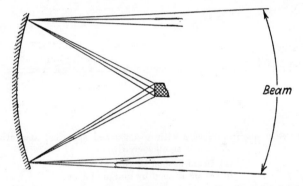

Beam

FIG. 8.3 Optical system of searchlight projector—Production of a beam of finite angle

source. Under these conditions any ray traced back from the eye through the system will end on the luminous source.

In such systems as searchlight projectors the aim (seldom completely achieved) is that an observer in the beam should see the whole aperture flashed with the source brightness. Such an optical system cannot increase the surface brightness of the source, but it can greatly magnify the angle subtended by the bright surface as seen by a distant observer. It can therefore increase the candle power (brightness × area) as seen from points in the beam, and the illumination of a distant surface in the beam. Fig. 8.3 is a diagram of a searchlight projector containing a source of finite area (as must always be the case).

The rays from opposite sides of the source diverge at a small angle, and if the optical aberrations are neglected, any eye within the beam of finite angle sees the mirror flashed with the brightness of the source. The *illumination* at a distant point is

$$\frac{\text{Brightness of source} \times \text{area of mirror}}{(\text{Distance})^2}$$

and cannot be increased by increasing the area of the source. The *area of the illuminated patch* at a given distance increases with the area of the source. It must be emphasised that the

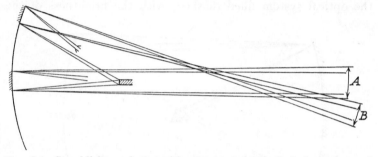

FIG. 8.4   Searchlight projector with exaggerated spherical aberration and small source

(a) Beam flashed by central zone
(b) Beam flashed by marginal zone

illumination at all distances large compared with the dimensions of the mirror follows the inverse square law ; it is not possible with a finite source to produce a parallel beam in which the illumination is constant.

   Fig. 8.4 shows the effect of spherical aberration on a mirror projector using a small source. There are now regions of the beam in which an observer sees the central part of the mirror flashed, but outer zones of the mirror are not flashed, and the illumination achieved in such regions is less than in the aberration-free case. It is true in general that aberrations of an illuminating system produce regions of partial flashing when a small source is used ; the light which would go into these regions in an aberration-free system is spread more diffusely over a larger patch. The importance of these

304

partially flashed regions becomes less when the size of the source is increased.

8.5 Typical Illuminating Systems

The mirror projector has been studied as the clearest example of the " flashing " principle. An elementary laboratory use of the principle is in the illumination of a spectrograph slit. It is required that the slit be flashed with the brightness of the source when seen from any part of the collimator lens and with a suitable source this may be accomplished by putting the source close up to the slit. A flame or arc cannot safely be placed in this position but one may employ a lens to form an image of the source on the slit, using a beam of such an angle that the collimator lens is filled with light. The most convenient method of adjustment is to set up the instrument without the illuminating lens, open the slit and reduce its length to the central part. Observe, either directly or through the prism, the patch of light thrown by the source on the collimator lens. When this patch lies centrally on the lens the source is in the axis of the collimator. The lens is now set up to focus the source on the slit, and it should be verified that the collimator lens is filled with light. The slit may now be adjusted to its working dimensions. If the lens and spectrograph are firmly set up the source can be readjusted or replaced at any time by moving the source to bring its image on the slit. Similar procedures may be devised for adjusting the illumination of other optical instruments.

It may be shown that the intensity of the final image in a spectrograph or spectroscope does not ordinarily depend on the collimator lens provided that it is large enough to allow the camera lens or the visual observer's eye to be filled with light. In a visual instrument the brightness of the image follows the same rules as in a telescope (§ 8.15) and is usually equal to the (monochromatic) brightness of the slit less the transmission losses.

In a spectrograph, as in a camera, the photographic intensity depends inversely on the square of the aperture ratio : (focal length of camera lens (f)/diameter of entrance pupil (d)).

Now the prism system of a spectrograph is usually its most expensive optical feature, so that the prism face should determine the entrance pupil of the camera. With a given prism, the focal length of the camera should be short if a high luminosity is required for weak spectra, but the resolution of spectral lines may be limited by photographic grain unless the focal length is long. With an emulsion capable of resolving, say, 100 lines per mm., the emulsion rather than diffraction phenomena will limit the resolution unless (the width of the diffraction image $\lambda . \dfrac{f}{d} > 10^{-3}$ cm. approximately). It follows that for a spectrograph faster than say, $f/20$, the requirements for luminosity and resolution make opposite demands on the focal length of the camera lens, and the actual value adopted must be a compromise.[*]

In a monochromator, or a spectrometric instrument using an energy detector such as a photoelectric surface, the output depends on the total flux of radiation through the exit aperture: it is characteristic of such instruments that output may be traded against resolution by opening the defining apertures (Jacquinot 1954, *see also* Jacquinot 1960 and Bellevue 1958).[†]

The condenser system used in a projection lantern is indicated in Fig. 8.5. Here the condenser forms an image of the source in the entrance pupil of the projection lens and every point in the lens covered by this image "sees" the condenser flashed with the brightness of the source, if the source is homogeneous and the condenser free from aberration. The transparent slide to be projected is put in the beam just after the condenser, and is therefore seen against the source brightness from every point of the lens. The imperfections of such systems in practice are :—

(*a*) The image of the source may not fill the entrance pupil of the projection lens. It will appear below that for maximum illumination of the screen, the projection lens

---

[*] The elementary design of spectrographs is discussed in Boutry 1946.

[†] Jacquinot goes on to show that the luminosity for given resolution may be much higher for certain interferometers than for slit spectrometers.

should be filled with light and if this cannot be done a cheaper lens of less aperture area could have been used.

(*b*) Aberrations of the condenser may give a partial flash of the condenser seen from some parts of the projection lens. In this case again, the projection lens is not being fully utilised. Further, there is a possibility of non-uniform illumination of the image, e.g. a reduction of intensity at the edge, due to partial flashing by the outer zones of the condenser. The condenser should therefore be designed to reduce spherical aberration as far as is economically possible.

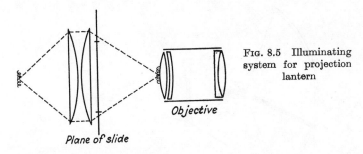

Fig. 8.5 Illuminating system for projection lantern

The illumination on the screen at an axial point corresponding to a clear area of the slide may be calculated as follows : this part of the screen receives light from the exit pupil of the projector lens (or such part of it as is flashed by the condenser) filled with the brightness of the source. The illumination is therefore $\dfrac{aB}{r^2}$, where a is the area of the exit pupil, B is the brightness of the source (diminished by reflection and absorption losses) and r is the distance from projector to screen. It is therefore advantageous to have a projector lens of large size (and necessarily of large focal ratio) if it can be flashed by the condenser system. The illumination will fall off at the margins of the screen, because of the increased distance of the marginal parts from the projector, the increased obliquity of the incidence, and the effect of the " cosine law " behaviour of the source. This effect, though quite large (the intensity falls off as $\cos^4 \theta$), usually goes unnoticed in ordinary projection. It becomes conspicuous

307

in the result if a projector is used for photographic enlarging, and a number of enlargements are mounted to form a mosaic.*

The illuminating system used with cinema projectors is usually rather different from that described above. In this case the object to be projected is small and the projection lens is large so as to obtain a high illumination of the screen. The image of the source is thrown by the condenser *into the plane of the film,* and the projector lens is in a wider part of the illuminating beam.

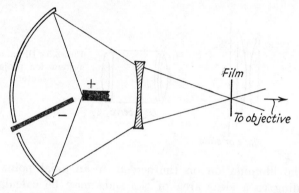

FIG. 8.6   Illuminating system for cine projector, using mirror and negative lens

It is necessary to have a uniform source, and this is provided by the positive crater of a carbon arc. In practice the crater image is a little larger than the film picture so as to allow for wandering of the arc, and the condensing lens is sometimes replaced by an image-forming system containing a lens and a curved mirror (Fig. 8.6).

The principles of the optical systems described above can often be used to project a profile (e.g. a vibrating string) in the laboratory. Where it is necessary to project the profile

* The same reduction of illumination at points off the axis takes place in the camera. In both camera and projection lenses there is usually an additional cut-off by diaphragms and mounts which act as restrictive aperture stops when seen from outer parts of the field (" vignetting "). This effect is often more important than the cos⁴ θ effect.

of a thick object, one must illuminate with a parallel beam of light and modify the projection lens system accordingly. This is done in projectors for engineering inspection purposes ; for an account of it see Cox and Habell (1948), p. 260.

In any projection system, the intense illumination of the slide or other object involves considerable heating. When the source is a tungsten projector lamp, each lumen is accompanied by about $1/40$ W of total radiation. It is found that a photographic film of ordinary density is damaged in a few minutes by a radiation flux of 0.3 W/sq. cm. Most of this radiation (about 88 %) * is infra-red and can be cut off by a suitable filter. A water cell 1 cm. thick cuts off about half the total radiation, and the cut-off of the infra-red is nearly complete if 3% of copper sulphate (with a few drops of sulphuric acid) is added to the water. A similar performance is given by a thickness of 2-3 mm. of a special heat-absorbing glass. Since all the radiation absorbed appears as heat in the glass, the latter should have a high resistance to thermal shock, and Chance ON20 glass has been recently developed for the purpose. The glass should be uniformly exposed to the beam and not screened at the edges, and it should be mounted without tight clamping.

The optical arrangement for producing a galvanometer " spot " are similar in principle to those for lantern projection (Fig. 8.7). The mirror at M, which may be concave but is more conveniently a plane mirror immediately behind a convex lens B of focal length roughly equal to the scale distance, is the projection system which images the mask at A on the scale. The lens A is the condenser which images the light source on the galvanometer mirror. An eye placed in the final image sees the galvanometer mirror flashed with the brightness of the source. If the best performance is required from the illuminating system, as when the mirror is very small, it is necessary to use a compact source of high brightness and to have a chromatically corrected lens at A. If the galvanometer mirror is completely covered with the image of the source, no choice of A makes any difference to the

---

* This figure is taken from Messrs. Chance's data sheets on heat-absorbing glass.

TABLE 8.2

Designation	Ratings available, 1950	Efficiency Lumens/W
Tungsten filament, general illumination types	230 V, 15-150 W 200-1500 W	8-13 14-20
Tungsten filament projector types.	Very numerous between 12 V, 12 W, and 250 V, 1000 W	Up to 28-30 for 25 hr. life—heavy current type
Tungsten arc " pointolite "	30, 100, 500, 1000 c.p.	
Carbon arc	5-50 A	Order of 12 overall on 100 V supply
Carbon arc (high intensity)	50-150 A	
Mercury arc. Pool electrodes in glass	Not now available commercially	15
High pressure. Type M.A. (street lighting lamp) in glass	250 W; 400 W	30-40
High pressure. Type M.B. in quartz	40, 50, 125 W	~30
Very high pressure Type M.E. in quartz	250 W	40-45
Water-cooled type M.D. (typical—not generally available)		~60
Sodium	40, 65, 80, 140 W	~70
Fluorescent tube (low pressure Hg with hot cathodes)	15, 20, 40, 80 W	40-45
Surface of the sun		

Light Sources

Surface brightness candles/sq. cm.	Spectrum characteristics	Operating notes
500-1000 filament 3 opal bulb	Continuous. Colour temp. 2500°-3000° K.	Direct use on A.C. or D.C. Low-voltage heavy-current lamps have higher efficiency, brightness, and colour temp. for a given life
1000-2000 filament	Continuous. Colour temp. 3200°-3400° K.	
1300 bead	Continuous	Obsolescent. Usually D.C. with resistance. A.C. types available
15-20,000 (positive crater)	Continuous. Colour temp. *ca.* 4500° K.	Usually D.C. with resistance. Arc voltage 40-50. Line voltage 80 upwards
70-100,000	*ca.* 6000° K.	
2-3	Mercury line spectrum. Resonance line at 2536 A.U. strong in a cooled quartz lamp	D.C. with resistance. Obsolescent
150 max.	Mercury line, appreciably broadened. Some continuous background	A.C. with choke
1000 max. ~1·5 in pearl bulb	Mercury lines, much broadened Continuous background	A.C. with choke
18,000	Mercury lines, much broadened. Continuous background	A.C. with choke
20-30,000	Mercury lines, much broadened. Continuous background	A.C. with choke
10	Sodium lines, predominantly yellow doublet	A.C. with transformer
~0·5	Continuous	A.C. with choke and starting arrangements
~150,000	Continuous (dark lines) Colour temp. ~ 5750° K	

TABLE 8.3

Notes on Special and Improvised Light Sources

(1)   Tungsten filament lamps (e.g. 100 W 100 V gasfilled) may be flashed with about twice normal voltage for times of the order of tenths of a second (e.g. for illuminating cloud chamber tracks). The peak voltage must not be sufficient to cause an arc discharge through the filling gas, which leads to the instantaneous destruction of the filament.

(2)   Flash discharge tubes filled with xenon are made commercially in straight and coiled forms. They are connected to a bank of condensers charged to several kilovolts, and the discharge is started by applying a triggering voltage to a special internal or external electrode. The efficiency is about 40 lumen.sec./watt.sec., and the duration of the flash, which depends mainly on the electrical constants of the circuit, is of the order of 100-200 μs. Because of the reciprocity properties of photographic plates (§ 8.26), it may sometimes be profitable to lengthen the flash by introducing inductance into the circuit. Quartz tubes have been made for which the permissible energy of the discharge is 10,000 joules or more. A different type of tube (Mitchell 1948 ; see also Chesterman 1951) produces an intense flash of about 1 μs duration.

(3)   Although the procedure is not recommended by the makers, the type MB quartz mercury lamp may be deprived of its outer glass casing and used as a laboratory light source. A reasonably long life is obtained. If the current through the lamp is reduced, or strong air-blast cooling is applied, the mercury lines are fine enough to show the hyperfine structure. MB lamps in clear glass envelopes can be obtained to special order. A small low-pressure hot-cathode lamp (Siemens M2) is a very convenient source for interferometry: it may be run on A.C. mains with a condenser in series to limit the current.

(4)   Discharge tubes containing neon, helium, may be run as spectroscopic sources from transformers as used for neon signs. These transformers have high leakage inductances, so that the open-circuit voltage of 2-5 kV, drops rapidly under load.

(5)   Lamps containing sodium, thallium, cadmium, or a cadmium mercury mixture, may be obtained commercially (from the G.E.C. London). Lamps containing caesium, or rubidium are also made. These lamps are run from A.C. with resistance or inductance in series, and some of them are available in a modified form to run on D.C. Very recently, lamps have been available filled with the pure 198 isotope of mercury, which gives the mercury spectrum free from hyperfine structure.

brightness of the final image.* The image of a bright line can, however, be converted into a bright point by putting a cylindrical lens in the final beam with the axis of the lens in the direction of deflection. Used in this way the cylindrical

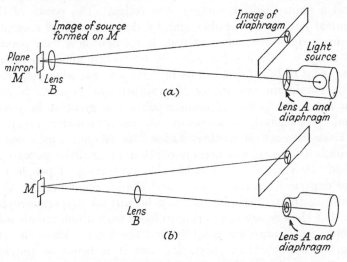

FIG. 8.7 Alternative systems for forming a galvanometer " spot "

  (*a*) Is simple and convenient

  (*b*) Avoids oblique aberrations of the lens

lens (unlike a spherical lens in a similar position) does not change the deflection and increases considerably the illumination of the spot. This device is valuable for photographic recording.

8.6   Light Sources

The illumination produced in any given case depends on the light source ; we have seen that in the case of direct illumination, the candle power is important and that in most optical illuminating systems the intrinsic brightness is the significant quantity. Tables 8.2, 8.3 give the properties of a number of useful light sources (see also Bourne, 1948).

 * The system of Fig. 8.7(*b*) has been recommended for galvanometer work. It has the advantage that it avoids oblique aberrations of the image-forming lens, but it is usually less convenient than the arrangement of 8.7(*a*).

8.7   The Eye as an Optical Instrument

Since the eye is often the final element in an optical system, it is well to have some quantitative idea of its properties. From our point of view, the eye consists of an optical system and a photosensitive surface—the retina. The power of the optical system is variable and by definition the "normal" (emmetropic) eye, when at rest, is focused on a "far point" at infinity. By a subconsciously controlled muscular effort, the point of best focus can be brought inwards when required. The maximum amount of this adjustment depends largely on age; the power of accommodation is greatest in youth and progressively disappears. A conventionally accepted "least distance of distinct vision" is 25 cm., which corresponds to maximum accommodation in an average eye at about 40 years. In a considerable proportion of people the eye departs from this normal, and the far point may be at a finite distance (myopia), or may be virtual (hypermetropia) so that the eye can only bring to focus rays which are already convergent towards a point behind the head. These defects can be corrected by spectacles, but it is usual to provide in the eyepieces of optical instruments an adjustment to allow myopic and hypermetropic eyes to focus on the graticule. A typical range of adjustment is $\pm$ 5 dioptres.

A further common defect of the eye, astigmatism, in which the refractive power of the eye varies in different meridians, is corrected by spectacles with cylindrical curvature properly oriented.

8.8   The Acuity of Vision

The resolving power of the eye, measured for example by the angular distance between two black lines which are just seen as separate under good conditions of contrast and illumination, is about 1' (1/3440 radian), and it appears that resolution of this order corresponds both to the resolution of the optical system and to the grain size of the retina, since these two factors are well balanced. This resolution is available only over a small field rather less than one degree wide, corresponding to a particular part of the retina, the fovea, which lies a little to one side of the optic axis of the eye ; and the eye moves so as to make any object which is examined minutely lie in this field. The outer part of the retina serves for warning and searching rather than for critical examination.

The resolving power measured in the way described is not always the best criterion of visual acuity, and the " vernier acuity ", measured by the angular magnitude of the least detectable break in a line (Fig. 8.8(a)) may be very much less than a minute. It is this quantity which decides the accuracy of eye settings on a properly designed scale and vernier, or in a coincidence range-finder. Values ranging

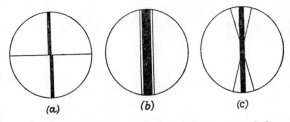

FIG. 8.8   Examples of " vernier acuity " and " symmetry judgment " of the eye

from 12″ to 1″ have been given as the performance of experienced observers with the latter instrument. It is known that in order to get the best values of vernier acuity the division between the two halves of the field must be very fine and the lines themselves must not be very short. These points, as well as the avoidance of parallax, must be taken into account in designing pointers and verniers. The eye can also make very accurate judgments of symmetry in such settings as are shown in Fig. 8.8(b), (c). In all these cases 10″ is a reasonable acuity to assume in calculations.

The eye is not free from spherical aberration, particularly when the pupil is large (the eye may then be working at about f/3) but the effects of this aberration are not very important. The chromatic aberration of the eye may be disturbing in visual measurements on strongly coloured objects. For example, if illuminated cross-wires are used in making a visual setting on a spectral line, and if the colour

315

of the illumination is different from that of the line, it will not be possible to focus the eye satisfactorily on line and pointer together (chromatic parallax). The difficulty may be avoided by using a wide slit with a wire down the centre, which usually provides an object clear enough to be observed without illuminated crosswires (Guild).

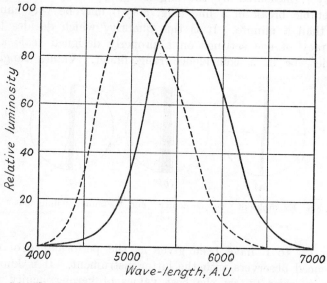

Fig. 8.9 The luminous effect of equal energies in different parts of the spectrum. Visibility curve of a standard observer, adopted by Commission Internationale de l'Eclairage 1924. See also Judd, 1931. The dotted curve shows the visibility curve for a dark adapted eye

8.9   The Colour and Intensity Response of the Eye

The eye, when adapted to fairly strong light (cf. § 8.10) is sensitive from the red end of the spectrum at about 7000 A.U. to the violet at about 4000 A.U., but the same illumination, measured in terms of energy, at different parts of this wavelength range, produces very different visual sensations of brightness. The relative luminosity of different spectral colours varies between individuals, and has several times been determined for batches of observers. A fictitious " standard observer ", obtained by averaging the results of testing many individuals, has a sensitivity curve shown in Fig. 8.9. The whole photometric system of Table 8.1 is based on the response of the eye, and in comparing sources of given spectral compositions the quantities of Table 8.1 can be translated into terms of relative energy by using a curve like Fig. 8.9. If an objective instrument like a photo-electric cell is used to compare illuminations of different spectral composition, its spectral response must be corrected by filters or by calculation to agree with that of the eye. The eye itself is often used as a comparison instrument in photo-metry ; it can detect differences of less than 2 % in the bright-ness of two closely adjacent areas (in the absence of colour differences). It is found that this fraction remains nearly constant over a large range of brightnesses but increases rapidly at low brightnesses. In practice, photometric matches can be made considerably more accurately than 2 % by taking the mean of a number of settings, preferably taken in rapid succession.

8.10 The Behaviour of the Eye at Low Intensity— Ultimate Sensitivity

At low illuminations the eye becomes " dark adapted ", and its sensitivity increases greatly. A small part of the change is due to the expansion of the pupil, but by far the greater part depends on changes in the retina which take a considerable time. Fig. 8.10 illustrates this, and shows that the eye should be adapted to the dark for about half an hour before doing work which involves perception of the faintest lights. In practice it is most comfortable to go into a room lit by artificial light and to reduce the illumination to zero in several steps ; an old-fashioned gas burner was used at the Cavendish Laboratory for this purpose. Dark adaptation may be achieved, and preserved in light, by wearing close-fitting goggles containing red filters.

In the dark-adapted eye, the predominant mechanism of the retina is not the same as at normal illuminations ; the change is apparently pronounced when the field brightness is re-duced to that of a diffuse reflector illuminated with about 0·1 ft.

317

candle (10^{-4} lambert). The dark-adapted eye is most sensitive at about 5050 A.U. and the relative sensitivity to red light is much less than normal (dotted curve of Fig. 8.9). This

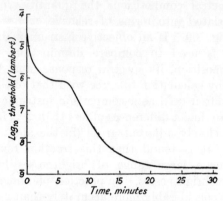

FIG. 8.10 Dark adaptation of the eye after Hecht and Schlaer, 1938. Ordinates are logarithmically plotted values of threshold brightness for a blue field 3° diameter. The eye had been light-adapted before the experiment with a field brightness of 1·55 lamberts

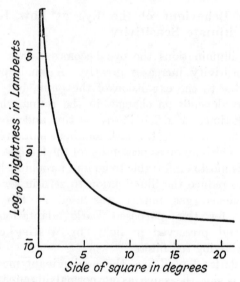

FIG. 8.11 Threshold intensity for visibility of square areas subtending different angles at the eye. (Dark-adapted eye.) After Reeves, *Astrophys. Jour.*, Vol. 47, p. 143, 1918

shift in sensitivity is called the Purkinje effect. At low brightnesses the sensation of colour disappears, and the resolving power of the eye is greatly reduced. Very faint objects disappear if looked at directly, since the fovea is not sensitive to weak light.* Appendix 1 gives a value for the minimum light detectable by the eye and compares it with other detectors. Fig. 8.11 indicates the order of magnitude of the threshold brightness of extended objects. It shows that an object subtending a large angle at the eye can be seen at lower brightness than one subtending a smaller angle. It is therefore profitable to use a properly designed telescope to view terrestrial objects at night although the telescope does not increase surface brightness (§§ 8.4, 8.14).

8.11 Image-Producing Optical Systems

In certain cases a relatively simple optical system can produce an image whose definition is limited only by the wave nature of light, but often the design of an image-producing system is a compromise between complexity and the effective control of aberrations. It is costly to use a large number of surfaces and each refracting surface produces some loss of light by reflection. More important, some of the lost light may, by further reflection, form flare spots or spoil the contrast of the image. These effects may be greatly reduced by anti-reflection coatings (§ 8.23).

8.12 Aberrations

The simple (Gaussian) theory of lens systems applies in strictness only to rays which (a) make very small angles with the axis, and (b) pass through the (spherical) surfaces at very small distances from the axis. It corresponds to using the approximation $\sin \theta = \theta$ for the angles which occur in the calculation. The next step is to use the approximation

---

* Histologically the retina contains two kinds of visual cells : cones which are supposed to be active at high levels of illumination, and rods which are responsible for vision at low levels. Cones are most densely distributed in the fovea ; rods are absent or rare there.

$\sin \theta = \theta - \dfrac{\theta^3}{3!}$ (" third order theory "). The modifications now imposed on the Gaussian image are classified by Seidel in terms of certain parameters which appear in the third-order equations for tracing a ray through the system. The Seidel aberrations cannot, in general, be separated physically in the image formed. They are, however, valuable for descriptive purposes as well as for detailed calculations, for each varies in a characteristic way with the aperture of the lens and with the obliquity of the rays, and it often happens that the reduction of one or two particular aberrations is the central feature of an optical design.

Suppose the image of a point, formed by a lens system according to Gaussian optics, lies at a distance h from the axis, then the linear size of the aberration patch produced by the Seidel aberrations in the plane of the Gaussian image depends in the following way on the radius r of the entrance pupil:—

Spherical aberration . . . . r^3

Coma . . . . . . r^2h

Curvature errors . . . . rh^2
(Astigmatism and field curvature)

Distortion. . . . . . h^3

Spherical aberration is independent of h and is therefore present even for an axial image. As we leave the axis, coma first appears, taking the form of an asymmetrical blurring of the image. The curvature errors become significant for images lying further from the axis. They are especially important when a beam goes through a system of moderate aperture at a large angle with the axis, as in an eyepiece, and in photographic lenses in which r and h may both be large. On account of astigmatism the image bundle of rays from a point object never goes through a point image, but concentrates successively through two " focal lines ". The nearest approach to a point image (disk of least confusion) lies between these (Fig. 8.12). The curvature errors involve two independent parameters of the lens system ; one of these parameters controls the curvature of a surface called the Petzval surface, and the other controls the separations between the Petzval surface and the curved surfaces in which lie the tangential and sagittal (radial) focal lines. It might be desirable to design a lens system so as to remove astigmatism, bringing the two focal lines to coincide in the Petzval surface, and also to remove the curvature of the latter, but it is not often possible to do this. The designer usually tries to bring the disks of least confusion into a nearly plane surface.

The distortion produced by an optical system is independent of r and is therefore present in general even when the lens opening is very small. (The coefficient of h^3 does, however, depend on the position of the aperture stop relative to the system. See below.)

In ambitious optical systems such as camera lenses of large aperture and high-power microscope objectives, aberrations of higher order than the third (zonal aberrations) become very important and the optical design is largely based on balancing the higher-order aberrations against those of lower order over a definite field. The performance of such systems usually goes rapidly bad outside the field which they are designed to cover.

In addition to these monochromatic aberrations, refracting optical systems show chromatic aberration due to the variation of refractive index with wavelength. If a lens is made of any ordinary glass, its focal length varies at least $1\frac{1}{2}\%$ from red to violet, and chromatic aberration is likely to be the most conspicuous fault of a single lens of moderate aperture used with white light. A thin doublet lens made of two different glasses can be made achromatic in the sense that it behaves alike for two selected wavelengths. In visual instruments red (λ 6563 A.U.) and blue (λ 4861 A.U.) rays are chosen, and the power of the lens is then a maximum in the brightest part of the spectrum and changes only slowly there. The difference between the maximum and the red-blue power is then of the order 1/2500. It is rarely necessary to correct a system for three colours (apochromatic correction) or to use achromatic lenses in the ultra-violet, though quartz-fluorite doublets have been used in small sizes for the latter purpose.

The condition for achromatism of a doublet involves only the powers of the lenses and the dispersive powers of the glasses : the other parameters of the lenses may be varied to

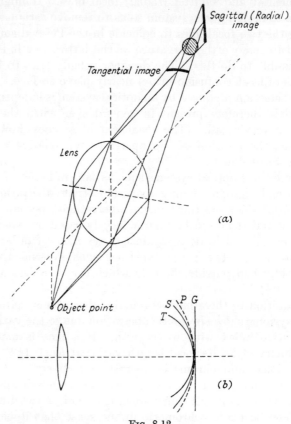

FIG. 8.12

(a) Diagram showing the formation of an astigmatic image by a lens

(b) Diagram to show the relative position of the paraxial image, the Petzval surface P, and the astigmatic surfaces for a normal case of uncorrected or undercorrected astigmatism

     G is the Gaussian image plane P is the Petzval surface

     S, T contain the sagittal and tangential images

reduce monochromatic aberrations. In particular, third-order spherical aberration can be annulled for a particular position of object and image.

Achromatism in a restricted sense, as used in eyepieces, can be obtained from a separated combination of lenses of the same glass. The *power* of the system is the same for all colours but the *positions* of foci and principal planes vary from wavelength to wavelength.

When lenses are used in laboratory experiments they should be chosen and placed with a view to the reduction of aberrations. The spherical aberration of a lens is minimised when the angular deviation of a ray is split as evenly as possible between the refracting surfaces, and a further reduction can be obtained if the deviation is spread over the

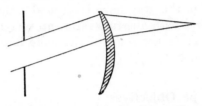

FIG. 8.13 Use of a stop to control aberration. The stop here requires oblique rays to fall on the margin of the lens. The coma is then balanced against the strong spherical aberration of the meniscus lens

surfaces of two or more lenses. A simple example is provided by the usual construction of a lantern condenser (see Fig. 8.5), for with glass of refractive index about 1·5 minimum spherical aberration is nearly achieved when parallel light falls on the convex surface of a plano convex lens. Two such lenses placed with their convex surfaces adjacent form a system of nearly minimum aberration for the case where object and image lie in positions corresponding to the focal planes of the separate lenses.

The position of the aperture stop has an important effect on the oblique aberrations of a lens system. A symmetrical lens or lens system, with a stop at its optical centre is automatically free from distortion, coma, and lateral chromatic aberration if it is used symmetrically, as in photographic copying at full size. It is often found that these aberrations are small for such a system, even if it is not used quite symmetrically.

The astigmatism of a lens can be suppressed for a particular position of object and image by choosing a particular position for the diaphragm, remote from the optical centre, so that the pencils coming from different parts of the object are diverted through different parts of the lens. When the tangential and sagittal images have been brought together in this way, the image lies in the Petzval surface, whose curvature is usually marked.

Alternatively, the position of a stop can be chosen so that the coma of a suitably shaped lens is balanced against the spherical aberration and the astigmatism is over-corrected to give a reasonable image on a flat plate. Meniscus lenses stopped down in this way have been used rather extensively in cheap cameras with aperture ratios up to f/11 (Fig. 8.13).

We may now review some of the more important image-producing systems.

8.13 Telescope Objectives

The normal function of these lenses is to accept nearly parallel beams from distant objects and bring them to a focus. They work at focal ratios of the order f/15-f/8, and cover angular fields of a few degrees (e.g. $\pm$ 1°-5°). These are rather easy conditions from the point of view of aberration control and in fact any well designed and well constructed small objective will show a star image surrounded by its diffraction rings so that its performance is limited by the wave nature of light rather than aberration (cf. § 8.14). Objectives of lower quality are likely to be limited by inhomogeneity of the glass and by local irregularities of working, and expensive astronomical objectives are worked locally by hand to compensate for inhomogeneities. In this case the final spherical corrections may be given during the hand retouching so that the finished surfaces are very slightly aspherical.

Ordinary telescope objectives are doublets made of crown (convergent) and flint (divergent) glasses, and in small objectives the components are cemented together so as to suppress two air-glass surfaces which would reflect light. With a given pair of glasses the designer has at his disposal four main parameters (the radii of the four surfaces) and he can also vary the thickness of the lenses and that of the air space in an uncemented objective. Considering only the radii as variables (i.e. the thin lens approximation), the requirement for a given focal length introduces one relation between the variables and the achromatic condition another. If the lens is to be cemented, the second and third radii must be equal and the one remaining degree of freedom is usually used to give zero (third order) spherical aberration for one (infinite) object distance.* If the lenses are uncemented the additional degree of freedom may be used to remove coma and this result may also be obtained with a cemented doublet if the refractive properties of the glasses are treated as available variables. Astigmatism, curvature of field and distortion are not normally considered in the design of telescope objectives, and they produce only small effects over the angular fields used in practice.

8.14 The Choice and Use of a Telescope

Whether a telescope is used to view distant objects, or as part of an optical system, e.g. in a spectrometer, the properties of the telescope must be chosen with the following considerations in view :

(*a*) The bundle of rays going through the instrument is limited by the entrance pupil, which is usually the rim of the objective, and the conjugate exit pupil, which is the image of the objective rim formed by the remainder of the optical system. This pupil usually lies just behind the eye lens, and its diameter is

diameter of objective /linear magnification.

(*b*) The angular resolution of the telescope is given by

$1 \cdot 22\lambda$/diameter of ray bundle entering instrument,

and the denominator is equal to the diameter of the objective, provided that the exit pupil formed by the instrument is

---

* An alternative is to balance first order aberration against the higher orders so as to secure a better overall performance. See, e.g. Dimitrov and Baker, p. 29.

smaller than the pupil of the observer's eye. If this condition is not met, the pupil of the eye acts as the aperture stop, and the objective is not fully utilised.

(*c*) The brightness of the image of a source which has resolvable angular size is equal to that of the source itself (less transmission losses) provided that the exit pupil of the instrument is *larger* than the pupil of the observer's eye. The telescope is said to have normal magnification when the exit pupil is just equal to the eye pupil (about 8 mm. diameter for the dark-adapted eye). The magnification is then about 3 for each inch of aperture.

Telescopes with less than normal magnification are only used as aids to night observation of terrestrial objects ; this is done to secure a large exit pupil, so that the eye may move slightly relatively to the telescope without losing brightness in the image. For other purposes it is preferable to increase the magnification above normal, thereby securing increased angular resolution at the expense of brightness. It is easy to calculate that the angular resolution of the objective ($1 \cdot 22 \, \lambda/d$, measured in the object space) corresponds with the resolution limit of the eye (about 1 minute of arc in the image space) when the magnification is such that the exit pupil has a diameter of about 2 mm. This is probably a good value to take for most instrumental uses of telescopes. It corresponds to a magnification of about $12 \times$ diameter of objective in inches.

The angular diameters of stars are always below the limit of resolution, but the diffraction disk is visible in a small telescope if the magnification is greater than that just given.

In large telescopes the effective size of a star image is controlled, not by instrumental diffraction, but by atmospheric disturbances ("seeing") which cause complicated variations in the position, size, and focus of the image. In certain astronomical studies, particularly of planets, the human observer has an advantage over photography in that he can select and interpret the image seen in the fleeting moments of good seeing. It is convenient to speak of a "seeing disk" which is the effective stellar image for a certain observatory, occasion, and method of observing. The seeing disk has often a diameter about one second of arc, which corresponds to the diffraction disk in a 4 inch telescope, so that in larger telescopes the star behaves as a small extended object. In visual observations astronomers frequently use magnification (e.g. 50 per inch of aperture) much greater than normal magnification or the minimum required for observation of the diffraction disk, finding that this leads to more comfortable observation.

8.15 Microscope Objectives

The resolving power of a microscope objective depends essentially on the angle of the cone of rays which can enter the lens from an object point. Microscope objectives therefore deal in the object space with rays making very great

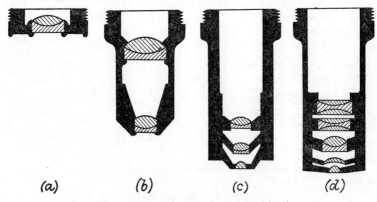

(a)   (b)   (c)   (d)

FIG. 8.14 Construction of microscope objectives

(a) $\times$ 3   2 in. focal length.   N.A. 0·1
(b) $\times$ 10 16 mm. focal length N.A. 0·25
(c) $\times$ 40 4 mm. focal length. N.A. 0·65
(d) $\times$ 80 2 mm. focal length. N.A. 1·4 (Apochromatic)

angles with the axis, but they are only required to form images of points very near the axis. The removal of spherical aberrations is therefore the key to the design of these lenses.

High power microscope objectives are usually designed to be used with the front lens connected with the object by a medium of homogeneous refractive index n. A drop of cedar-wood oil (or a synthetic substitute) is used between cover glass and objective, and the object is mounted in a refracting medium (e.g. Canada balsam). The limit of resolution of a dry microscope objective is given by $\lambda/\sin\theta$ where λ is the wavelength of light in air and θ is the semi-angle

TABLE 8.4

Typical Performance of Microscope Objectives

Designation	Conventional magnification	N.A.	Wave theory depth of focus	Eye-accommodation depth of focus ($\times 10$ eyepiece)	Working distance mm.
2 in. Achromatic	3	0·1	50 μ	250 μ	—
⅔ in. Achromatic (16 mm.)	10	0·25	12·5 μ	25 μ	—
4 mm. Achromatic . .	40	0·65	1·1 μ	1·5 μ	0·6
4 mm. Apochromatic . .	40	0·9	0·4 μ	1·5 μ	0·1
2 mm. Fluorite (oil) . .	80	1·3	0·3 μ	0·4 μ	0·3
2 mm. Apochromatic (oil) .	90	1·4	0·2 μ	0·4 μ	0·25

The field of view of a microscope is always defined by the eyepiece and is given by

$$\frac{250 \text{ mm.} \times 2 \tan (\text{half angular field of eyepiece})}{\text{Conventional magnification of whole system}}$$

which in normal cases is about

$$\frac{130 \text{ mm.}}{\text{magnification}}.$$

of the cone accepted by the objective. The resolution is improved to $\lambda_{air}/n \sin\theta$ by homogeneous immersion, and $n \sin\theta$ is called the numerical aperture (N.A.) of the objective. Oil immersion brings the further advantages that the design of the objective is greatly simplified and the troublesome effect of variations in the thickness of the cover glass on the correction of the system is eliminated.

Fig. 8.14 shows the usual construction of lenses of different powers, and Table 8.4 gives some particulars of their performance. In many high power objectives the corrections are improved by using fluorite, which has an extremely low dispersion, for the front lenses. "Apochromatic" lenses are made in which added complications are used to obtain a better colour correction (equal power for three colours, correction of spherical aberration and coma for two colours), and at the same time to obtain a slightly higher N.A. Apochromatic objectives show a chromatic difference of magnification which should be compensated by using a special eyepiece.

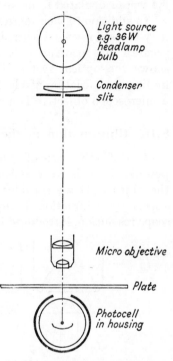

Messrs Cooke have introduced a "fluorite" objective with specially long working distance ; it has been valuable for examining nuclear tracks in thick photographic emulsions (§ 11.18). A reflecting optical attachment has been devised which lengthens considerably the working distance of a high-power dry objective and this is now made commercially. It was devised for studying surfaces inside vacuum tubes

Fig. 8.15 Optical system of micro-photometer, using microscope objective to form reduced image of slit on photographic plate

and has also been used for nuclear emulsion work (Dyson 1949).

The depth of focus of a microscope objective, as calculated from wave theory considerations, depends on the angular size of the pencil (θ on either side of the axis) admitted by the objective. It is given by $\pm\,\lambda/(8\sin^2\theta/_2)$ or roughly by $\lambda n^2/[2\times(\text{N.A.})^2]$. There is a further depth of focus, important for low powers, due to accommodation of the observer's eye. It is given (in microns) by $10^8 n/16M^2 \; \delta$ where the overall magnification is M and the least distance of accommodated vision is δ. It is not, of course, available when the microscope is used photographically. The depth of focus data of Table 8.4 were calculated from these formulae.

In addition to their more normal uses, microscope objectives may be used reversed when it is necessary to form a very small accurate image of an object, e.g. a light source. Fig. 8.15 shows the optical system of a simple microphotometer for finding the variation of blackening over a photographic plate; a microscope objective is here used reversed.

8.16   Illumination in the Microscope

The effective use of the microscope, especially the high powers, depends very much on the correct illumination of the object. If we consider the usual case of a transparent object the diffraction beam method of considering microscope resolution, introduced by Abbe, shows that the resolution

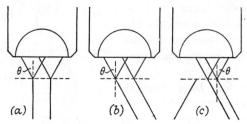

FIG. 8.16   Diagram to show principle of microscope illumination and its effect on resolution
  (a) Axial parallel illuminating beam
  (b) Oblique parallel beam   (c) Solid illuminating cone

of a grating structure in the object depends on the passage into the optical system of the diffracted beams which, in effect, carry the information characteristic of the structure. If the object is illuminated with an axial parallel beam the condition for resolution $d = \lambda \sin \theta$ is obtained when the first two diffracted beams enter the objective. If the illuminating rays enter the objective as shown in Fig. 8.16, we can obtain resolution with the central beam and one lateral diffracted beam, giving $d = \lambda/2 \sin \theta$. The resolving power of the objective is therefore doubled. In practice, in order to obtain resolution of structures lying in any direction we illuminate the object with a solid cone of rays, and Fig. 8.16 shows that for maximum resolving power the illuminating cone must have an angle as great as the cone accepted by the objective.

The normal illuminating system of a microscope is a condenser mounted with focusing and centring adjustments in a substage. A microscope objective can be used as a condenser, but since the source of light always possesses considerable area there is no need to form a completely aberration-free image, and the high correction of an objective makes it an unnecessarily expensive condenser. Furthermore, the corrections of a high-power dry objective allow for a thin cover-glass over the object and would be completely spoiled by the interposition of a glass slide of normal thickness. Special condensers are therefore supplied for substage use. The systems

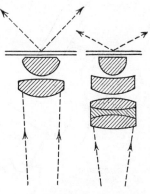

FIG. 8.17   Condenser systems used with the microscopes

shown in Fig. 8.17 differ in the degree of spherical and chromatic correction which has been applied to them. It will be noted that when an oil-immersed objective is in use the production of a full illuminating cone demands that the condenser be also designed and used as an oil-immersion system. In hurried work which demands only a considerably reduced performance from an objective the oil is sometimes omitted between condenser and slide (an immersion objective is of course unusable unless oiled on).

8.17   The Use of the Microscope

Fig. 8.18 shows diagrammatically an ordinary microscope with its adjustments. For very low power work the image

of a " pearl " or better, " opal " lamp bulb may be thrown
roughly on the object by means of a concave mirror below
the stage ; for all other purposes one of the condenser
systems of Fig. 8.17 is used.   The source of light may be an
opal lamp in a screening box ;   for high powers and rather
opaque objects a source of high brightness such as a filament (preferably a low-voltage heavy-current type) or a
high pressure mercury arc may be used in conjunction with
a lens which focuses an image of the source on the condenser.

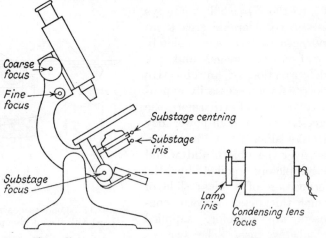

FIG. 8.18 The adjustments of the microscope. A lamp without a condensing lens may be used.   In this case it should have an opal bulb
  and an iris should be provided

This lens becomes flashed with the brightness of the source.*
The light source should be provided with an iris diaphragm.
The light is thrown, usually by an adjustable plane mirror,
into the condenser, which forms an image of the primary or
secondary source in the plane of the object.   In setting up the
microscope the condenser should be brought nearly into
contact with the slide, and if an immersion objective is to be
used a drop of oil should be introduced between the face of
the condenser and the slide.   The microscope is then focused

* This system is also used for photomicrography. Lamphouses with
built-in lenses are available commercially.

on the object, using a fairly low power (e.g. $\frac{2}{3}$ or 1 in.), and the condenser focused to form an image of the source on the object. On removing the eyepiece and looking down the tube, the back lens of the objective should be seen filled with light. The iris diaphragm of the condenser is now partly closed and the image of this diaphragm should be seen concentric with the objective.* The condenser is centred by its adjusting screws until this is so. The full resolution of an objective is attained when its angular aperture is filled with light and the condenser iris may be adjusted to this end. If it is opened too wide, unnecessary light will be scattered into the field of view, spoiling the contrast, so that the opening of this iris is important in critical microscopy and may need adjustment during an observation. Further to avoid scattered light, it may be necessary to use the lamp iris so as to illuminate only the small part of the field which is under close observation. A well-corrected condenser is required to produce a small image of the source with an illuminating cone of wide angle.

When the illumination has been adjusted the microscope is focused critically. The depth of focus under various conditions is indicated in Table 8.4 and in using high powers it is usually necessary to focus up and down, examining successive layers of a transparent object.

8.18 Eyepieces

The conditions for image formation by the eyepiece are nearly the same in telescope and microscope ; cones of small angular aperture come from the objective, and the final image is formed somewhere between infinity and the least distance of distinct vision.

With monocular instruments it is least fatiguing to have the image at infinity (or at the far point of the eye) and the instrument should be focused slowly, with the final movement downwards in the case of a microscope or pushing in the eyepiece of a telescope. The adjustment is checked by looking at a distant object and transferring the gaze abruptly

---

* An alternative and more sensitive method consists in focusing the image of this diaphragm with the microscope, using an eyepiece and a low power objective, and racking the microscope tube well up.

to the image, which should immediately be seen in focus. When there is a graticule with separate eye-focusing, this should first be adjusted as above with the main image thrown far out of focus ; the instrument as a whole is then adjusted to bring the image to coincide with the graticule. In binocular instruments where the two directions of viewing are convergent the images should not be formed at infinity, but nearer the eyes, since the convergence and accommodation are psychologically coupled.

The apparent field of view in an eyepiece is usually less than $\pm 20°$; it may go up to perhaps $\pm 35°$ in rather special designs.

The oblique corrections of an eyepiece depend on the position of its aperture stop, which is normally the objective of the instrument. The detail design of the eyepiece therefore depends on the relation between its focal length and the tube-length of the instrument. The changes involved are not very important except for low-power eyepieces, and eyepieces may often be regarded as interchangeable optical units available for use with different instruments.*

Ordinary eyepieces are derived from the traditional Huyghens and Ramsden forms (Fig. 8.19). The former has its first focal plane inside the eyepiece, and graticules cannot be put into this plane. Huyghens eyepieces are normally used in ordinary biological microscopes, and simple graticules, e.g. short scales, squared grids for blood counts, are mounted in the focal plane of the eye lens and viewed through that lens only. The aberrations of the eye lens are then quite apparent in the image of the graticule, especially in the outer parts of the field.

For accurate sighting, and especially for use with travelling wire micrometers, the Ramsden eyepiece with an external principal focus is required. A micrometer used in this way is independent of any distortion introduced by the eyepiece, since cross wire and image are observed in exactly the same way, and the distortion introduced by the objective is usually negligible both in telescopes and microscopes.

* The external diameter of eyepieces has been standardised at 0·917 in. (28·3 mm.) for microscopes, and 1·25 in. (31·8 mm.) for telescopes.

The Huyghens eyepiece is chromatically self-corrected in the sense that it has the same focal length and hence the same magnification, for all colours (except for compensating eyepieces). The Ramsden eyepiece, constructed as in Fig. 8.19, is not completely free from colour. Chromatic correction

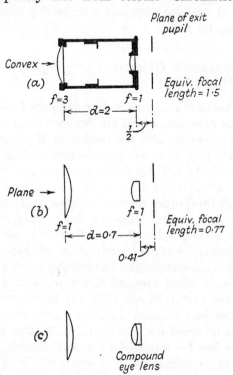

Fig. 8.19 Typical forms of ordinary eyepieces
(a) Huyghens   (b) Ramsden   (c) Kellner

can be secured by the use of a doublet eye lens (Kellner eyepiece), but it is then necessary to take special precautions to control the curvature errors of the eyepiece ; this is done by a proper choice of glasses for the eye lens. Glasses with a small difference of refractive index are required, and barium glass is usually used. These eyepieces are usual in prism binoculars and small sighting telescopes : they are sometimes used with the microscope.

The eyepieces described cover most laboratory uses ; more elaborate designs are occasionally used to cover a large angular field. Very high power eyepieces cover only a small area of the primary image formed by the objective, and it is not necessary to use a field lens. The eyepiece then consists of a corrected eye lens only and a cemented triplet is some- times used in this way.

8.19 Photographic Objectives (see Cox 1943 ; Cox and Martin 1945)

These lenses are comparatively complicated combinations, often of large aperture, which are designed to give a working definition comparable with the resolution of a normal photo- graphic emulsion over a flat plate corresponding to a rather large angular field (cf. Table 8.5).   The design of photographic lenses involves much balancing of aberrations, necessarily going beyond third-order aberration theory.   It is clear that different lenses represent different design compromises, and no ordinary photographic lens used at full aperture shows definition limited solely by diffraction phenomena. Many photographic lenses may give images comparable * with the diffraction limit when stopped down to, say, f/12, but it must be noted that it is normally less satisfactory to use a large aperture lens stopped down to a given aperture than to use a lens designed for that aperture, because the designer of the former lens has striven for the best compromise between aberrations at something like full aperture.   It is also wrong to use a lens to cover an angular field greater or less than that for which it was designed, for in balancing aberrations near the edge of the field the intermediate portion has prob- ably had to suffer to some extent, while in practically all photographic anastigmats the aberrations increase very rapidly indeed outside the designed field. Photographic lenses are normally designed for a distant object, and the corrections may be decidedly less perfect if they are used to

---

* The diffraction disk has a *diameter* given by $2\cdot4\,\lambda f/D = 2\cdot4\,\lambda F$ where F is the focal ratio.   It may be taken as 12μ for a lens working at f/10 and 5μ at f/4·5.

photograph objects nearer than, say, 8 times the focal length
(or in enlarging by a factor less than 8 : 1).

8.20 Depth of Focus

It is only in special cases that a photographic lens is used
to form on the plate an image of a strictly plane object, and
in general some part of the image must be out of focus according to the rules of geometrical optics. We may find
the geometrical size of the disk which represents the out of
focus image of a point and use the result to calculate the
depth of focus corresponding to a given tolerance on definition.

We have $\dfrac{1}{l_2} - \dfrac{1}{l_1} = \dfrac{1}{f_2}$ where l_1, l_2, are measured from object,
image to the appropriate principal points

$$\frac{dl_1}{l_1{}^2} = \frac{dl_2}{l_2{}^2}$$

and if δ is the diameter of the image, disk D that of the exit
pupil

$$\delta = \frac{D}{l_2} \cdot dl_2.$$

For a fairly distant object l_2/D may be replaced by the focal
ratio F and we have

$$\delta = \frac{1}{F} \cdot \frac{l_2{}^2}{l_1{}^2} dl_1$$

which allows us to calculate the depth of focus in the object
space.

It is interesting to compare the depth of focus of two lenses
of different focal length on the assumption that we intend
to enlarge the final negatives to the same size and tolerate
the same final disk in each case.

The formula above may be written

$$dl_1 = \delta \frac{F}{m^2}$$

where m is the magnification (normally < 1) of the camera
lens.

337

TABLE 8.5

Representative Performances of Photographic Lenses

(See also Cox 1943 ; Cox and Martin 1945)

	Focal length	Angular field	Aperture (F-number)
(1) General purpose lenses, usually Triplet and Tessar types	1·5-5 cm. 5·0-30 cm. 50 — 70 cm.	± 24° ± 26° ± 20°	2·7 4·5 5·0
(2) Special lenses. Process, air survey, etc. T.T.H. Aviar T.T.H. Cooke series IX. with apochromatic correction	6-15 in. and longer 13-48 in.	± 26° ± 20°	4·5 10-15
(3) Large and extreme aperture lenses— T.T.H. Special Speed Panchro Zeiss Biotar R-Biotar T.T.H. radiography lens	2¼ in. 2-7 cm. ∼ 5 cm. 2 in.	(35 mm. film) ± 4° ∼ ± 8°	1·3 1·4 0·85 * 0·8 *
(4) Wide angle lenses— Ross Xpress. Wide-angle Goerz Hypergon	5 in. also 4-10 in. 6-12 cm.	± 35° ± 70°	4 22
(5) Projection lenses— Petzval type		± 5°- ± 8°	2-3

* These lenses are related to the Petzval lens ; they were designed for screen radiography and are valuable, e.g. for rapid photography of cathode ray tubes.

338

Now if m_e is the magnification due to enlargement

$M = mm_e$ the final overall magnification,

$\varDelta = m_e\delta$ the size of the confusion disk in the final image, we have

$$dl_1 = \frac{\varDelta F}{m_e m^2} = \frac{\varDelta F}{Mm}$$

so that for a given F number of the camera lens the depth of focus is increased if the initial photograph is taken with a lens of short focus for which m is small.

The geometrical calculation of depth of focus is a useful practical guide to the behaviour of a lens, although it neglects the aberrations of the lens and the effects of diffraction. In some cases it may give a pessimistic result, for in the three-dimensional diffraction pattern which is the actual image, there may be a marked cylindrical concentration of intensity along the optic axis (Conrady 1923).

8.21 Projection Lenses

The function of a projection lens in an enlarger or projector is nearly that of a camera lens with reversed direction of the light. An enlarger lens ought to be corrected for the object and image distance at which it is to be used (cf. § 8.19). A lens for slide or film projection may be similar to a photographic anastigmat, but projection lenses usually cover a fairly small angular field ($\pm 12°$ is typical), and an older type of lens, the Petzval portrait combination, gives a satisfactory performance under these conditions, and is most commonly employed, working at apertures up to about f/2.*

8.22 Reflecting Optical Systems

Although reflecting optical systems have important advantages, including of course complete intrinsic achromatism, they have as yet been little used in general laboratory work. Their limitations arise partly from the inconvenient overlapping of object and image spaces, partly from the difficulty of preparing a permanent reflecting surface of high

* The principles of this lens have been applied to photographic objectives of large aperture and small angular field (Table 8.5) (Cox 1943).

efficiency. The latter problem is partly solved by the use of evaporated aluminium (Appendix 3).

Well-established reflecting systems are the astronomical telescope with parabolic mirror working usually at about f/5, and the reflecting concave grating which is a normal method of obtaining spectra of wide range and high resolving power. In infra-red spectroscopy concave mirrors are usually used with prisms and plane gratings since achromatic lenses cannot be constructed to cover a sufficient frequency range. Effort has recently been put into reflecting microscopes which have as a great advantage optical settings which are independent of wavelength into the ultraviolet (Burch 1946).

There are signs of an increasing interest in reflecting systems (Bouwers 1946). The spherical aberration on the axis of a concave mirror is zero for the special cases of a spherical mirror used with coincident object and image, a paraboloid used with parallel light, or an ellipsoid used with image and object at its foci. The spherical aberration of a spherical mirror used with parallel light is much less than that for any single lens of the same focal length and aperture.†

As we leave the axis, first coma and then astigmatism become important. (For the dependence of these aberrations on aperture and angular field see § 8.12.) The actual magnitude of these errors may be inferred from some figures relating to astronomical telescopes (cf. Dimitrov and Baker). For an f/3 parabolic mirror, 1° away from the axis, the astigmatism is about 1·2 sec. of arc and the coma about 19 sec. It is interesting to note that coma, astigmatism, and distortion (but not curvature of the field) may be removed from a field of any extent by diaphragming the mirror nearly at its centre of curvature.

A number of optical systems have been devised for astronomical telescopes in which the aberrations of the mirror are corrected by a further optical surface (see Dimitrov and Baker for an account of these). At present the most important of these developments is the Schmidt telescope which has already

---

† The numerical value of the longitudinal aberration at the focal plane is $h^2/8f$ for a ray which strikes a mirror of focal length f at a height h from the axis.

been used for several purposes besides its original astronomical one. A typical performance is a useful field of $\pm$ 12° at f/1, and the applications include meteor cameras, high-speed spectrographs, and the projection of cathode-ray tube displays for television.

The principle of the Schmidt camera is as follows : when a spherical mirror is " parabolised ", the intention is to equalise all the optical paths from a distant object point to the focus. This result may be also obtained by putting in front of the mirror a plate of refracting material whose thickness is varied to introduce the correct path differences at every point. This plate has aspherical surfaces, and of course introduces some chromatic aberration, but since only a small correction is required, this aberration is not serious. If the plate is placed in the plane through the centre of curvature of the mirror the correction is given very approximately for all angles of incidence and aberration-free images of, say, a star-field are formed on a spherical surface concentric with the mirror. This curvature of the image surface is one major drawback of the Schmidt system ; another is the difficulty of figuring the corrector plate. It is, however, certain that the Schmidt and modifications of it will be increasingly used in a number of fields.

The Maksutov system (Maksutov 1944), which does not involve an aspherical surface, could perhaps be made the basis of high aperture laboratory systems, and in fact several systems of this type are described by Bouwers (1946), who invented independently the method of correcting a concave mirror by a concave meniscus lens.

8.23 Anti-Reflection Coatings

The evil effects of surface reflection in refracting optical systems have been noticed in § 8.11. The light reflected from the surface of separation of two media is given for the case of normal incidence by

$$\left(\frac{n_1 - n_2}{n_1 + n_2}\right)^2$$

where $n_1 n_2$ are the refractive indices. The reflection at each glass-air surface is therefore about 4 %. The reflection is reduced to zero by interference if the surface is coated with a layer of a transparent substance of thickness $\lambda/4$ and refractive index $\sqrt{n_1 n_2}$ and may be greatly reduced if these conditions are approximately fulfilled. In practice, films of substances like cryolite ($n = 1\cdot34$), magnesium fluoride ($n = 1\cdot38$) are applied to glass surfaces by vacuum evaporation.* A number of firms undertake this work commercially. The main importance of this treatment is that it allows the optical designer to use systems containing more air-glass surfaces. For example, in a system with 10 air-glass surfaces, about 34 % of light is lost by reflection, and this could be reduced to about 14 % by surface treatment. The reduction in light scattered about the system or reflected into flare spots is always more important than the increase in transmission.

This use of anti-reflection coatings is the simplest application of an important technique involving interference between the waves reflected at the interfaces of a series of layers of controlled thickness and appropriate refractive index (Fig. 8.20). The layers are supposed to be thin and uniform so that coherent waves are reflected: the simplest results are obtained for normal incidence and strictly monochromatic light, as in the qualitative discussion below. More detailed information for more general cases can be obtained from books by Heavens (1955) and Vasicek (1960). A single $\lambda/4$ layer of *higher* refractive index than the glass on which it is deposited gives additive interference from its two boundaries, and hence gives an enhanced surface reflection. It is useful as a partially reflecting mirror (beam splitter) which has considerably smaller absorption losses than a partially reflecting film of silver or aluminium. An example of performance is given in Table 8.6.

A series of alternate high and low index layers gives a high reflection coefficient with very little absorption, and can act as an extremely effective coating for Fabry Perot interferometer plates. Fig. 8.20 indicates qualitatively the way in which the

---

* The values of n are those for the bulk material. It is known that the values obtained from a film vary slightly with the thickness and the method of deposition. In this section the lengths $\lambda/4$ etc. refer to wavelengths in the material of the film.

multilayer coatings work, but in practice the multiple reflections must be taken into account: the calculation becomes rather complicated, and is best attacked by matrix methods.   Table 8.6 gives examples of results obtained.

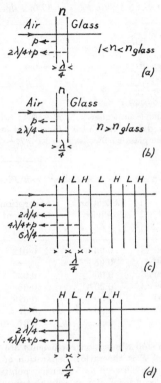

FIG. 8.20   Diagrams to show principle of thin-film systems

(a) Anti-reflection layer
(b) Reflection-enhancing layer
(c) Reflection from first stack of interference filter described as 3-L-3
(d) Reflection from first stack of interference filter described as 2-H-2

A dotted line indicates a beam whose phase has been reversed by reflection, and p is the path difference $= \lambda/2$ corresponding to this

If a spacer layer of dielectric is deposited between highly reflecting layers, the combination (which is essentially a low-order Fabry Perot étalon) can be used as a wavelength filter whose pass bands at normal incidence are defined by the relation $2nt = m\lambda$ (where n is the refractive index of the spacer, t its thickness, m is an integer and λ is a wavelength measured in vacuum).

TABLE 8·6

Optical Applications of Thin Films

(a) *Single Reflecting Films*

ZnS on crown glass $\quad n = 1\cdot5$	$R \sim 0\cdot3$	at design wavelength
TiO on crown glass	$R \sim 0\cdot4$	at design wavelength

(b) *Single Anti-Reflecting Films*

MgF_2 on very dense flint glass	$R \sim 0$	at design wavelength
MgF_2 on crown glass $= n = \lambda\,1\cdot5$	$R \sim 0\cdot014$	at design wavelength

(Cf. one glass surface at $n = \lambda\,1\cdot5$ $R \sim \lambda\,0\cdot04$)

(c) *Selected Semi-reflecting Films for Fabry Perot Plates* (Jacquinot 1960)

Nature of Film		Reflection Coefficient R	Absorption Coefficient A	Fabry Perot Performance F	τ
Fresh silver at	6800	0·95	0·012	60	0·6
Aged silver at	6800	0·95		60	0·4
	5200	0·95	0·027	60	0·2
	4200	0·90	0·068	30	0·1
Aluminium at	3200	0·90	0·078	30	0·05
5 layers ZnS-cryolite		0·90	0·01	30	0·8
7 layers ZnS-cryolite		0·95	0·01	60	0·7

Note.—The reflection and absorption coefficients are those for intensity. The " finesse " F is the ratio: Separation of consecutive orders/ width of an order between half-intensity points, and τ is the transmission of the interferometer at a maximum.

(d) *Typical Interference Filters in Visible Spectrum.   Zinc Sulphide and Cryolite in reflecting stacks as indicated.*

Type of filter	Width to half intensity	transmission %
5—C—5	110	85
6—Z—6	85	78
7—C—7	50	65
9—C—9	15	20
11—C—11	15	50
10—Z—10	7	50

The reflecting layers may be of metal such as silver, or may consist of multilayer dielectric stacks. As might be expected from the discussion above, the all-dielectric filters have better properties of narrow transmission band and low absorption, but the reflecting properties of the dielectric stack become poor at wavelengths removed from that for which they were calculated and the complete filter has " side band " transmission regions as well as the narrow main maximum. These side bands, as well as any undesired maxima of the main interference pattern, must usually be removed by auxiliary glass or dye filters.

In the visible spectrum, ZnS is the most used high-index layer and cryolite the most popular low-index substance for multilayers (MgF_2 has superior hardness and is used for single anti-reflection coatings on this account). These substances can all be evaporated without much difficulty and the layers are fairly stable in the atmosphere. It is not so easy to find layers as suitable for the ultra-violet and infra-red parts of the spectrum; reports on a number of substances are to be found in Bellevue 1957. (Summarised in Jacquinot 1960.)

In parts of the infra-red, semi-conductors such as germanium, silicon, and tellurium transmit freely and have a high refractive index, so that efficient interference filters can be made by combining these metals with dielectric substances such as cryolite.

All these devices require the deposition of uniform films of controlled thickness. These are usually obtained by evaporation in a good vacuum (Strong 1938, Heavens 1955, Ring and Lissberger 1955), but certain kinds of single-layer reflecting and anti-reflecting films have been produced by chemical methods—e.g. TiO_2 by reacting together $TiCl_4$ and water vapour, TiO_2 and Fe_2O_3 by oxidising evaporated films of the metals, Bi_2O_3 by " reactive sputtering " of the metal in an oxidising atmosphere.

8.24 Photography

The general features of the photographic process are well known and are indicated in Fig. 8.21. The photographic emulsion was highly developed empirically long before any theory of the latent image was available. Quite recently, considerable progress has been made with the explanation of the latent image in terms of the quantum theory of crystal lattices (Mott and Gurney 1948) and (Berg 1948), but the preparation of an emulsion with any particular properties is still a very technical matter on which information is not

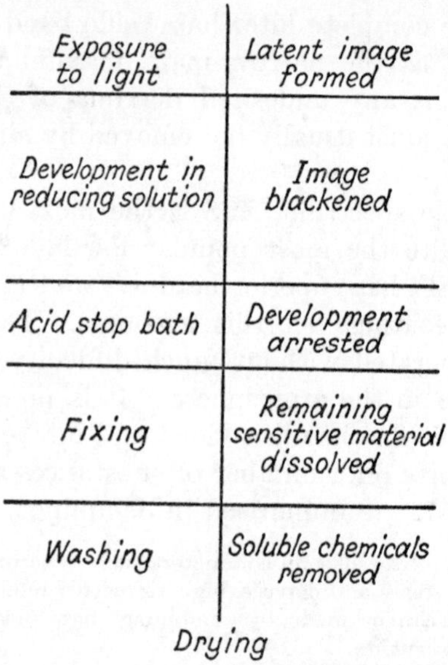

Exposure to light	Latent image formed
Development in reducing solution	Image blackened
Acid stop bath	Development arrested
Fixing	Remaining sensitive material dissolved
Washing	Soluble chemicals removed

Drying

FIG. 8.21 The photographic process

freely published. The manufacturers now describe in some detail the properties of the emulsions they make, and their publications must be consulted for quantitative data. This section is to be regarded as a general guide to the laboratory use of photographic materials.

8.25 The Quantitative Behaviour of Photographic Materials

The properties of an emulsion are conveniently discussed in terms of the " characteristic curves " connecting the density of the final image with the exposure. The exposure may conveniently be taken as the product of the light intensity

during exposure and the time of exposure. For the moment
we suppose the exposure time to be constant so as to avoid
the complications discussed in § 8.26.

The density is defined as the common logarithm of the
ratio :

$$\frac{\text{light incident on blackened plate}}{\text{light transmitted by plate}}$$

and the conditions of measurement have to be defined, since
the blackened emulsion absorbs a part of the light which
falls on it and scatters another part. If the incident light is
confined to a narrow beam and the transmitted light is also

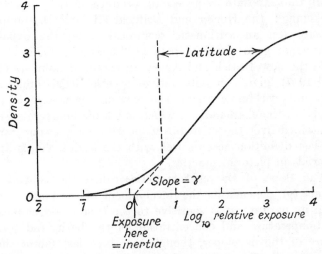

FIG. 8.22 The characteristic curve of a photographic emulsion. The curve
given is schematic, but an idea of the absolute sensitivity can be given : for
a particular fast orthochromatic emulsion the abscissa O corresponds
to 0·01 metre-candle-second. For exposures beyond the greatest shown
here the density may decrease with increasing exposure (solarisation)

measured in this beam, as in some forms of microphotometer,
the density is the *specular density;* if the incident light is
in a beam, but the whole of the transmitted light is measured,
including that scattered by the emulsion, the density is the
diffuse density (notation of B.S. 1384) and it is this lower
value which is significant in contact printing.

The characteristic curve is not of simple shape, and its main features are indicated in Fig. 8.22. In pictorial photography the time of exposure is chosen so that the range of exposures on the plate lies at least in part in the nearly linear part of the curve, but in scientific photography (e.g. astronomy ; the spectroscopy of faint lines) this is not always possible, and this circumstance sometimes leads to confusion in comparing the useful sensitivities of different plates (see § 8.29). The numbers used to specify the speeds of plates depend on particular features of the characteristic curve, and it is not therefore possible to compare them accurately. The old German Scheiner numbers give (on an inverse logarithmic scale) the exposure required to produce a just detectable blackening ; the Hurter and Driffield (H. and D.) numbers measure (on an arithmetic reciprocal scale) the exposure corresponding to the extrapolated " inertia " of Fig. 8.22 ; while the new British and American standard numbers (B.S. 1380/1947) give, on alternative inverse logarithmic and reciprocal arithmetic scales, the exposure necessary to give a slope to the characteristic which is 0·3 of the average slope maintained over the next 1·5 of logarithmic exposure range. The last definition accords well with the use of photographic materials in pictorial practice.

The slope of the characteristic, called the contrast or gamma (γ), depends on the development of the plate as well as on its nature ; it is sensitive to the time of development, the temperature and concentration of the bath, and to the nature of the developer, though the three last factors have only a small effect on the ultimate contrast obtainable from a given emulsion. There is a limiting value γ_∞ to which the plate tends on long development and in practice the γ-value attained is $0·7\,\gamma_\infty$-$0·8\,\gamma_\infty$, since further development leads to excessive background fog.

When a photographic image is printed or re-photographed the effective contrast given by the double process is the product of the gammas of the component processes, so that in pictorial photography the dual choice of negative material and printing paper allows the brightness scale of the original to be reproduced in a realistic way. This requires, ideally, a gamma-product value of unity, and a rather higher value is usually chosen. On the other hand, photography on a high contrast emulsion followed by printing on high contrast material provides a useful means of increasing small differences in brightness (e.g. in a very transparent microscopic preparation) to an easily visible level.

A further property of a photographic plate obtainable from the characteristic curve is the *latitude*, which may be defined (rather indefinitely) as the ratio of the exposure at the upper end of the straight portion of the characteristic curve to the exposure at the lower end. The latitude tends to be greater for emulsions of high speed and low contrast than for the slow emulsions of high contrast used, for example, on process plates.

8.26 The Reciprocity Law

While it is convenient to plot the abscissae of Fig. 8.22 in terms of the product It, the photographic effect of a given time-integrated quantity of light depends appreciably on the

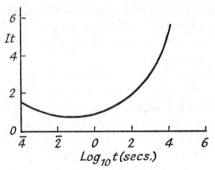

FIG. 8.23 Typical reciprocity failure curve. Exposure product (relative values) required to give constant density at various illuminations

rate of exposure. This effect is known as the "departure from the reciprocity law". The reciprocity law states that the effect of an exposure depends only on the time-integrated value of the energy flux, and it holds for many photochemical processes, for the response of photographic emulsions to X-rays, and as a rough approximation for the response of emulsions to visible light. More accurately, the conditions for constant photographic effect are represented by a curve like Fig. 8.23. It appears that a given dose of light energy is most effective when administered in a time of the order of tenths of a second. For exposures of, say, one hour, the reciprocity failure may require 2-5 times the integrated light flux to produce a given blackening, and the factor of increase varies from emulsion to emulsion. For astronomical purposes (i.e. for exposures up to several hours) the empirical law of Schwarzschild has been used as a guide. It states that the effective exposure depends on It^p where the exponent p is of the order 0·8. In astronomical terms this means increasing the exposure by a factor about 3 for each stellar magnitude.[*]

Certain commercial plates, intended particularly for astronomical purposes, have reduced reciprocity failure i.e. their sensitivity is well maintained at low light intensities. (See in particular the Kodak, Rochester, data on plates for scientific purposes. This firm includes the letter A in such plate designations as 103AO to indicate astronomical plates with reduced reciprocity failure.)

It is sometimes stated that the reciprocity failure curve steepens at very low intensities and that no photographic image is produced by very weak light acting even for an indefinitely long time.

At high intensities there is also a departure from the reciprocity law, and more energy is required to produce a given photographic effect in an intense flash than in a longer exposure at moderate intensity. The increase may be of the order five-fold at 10^{-6} sec. Reciprocity failure depends considerably on the temperature of the plate during exposure, and this fact has been shown to be significant in the theoretical interpretation of the behaviour of emulsions (Mees 1944).

8.27 Characteristics of Emulsions—Colour Sensitivity

An untreated photographic emulsion has a spectral region of sensitivity which starts from the gelatine limit in the

[*] An increase of one stellar magnitude corresponds to a decrease in luminosity in the ratio $\sqrt[5]{100}$, or very nearly 2·5 : 1. The corresponding logarithmic decrease is 0·4.

ultra-violet (see below), has a maximum in the near ultra-violet at about λ 3600 A.U., and extends on the long wave side to about λ 4900 A.U. The region of sensitivity can be extended to the red and beyond by treating the emulsion with certain dyes, and most of the recent improvements in the sensitivity of plates to white light have been achieved in this way. The spectral sensitivity of typical " orthochromatic " and " panchromatic " emulsion is indicated in Fig. 8.24. Materials with these characteristics are generally available, but the makers have a considerable variety of sensitising dyes

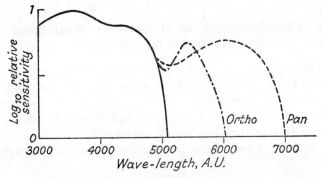

FIG. 8.24   Sensitivity of photographic emulsions to equal energy throughout the spectrum

————— Unsensitised emulsion
— · — · —   Typical orthochromatic sensitisation
— — — —   Typical panchromatic sensitisation

which can be applied to standard emulsions for particular purposes (see, e.g. Kodak catalogue sheets), including the photography of the infra-red spectrum to about 9000 A.U. (with extreme dyes and long exposures to about λ 12000 A.U.).

In the ultra-violet the sensitivity and contrast of photographic emulsions falls off rapidly below about λ 2300 A.U. because of absorption in the gelatine. The Schumann plates for the extreme ultra-violet were made with an absolute minimum of gelatine to stick the silver halide grains to the glass ; they have been made commercially (by Hilger) but are delicate and expensive. Certain slow plates (e.g. Ilford Q) are made with emulsions very rich in halide grains ; they were originally intended for recording particulate rays, but they work well for ultra-violet spectroscopy. An alternative method of increasing sensitivity in the further ultraviolet is to coat the plate with a fluorescent substance ; this has been done commercially (by Kodak) but satisfactory results are obtained with petroleum oils (liquid paraffin, warm yellow vaseline) applied by bathing the plate in the oil or in a solution of it ; the writer found that the best uniform layer for photometric plates was obtained with vaseline without solvent. After exposure and before development, the fluorescent layer is washed off with a solvent.

8.28 Characteristics of Emulsions—Graininess and Turbidity—Resolving Power

The resolving power of a photographic emulsion is limited by the finite size of the halide grains and by the scattering of light in the emulsion. Some makers quote the number of lines per millimetre which their emulsions will resolve ; it is broadly true that fast emulsions have low resolving power and that high resolution is obtained from slow " process "

TABLE 8.7

Typical Characteristics of Negative Materials

Makers' description	Resolving power lines/mm.	Working γ (rough values)
Slow process . . .	80-100	3·0
Rapid orthochromatic . .	40-50	1·2
Ultra-speed ortho. . .	30-40	0·9
Half-tone panchro. . .	80-100	6·0
Rapid process panchro. .	30-40	4·0
Commercial panchro. . .	30-40	0·9
Fastest panchro. . . .	30	1·0
Maximum resolution . .	>1000	5·0
Positive film . . .	50-60	1·5
Micro-file film (pan.) . .	120-130	1·3
Recording film (ortho.) .	40-50	1·5
High-speed panchro. film .	30-40	0·7
Fine grain panchro. . .	70-80	0·8

plates (Table 8.7). In agreement with this table, 20 μ is regarded as an average size for a star disk photographed on a normal emulsion. High resolution emulsions are made for such purposes as photographing graticules; their resolution is so high that it is difficult to devise optical arrangements to use it to the full, but these emulsions are extremely slow.

The photographic image is sometimes further spread by the reflection of light from the glass-air surface of the plate back into the emulsion; this produces the effect called "halation",* in which the regions of high exposure appear to spread at the edges. It is worse with glass plates than with films because of the greater separation of the surfaces of the plates; it can be abolished by backing the glass side of the plates with an opaque pigment, or by casting under the emulsion an opaque layer or a special emulsion layer. In all modern plates the anti-halation pigment layer comes away in processing.

8.29 The Choice of a Photographic Material

In many laboratory applications the conditions are similar to those of general pictorial photography, and the requirements for speed, contrast, and latitude may be inferred from § 8.25. The grain size of the emulsion must also be taken into account (§ 8.28). Often, however, the light available is not sufficient to bring the emulsion to the linear part of its characteristic curve. We then need a plate in which a minimal exposure will produce a blackening clearly detectable above the background fog, and emulsions of high contrast and low background density may be preferable to plates of high speed as rated for pictorial purposes. High-speed panchromatic plates often show relatively low contrast and high background. We have found at Manchester that the best emulsions for flash photography of cloud chamber tracks are those evolved for recording purposes (e.g. Kodak R 55, Ilford 5G 91), and these emulsions are also specially suitable for recording cathode-ray tube traces (Hercock 1947). For spectroscopy in the blue

---

* The refractive index of gelatine is about 1·53, so that the reflection at the gelatine-glass interface is small.

and ordinary ultra-violet regions " process " plates are the most generally useful and panchromatically sensitised process plates are available for work in the other parts of the spectrum. It must be remembered that special dye sensitisation is available to give particular spectral characteristics (cf. § 8.27).

8.30 The Manipulation of Photographic Materials in the Laboratory

The general handling of photographic plates and films is described in many books ; there are, however, special points which arise in laboratory work.

Exposure.

The exposure must usually be found by trial ; since the response of a plate depends more or less logarithmically on the exposure, it is useless to make trial exposures varying in small steps and it is convenient to make the exposures increase geometrically, say, by a factor of two. A larger factor than this should be used if the exposure is quite unknown ; a smaller factor is required in final trials in those cases where the density of some feature of the negative must be held within narrow limits, e.g. in precise photometric work.

Development

In laboratory development the important thing is uniformity and reproducibility ; the method of developing for a fixed time depending on the known temperature is therefore always used. The ideal arrangement is to have a temperature-controlled dark room (conveniently at 65° F = 18° C.) in which the solutions are stored, and the development carried out. It is difficult to work in a room where the temperature is very different from that of the solutions. Something may be done by using an outer dish filled with water at a measured temperature ; anything more elaborate usually involves more complication than a room thermostat and heater. It is our experience that a high-contrast metol-hydroquinone developer (e.g. Kodak D 19b) meets a very large proportion of laboratory requirements. Single plates are developed in dishes with frequent rocking ; in photometric work and in some other cases where plates are to be measured accurately, special precautions must be taken to avoid the Eberhard effect. This is a kind of uneven development due to the fact that the action of the developer on developable silver halide causes a change in the composition of the developer, exhausting the reducing agent and producing soluble bromide which restrains development. The result is that high-density regions of the plate and their immediate neighbourhood are less developed than the remainder. The effect is avoided by brushing the plate during development with a camel-hair brush or by using a special tank in which a piston or scraper passes within a millimetre or so of the plate and produces a powerful turbulent flow over its surface (Dobson, Griffith and Harrison 1926). Short lengths of film are best developed in a spiral tank, large quantities by winding on a frame and immersing in a very narrow deep tank.

Fixing

It is normal practice to remove the plate from the developer, wash it for a few seconds in water and transfer it to an acid hypo. fixing bath. In accurate photometric work with a turbulent flow tank, we preferred to run off the developer and flood the plate at once with acid hypo., which was only used once for this purpose. Development may also be stopped very definitely by using an intermediate stop bath of weak (acetic) acid. In any case the important fact is that developers only act in alkaline solution. It is usual to leave the material in the fixing bath for at least twice the time required to remove all the visible silver halide ; normal plates should not be left for more than a few hours in a fixing bath. The next process is washing in running water to remove all traces of thiosulphate. The minimum washing time depends on the nature and thickness of the emulsion, but one hour is normally safe. Plates for quantitative work should finally be washed in distilled water, preferably containing a little of a " wetting " agent which causes the liquid to form a uniform film instead of droplets. The drying of plates in an English urban laboratory, without risking dust deposits, is not easy ; the best arrangement is probably a box through which a stream of muslin-filtered warm air is drawn by a fan or blown by a hair-dryer.

8.31   Photometry—The Measurement of Light Intensity

The measurement of stellar magnitudes, light intensities in spectrum lines, and the like is a matter of considerable and increasing importance. The eye can decide with considerable accuracy the equality of brightness of adjacent fields (§ 8.9), and a number of optical instruments depend on using it in this way (e.g. polarimeter, some spectrophotometers). The practical alternatives to the eye are the photocell or thermocouple which transform radiant energy into electric current ; they have the advantage of linear response and more certain standardisation so that they are not confined, like the eye, to detecting equality of illumination but can make direct measurements.

The photographic plate may sometimes serve as an intermediary, as when a spectrum or a field of stars is recorded on a plate and measured at leisure. The characteristic feature of photographic methods is that the actual record is made with comparatively simple apparatus, which may, for example, be used in the field, and the record is examined at leisure with all necessary refinements. The light which is studied may last a very short time, or it may be so weak that it can only be recorded with a very long exposure, or may fluctuate so as greatly to complicate direct measurements (e.g. if one attempts to compare line intensities in the spectrum of an unsteady discharge). In all these cases the approximate integration effected by the plate is most valuable.

On the other hand, the photographic method is indirect and therefore gives increased opportunity for error ; it will be seen that very considerable precautions are necessary. In recent years there has been a definite tendency to expand the use of photocells—especially electron multiplier photocells—for astronomical and spectroscopic measurements formerly performed photographically.

8.32 Photographic Photometry

(See Dobson, Griffith, and Harrison 1926 ; Harrison 1929).

We shall refer directly to the photometry of spectra, which illustrates well the principles involved, but of course these principles can be applied to other problems.

Each plate must contain, as well as the spectra to be measured, calibration marks which give the blackening corresponding to known relative light intensities. Where we compare intensities of the same wavelength (homochromatic photometry) the calibration marks are obtained by making a series of exposures with the light cut down in a known ratio, and Table 8.8 gives several methods for doing this. In the much more difficult (and less common) problem of heterochromatic photometry, it is necessary to find the relative photographic effects of radiant energy of different wavelengths. This must be done by using a source whose energy distribution is known. Over part of the wavelength range, the continuous spectrum from a tungsten lamp may be used in this way.

In this case the light may very conveniently be weakened by method 4—the variation of the slit width of the spectrograph. Because of the Eberhard effect, the density of a narrow blackened strip should not be compared with that of a large area, and it is therefore good to break up continuous calibration spectra into lines by means of a mask if they are to be compared with spectrum lines.

In the ultraviolet the spectrum of heated tungsten is too weak to be used as a source of known energy distribution, and it is usually necessary to find the energy distribution of a suitable source experimentally, using a thermocouple or its equivalent. It should be noticed that the calibration can be performed with a strong steady source and the result applied to the photographic photometry of a weak or fluctuating source.

The exposure and processing of the plate must be carefully planned to secure uniformity ; * spectra to be measured

---

* Plates may be obtained coated on "patent plate" glass to improve the uniformity of the emulsion layer. Dobson, Griffith, and Harrison (*loc. cit.*) found density differences of about 0·05 in a uniformly exposed plate carefully developed in a special dish, and differences of 0·02 in a plate developed in their tank with plunger. The latter difference they attribute, in part at least, to the plate itself.

TABLE 8.8

Methods of Attenuating Light for Plate Calibration

(1) Rotating sector giving intermittent exposure . .	Effect on plate characteristic is complicated. (Intermittency effect.) The error is small if the exposure is cut into 100 or more flashes.
(2) Reduction of aperture of an optical system (usually interposed in a parallel beam)—	
(a) Fixed sector system .	Uniformity of beam must be good and tested.
(b) Rotating sector system	Non-uniformity of beam produces a second order intermittency error.
(c) Wire gauzes and gratings . . .	Precautions required to avoid diffraction errors. See **Harrison 1929**.
(3) " Neutral " and other filters, e.g. Grey glass . . Step wedge . . Continuous wedge .	Absorption must be known at required wavelengths. Platinum sputtered or evaporated on glass or quartz is neutral over a wide range. Gelatine wedges which are nearly neutral over visible spectrum are available commercially (e.g. from Ilford).
(4) Variable slit width in spectrograph (step slit) . .	Used only with continuous spectrum.
(5) Polariser and analyser at variable angle . .	Not usually convenient.
(6) Temperature variation of filament source . .	Not usually convenient.
(7) Theoretical relation between intensities, e.g. of line components . . .	Very special applications.

should not appear near the edge of the plate, and the exposures should be distributed so that a small systematic variation of properties over the plate gives a random rather than a systematic error in the results. The precautions mentioned in § 8.30 should be taken in development.

The final experimental step is the measurement of the blackening of the plate with a microphotometer. The optical arrangement of a simple microphotometer is shown in Fig. 8.15. Slits may be introduced to obtain higher resolution : the design should be such that light is not scattered into the detector from parts of the plate near that being measured ;

TABLE 8.9

Detectors for Microphotometers

Detecting element	Auxiliary equipment	Advantages	Disadvantages
Thermopile.	Galvanometer	Simple Very stable	Response time not very short. Focusing of optical system complicated by maximum response in infra-red.
Barrier layer cell . .	Galvanometer (low resistance for linearity)	Simple	Sensitivity not very high. Shows some fatigue, and long term stability not perfect.
Photocell .	Electrometer D.C. amplifier A.C. amplifier with chopped light.	Sensitivity high so that narrow slits can be used. Stability of cell good.	Detecting system complicated and may include elements—high resistances, D.C. amplifying stages—which require care to make them stable.
Photo-multiplier	Galvanometer	Very high sensitivity. Fairly simple.	Complications of power supply. May show "fatigue" at high currents.

this will take place if a considerable area of the plate is illuminated and the resolution is obtained by a slit over the detector. Measuring detectors for microphotometers are discussed in Table 8.9. Microphotometers may be made automatically recording or not ; the benefits of recording are considerable when complicated spectra are recorded or when it is necessary to integrate the effect on the plate over a length of spectrum, but direct reading is a quicker method for comparing the intensities of a few spectral lines. In this case the spectra are recorded with a wide slit so as to obtain flat-topped photometer curves. The blackening measurements obtained from the calibration exposures are used to prepare a curve connecting the blackening of the plate with the intensity of the radiation which caused it. The unknown intensities recorded in the experimental exposures are then evaluated from the curve.

APPENDIX 1

The Setting Up of Optical Systems

It is useful to have a systematic procedure for setting up systems of lenses and other optical components, since the behaviour of such systems can be seriously spoilt if the optic axis of a lens does not coincide in *position* and *direction* with the axis of the system. If there is a straight train of optical components it is convenient to mount them on an optical bench (based on the kinematic slide, § 3.4) ; in other cases they may stand on a rigid table. A preliminary adjustment of height (and sideways position on an optical bench) can be made by bringing the components in turn up to a point held in a fixed clamp, but this must be followed by optical adjustment.

(*a*) An important operation is to set up a convergent lens so that its optical centre moves on a line parallel to a slide and that the line so defined passes through a particular point, e.g. a small hole. The latter is brightly illuminated and its image is formed by the lens on a ground glass screen or in the focal plane of an eyepiece. The distance between object and image must be greater than four times the focal length, and there are two positions of the lens which form an image in the chosen plane. The lens must then be adjusted systematically until the image is in the same lateral position for the two positions of the lens.

(b) The operation just described does not secure that the optic axis of the lens lies in the required direction. This adjustment is made by using the ghost images produced by reflection at the lens surfaces, as seen by an eye placed on the axis near the primary image. The lens must be turned, without moving its optical centre, until these images are superposed. The position of the lens centre may then be tested as in (a). These operations are repeated for all the lenses of a system ; it is obviously almost essential to be able to remove lenses from the bench and replace them without altering the adjustments.

Divergent lenses may be centred by combining them with a previously centred convergent lens to form a convergent system, or by the method given below.

(c) A method which can be used to set up optical elements of any kind even in the absence of an optical bench is the following :—

An illuminated hole is put in the focal plane of a lens, set up if possible by the method given above. The lens is then provided with a diaphragm with a small central hole. The narrow beam of light obtained defines the optic axis of the system ; if great precision is required the first hole is made very small and diffraction rings due to the second hole can be seen at any point along the beam by means of a magnifier. Lenses can be inserted and centred by moving them until they produce no deflection of the beam. Other optical components such as slits, prisms or mirrors may be centred about the beam, if their optical centres are marked, e.g. by temporary diaphragms or cross wires. The orientation of the lenses must again be adjusted by flare spots though sometimes, with lenses of high quality and long focal length, the symmetry of the image of a small hole, observed at full lens aperture, is a sensitive test of orientation.*

* For a more complete treatment, see Surugue 1947.

APPENDIX 2

Optical Materials

In this section we have collected for reference the properties of some of the most important materials. The data given are those required for understanding the general principles of optical systems and for planning design. Detailed information for final design purposes must usually be sought elsewhere.

Reflecting Surfaces

The most important reflecting surfaces in precision optical systems are silver and aluminium deposited on glass by vacuum evaporation. Silver can be deposited by cathode sputtering or by chemical methods, but these methods are not recommended where the best reflecting films are required. There is some dispute about the exact efficiency obtainable with the best silver films for Fabry Perot interferometers. In these instruments the resolving power depends on the reflection coefficient of a partially transmitting film and the brightness of the maxima depends strongly on the transmission coefficient. It is probable that about 4% of the (green) light is absorbed in the film, but some workers claim that the sum of reflected and transmitted intensities differs from the incident intensity by less than this. The point only becomes important when very high performance is demanded from an interferometer. The low reflection of silver around $\lambda.U. 3200$ A.U. is due mainly to transparency of the silver in this region but if the film is thickened up to reduce the transmitted light the absorption becomes important.

Aluminised mirrors tarnish less than silver in most atmospheres and may be preferred for applications (e.g. telescopes) where a high reflectivity is required throughout a reasonable life. They do not compete with silver for interferometers in the visible spectrum, but may be used for this purpose in the ultra-violet (to, say, $\lambda 2200$). Metallic mirrors made of specially pure aluminium brightened by an anodic process are sometimes useful for condensers ; their reflection co-efficient is about 85 % and they cannot be polished without disturbing their shape, so that they are not used in precision optics.

In the infra-red spectrum most metals have high reflection coefficients ; gold films have sometimes been used because they do not tarnish readily. Beyond about $\lambda\ 10\mu$ the reflection from a metal surface depends on the electrical conductivity of the metal and is nearly 100 % for most ordinary metals.

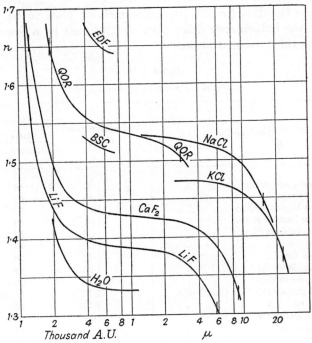

FIG. 8.25 Variation of refractive index with wave-length for some optically important materials. In certain cases vertical lines indicate limits of transparency (for practical use in thickness of about 1 cm.)

Refracting Media

Fig. 8.25 shows for certain materials the variation of refractive index with wavelength ; in some cases the ultra-violet and infra-red limits for their practical application are shown ; they coincide roughly with the wavelengths for which the radiation is half absorbed in a path 1 cm. long. The two glasses, extra dense flint (EDF), and borosilicate crown (BSC) are typical of the " old " achromatic pairs. They are still advantageously used for telescope objectives and lenses of similar function. Table 8.10 shows the refractive indices and the Abbe reciprocal dispersion numbers for a rather wider range of materials. The properties of these and other glasses are obtainable from the makers' catalogues. For final optical design calculations it is necessary to get from the makers the data for the particular melt of glass to be used, since the indices may differ from melt to melt by a few units in the third decimal place.

TABLE 8.10

Refractive Properties of Glasses, etc.

Designation	Refractive index $n_{\lambda 5893}$	Abbe ν $\dfrac{n_{\lambda 5893} - 1}{n_{\lambda 4861} - n_{\lambda 6563}}$
Borosilicate crown . . .	1·51	64
Hard crown	1·52	60
Light barium crown . . .	1·54	59
Dense barium crown . . .	1·61	60
Light barium flint. . . .	1·56	55
Light flint	1·58	40
Dense flint	1·62	36
Extra dense flint	1·65	34
Very dense flint	Up to 1·79	25
1945 glasses (Kodak) (Lee 1946) .	1·7-2·0	55-20
Fluorite	1·434	95
Lithium fluoride . . .	1·392	98·5
Fused quartz	1·458	67
Quartz (ordinary ray) . . .	1·544	72
Methyl methacrylate (Perspex) .	1·49	56
Polystyrene	1·59	31

It is convenient, and is becoming usual, to specify optical glasses by a six-figure code comprising three significant figures of $(n - 1)$ and three figures of the Abbe reciprocal dispersion. A borosilicate crown would thus be denoted by 510644.

The quartz used in optical equipment is usually the natural crystal, which is birefringent. The index for the ordinary ray is given in Fig. 8.25 (QOR). Even when the light passes along the optic axis, quartz produces a separation of circularly polarised components and in certain instruments, particularly 60° spectrograph prisms, this must be compensated by making the optical path half of right and half of left-handed quartz. Fused quartz (which is of course isotropic) is still not made homogeneous enough for precise optical elements of any size. Its refractive index is much lower than that of the crystal, and its spectral transmission about the same as the crystal. Fluorite, which is optically isotropic except for strain, is used in optical systems for the infra-red and the vacuum ultra-violet (Bomke 1937), as well as in microscope objectives where its low dispersion in the visible spectrum is exploited (Table 8.10). It is very rare in any but small pieces, but artificially grown crystals are now being made. Lithium fluoride transmits light beyond the fluorite limit in the ultra-violet and is also useful in the infra-red. The crystals are grown artificially, and more easily than those of fluorite. Rocksalt prisms can be used in the infra-red to about λ 15 μ, but as shown in Fig. 8.25, the dispersion at shorter wavelengths is smaller than that of fluorite, and the latter may be preferred for infra-red prism spectroscopy at intermediate wavelengths (Gore *et al.* 1949). Rocksalt is hygroscopic, and a spectroscope using rocksalt prisms must be arranged to contain dry air. It is convenient to warm the instrument, before opening it, by means of a built-in heating element. The transparent plastics have not yet been found suitable for precise optical elements ; they are soft and difficult to form with the required accuracy and they have very large temperature expansion. On the other hand, they are extremely transparent and are used in devices in which light is conducted along a rod by repeated total internal reflection. This arrangement can be used to illuminate inaccessible corners (e.g. in surgery) or to bring light from a scintillation screen to a photomultiplier.*

* There is at present a development of " fibre optics " (see Kapany in Strong 1958) in which an image is transferred from place to place by a bundle of transparent fibres, which are preferably " insulated " from one another by sheaths of different refractive index. The fibres are usually of glass; they may be flexible, curved, or tapered in certain applications.

Infra-red Materials

The commercial and military use of infra-red instrumentation has directed attention to a number of materials additional to those shown in Fig. 8.25: some of these have extended infrared transmission, and some are distinguished by withstanding exposure to the elements. Descriptions are given in Smith Jones and Chasmar (1957), and a rather complete survey has been made in an (unclassified) report to the U.S. Government from the University of Michigan.

Ordinary optical glasses begin to absorb strongly at about $2 \cdot 7 \mu$: the properties of quartz and certain halides are shown in Fig. 8.2. TiO, A_2O_3 (sapphire) and MgO transmit rather longer wavelengths than quartz. AgCl, KBr, CsBr, CsI go to still longer wavelengths. CsI has useful transmission to 50μ. AgCl, the synthetic mixed crystal TlBr/TlI called KRS5, transmitting to about 40μ, and the glass obtained by melting As_2S_3 which transmits to about 11μ have some importance for infra-red windows and optical components which are not readily attacked by damp. Films of polyethylene and polypropylene can be used as thin windows and as substitutes for deposited films in a region beyond about 14μ, where they are free from absorption bands.

Optical Filters

Filters of coloured glass are made (in this country by Chance) and transmission data are available from the makers. The transmission is usually of high- or low-pass type but with fairly gradual cut-off. An exceptional case is that of didymium glasses which have a narrow absorption region in the yellow, and may be used to suppress the yellow mercury lines. Filters may of course be combined with advantage in many cases. A greater range of characteristics is available in dyed gelatine filters by Wratten (Kodak) and by Ilford. The gelatine film may be used alone ; it is of course delicate but is sufficiently uniform to be put into many optical systems without loss of definition. The film can also be obtained cemented between glass plates of various optical qualities. Liquid solutions can be used in parallel-sided glass cells (Strong 1938) ; they are usually rather inconvenient, but certain special characteristics are obtainable only in this way, and in certain cases (e.g. infra-red absorption, didymium), the liquids are much cheaper than their equivalents in glass.

Many semiconductors transmit radiation if the quantum energy is insufficient to transfer electrons from the filled energy band, and they can therefore be used as long-wavelength-pass filters. The cut-off wavelengths for Ge, Si are about $1 \cdot 8 \mu$, $1 \cdot 2 \mu$ respectively but depend on temperature and the purity of the material. Other substances such as Se, Te, InSb, InAs, GaSb, GaAs, have analogous properties. They are used in single crystals or as deposited layers. In the transmission region they have high refractive indices and reflection losses can be reduced by a suitable anti-reflection coating. Interference filters (see p. 344) are now produced commercially. A very beautiful filter, depending on the birefringent properties of crystals and combining small band-width with large aperture, has been invented by Lyot, but it lies rather beyond the scope of this book (B. Lyot 1944; see also Evans 1949).

CHAPTER 9

THE DETECTION OF
ELECTROMAGNETIC RADIATION

9.1 Introduction

Electrical detectors for light and other electromagnetic radiations have a great and increasing importance. In the visible and ultra-violet direct photoelectric measurement competes strongly with the photographic methods discussed in § 8.32. Its advantages are intrinsic linearity and high quantum efficiency, and the information which comes out in electrical form is available for direct recording, for automatic computation, or to provide control signals. When the quantum energy of the radiation is below about 1 volt, photographic methods cannot be used, but electrical quantum detectors are available to much longer wavelengths.

In this chapter we shall deal with the detection and measurement of electromagnetic radiation in a range of frequencies which is bounded at the lower end by the availability of tuned radio frequency devices. At high frequencies the methods used merge with those employed in nuclear physics and discussed in Chapter 11. There is of course an essentially technical problem in obtaining an adequate response of a detector to a given signal, but in the last resort the effective sensitivity of any detector is limited by fluctuation phenomena—noise in the sense discussed in Chapter 10. A perfect detector would give a characteristic response for every quantum of radiation which fell upon it, and the accuracy of measurement would be limited by the fluctuations in the incident radiation.

It appears on p. 402 that this leads to a ratio of " signal " to r.m.s. noise $(nS)^{\frac{1}{2}}$ where n is the rate of arrival of quanta and S is the time of observation. Actual detectors give a worse relation between signal and noise for several reasons.

(a) They have a quantum conversion efficiency ϵ which is less than unity, and this reduces the signal/noise ratio to $(\epsilon nS)^{\frac{1}{2}}$.

It must be noted that ϵ refers to the average number of *independent events* produced by each incident quantum, and this noise ratio is not improved if each " event " is larger than the liberation of a single electron.

(*b*) In amplifying the initial events the fluctuations are increased by random variations in the ratio of amplification as between events.

Wavelength		Frequency wave number		Quantum energy		Quantum detectors available
$\log \lambda$ cm.	usual form	$\log c/s$	cm^{-1}	eV	Temp. $h\nu = kT$	
-6	$100\,AU$			100		
		16				
-5	$1,000\,AU$			10		
		15				
near uv visible						
-4	1μ		$10,000$	1		
		14				
-3	10μ		$1,000$	0.1		
		13			$300°K$	
-2	100μ		100	0.01		
		12			$30°K$	
-1	$1mm.$			0.001		

Detectors listed: Eye, Photoplate, Fluorescent conversion, Photocathode, Gas ionisation, Solid state

Fɪɢ. 9.1 Nomogram for electromagnetic radiation and key to quantum detectors

(*c*) The detectors may introduce noise arising from their own mechanism and not related directly to the incident radiation.

(*d*) They may detect and amplify fluctuations of background radiation which cannot be excluded but which is not relevant to a particular investigation.

Radiation detectors can usefully be divided into those which absorb all the energy which falls upon them and measure it as heat, and those which make use of some distinctive quantum process and whose efficiency varies strongly with frequency. It will appear that most of the non-selective detectors are quite severely affected by noise of type (d), and that quantum detectors can usually surpass them in ultimate sensitivity.

The availability of quantum detectors for different parts of the spectrum is shown in Fig. 9.1: non-selective detectors are discussed in § 9.8.*

9.2 Photocathodes and Photoemissive Cells

In photoemissive cells electrons are extracted from the surface of the cathode. The average number of electrons produced per incident quantum (the quantum efficiency) varies with the frequency of the radiation and determines the fundamental behaviour of the cell.

If the cathode is a *pure metal* there is a threshold frequency, corresponding closely to the work function of the metal, below which there is no emission. The extraction of photoelectrons by light of frequency near the threshold is confined to a thin surface layer; reflection of light is a process which competes strongly with the production of photoelectrons, and the photoelectrons are scattered by other electrons on their way out. The maximum quantum efficiency is about 10^{-4}. Photocells with pure metal cathodes are not very important technically, though cells with e.g. sodium or zirconium cathodes have been used for measuring ultraviolet light in meteorological and biological experiments where their insensitiveness to longer-wave radiation is an advantage.

Photocathodes of present technical importance are semiconductors of more or less complicated structure which have been developed empirically. They have much higher quantum efficiency than pure metals, and the work needed to extract an electron from certain composite cathodes is less than for any pure metal, so that photoemission is possible for light of longer wavelength.

* R. Clark Jones (numerous papers in *J.O.S.A.* from 1949) has given much attention to defining and clarifying the sensitivity parameters of radiation detectors. In particular he introduces the terms " responsivity " for " output per unit energy input " and " detectivity " for the reciprocal of that input power which gives a response just equal to the rise.

9.3 Note on Photocathodes Obtainable in Commercial Tubes

The characteristics of the principal cathodes available in commercial tubes are shown in Fig. 9.2. The quantum

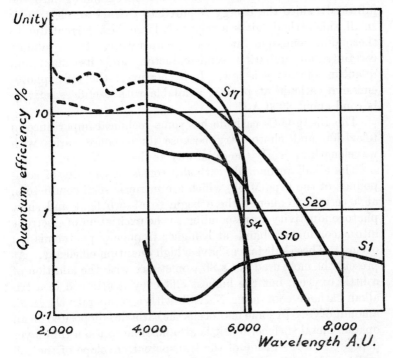

FIG. 9.2 Approximate quantum efficiency of commercial photocathodes (plotted against wavelength). The cathodes are denoted by their (American) commercial symbols

$S1$ is Ag–0–Cs. Its response decreases gradually beyond the diagram and extends to nearly 12,000 A.U.

$S4$ is CsSb on a metal backing. The semitransparent cathode denoted by $S11$ has a similar characteristic

$S10$ is Bi–0–Ag–Cs in semitransparent form

$S17$ is tri-alkali (semitransparent)

The dotted parts of the curves are obtained with a cell or window of fused quartz

efficiency obtained varies from tube to tube, and the published values (e.g. Sommer 1960; Sharpe 1961) vary accordingly, experimentally cathodes have been made, particularly by Lallemand (1953) with quantum efficiency rising to about 50 % at the most favourable wavelength.

The Cs-O-Ag cathode, prepared by depositing caesium on oxidised silver, has photoelectric response extending into the infra-red: since the energy required to extract an electron is small, this cathode gives a relatively large dark current due to thermionic emission at room temperature. It is almost certainly an impurity semiconductor, and its maximum quantum efficiency is low. It is, however, the only photoemissive cathode at present available with useful sensitivity beyond about 8000 A.U.

The Bi-Ag-O-Cs cathode has some technical importance in television and photometry because its response varies with wavelength in nearly the same way as that of the eye.

The alkali-antimonide cathodes consist essentially of compounds of the type M_3Sb, which are intrinsic semi-conductors: at a certain frequency these begin to absorb light and show photoconductivity corresponding to the excitiation of electrons into a conduction band, at a higher frequency photoemission occurs. These substances have a high quantum efficiency. At present the most used is Cs_3Sb, sometimes with the addition of a little oxygen, but the highest efficiency is attained in a tri-alkali cathode containing Na_2KSb with a comparatively small amount of Cs. In some photocells the cathode is deposited on an opaque metal surface, but it is also possible to use a thin layer deposited on the inside of the transparent envelope of the cell and to collect the electrons from the face opposite to that on which the light is incident. This arrangement is particularly valuable in photomultiplier cells with large cathodes used in nuclear scintillation experiments (§11.9). It does not seem that the sensitivity of such semi-transparent cathodes is very different from that of thick layers: in certain cells an opaque cathode of high efficiency is obtained by depositing a thin layer of photoelectric material on a highly reflecting backing so that the light not absorbed on first passage through the layer is returned through it.

9.4 Photocells and Photomultipliers

In a simple vacuum photocell, electrons from the cathode are collected by an electrode held at positive potential: since the currents are normally small, space charge effects are small, and saturation is obtained with small electric fields.

Amplification of the current within the cell can be obtained by introducing an inert gas at a low pressure and applying a voltage sufficient to produce ionisation when the electrons collide with gas atoms. The amplification obtained is very dependent on the gas pressure and the voltage, and it is subject to statistical variations from electron to electron. In practice the amplification obtainable with stability is very limited (to about 10 under commercial conditions) and gas filled cells are now rarely used in laboratory work. They are of technical importance when an all-or-none response is required, and they are usually used in sound-film reproduction.

Amplification of a very favourable kind is obtained by accelerating the electrons and allowing them to fall on a prepared surface (dynode) which gives a large secondary emission of electrons. An amplification of 3-5 is obtained in a single stage, and "photomultiplier cells" with numbers of stages between 9 and 19 are in regular use, the dynodes being fed from a potential dividing chain which usually provides 100-200 V per stage.

The geometry of the dynode system must be such that the secondary electrons are accelerated away from the surfaces: some dynode systems are shown in Fig. 9.3. In certain of these the electrostatic fields have a focusing action, so that the descendants of a particular primary electron form a compact bundle at every stage: this property is not usually important in photometry, but it decreases the spread in the transit times through the multiplying system and therefore improves the high frequency response of the cell. The only noise introduced in this form of amplification arises from statistical variations in the number of secondaries produced by a single electron; this happens mainly in the first few dynodes and results in practice in an increase in the primary fluctuation noise by a factor of about 1·2. The amplification is available over a wide frequency

373

band between zero and a limit set by variations in the time between the emission of the photoelectrons and the collection of the corresponding electrons from the last dynode. This limit may lie in the region 10^8-10^9 c/s.

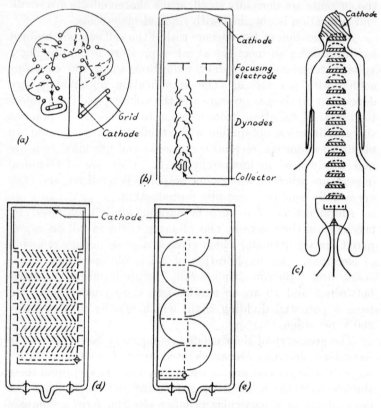

FIG. 9.3   Dynode systems for photomultipliers
(a) Compact focused system (Rajchman, R.C.A.)
(b) Linear-focused system
(c) Venetian blind with focusing grids (Lallemand 1949)
(d) Venetian blind with flat grids (E.M.I.)
(e) Box and grid system (Du Mont, E.M.I.)

9.5   The Application of Photocells and Photomultipliers

Vacuum photocells give very reproducible currents and can be used for precise photometry, under certain precautions, which

374

are mainly concerned with avoiding disturbances caused by
stray electric charges on the windows and other insulating
surfaces of the cell. It is necessary to avoid exposing the cells
to high temperatures (or strong light) which may cause migra-
tion of caesium within the cell.

Technical photocells are commonly operated with about
100 V between cathode and anode; since the photocurrent is
nearly saturated, no special stabilisation of this voltage is required. The current in a photocell may be measured with a sensitive galvanometer, but it is more common to pass the current
through a high resistance and
to measure the potential difference with an electrostatic
device: this is now frequently
an electrometer valve (§6.16).
It is often advantageous to
" chop " the light periodically
and to use an A.C. amplifier.
The A.C. amplifier can be
made to be robust and to have
a stable gain: if it is made
frequency-sensitive, or followed by a phase-sensitive

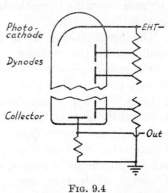

FIG. 9.4

rectifier operated in synchronism with the chopper, the system
discriminates against small amounts of stray light which are
not chopped at the right frequency.

It is not possible in practice to reach with a simple photocell
the limit of sensitivity set by fluctuations in the cathode
emission (§10.10), and the photomultiplier cell has revolutionised the measurement of weak light, particularly in astronomy.
The usual circuit arrangement for using a multiplier cell is
given in Fig. 9.4, which shows the potential divider to supply
the dynodes and an output resistor across which a high-
impedance measuring device is connected: alternatively a
galvanometer can be used to measure the current directly. It
is sometimes desirable to keep the cathode at earth potential
(e.g. where a tube with cathode on the wall is operated in contact

with a tank of liquid). The output circuit must then be at a rather high positive potential: if a galvanometer is used to measure the current it must be properly insulated and electrostatically screened. If the input light is modulated, the output signal from a resistor may be taken to an amplifier through a condenser which has good insulation.*

It is possible in a photomultiplier to detect the burst of electrons resulting from the amplification of a single photoelectron and therefore to measure the photoelectron rate with the counting techniques described in Chapter 11. These " photon counting " methods have some advantages at the weakest illuminations.

The amplification in a photomultiplier increases rather rapidly with the voltage applied to the dynodes. 0·1 % voltage change gives 0·8 % change of amplification in a typical 11-stage tube, so that a well-stablished power supply (usually of 1000-2000 V.) is required. The overall sensitivity of a photomultiplier tube is fairly stable if only small currents (e.g. 1 μA) are drawn from the collector. " Fatigue " effects of uncertain origin are observed with larger currents, and the makers' maximum currents, set apparently by considerations of energy dissipation, are much larger than is desirable in quantitative work. Most photomultipliers behave rather irregularly when they are first shut up in the dark with voltage applied to the electrodes, and it may be necessary to keep them for many hours in this condition before the most consistent response to weak light is obtained. They should never be exposed to temperatures much above ordinary room temperatures, nor to strong light with the voltages applied. Some irregularities can be traced to electrostatic disturbances due to the glass of the cell, especially when a cathode formed on the glass is maintained at a potential very different from earth. It may be necessary to use an external guard-ring at cathode potential.

Photocells and photomultipliers give a " dark current "

---

* When photomultipliers are used to detect flashes of light, as in nuclear scintillation counters, it is sometimes advantageous to take a positive-going output from the last dynode rather than the negative pulse from the collector. The dynode pulse is of course rather smaller than the collector pulse.

whose fluctuations set an important limit to the detection of weak light. Part of this current is due to insulation leakage, ionisation of residual gas, and field emission from the electrodes: these can be reduced by selection of the cells. There is, however, a more fundamental dark current which arises from thermionic emission from the cathodes (and dynode surfaces) at room temperature: this current can be greatly reduced by cooling with solid carbon dioxide or liquid air. This is necessary when the weakest light is being measured, especially with red-sensitive cathodes (Cs-O-Ag) but it involves considerable technical complication in keeping windows and insulation free from condensed moisture, and in keeping the tube free from dangerous thermal stresses.

The energy sensitivity of the photomultiplier probably exceeds that of any other physical instrument, but it must be stated again that the sensitivity, dark current, and steadiness vary considerably from cell to cell in the present state of the manufacturing art (cf. Engstrom *et al.* 1952), and selection among a number of cells is a great advantage in securing the highest performance.

9.6 Photoelectric Detectors in the Ultra-violet

Photocells and photomultipliers are made with caesium-antimony cathodes and bulbs or windows of special ultra-violet-transmitting glass or of fused quartz: the sensitivity then remains high to 2500 Å and 2000 Å respectively: tubes have been made with windows of synthetic sapphire and lithium fluoride but they are not normally purchasable.

At shorter wavelengths (vacuum ultraviolet) a simple and efficient method is to use a fluorescent substance (e.g. sodium salicylate crystals deposited from methyl alcohol solution) to convert the radiation into light which can be detected by an ordinary photomultiplier tube; the difficulty of finding a window material transparent to short-wave radiation is thus evaded.

It has been found possible to make photocathodes and photomultipliers which work directly in the vacuum of a spectrograph. At short wavelengths the photoemission from a metal is not confined to the surface, and the quantum efficiency rises considerably, so that simple metal cathodes may be used and they remain active even after exposure to air for short periods. There are also dynode materials (e.g. beryllium copper) whose secondary emission is not destroyed by exposure to air or which can be revived by simple heat treatment. A further technique, which, however, requires a window, uses the photoionisation of gases, which may be used in the filling of a Geiger counter. Such counters may be made to some extent wavelength selective. References are given in Braddick 1960.

9.7   Solid-state Photoelectric Detectors

The red sensitivity of known photoemissive cathodes ceases at about $1\cdot2$ μ (Cs-O-Ag cathode) and quantum detectors for longer wavelengths than this depend on internal photoelectric processes in semi-conductors. These produce an increase of conductivity on illumination (photoconductivity) or a voltage (photovoltaic effect).

Photovoltaic (barrier layer) cells, which have been available for many years, consist of a thin (polycrystalline) layer of copper oxide, selenium, or lead sulphide formed on a metal surface and covered with a transparent conducting layer or mesh. The interface between semiconductor and metal acts as an electrical rectifier; when illuminated it generates an e.m.f. and will yield a current which is proportional to the flux of incident light if the external resistance of the measuring circuit is low. Typically, these cells give about 100 μA per lumen of incident light as obtained from a black body at 3000° K.

The spectral sensitivity begins in the near infra-red and extends into the visible spectrum, and that of the selenium cell is not very different from that of the human eye. It may be adjusted by means of filters to agree closely with that of the eye or a given photographic emulsion. These cells, connected to simple microammeters, have long been used as photographic exposure meters and in illuminating engineering measurements, but their sensitivity varies with temperature and is not very constant with time: it also varies in a complicated way with the angle at which the light is incident. The cells may, however, be used for quite accurate photometry by comparative methods.

Photovoltaic cells of a newer type consist of single crystals of silicon " doped " with other elements in such a way that a layer of n-type semi-conductor is formed on the surface of a p-type semiconductor. When the junction layer is illuminated, quanta are absorbed and hole-electron pairs are produced and separated, so that a current is available to do work in an external circuit. These cells are used as " solar batteries " to obtain electrical power from sunlight with an energy efficiency of the order 10 %. The same principle of photoproduction of hole-electron pairs in the immediate neighbourhood of a p-n junction is used in photodiodes and phototransistors used as detecting and measuring instruments. In the latter the connection to the base is formed by a second p-n junction, and current amplification is obtained as in the common-emitter use of a triode transistor (§ 7.27). The overall sensitivity of commercial devices is of the order 1 A per lumen of tungsten light and the maximum sensitivity is in the red part of the visible spectrum. The active area of the devices is small, and they are particularly useful for such applications as digital decoders and punched tape readers. Other semi-conductors such as indium antimonide, can in principle be used as junction photovoltaic cells in the same way.

In other solid state devices the primary process is the photoconduction produced by the excitation of electrons either from the valency band of energy levels (as in PbS, CdS, InSb), or from impurity levels (" doped " Ge). If the semiconductor is provided with contacts which can supply electrons freely, the conductivity persists until the electrons are recaptured into deep-lying levels, so that the current which flows is not limited to the rate of excitation of primary electrons. The current is usually proportional to the applied voltage, so that the phenomenon can properly be described as photoconductivity: it decays with time, not necessarily exponentially, since several decay processes may be involved, but in a way roughly specified by a time constant. The fundamental noise in the photocurrent due to fluctuations in the generation and recombination of electrons is only exceptionally observable: it is usually overlaid by noise whose origin is not yet fully known, and whose frequency distribution curve rises at low frequencies.

The properties of important detectors of this type, available in 1960, are summarised in Table 9.2. Cadmium sulphide photoconductive cells are used as sensitive detectors for visible light when their slow response can be tolerated: they are in practice used mainly for working relays in various technical applications.

TABLE 9.1

Solid-state Radiation Detectors

Type of cell	Wavelength for maximum sensitivity	Long wave limit	Time constant
	μ	μ	
CdS	0·7	0·9	ca 50 msec.
Ge (phototransistor)	1·6	2	ca 100 μsec.
PbS room temp.)	2·5	3·5	50-500 μsec.
(cooled to 90° K.)	3·5	4·5	
PbSe (room temp.)	3·5	5	1-10 μsec.
(cooled to 90° K.)	7	8·5	10-50 μsec.
PbTe (90° K.)	4·5	5·5	20-100 μsec.
InSb (photoconductive)	6·5	8	< 1 μsec.
Ge (doped Au)		9·5	
(doped Au, Sb)		6	
(doped Zn, 4° K.)	35	40	≪ 1 μsec.
(doped Sb)		118	

The lead salt cells consist of polycrystalline layers deposited chemically or by evaporation on glass or a similar substrate between metal or graphite electrodes: they do not develop their full sensitivity until they have received an empirical treatment with oxygen. The sensitivity of some of these cells is greatly increased by cooling to 90° K. (liquid air) or lower. The noise is reduced and the limit of sensitivity may be shifted towards longer wavelengths. The time constant of PbS cells is a few hundred microseconds at room temperature and longer at low temperatures. They are usually used with chopped radiation, and since their impedance is fairly high (order 1 megohm), they can be coupled directly to valve amplifiers. The choice of chopping frequency is important: it should be high enough to reduce the effect of flicker-type noise whose spectral density increases with decreasing frequency, but if it is too high, the sensitivity of the system will fall, because of the time response of the photocell. In practice a chopping frequency of a few hundred cycles per second gives the best advantage.

Lead selenide and telluride cells are similar in their general characteristics to lead sulphide: lead selenide cells can be used at room temperature as well as at low temperature, but lead telluride is only useful when cooled. These two detectors have been used for spectroscopy down to about 7 μ.

More recently, monocrystalline indium antimonide has been developed as a detector for this region. The fundamental process involved is the excitation of electrons from the filled band of main levels, and the detectors respond out to about 7·5 μ when used at room temperatures. When InSb is cooled, the limit of spectral response moves to *higher* frequencies and if the cells are cooled to liquid air temperature to reduce noise, they are only useful to about 5·5 μ.

Single crystals of germanium, containing controlled impurities, require very little excitation energy and are sensitive to very long wavelengths, but the quantum efficiency is less than that of intrinsic semiconductors. Thermal excitation takes place at quite low temperatures in these substances; it can be taken as a rough rule that detectors sensitive beyond about 5 μ must be cooled in practice with liquid air, while zinc- and antimony-doped germanium detectors must be cooled in liquid helium.

9.8   Non-selective (Thermal) Detectors

Radiation of any frequency can in principle be detected by absorbing it and measuring the heat produced: detectors working in this way have a theoretical limiting sensitivity set by fluctuation noise in the energy exchange between the detector and its surroundings. This noise limit is in general worse than that of a selective quantum detector, but it is difficult to approach in practice because of extra noise incidental to the particular detector (e.g. thermal noise corresponding to its electrical resistance). The relation between such noise and the signal depends on the properties of available materials, and if the detector is cooled to reduce the energy exchange fluctuations, the relation between parasitic noise and signal often becomes worse.

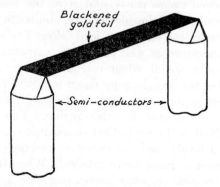

Fig. 9.5 Principle of Schwartz thermocouple.

The temperature-sensitive element in these detectors may be a thermocouple or a resistance thermometer (bolometer) and there is no decisive difference between the sensitivity attained with the two devices (Smith, Jones, and Chasmar 1957 which gives a comprehensive study and theoretical treatment of available detectors).

In designing a sensitive thermocouple materials must be chosen to give a high thermoelectric power combined as far as possible with high electrical conductivity and low thermal conductivity; the two latter properties tend to be incompatible. Some advantages are obtained by using semiconductors as in the Schwartz (Hilger) and some other commercial detectors: these advantages arise mainly because the dimensions and mechanical design of the " optimum " detector (cf. Fig. 9.5) are favourable compared with the assembly of very fine metal wires or films.

Semiconductors can also be used in bolometers: flakes of a mixture containing metallic oxides (thermistors) show a large decrease of resistance with increasing temperature, and at low temperatures slips of carbon composition as used in radio resistors make effective bolometers. Very sensitive detectors have been made by using substances maintained at the threshold of superconductivity, where over a short temperature range the resistance changes very rapidly. These devices are at present subjects for research rather than practical tools, but probably have the lowest noise level of any known thermal detector.

Thermocouples and bolometers are now usually used with chopped radiation and A.C. amplifiers. They must be designed with short time constants since 5-10 c/s is about the lowest frequency for convenient amplification and valve flicker noise (§ 10.6) becomes important at low frequencies. One of the difficulties in designing the detectors lies in obtaining a receiving element of low heat capacity which is nearly black (absorbing) at long infra-red wavelengths.

A special form of differential gas thermometer, the Golay cell, has ben used rather extensively as a spectroscopic detector in the far infra-red, and it is made commercially. It consists of a thin flat gascell containing a radiation absorber, surrounded by an annular cell which is not exposed to the radiation. The pressure difference produces in a thin membrane a deformation which is detected optically with a photocell. The detector is used with chopped light and is made insensitive to slow changes in temperature of the cells by providing a small leak between them.

It is clear that thermal detectors of high sensitivity are rather difficult instruments and it is advantageous to use quantum detectors where possible. Thermal detectors are important for calibrating other detectors, since their energy sensitivity is constant over long spectral ranges; this use does not necessarily involve very weak radiation since in calibrating a sensitive detector the radiation can be attenuated in a known ratio. Thermal detectors must also be used for those parts of the infra-red spectrum for which convenient quantum detectors are not available, and for most laboratories this implies at present wavelengths longer than about 7 μ.

APPENDIX 1

Note on the Comparison of Detectors for Small Amounts of Light

(a) One quantum of green light (λ 5550 A.U.)

$$= 3\cdot5 \cdot 10^{-12} \text{ ergs}$$
$$= 3\cdot5 \cdot 10^{-19} \text{ W sec.}$$
$$= 2\cdot22 \cdot 10^{-16} \text{ lumen sec.}$$

(b) Sensitivity of the eye to a point source—from astronomical data.

The eye can detect a star of magnitude 6. The corresponding flux into an 8 mm. diameter pupil is $4\cdot2 \cdot 10^{-13}$ lumens. Under very favourable conditions a star of magnitude $8\cdot5$ can be detected, corresponding to a flux of $4\cdot2 \cdot 10^{-14}$ lumens. If the light were all of the most favourable wavelength, this would be about 200 quanta/sec.

(c) A fairly fast photographic emulsion gives a detectable blackening with about $0\cdot004$ metre-candle-sec. This corresponds to $4\cdot10^{-7}$ lumen sec./sq. cm., and if this light is in a star image of area $3\cdot10^{-6}$ sq. cm., the exposure required is $1\cdot2 \cdot 10^{-12}$ lumen secs. This agrees very roughly with the astronomical rule of thumb that a just visible object can be photographed in about one minute. Taking account of reciprocity failure, the flux into a star image which was just detectable after an exposure of 10^4 sec. would be $6\cdot10^{-16}$ lumens, or about 3 quanta/sec.

(d) With photo-cathodes now available, 10 quanta of light of the most favourable wavelength give 1 photoelectron. In photomultiplier cells an amplification of 10^6-10^7 is obtainable in the electron multiplier, so that 1 quantum/sec. incident on the cathode gives an ultimate response of 10^5-10^6 electrons/sec. The higher figure corresponds to a current of $1\cdot6 \cdot 10^{-13}$ A, which is not very difficult to measure electrostatically. The current is subject to large fluctuations and would have to be integrated over a period of many seconds. With a photocathode at ordinary temperatures the emission would be completely swamped by thermionic emission; the

384

dark current of the best available multipliers at room temperature is of the order 0·01 μA-0·1 μA, after amplification. Measurements have been made which appear to show that the thermionic emission from a cathode can be reduced to one electron in many seconds, using liquid air cooling (Engstrom 1947).

It will be seen that the photomultiplier is much more sensitive than the photographic plate or the eye in the detection of a small image ; the plate can, however, record detail over a large area at once. Experimental tests show that if a small pattern (an interference pattern about 1 mm. wide) is scanned by the photocell, the time taken to detect given detail is about 100 times less than that required by the photographic plate. Corresponding figures can be deduced for other patterns such as spectra. The photocell of course gives the intensity distribution much more directly than the plate.

CHAPTER 10

THE NATURAL LIMITS OF MEASUREMENT

10.1 The Natural Limits of Measurement

It is nowadays accepted that the accuracy of physical measurements is ultimately limited by causes which arise from the nature of the measurement rather than from instrumental limitations (Barnes and Silverman 1934). In principle even a simple measurement of length is made on a lattice of vibrating atoms, and the best we can do is to take a time-average of their positions.

Spontaneous fluctuations which occur in amplifier systems can give rise to audible noise in telephones, and it is convenient to use the term " noise " to embrace all the fluctuation phenomena we are going to consider. We may divide the causes of noise into

(1) Thermal agitation.

(2) The particulate nature of matter and electricity.

(3) The " uncertainty " limitations of quantum mechanics.

The third group does not yet seem to have provided a limitation to practical measurement of the kind considered here, but it must be borne in mind as a potential limiting factor ; it might, for example, become important in resistor noise at very low temperatures.* We shall see that phenomena of groups (1) and (2) often act as limiting factors in measurements which seek to combine high sensitivity with rapid response. It should perhaps be stated that while noise, in the sense of this chapter, is always the ultimate limit to accuracy, it is rather exceptional in ordinary laboratory work for this limit to be operative, since a grosser limit is often set by uncontrolled external factors (e.g. mechanical vibration, electrical pick-up, temperature effects). In high-frequency technique, where a system may respond over a large frequency band, we shall

---

* Quantum limitations are approached in the most elaborate measurements of the width of spectral lines.

see that the noise is quite large, and may be appreciable in very ordinary work.

10.2   Thermal Agitation

It is well established that in any system with a number of independent degrees of freedom which is in thermal equilibrium with its surroundings at a certain absolute temperature T, the kinetic energy associated with each degree of freedom is $\frac{1}{2}kT$, where k, Boltzmann's constant, is the gas constant referred to a single molecule. The numerical value of k is $1\cdot4 \cdot 10^{-16}$ ergs/°C.*

Because of this thermal motion, the co-ordinate corresponding to any degree of freedom shows random fluctuations. The Brownian motion seen in small particles suspended in a fluid is typical of the case where the motion is subject to no definite restoring force.† The particles experience molecular impacts which drive them hither and thither. In the mathematical treatment of this phenomenon (Einstein 1906) the molecular impacts are treated partly as driving and partly as damping forces, and the resulting motion is shown to be a " random walk " in which the average displacement of a number of particles from their initial positions increases with the square root of the time.

More typical of the effect of thermal agitation on measurements is the motion of a torsional suspension which has a restoring couple proportional to its displacement from a zero. Here the molecular bombardment acts in part as a disturbing, and in part as a damping force, and a detailed account of the motion can be made by a statistical analysis of the process. The character of the motion depends on the gas pressure ; at high pressures the molecular impacts are frequent and the motion of the suspended system appears completely irregular, though (unlike the Brownian motion) it takes place about a definite zero. At low pressures the molecular impacts are

* The quantum theory requires modifications of the equipartition law when kT is comparable with $h\nu$. These are not normally important in the calculation of noise since at 300° K. the frequency corresponding to kT is about 10^{13} c/s.

† The name Brownian motion is sometimes applied to thermal agitation in general.

rare, but the damping effect of the collisions is small, and the motion is largely harmonic with the natural frequency of the system. There are, however, irregular changes in amplitude and phase. The average kinetic energy (and the average potential energy which is equal to it in a system of this kind) are independent of the changes in pressure, and can be calculated without any reference to the mechanism involved. *It is true in general that the kinetic energy $\frac{1}{2}kT$ is associated with a co-ordinate at temperature* T, *independent of the number or type of disturbing mechanisms acting.*

In this case of a suspended system with a restoring couple, the random deflections take place about a mean position, and this mean position may be found with any desired accuracy by averaging the positions over a long enough period. If, then, we *assume* that a deflection imposed on the system is steady, we can measure it by averaging a long series of readings, but rapid changes of deflection are entirely masked by the random deflections.

If the moving system is that of a galvanometer, the random deflections set a limit to the smallest current or voltage which can be observed in a finite time. We shall see that this limit is imposed on all methods of measuring current, and may be considered as due to the random motion of electrons in the circuit. In a galvanometer the electrical and mechanical disturbances are closely coupled, and the motion can be considered from either the mechanical or the electrical standpoint.

10.3 Thermal Noise in Electrical Circuits

The theory of thermal noise in electrical circuits was originally invented by Nyquist to deal with valve amplifier circuits. A resistance R at temperature $T°$ K. is known experimentally to be the seat of a random noise voltage, which is due to the conduction electrons sharing in the distribution of thermal energy. Nyquist (1928) applied a simple thermodynamic argument to show that the magnitude of the noise voltage and its frequency distribution are independent of the construction of the resistor and depend only on R and T.

The random noise can be represented by a continuous frequency spectrum. When a number of superposed harmonic disturbances are unrelated in frequency the "effective" value of the resultant is obtained by taking the root of the sum of the squares of the amplitudes of the components. It is therefore convenient to define a distribution function $E^2(\nu)$, such that $E^2(\nu)d\nu$ is the contribution to the squared effective voltage made by the components lying in the frequency range between ν and $\nu + d\nu$, and $\int_{\nu_1}^{\nu_2} E^2(\nu)d\nu$ is the contribution made by the components in the finite range between ν_1 and ν_2.

Suppose that two resistors of magnitude R kept at the same temperature T are connected by a loss-free transmission line which includes a matched, non-dissipative filter which allows power transfer only in a restricted frequency range between ν_1 and ν_2. The power transferred from one of the resistors to the line is

$$\frac{1}{2} \cdot \frac{1}{2R} \int_{\nu_1}^{\nu_2} E^2(\nu)d\nu$$

in this range. If the distribution function is not the same for the two resistors, we could by choosing the pass band of the filter correctly, obtain a net transfer of energy between the resistors, which is not compensated in any other frequency band. Such a transfer is contrary to the Second Law.

The argument may be extended to show that the noise from an impedance $Z_\nu = R_\nu + jX_\nu$ is at every frequency the same as that for a pure resistance of magnitude R_ν. The actual form of the distribution may be shown to be

$$E^2(\nu) = 4kTR_\nu.$$

For a pure resistance R_ν is constant over the frequency spectrum, and $E^2(\nu)$ has the value $1 \cdot 6 \cdot 10^{-20}$ (volts)^2 per cycle per ohm at 300° K.

This noise voltage integrated over all frequencies would be infinite, but in practice there is always a capacity C in parallel with the resistance R, and we have

$$Z_\nu = 1 \Big/ \left(\frac{1}{R} + j2\pi\nu C\right) = R/(1 + j2\pi\nu RC)$$

$$R_\nu = R/(1 + 4\pi^2\nu^2 R^2 C^2)$$

and the noise voltage spectrum given by

$$E_\nu^2 = 4kTR/(1 + 4\pi^2\nu^2R^2C^2)$$

cuts off at high frequencies which make $4\pi^2\nu^2R^2C^2 \gg 1$.

If we integrate the noise spectrum from ν_1 to ν_2, we obtain

$$\overline{E^2} = \int_{\nu_1}^{\nu_2} E^2(\nu)d\nu = \int_{\nu_1}^{\nu_2} 4kTRd\nu/(1 + 4\pi^2\nu^2R^2C^2)$$

$$= \frac{4kTR}{2\pi RC} {}_{\nu_1}^{\nu_2}[\tan^{-1} 2\pi\nu RC].$$

If the band extends from 0 to ∞, we obtain

$${}_{\nu_1}^{\nu_2}[\tan^{-1} 2\pi\nu RC] = \frac{\pi}{2}$$

and

$$\overline{E^2} = \frac{kT}{C}$$

which is the value we obtain by setting the energy of the condenser

$$\tfrac{1}{2}C\overline{E^2} = \tfrac{1}{2}kT.$$

If the RC circuit is followed by an amplifier or filter for which the voltage gain at frequency ν is $g(\nu)$, the output noise voltage is given by

$$\overline{E^2} = 4kTR\int_0^\infty \frac{g^2(\nu)}{1 + 4\pi^2\nu^2R^2C^2}d\nu$$

10.4   Thermal Motion in Galvanometer Measurements

Using the notation of § 6.7, the motion of the galvanometer coil is given by

$$I\frac{d^2\theta}{dt^2} + \left(\beta + \frac{n^2A^2H^2}{R}\right)\frac{d\theta}{dt} + c\theta = nAHi.$$

The current sensitivity

$$\frac{\partial\theta}{\partial i} = \frac{nAH}{c}$$

and the voltage sensitivity

$$\frac{\partial\theta}{\partial v} = \frac{nAH}{Rc}.$$

Now equating the (potential) energy of rotation of the coil to $\frac{1}{2}kT$ we have

$$\tfrac{1}{2}c\bar{\theta}^2 = \tfrac{1}{2}kT$$

where $\bar{\theta}^2$ is the mean square deflection of the coil. This deflection corresponds to a random current of mean square value

$$\bar{i}^2 = \frac{kT}{c} \cdot \left(\frac{c}{nAH}\right)^2$$

or to a random voltage of mean square value

$$\bar{v}^2 = \frac{kT}{c}\left(\frac{Rc}{nAH}\right)^2.$$

These values are, in fact, not very conveniently expressed for ordinary use. The voltage relation takes a very simple form for the case where the damping of the system is entirely electromagnetic and is critical. This case was worked out by Ising in the paper which first called attention to the role of the thermal motion in electrical measurements.

We have

$$\left(\frac{n^2A^2H^2}{R}\right)^2 = 4Ic$$

$$\frac{n^2A^2H^2}{R} = 2c\sqrt{\frac{I}{c}} = 2c\frac{\tau}{2\pi}$$

where τ is the undamped time of swing.

Re-writing the expression above for $\bar{v}^2$

$$\bar{v}^2 = \frac{kT}{c} \cdot Rc^2 \cdot \frac{R}{n^2A^2H^2} = kTRc \cdot \frac{}{c\tau}$$

$$= \frac{\pi kTR}{\tau}.$$

This relation has an obvious affinity with the Nyquist result for the random voltage in a resistive circuit, and can in fact be deduced from it by multiplying the resistor noise spectrum by the voltage response of the galvanometer calculated for each frequency, and integrating over all frequencies.

These results give the order of magnitude of the zero fluctuations of a galvanometer. If measurements are being made with such sensitivity that the thermal motion is apparent, it is necessary to consider choosing the constants of the system and the method of observation so that the thermal fluctuations are removed as completely as possible from the mean of readings taken over a finite time of observation. The problem has been studied by Zernicke (1932) who works out the correlation which exists between two readings separated by a time interval, because each element of the thermal motion decays with the characteristics of the natural motion of the system. The best estimate of the position of the indicator, obtainable in a given time S, is got by integrating the reading with respect to time, and its mean square error is given by

$$\bar{v}^2 = \frac{2kTR}{S}.$$

This result is independent of the damping or the period, if this is short compared with S. The mean of a number of readings taken at intervals of, say, half an undamped period over the time S is not much worse than the value obtained by integration.

In practice, it is not often possible to take readings over so long a period as is envisaged here, and it is usually necessary to take alternate readings of the deflected and undeflected system. Zernicke has calculated the best times at which to take readings, so as to take advantage of the correlation between the positions of the system at different times. The original paper, or the summary in Barnes and Silverman, should be consulted for details.

10.5 Further Fluctuation Phenomena in Electrical Circuits *

Shot Noise and Partition Noise

A source of noise not yet considered arises from the fact that an electric current involves a transfer of discrete electrons.

---

* See Moullin (1938).

The effect is found in its simplest form in a diode valve used in such a way that the space current is electrically saturated and is limited by the emission from the cathode.   In successive short intervals of time the number of electrons emitted fluctuates in the same way as the emission from a radio-active source (§ 2).

Schottky (1922) showed how the variations in current could be obtained as a distribution function in frequency by Fourier analysis.   In a valve the passage of an electron from cathode to anode gives rise to a pulse of length equal to the transit time.   If we assume that this is short compared with the reciprocal of any frequency we are considering, each electron pulse may be treated as a Dirac δ function and gives a uniform distribution of I^2 over all frequencies.   If we have a current of uncorrelated electrons, we may simply superpose their frequency distributions in I^2 and obtain

$$I_\nu^2 \, d\nu = 2ei d\nu$$

where $I_\nu^2 d\nu$ represents the contribution to the squared current noise from a frequency range $d\nu$, and e is the electronic charge.

The valve acts in fact as a constant-current generator of alternating currents covering a continuous frequency spectrum according to this law.   If these currents are passed through a pure resistance R, we have for the e.m.f. developed across the resistance

$$E_\nu^2 d\nu = 2ei R^2 d\nu$$

and the e.m.f. developed across an impedance consisting of a resistance R and capacity C in parallel is

$$E_\nu^2 d\nu = 2ei \frac{R^2}{1 + 4\pi^2\nu^2 R^2 C^2} d\nu.$$

A saturated diode may be used in measurement work, e.g. on radio receivers, as a calculable source of noise, and if the associated circuit is carefully designed, it can give satisfactory results up to at least 200 Mc/s (Moffatt 1946).

In a valve where the emission is limited by space charge —this is necessarily true of triodes used as amplifiers—the shot effect of the anode current is much less than it is in the

TABLE 10.1

Noise in Valves—Empirical Data

For a triode $R_{eq} = \dfrac{2 \cdot 5}{g_m}$ (shot noise).

or a pentode $R_{eq} = \dfrac{2 \cdot 5}{g_m}$ (shot noise) $+ \dfrac{20}{g_m} \dfrac{I_{g_2}}{I_k}$ (partition noise).

Where g_m = mutual conductance, I_{g_2} = screen current, I_k = total cathode current.

(W. A. Harris, quoted in Valley and Wallman, 1948.)

Values calculated from this for representative valves

Valve designation	g_m mA/V	$\dfrac{2 \cdot 5}{g_m}$ ohms
6C5	2	1250
6J6 (CV858)	5·6	450
Mullard EF37 as triode	2·8	900

Valve designation	g_m mA/V	$\dfrac{2 \cdot 5}{g_m}$ ohms	$\dfrac{I_{g_2}}{I_k}$	$\dfrac{20}{g_m} \cdot \dfrac{I_{g_2}}{I_k}$ ohms	R_{eq} ohms
Mullard EF37 as pentode	1·8	1400	0·21	2340	3740
EF50	6·5	390	0·2	710	1100
EF54	7·7	325	0·12	470	795
EF91 (CV138)	7·5	330	0·2	535	865

The *experimental* values of R_{eq} in some cases agree with those given and are sometimes appreciably higher. The reason for this is obscure.

At very high frequencies, noise calculations are complicated by the internal coupling between electrodes and the effect of lead inductance, and the noise is greater than that calculated for lower frequencies.

temperature-limited case.* Theoretical calculations for the shot noise of amplifying valves of different geometrical forms have been made, but the agreement with experiment is not very good.

In a tetrode or more complicated valve, a new statistical source of noise appears in the random distribution of the space-current between the electrodes (normally between anode and screen). On account of this " partition noise ", a properly used triode may be preferable to a pentode in the early stages of a high gain amplifier, and the noise in a pentode is reduced by designing the valve so that the screen current is as small as possible a part of the total space current.

Shot noise and partition noise have the same frequency characteristics as thermal noise, and it is convenient to specify them in terms of the resistance which, when maintained at room temperature and connected across the grid and cathode of the valve would produce the same output noise. Table 9.1 gives approximate (empirical) formulae for calculating valve noise and the equivalent noise resistances deduced for several representative valves. It will be seen that these are of the order of a few thousand ohms. In low-frequency circuits valve noise can usually be made small compared with thermal noise, but this is not necessarily true at high frequencies, where it is hard to obtain high circuit impedances.

In some cases the shot noise of the grid current may be important ; it is given by

$$E_v^2 d\nu = 2ei_g Z_g^2 d\nu$$

where Z_g is the grid circuit impedance. If i_g is made up of an electron current and an ion collection current which partly or wholly cancel one another, the shot fluctuations of the two currents are nevertheless additive, and this fact is important in cases when a vacuum tube is used as an electrometer with a high resistance grid circuit and the grid operated near the " floating " potential (§ 6.17).

---

* In a metallic conductor the mechanism controlling the passage of electrons is such that shot noise is utterly negligible.

10.6   Flicker Noise and Noise in Semiconductor Devices

A further source of noise in valves is the emission mechanism of the coated cathode. The theory of this " flicker noise " is not yet fully established. Empirically the noise is approximately represented by a current fluctuation

$$I_\nu^2 d\nu = K \cdot \frac{i_a^2}{\nu} d\nu.$$

Unlike shot and thermal noise, this noise is not uniformly distributed over the frequency spectrum, and the contribution to I^2 from a frequency band of given width increases as the frequency falls.* Flicker noise is in practice usually small compared with other noise from other sources at frequencies greater than 1000 c/s, but may become dominant in systems which have a selective response at low or very low frequencies, for example, it is greater that the shot noise in an oxide cathode valve at 10 c/s and 1 mA anode current. Valves, even of the same type, give distinctly different amounts of flicker noise: it is small or absent in the emission from pure tungsten cathodes or from photocathodes.

A fluctuation noise voltage called " excess noise " whose frequency density increases at low frequencies occurs when a current passes through resistors made of semiconductors or thin deposited films. It is therefore good to use wire-wound resistors to carry current in the low-level circuits of amplifiers, especially when they have low-frequency response.

Noise in semiconductor devices

Semiconductors of course produce the thermal noise voltage distribution appropriate to their resistance: they also produce current fluctuations analogous to shot noise, due to fluctuations in the production and recombination of mobile carriers. As in the case of shot noise, the trajectory of a carrier between

---

* A simple approximate formula for flicker noise, expressed as an equivalent grid voltage, is quoted by Kandiah and Brown (1952)

$$E^2 = \frac{10^{-13} \, \delta\nu}{\nu} \text{ (volts)}^2.$$

generation and recombination can be regarded as a current pulse and the noise frequency spectrum calculated by Fourier methods.   The pulses are usually longer than the transit time of an electron in a valve, so that the spectral density is not uniform over the range of practical interest.   Furthermore the " excess noise " of semiconductors, with a spectral density increasing at low frequencies, is rather large in point contact devices and quite considerable in junction transistors.   As an indication of order of magnitude, this noise in a junction transistor amplifier at a frequency about 1000 c/s may be 10-15 decibels above the thermal noise in its input impedance at room temperature.

10.7   Examples.   An Audio-Frequency Amplifier

It is useful to give some calculations of noise in normal amplifying systems since this will exhibit the relative importance of different kinds of noise.

Consider an audio frequency amplifier, amplifying from 100-10,000 c/s and cutting off sharply at the ends of this band. The input circuit consists of a 500 kΩ resistance in parallel with 20 pf.

Since the impedance of 20 pf. at the highest frequency, 10 kc/s, is about 750,000 ohms, which is higher than the grid leak, the thermal noise in the input circuit may be calculated fairly closely from the formula

$$\bar{E}^2 = 4kTR(\nu_2 - \nu_1).$$

Putting in numerical values

$$(kT = 4 \cdot 10^{-14} \text{ erg} = 4 \cdot 10^{-21} \text{ joule at } 290° \text{ K})$$

this gives $(\bar{E}^2)^{\frac{1}{2}} = 126$ microvolts for $R = 10^6$ ohms and $\nu_2 - \nu_1 = 10^6$ c/s.*   For $\frac{1}{2}$ megohm and 1/100 megacycle the r.m.s. value is 9 μV.   Using the more accurate formula

$$\bar{E}^2 = \frac{4kTR}{2\pi RC} {}_{\nu_1}^{\nu_2}[\tan^{-1} 2\pi RC\nu]$$

---

* This is a convenient result to remember : r.m.s. thermal noise at room temperature for 1 megohm and 1 megacycle = 126 μV.

we obtain for the r.m.s. noise

$$\frac{4kTR}{2\pi \cdot 10^{-5}} \tan^{-1} 0.62$$

so that the effective band width for noise calculations is about 9000 cycles and the r.m.s. noise about 8·5 μV.

It is clear from the values given in § 9·5 that anode shot noise is small compared with this, and flicker noise is also unimportant. The shot effect of grid current may be considered. It is given by

$$\overline{E}^2 = 2ei_g R_g{}^2(\nu_2 - \nu_1)$$

where R_g is the grid resistance,

i_g is the grid current,

e is the electronic charge.

The effect is small compared with the thermal noise if i_g is of the order 10^{-9} A but may become dominant in a valve with abnormally large grid current.

10.8   A Radar Receiver

The receiver is connected to an aerial, and for purposes of calculation the radiation resistance of the aerial may be regarded as a source of thermal noise at (conventionally) 290° K.

Physically the aerial is a coupling between the receiver and the temperature radiation of the outside world, and for a directive aerial the effective temperature depends markedly on the way in which the beam is directed. It is quite high, for example, if a narrow collecting beam includes certain " noise sources " in the heavens.

The frequency band width of the receiver is large so as to allow the reproduction of pulses accurately defined in time (§ 7.3).

Putting $R = 80$ ohms, $(\nu_2 - \nu_1) = 2 \cdot 10^6$ cycles,   the resistance noise formula gives a r.m.s. voltage at 290° K.

$$126\left(\frac{80}{10^6} \cdot 2\right)^{\frac{1}{2}} = 1.6\,\mu\text{V}.$$

In practice the noise from the receiver is considerably larger than this, and it is useful for engineering purposes to define a " noise factor ".

$$k = \frac{\text{mean square noise voltage observed}}{\text{mean square noise voltage calculated for aerial at 290}^\circ \text{K}}.$$

The noise factor is usually expressed in decibels, i.e.

$$k_{db} = 10 \cdot \log_{10} k.$$

10.9 An Amplifier used in conjunction with an Ionisation Chamber, e.g. for counting α Particles

The design of amplifiers for this purpose is considered in § 10.13. A charge is collected in the chamber over a time τ which may be a few microseconds (electron collection) or about a millisecond (ion collection). The amplifier includes circuits which limit its frequency response at both high and low frequencies. The low frequency cut-off converts the pulses into sharp kicks

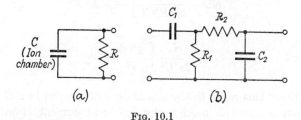

(a) (b)

Fig. 10.1

(a) Input

(b) Pulse forming circuits of ionisation chamber amplifier

For simplicity of calculation, take $R_1 << R_2$. This is usually true of practical systems

suitable for counting, whose height should be proportional to the initial ionisation (clipping). The high frequency cut-off controls the rise time of the pulse and we shall see that it has an important effect on the noise. In order to secure a well-shaped pulse the circuits which limit the frequency response are often deliberately inserted at a particular point, the rest of the amplifier being designed to have a wide response band.

The frequency limiting circuits in a simple case are those given in Fig. 10.1.

When a charge q is placed upon the condenser C in a time short compared with RC the signal voltage produced is q/C and its squared value, which may be compared with the noise, is q^2/C^2. In a typical case $C = 50$ pf. $R = 10^{10}$ ohms, so that $2\pi RC\nu \gg 1$ for any value of ν within the amplifier frequency range. The thermal noise formula (p. 390) then becomes

$$\overline{E}^2 = \frac{4kT}{4\pi^2 RC^2} \int\limits_0^\infty \frac{g^2(\nu)}{\nu^2} d\nu.$$

The thermal noise is therefore diminished, relative to the signal, by making R large, and the signal/noise ratio is independent of C. If R is given a high value, the first valve must be selected and arranged to work with a low grid current, and even so the grid shot noise will be important. Its value is given by

$$\overline{E}^2 = \frac{2ei_g R^2}{4\pi^2 R^2 C^2} \int\limits_0^\infty \frac{g^2(\nu)}{\nu^2} d\nu$$

$$= \frac{ei_g}{2\pi^2 C^2} \int\limits_0^\infty \frac{g^2(\nu)}{\nu^2} d\nu.$$

The ratio of this noise to the signal does not depend on R or C.

When a valve is used under low grid current conditions with low anode voltage, its mutual conductance is small, and the anode shot noise is considerable when stated in terms of an equivalent grid resistance. 10,000 ohms (corresponding to $g_m = 0.25$mA/V) is a representative figure for a selected triode. The noise produced is

$$4kT.R_{eq} \int\limits_0^\infty g^2(\nu)d\nu$$

where R_{eq} is the equivalent grid resistance. This noise becomes worse, relative to the signal, as C increases.

Flicker noise may be appreciable in an amplifier designed to have a pass band at relatively low frequencies, as is required when an ion collection chamber is in use.

$g^2(\nu)$ can be calculated for the system of Fig. 10.1; it is the product of two factors $\dfrac{p^2T_1{}^2}{(p^2T_1{}^2 + 1)}$ and $\dfrac{1}{(p^2T_2{}^2 + 1)}$ corresponding respectively to the differentiating (clipping) circuit determining the L.F. response and to the integrating circuit determining the H.F. response. p is the angular frequency $= 2\pi\nu$, $T_1 = R_1C_1$, and $T_2 = R_2C_2$.

The integral

$$\int_0^\infty \frac{g(\nu)}{v^2}d\nu \quad \text{becomes} \quad \pi^2 \frac{T_1{}^2}{(T_1 + T_2)}$$

and the integral

$$\int_0^\infty g(\nu)d\nu \quad \text{becomes} \quad \frac{T_1}{4T_2(T_1 + T_2)}$$

so that the thermal noise is

$$\frac{kT}{C^2R} \frac{T_1{}^2}{(T_1 + T_2)}$$

the grid shot noise is

$$\frac{ei_g}{2C^2} \frac{T_1{}^2}{(T_1 + T_2)}$$

and the anode shot noise is

$$kTR_{eq} \frac{T_1}{T_2(T_1 + T_2)}.$$

In a practical amplifier, T_1 and T_2 are often made equal and rather longer than the time of collection τ (§ 10.13). Let us consider an amplifier to be used with an ion collection chamber ($\tau = \frac{1}{2}$ to 1 millisec.), and take the following values : $T_1 = T_2 = 1\cdot5 \cdot 10^{-3}$ sec., $C = 50$ pf., $R = 10^{10}$ ohms, $i_g = 5 \cdot 10^{-12}$ A, $R_{eq} = 10^4$ ohms.

We have kT (at $290°$ K) $= 4 \cdot 10^{-21}$ joules, $e = 1\cdot6 \cdot 10^{-19}$ coulomb.

With these values, the thermal noise is negligible, the r.m.s. anode shot noise is about $0\cdot12$ μV and the r.m.s. grid shot noise is about $0\cdot35$ μV. It is found that the flicker noise in this case is about $0\cdot2$ μV. The grid shot noise is then the leading noise component, and the total r.m.s. noise is about $0\cdot4$ μV.

This must be compared with the pulse obtained by collecting ions, as attenuated by the filter circuits. For a pulse which rises in about $\frac{1}{2}$ millisec., the attenuation by integrating and differentiating circuits of time constant 1·5 millisec. is about 2·5 : 1. If therefore we assume that we can distinguish a pulse which after attenuation is about 3 times the r.m.s. noise, the corresponding charge is

$$5 \cdot 10^{-11} \times 4 \cdot 10^{-7} \times 3 \times 2\cdot5 = 150 \cdot 10^{-18} \text{ coulomb.}$$

This corresponds to the collection of about 1000 ions.

10.10 A Photocell used with an Electrometer Tube and Amplifier to detect Weak Light

The ultimate limit is here set ideally by the arrival of discrete light quanta at the photoelectric surface, for if on the average n light quanta arrive in unit time, the signal/noise ratio for a time of observation S is

$$\frac{nS}{(nS)^{\frac{1}{2}}} = (nS)^{\frac{1}{2}}.$$

The quantum efficiency ϵ of the best available photocathodes is of the order 10-15%, so that the shot effect of the photocell current gives a signal/noise ratio $(\epsilon nS)^{\frac{1}{2}}$, which is considerably worse than the photon shot effect. If there is a parasitic

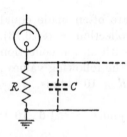

"dark" current from the cathode, due to thermionic emission, its shot effect will, of course, contribute to the shot noise, and, in fact, with the sensitive cathodes at present available (Sb—Cs, Cs—O—Ag) this effect is decisive unless the cathode is cooled. If the photocell is connected direct to an electrometer, the thermal fluctuations of the latter will set a limit to the current measurement, and if an electrometer valve is used to measure

FIG. 10.2 Coupling circuit between photocell and amplifier

the current, we shall see that additional noise in the valve circuits will usually set the limit. If the photocell contains electron multiplying stages which contribute little to the noise, it is possible nearly to reach the limit imposed by the photo-current shot noise.

If the circuit used to couple the phototube to an electro-meter valve is as Fig. 10.2, the r.m.s. thermal noise voltage has the value

$$\overline{E_e^2} = 4kTR \int_0^{\nu_1} \frac{d\nu}{1 + 4\pi^2 C^2 R^2 \nu^2} \tag{a}$$

and the shot effect voltage due to grid current is

$$\overline{E_g^2} = 2ei_g R^2 \int_0^{\nu_1} \frac{d\nu}{1 + 4\pi^2 C^2 R^2 \nu^2} \tag{b}$$

while the noise voltage due to the shot effect of the photo-current itself is

$$\overline{E_p^2} = 2eM^2 i_p R^2 \int_0^{\nu_1} \frac{d\nu}{1 + 4\pi^2 C^2 R^2 \nu^2}. \tag{c}$$

Here M is the internal multiplication provided in the photo-cell and ν_1 is the upper response frequency of the system, set probably by the galvanometer used as the final indicator. The signal which is to be compared with the noise above is

$$\overline{E^2} = M^2 i_p^2 R^2.$$

It appears at once that i_g and $M^2 i_p$ enter similarly into equations (b) and (c), so that $M^2 i_p$ must be much greater than i_g if the system is to approach the sensitivity limit set by the photocell itself. Since i_g is of the order 10^{-15} A for electro-meter tubes at present available, this means that internal multiplication in the cell is indispensable at low light levels for the primary photocurrent will then be small compared with 10^{-15} A.

If $2\pi RC\nu_1 \gg 1$, so that the speed of response of the system is limited by the input circuit and not by ν_1, the noise formulae take the simple form

$$\overline{E_{\text{thermal}}^2} = \frac{kT}{C} \; ; \quad \overline{E_{\text{grid shot}}^2} = \frac{ei_g R}{2C} \; ; \quad \overline{E_{\text{photocell}}^2} = \frac{eM^2 i_p R}{2C}$$

and the comparable signal is given by

$$E_{\text{signal}}^2 = M^2 i_p^2 R^2.$$

403

The thermal noise tends to be dominant with practical values of R, C, i_g. If R is increased, the shot noise, the photocell noise, and the signal, increase relative to the thermal noise. With $i_g = 10^{-15}$ A the grid shot noise becomes equal to the thermal noise when R is about 10^{13} ohms, and with a non-multiplying photocell the shot noise remains an irreducible limit to the useful sensitivity. With 10^{13} ohms, and the practical value $C = 20$ pf., the time constant is 200 sec., which is inconveniently long for many purposes. It has been suggested (H. L. Johnson 1948) that the electrometer tube should be followed with an amplifier having a rising frequency characteristic, so that the combination of input circuit and amplifier has a wider pass band and hence a quicker response. It may then be shown that the thermal noise becomes subordinate to the grid shot noise without the necessity for a very slow response. We must, however, use a photocell with internal multiplication if the photocathode noise is to dominate rather than the grid shot noise, and we can then satisfy the further condition that $E_{\text{photocell}} > E_{\text{thermal}}$ by a value of R, which makes the time constant of the input circuit moderate.

Thus for $M = 10^6$ and $R = 5 . 10^{10}$ ohm which gives with $C = 2 . 10^{-11}$ farad a time constant 1 sec. the condition becomes

$$1{\cdot}6 . 10^{-19} . 10^{12} . 5 . 10^{10} i_p > 2 . 1{\cdot}4 . 10^{-23} . 300 . \text{amp.}$$

$$i_p > 10^{-26} \text{ amp.}$$

The photocathode shot noise now dominates for any practical photocurrent and the considerations of p. 340 apply.*

10.11. The Coherent Rectifier Systems

The coherent detector, or phase-sensitive rectifier, is an important device for measuring an alternating signal, especially in the presence of noise. The frequency and phase of the alternating signal must be available at the detector, so that it

---

* There does not seem to be any information about the flicker noise of electrometer tubes and this factor is neglected in all calculations available. It is possible that flicker noise may be even more important than shot noise at the very low frequencies involved.

is normally obtained from a quasi-steady signal by a "chopping" process. After amplification, the signal is rectified by an electromechanical or by an electronic commutator operated in synchronism with the chopper. The wanted signal then appears as unidirectional: it can be smoothed by an "integrating" circuit and measured by a D.C. instrument. Parasitic signals of other frequencies, including most of the noise components, give rise to alternating ouputs which integrate to zero (compared to the wanted signal) over a sufficiently long period.

The properties of the device may be investigated if we treat the switching process as multiplication by a periodic function which can be represented by a Fourier series $A_1 + \Sigma A_n \cos n\omega t$.* If the signal contains a component $S_v \cos vt$, the output of the rectifier contains terms

$$S_v A_0 \cos vt, \tfrac{1}{2} S_v A_n \cos L(v + n\omega)t, \tfrac{1}{2} S_v A_n \cos L(v - n\omega)t.$$

This output may be smoothed, e.g. by an R.C. circuit which attenuates the high frequency components but passes the frequencies near zero which arise when v lies near ω and its harmonics $n\omega$ (cf. § 7.2).

Alternatively the ouput of the rectifier may be integrated by an electronic circuit (e.g. a Miller integrator p. 270) or by an electromechanical device such as a motor whose speed is accurately proportional to the applied e.m.f.† In this case the integrated effect of the difference term over time T is $S_v A_n \sin (v - n\omega)T/(v - n\omega)T$, and the other terms may usually be neglected. The function $\dfrac{\sin \theta}{\theta}$ plotted in Fig. 10.3 tends rapidly to zero as its argument increases.

In the important case where the background against which we discriminate is noise with a uniform distribution of squared amplitude in frequency it may be shown that the R.C. filter

---

* The implied restriction to an even function is unimportant: for the common case of simple square wave switching with equal on and off periods $A_0 = \tfrac{1}{2}$, $A_n = \tfrac{1}{2}$ (n odd), $A_n = 0$ (n even).

† Integrating motors developed from a German invention of 1939-45 are made commercially; the Velodyne (Williams and Uttley 1946) is an electronically-controlled D.C. motor with accurate integrating properties.

following a phase-sensitive rectifier accepts noise with an effective bandwidth $\frac{2}{RC}$ and that time integration over time T gives an effective bandwidth $\frac{2}{T}$. The integrating device, for which T may be made large, is therefore valuable when a very weak signal must be measured in the presence of relatively strong noise.

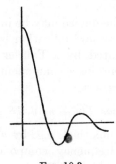

FIG. 10.3

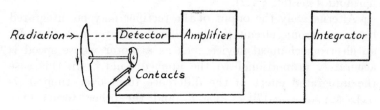

FIG. 10.4 A simple application of the phase-sensitive rectifier. Radiation is chopped by a sector disk, the phase sensitive rectifier is a mechanically-driven contact interrupting the input to the integrator

Fig. 10.3 indicates how the principle of phase-sensitive detection may be used. The rectifier may be a relay driven synchronously with the chopper: this method has the advantage that it will commutate correctly signals of any amplitude, but the relay requires careful design and adjustment, and it cannot be used at frequencies higher than a very few hundred cycles per second. Bridge circuits using diodes can be used as switches up to much higher frequencies: a particularly favourable arrangement has been devised by Noble and is described in Smith, Jones, and Chasmar (1947).

As an alternative to the rectifier, the signal can be multiplied by a sinusoidal reference voltage by applying the signal and reference voltages to the coils of a dynamometer, or by using an electronic multiplying circuit followed by an integrator. It will be clear from the analysis above that this arrangement has an acceptance band around the fundamental frequency *only*: it has been used less than the switching device because of the paucity of available multiplying devices. It must be noted that though the final response to noise depends on the integrating properties of the output circuit the amplifier and rectifier are required on deal linearly with the much larger noise amplitude corresponding to the bandwidth of the amplifier itself, so that it is advisable to limit the frequency response of the amplifier and to do so in early stages. This is conveniently done by shunting the anode resistors with condensers, but a more elaborate selective amplifier may be used.

Phase sensitive detection can be used with a photocell or quick acting thermopile to detect weak radiation, the chopper* being inserted in the beam of radiation: it has been applied to the measurement of small alternating voltages induced by rotating weakly magnetised rock specimens in a pick-up coil (Johnson *et al.* 1949). One of the most sophisticated applications is in radio astronomy, where in effect an aerial looks alternately at two parts of the sky and the difference due to a celestial source is treated as a signal: very long integration times are employed, and weak sources detected in the presence of almost overwhelming noise.

The problems of designing a chopper when the initial signal is a small voltage are discussesd in § 6.17.

---

* Some detectors have a non-uniform frequency distribution of noise: it is then desirable to choose the chopping frequency so that the pass band does not include the strongest noise (see p. 380).

CHAPTER 11

SOME TECHNIQUES OF NUCLEAR PHYSICS

11.1   Ionisation by Ionising Particles

The counting of ionising particles is a distinctive technique of nuclear physics, and the increasing importance of applied nuclear physics justifies a special section devoted to the subject.

The particles with which we are concerned are :

(1) Electrons of all energies from a few thousand volts upwards.

(2) Protons and α-particles.

(3) Heavily ionising fission fragments.

Fast and slow neutrons and γ-rays, which are not themselves ionising particles, are counted by means of the secondary ionising particles which they produce in suitable interactions.

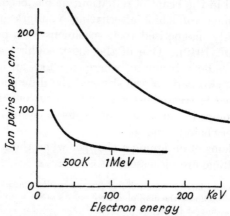

Fig. 11.1   Ionisation density (total ion pairs per cm.) for electrons of given energy in air.   Upper curve—electron energy to 250 KeV.   Lower curve—electron energy to 2 MeV.

In most applications, electrons, protons, or α-particles are counted.   The linear density of ionisation produced by these

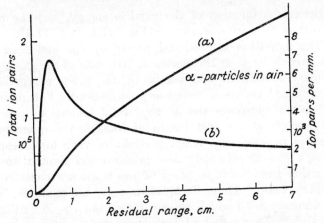

Fig. 11.2   (a) Total number of ion pairs produced
             (b) Ion pairs per mm.

Plotted against residual range for α-particles in air

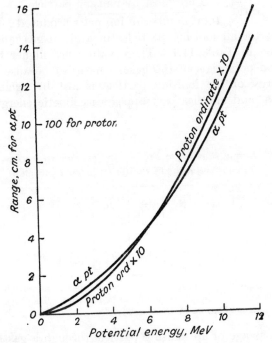

Fig. 11.3   Range in air for α-particles and protons.   Approximate data for
design purposes.   For accurate information see Livingston and Bethe, 1937,
Taylor, 1952.

409

particles is a function of the particle energy, and the most important data are presented in Figs. 11.1, 11.2, 11.3.

The ionisation is produced partly by the action of the fast particle itself on the electronic structure of the gas atoms (primary ionisation) and partly by the more energetic of the expelled electrons (secondary ionisation). For most of our present purposes the average total ionisation (primary and secondary) per unit length of track is the quantity of practical importance. When particles of very high velocity ionise a gas at relatively low pressure the fluctuations of ionisation from point to point of the track are considerable (Landau 1944). These fluctuations may, for example, limit the accuracy with which we can infer from the ionisation in a chamber the number of ionising particles crossing it; as one might expect, this limitation is encountered chiefly in cosmic ray physics.

The ratio $\dfrac{\text{energy lost by ionising particle}}{\text{total number of ion pairs produced}}$ is fairly constant for all ionising particles in a given gas, and values are given in Table 11.1. These values are higher than the ionisation potentials of the gases concerned because some of the energy of the ionising particle is lost by excitation of radiation, and another part appears as kinetic energy of the ions.

TABLE 11.1

Average Energy Required to Produce an Ion Pair in Various Gases
(From experiments by Stetter (1943) on α-particles)

Gas	Air	N_2	H_2	He	Ne	A	Kr	Xe
Energy in electron volts	35·6	37·1	36·0	30·0	29·7	28·2	26·2	23·6

The corresponding values for fast protons, electrons, are within a few per cent. identical with those given for α-particles. The best value for electrons in air is about 32 eV.

The passage of an ionising particle through a gas leaves a trail which consists initially of electrons and positive ions.

In practical ionisation chambers an electric field is applied between a high voltage electrode and an insulated collecting electrode which is usually near earth potential.   The potential changes of this electrode, due to the motion of the ions and electrons, are recorded.   By amplifying the potential changes it is possible to study the ionisation produced by a single particle ; alternatively, the integrated ionisation current may be used as a measure of a quasi-steady ionising radiation.

Again, amplification may be achieved within the counter by using an electric field sufficiently intense to produce ionisation by collision.   If the amplification is uniform from one particle to another, so that the measured potential change is proportional to the initial ionisation, the device is a *proportional counter*. If the amplification is such that a saturated pulse is produced by a particle irrespective of the initial ionisation, the device may still be used as a *counter*.

11.2   The Motion and Collection of Ions

When the ion density is very high, as in an α-particle track, some of the positive and negative ions may be lost by combination (Jaffé 1913), but in a practical ionisation chamber most of the ions move under the applied electric field towards the appropriate electrodes.   In the course of their motion they induce potential changes on the collecting electrode, and these changes are completed when the ions are finally collected.

In purified H_2, He, A, N_2, CO_2, the electrons remain free long enough to reach the collecting electrode, but in many gases, particularly oxygen and water vapour, the electrons are readily captured by gas molecules with formation of negative ions.   These ions are much less mobile than electrons.*

The motion of ions and electrons is controlled by collisions with gas molecules.   As a result of these collisions the motion becomes a random agitation on which is superposed a drift in the direction of the electric field : the random velocities

---

* For quantitative data on attachment, see Healey and Read 1941. The mean free path for capture is of the order 1 mm. for air at atmospheric pressure and an electric field of 1000 V/cm.

may be much greater than the drift velocity. For a given gas under a moderate electric field, the drift velocity is proportional to the field divided by the gas pressure, and the mobility is defined as the velocity per unit field at standard atmospheric pressure. For the field strength of 1000 V/cm., common in ionisation chambers, the positive ion velocities are of the order of 1000 cm./sec. (Quantitative data in I.C.T., Vol. VI).

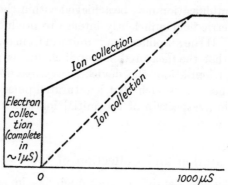

FIG. 11.4 Diagrammatic representation of voltage pulses from ionisation chambers. Upper curve—electron collection chamber. Lower curve—ion collection chamber

The drift velocities of unattached electrons in suitable gases are about a thousand times greater than this, and this fact has an important application in ionisation chamber technique, since it allows the electrons to move across a chamber in a time of the order 1 μS, thus producing a very sharp pulse.

In pure argon, under electric fields of the order given, the random velocities of electrons become high, because collisions between electrons and argon atoms are strictly elastic over a wide energy range. Rather paradoxically, the *drift* velocity of the electrons can be increased by decreasing the random velocity. If a few per cent. of CO_2 is added to the argon, inelastic collisions between electrons and CO_2 molecules keep the electron agitation velocity low. The cross-section of the argon atoms is peculiarly low for collision with low energy electrons (Ramsauer effect): both the increased free path and the reduced random velocity lead to an increased drift velocity in a given field, so that the addition of a little CO_2 is a valuable technical device where fast electron collection is required.

As the charged particles move under the electric field in an ionisation chamber, they induce charges on the collecting electrode, and these charges are responsible for the recorded pulse. If the electrode were insulated, its potential changes would take the form indicated in Fig. 11.4. In practice, the shape of the pulse is modified by the action of the leak resistance connected to the collecting electrode, which gives the collecting system a finite C.R. time constant, and again by the characteristics of the amplifier which follows. It will be seen that where the conditions in the chamber allow of electron collection, the initial pulse has a rise time of the order of a microsecond, and that it is followed by a much slower pulse, due to the positive ions, with rise time of the order of a millisecond. If electron attachment takes place and negative ions are collected, the whole pulse has a rise time of the order of a millisecond.

11.3 Electron Collection Chambers

Ion collection was always used in the older technique of the ionisation chamber and linear amplifier (Lewis 1942), but the use of electron collection with appropriate electronic circuits has certain important advantages.

(a) Particles may be counted in very rapid succession.

(b) The ionisation chamber may form one element of a coincidence counting system of high resolving power ; this has proved valuable in cosmic ray investigations.

(c) The amplifier used may be made quite insensitive to disturbances of frequency below, say, 10 kc/s, and microphonic effects, electrical pick-up at mains frequency, etc., may be eliminated.

In Fig. 11.4 the potential changes due to the collection of electrons and the collection of positive ions are shown as equal, but this is not true in general. The potential change induced by the movement of a charged ion from its place of formation to its place of collection depends upon the initial position of the charge. Nevertheless, if both ions of a pair are collected, the final potential change is e/C where e is the ionic charge and C the electrical capacity of the collecting electrode. In an electron-collection chamber, the observed potential change is due only to the movement of the electrons, the ion collection being too slow to be detected by the amplifier. In this case the size of the pulse depends upon where in the chamber the ions were formed. This variation is small in a cylindrical chamber with central electrode of small diameter, since most of the potential drop is concentrated in a small

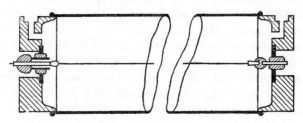

FIG. 11.5   Diagram of γ-ray ionisation chamber designed by Rossi. Outer parts are of brass with soft soldered joints. Wire is Kovar, 0·625 mm. diameter. Seals are Kovar-glass and arranged to provide an earthed guard ring between the high-potential outer case and the wire. The filling is argon with 3 % CO_2 at about 4 atmospheres

volume (Fig. 11.5). It may be avoided in a parallel plate chamber by arranging a grid, held at an intermediate potential, between the region where ionisation is produced and the collecting electrode (Rossi and Staub). The grid is made with a high transparency ratio, so that it collects very few of the electrons, but it screens the collector electrostatically from the positive ion distribution and from the electrons until these enter the space between grid and collector. The observed potential change is then due solely to the motion of the electrons from this moment until they are collected (Fig. 11.6).

In the practical use of an electron-collection chamber, the gas filling must be kept free from impurities which could give rise to electron attachment. The filling is typically argon with 2-4 % CO_2 under a pressure of several atmospheres. The gas mixture may be circulated over hot calcium, either continuously during use or for several hours before closing off the chamber, but good quality oxygen-free argon can be used, at least at moderate pressures, without this precaution, if the chamber is designed so that it can be freed from electro-negative gases (e.g. by heating before filling). At atmospheric pressure, cylinder argon is an

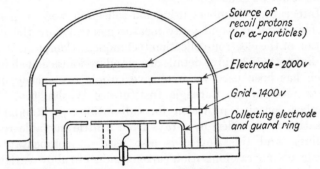

FIG. 11.6 A gridded electron collection ion chamber (based on a design by Rossi for recording fast neutrons)

effective filling and in some applications a slow stream of this gas may be passed through the chamber during the measurements.

Electron-collection chambers are particularly suitable for observing rapidly changing γ-ray intensities and cosmic ray bursts. Fig. 11.5 shows the general design of a chamber used by Rossi for these purposes.

Although electron collection chambers work well for counting α-rays and the determination of α-particle energies by measurement of total ionisation, they are rather inconvenient for these purposes (cf. § 11.4) unless they are used under atmospheric pressure with a slowly flowing stream of pure argon.

Electron-collection chambers can be used for ionisation measurements on neutron recoils, since the neutrons can enter the chamber without difficulty and knock protons out of a wax film into a medium-pressure gridded ionisation chamber.

11.4 Ion-Collection Chambers

It is a technical disadvantage of the electron-collection system that it requires a special atmosphere, so that radio-active sources (in particular α-ray sources) cannot be introduced into it without some trouble. In α-ray counting and range measurements it may be convenient to use ion collection in a chamber containing air at atmospheric pressure. The amplifier must then respond to pulses which have a rise time of the order of milliseconds.

Integrating chambers using ion-collection were in general use for cosmic-ray and γ-ray measurements before the introduction of the electron-collection technique. Compton, Wollan and Bennett (1934) give details of a standard ionisation chamber which has been used for extensive cosmic ray survey under the auspices of the Carnegie Institute of Washington. This chamber contains provision for calibration ; a standard of ionisation is provided by β-rays from a little movable rod of uranium, and this device is also used to compensate the average cosmic ray ionisation current and so to allow variations in the ionisation to be detected with high sensitivity. This chamber is used with a Lindemann or similar electrometer.

Simple chambers or electroscopes containing air at atmospheric pressure are commonly used for the routine measurement of radium and other radioactive sources by comparison of γ-ray activity. Small ionisation chambers are regularly carried by workers in medical X-ray departments and atomic energy installations as monitors against dangerous exposure to γ-rays. The electrodes of these chambers have excellent insulation (now usually polythene or PTFE) and in the absence of undue ionising radiation they lose only a small fraction of their charge in the course of a day. They are connected from time to time with an electrostatic or a valve electrometer which measures the residual charge. They might have research applications in addition to their normal use as routine health safeguards.*

---

* An alternative radiation monitor consists of a small piece of photographic film, worn in a holder. From time to time the film is withdrawn and developed.

11.5   Gas Multiplication—Proportional Counters

It is possible to obtain a useful amplification of the ionisation produced in a chamber if the electrons produced by the ionising particle pass into a region of comparatively strong electric field, where they acquire velocities sufficient to produce further ionisation by collision. In all counters so far found useful, this is achieved by making the positive electrode a fine wire. Multiplication then takes place in a comparatively small region (a few wire diameters) round the wire. Except for secondary effects, all electrons produced in the counter outside the multiplication region receive equal treatment. If this is to be accurately true, the gas filling must be such that negligible electron attachment takes place. Hydrogen, argon, argon-CO_2 mixture, methane, and boron trifluoride have all been used in counters using gas multiplication. The pressures range between 10 cm. Hg and a few atmospheres ; methane at a pressure near atmospheric seems to be a good filling for general purposes, e.g. β-ray counting, measurement of the ionisation of cosmic-ray particles, since the change of amplification with voltage is relatively slow in this gas.

For a given counter the gas multiplication is a rapidly increasing, roughly exponential, function of the applied voltage, and a very steady voltage source is perhaps the most important practical requirement in the use of the proportional counter. The stable multiplication obtainable is usually of the order of a few hundred, but much higher amplification has been achieved by taking special precautions ; see, e.g. Curran et al. (1949).

The simplest construction for a proportional counter (for penetrating rays) is identical with that of a Geiger counter (§ 11.7, Fig. 11.8). Since the gas multiplication takes place near the positive electrode in a small region whose configuration depends very little on the size and shape of the rest of the counter, cylindrical symmetry of the whole counter is not necessary, and proportional counters can be made with one or more wires in a chamber of nearly any shape. It is, however, necessary to have a high degree of symmetry if it is required

417

to keep the multiplication very constant from particle to particle. Rossi and Staub emphasise the bad effects of dust on the wire in causing random variations of multiplication. They found that under reasonably good conditions, 50 % of the pulses observed in a proportional counter with a homogeneous source lie in a band of width 5-10 % of the average size. The construction and calibration of proportional counters is discussed in a review article by West (1953).

11.6 The Geiger Counter

If the voltage applied to a fine-wire gas-multiplication counter is increased, a new régime appears in which the charge collected for each incident particle is not at all proportional to the initial ionisation. When the " Geiger " régime is fully established, the pulse size depends only on the counter and the applied voltage, and a characteristic pulse is initiated even by a single ion pair. This behaviour persists over a considerable voltage range, going over at higher voltages into an uncontrolled discharge.

The mechanism of the Geiger discharge is fairly complicated. Electrons from the initial ionisation produce more ions by collision in the neighbourhood of the central wire. The positive ions form a sheath which grows in thickness until its space charge prevents further ionisation by electrons in that part of the counter, but the discharge is propagated in both directions along the counter by the action of the light quanta produced. In the presence of a quenching gas (see below) which absorbs the photons strongly, the spread takes place entirely by photoionisation of the gas near the wire, but if no quenching gas is present, photoelectrons produced at the cathode play an important part in the spread. In support of this it is known that the propagation of the discharge can be arrested by a glass or metal bead on the wire only if a quenching gas is present.

The positive ion sheath now moves outward, reaching the cathode in a time of the order 10^{-4} sec., during which a negative-going pulse is induced on the wire. When an ion reaches the cathode, it may produce an additional electron if the energy of neutralization ϵ of an ion by a free electron derived from the metal, less the work ϕ necessary to detach the electron is sufficient to detach another electron, i.e., if

$$\epsilon - \phi > \phi$$
$$\epsilon > 2\phi.$$

In the absence of some quenching mechanism, the electron thus liberated re-starts the discharge.

Quenching may be effected by putting a high resistance in the circuit. The negative charge collected on the wire then leaves it relatively slowly. The positive ions therefore reach the cathode while the voltage across the counter is too low to produce effective multiplication, and the discharge does not re-strike. The resistance required is of the order 10^9 ohms and the recovery of the circuit after a pulse is therefore slow ; the time constant may be of the order 10^{-2} sec. A number of valve circuits have been devised to reduce the applied voltage wherever a pulse occurs and to restore it more rapidly than does the simple high resistance feed.

Externally quenched counters are, however, little used in present practice, for the counter can be made self-quenching if its gas filling contains a suitable vapour. A typical filling is argon to a partial pressure of 10 cm. Hg and ethyl alcohol to 1 cm. Hg. The discharge in such a counter is self-quenching whatever the value of the external resistance, and 1 megohm is a convenient value across which to take a voltage pulse. The mechanism of the quenching seems to be that the argon positive ions are neutralised by exchange of charge with alcohol molecules, giving molecular ions which are incapable of producing additional electrons when they reach the cathode. Furthermore, radiation which would produce photoelectrons at the cathode is absorbed in the vapour by a dissociation process without the production of an electron.

Since a high quenching resistance is not now necessary, the recovery of the applied voltage is rapid, and the counter is ready for another count in a time set by its internal mechanism rather than by the recovery of the voltage. The dead time actually found is due to the effect of the positive ion sheath in reducing the field near the wire. At first the multiplying mechanism is completely suppressed ; the electric field near the wire increases as the sheath moves outwards and after a time of the order 10^{-4} sec. the counter is again capable of giving a small pulse. After a further time of the same order, the counter has recovered completely, the ion sheath having been collected at the cathode.

The main disadvantage of this method of quenching is that the counter has a finite useful life (in counts) because the vapour is decomposed in the discharge. For a typical

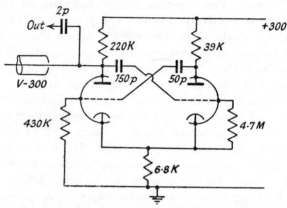

FIG. 11.7 Multivibrator circuit for quenching Geiger counters (Elliot, 1949). The voltage to be applied to the counter cathode is less than the working voltage by the amount of the valve H.T.

cosmic-ray counter (60×4 cm.) the life is of the order $2 \cdot 10^{8}$ counts, corresponding to a few months' use in a sea-level experiment. Although counters containing an organic vapour are self-quenching without the aid of a valve circuit, it is often advantageous to employ a quenching circuit (e.g. Fig. 11.7) (Elliot 1949). It has been shown that this circuit suppresses the discharge before it has spread far along the counter : the total charge passing is thereby reduced and the useful life of the counter greatly increased. A 60×4 cm. counter tested by Elliot had its life increased to about $3 \cdot 10^{9}$ counts. It is furthermore found that " bad " counters showing short and sloping voltage plateaux in the ordinary circuit often behave satisfactorily with the multivibrator quenching arrangement. When the multivibrator is used, the dead time of the arrangement is decided by the recovery time of the multivibrator which is constant, so that the dead time loss of counts may be estimated if necessary.

11.7 The Construction of Counters

Fig. 11.8 indicates the mechanical features of several useful types of Geiger counter. Glass counters with internal cathodes are used for relatively penetrating radiation (cosmic-rays, γ-rays). Alternatively, the cathode may be the outside

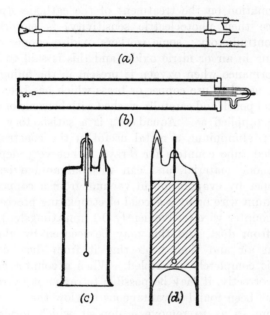

FIG. 11.8 Forms of Geiger counter
(a), (b) for penetrating radiation
(c), (d) with thin window for β-rays

metal shell of the counter. The wire is then insulated by the use of Kovar-glass or similar seals. The simplest construction of all, due to Maze (1946), employs a thin-walled (*ca.* 0·8 mm.) soda glass tube coated *externally* with graphite (Aquadag). The conductivity of the glass is sufficient to allow counting at cosmic-ray rates without serious loss of voltage.

P

Counters with a thin wall or thin window must be used for β-rays. A number of special counters have been made for use in applied nuclear physics, especially in biological applications of tracer elements. They include glass immersion counters with thin walls designed to respond to β-rays from radio-active liquids, and very small counters down to 0·8 mm. diameter. Some of these counters can be obtained commercially but many laboratories find it necessary to make their own counters, especially when they are of special shapes and sizes.

Information on the treatment of the cathodes (primarily to reduce their photoelectric sensitivity) is empirical and rather contradictory ; some workers oxidise copper cathodes by heating in air or nitric oxide, and this is said to stabilise the performance when oxygen is present in the filling. It is, however, usual to use copper or brass which has been cleaned with metal polish and carefully washed with benzene or acetone. Graphite (applied as " Aquadag ") is a satisfactory cathode material ; aluminium, a metal useful in the construction of thin-walled tube counters for β-rays, is not very dependable as a cathode material, and can with advantage be coated with copper by evaporation in vacuum from a copper-plated molybdenum wire or by a special electroplating process.

The counter wire (conveniently 0·1 mm. tungsten), should be free from dust, and this may be secured by glowing it gently in air and then protecting it from dust until the counter is completely assembled. When a counter ceases to operate correctly, it may be possible to revive it by re-filling, and it has been found advantageous to glow the central wire in vacuum so as to remove a deposit which forms on it. Counters intended for this treatment should have both ends of the wire brought out of the envelope.

It is certain that the gas filling of an argon/alcohol counter should be free from gases giving negative ions, in particular oxygen and water vapour.* The vacuum system and the

---

* If some of the electrons form negative ions, the multiplication process may fail and the efficiency of the counter be lowered. Further, some negative ions may release electrons after the main discharge is over and cause a parasitic count. This is one of the causes of the plateau slope. (See p. 360.)

counter construction should allow partial degassing to reduce the concentration of these substances, but no certain advantage has been obtained by using rigorous vacuum technique. Oxygen-free argon (which is a commercial product) and carefully purified alcohol should be used. The alcohol reservoir on the counter-filling system should contain calcium oxide as a dehydrating agent. Some workers treat the alcohol by freezing it and pumping off the gases. Ethyl ether has been used as a quenching gas ; it seems to be equivalent to alcohol and to allow the counter to operate at lower temperatures. Ethyl formate has recently been used extensively and low-temperature counters have been made using ethylene dibromide as a quenching agent, but the performance is impaired by negative ion formation. Counters are made containing a small proportion (0·1 %) of halogen in an inert gas mixture, and these are now rather extensively used, particularly since the working voltage with a well-chosen gas mixture is only a few hundred volts. The counters are made commercially. The cathode material must be chosen to avoid reaction with the halogen (graphite, stainless steel, and tantalum have been used); the life of the filling is then indefinitely long. With such a small concentration of halogen the behaviour of the counter is not strongly influenced by negative ion formation, but it is not certain whether the counters are suitable for high-performance coincidence arrangements.

11.8 The Geiger Counter in Use

The following are the important characteristics which determine the use of the Geiger counter :—

(a) *Efficiency*

A good Geiger counter has nearly 100 % probability of response if an ion pair is produced in it. Very fast ionising particles produce only a few ion pairs per cm. in the gas mixture used, and particles which go through the counter in very glancing trajectories have a certain chance of being missed altogether. This effect is not usually important. When a counter is exposed to γ-rays, the probability that a quantum will produce an electron capable of setting off the counter is not usually very large : it depends on the energy of the γ-ray quantum and on the materials in the counter. It may be advantageous to use heavy elements, e.g. Pb, for the wall or the cathode. If soft X-ray quanta are to be recorded, a good efficiency may be obtained by using a filling containing krypton or xenon and by arranging the path of the X-rays so that they have a good chance of being absorbed in the gas.

(b) *Pulse Shape*

The pulse from a counter develops relatively slowly and the interval between the passage of an ionising particle and the observed response therefore depends upon the sensitivity of the recording amplifier. This interval, and more especially the variability of the interval from counter to counter and from pulse to pulse, is important in high-resolution coincidence experiments. It is probable that with all precautions (counter free from negative ions, high gain amplifier) these uncertainties are of the order of a few tenths of a microsecond. (Cf p. 422).

(c) *Dead Time*

As described on p. 420 the dead time of a counter in a simple circuit is of the order of a few tenths of a millisecond, and particles go uncounted if they arrive before the counter has recovered enough to give a recordable pulse. When a quenching multivibrator is in use its characteristics determine the dead time.

A number of methods of measuring dead time are given in Craggs and Curran (1949). The simplest overall check of the dead time losses of a counter and recording system is an addition test using a number of small radioactive sources in well-defined positions around the counter. They are first applied separately and then together. The counting rates due to the sources should be additive, and any dead time loss appears as a reduction of efficiency at high counting rates.

(d) *The Plateau*

The misbehaviour of counters is often manifest in the short length and high residual slope of the " plateau curve " connecting applied voltage with number of counts (with a given source of ionisation and a definite recording sensitivity). For a good counter of " ordinary " size and shape the plateau may have a length of 200 V and a residual slope of 0·02 % per volt, but in small or peculiarly shaped counters it is not possible to obtain a plateau as good as this.   When a counter is in use the voltage must be supplied from a stabilised source, which need not, however, be very accurate in view of the plateau characteristics.   The behaviour of the counter must be checked from time to time : in long-continued coincidence measurements it is usual to test daily to see that each counter is counting normally as judged by rate and apparent random-ness, and to verify occasionally that each counter is working, say, 50 V above the threshold at which counting begins.   A further useful check is to examine the pulses on an ordinary oscilloscope since most sorts of bad behaviour are associated with multiple or ragged pulses.

11.9   Scintillation Counters

When an α-particle strikes a crystal of zinc sulphide, activated with traces of certain foreign elements, a bright scintillation is produced. The energy efficiency of this process is surprisingly high.

The counting of α-particle scintillations by eye was one of the most important techniques of classical radioactivity research. It is now obsolete, but the application of the electron multiplier photocell has revived the scintillation method and has extended its scope to β-ray and γ-ray counting.

A photomultiplier with a thin layer of activated zinc sulphide crystals mounted just outside the envelope is prob-ably the most satisfactory device available for counting α-particles : the scintillations are so bright that the noise generated in the photocell is unimportant and the maximum amplification is not required. α-scintillations can be counted in the presence of β or γ rays.*

β-rays lose much less energy per unit path in the phosphor

---

* Activated zinc sulphide is obtainable commercially : in a suitable specimen the duration of the light pulse produced by an α-particle is about 10-15 μS.

than do α-rays, and the scintillations are very much weaker. It is therefore necessary to use the phosphor in such a form (a large single crystal) that light can be collected from an appreciable thickness of material, and to arrange effective optical coupling between this and the photocathode. It is necessary to use high amplification in the photomultiplier and to discriminate against noise pulses, but it is not usually necessary to cool the photocathode. A device which has been employed to detect weak scintillations in the presence of noise is to couple two multipliers in coincidence to a single crystal so that scintillations are recorded as coincidences while noise pulses are in general not recorded. The phosphors at present used for β and γ ray counting are of three main types, and their characteristics are set out in Table 11.2.

Gamma-rays are counted *via* secondary electrons produced by the processes discussed on p. 428; since the organic phosphors contain no heavy elements, they do not respond efficiently to γ-rays unless very thick layers can be used. Sodium iodide containing 1 % or less of thallium iodide responds well to X and γ-rays: the crystals are hygroscopic and are usually sealed in a container with some transparent oil to couple them to a glass window and thence to the photocathode. Because of the high volume efficiency of absorption and conversion in these crystals, the active portion of the detector can be very compact; this is particularly advantageous in experiments in which the angular distribution of the radiation is measured.

The liquid scintillators are versatile in shape and size ; in particular they can be made very large. Large liquid counters are valuable in cosmic ray experiments and some others in which widespread weak γ-rays are measured. The efficient collection of light from a large volume of liquid presents some difficulty. Photomultipliers with large cathodes (e.g. 5 inches diameter) are used for the purpose, and of course a number of photocells may be applied to a tank of liquid. Loss of light from the rest of the surface of the tank is minimised by shaping the vessel to encourage total reflection (Garwin 1952), or by coating the surfaces with an efficient diffuse reflector (MgO). The efficiency of these devices is limited by self absorption of the scintillation light in the liquid.

The shortness of the light emission from organic scintillations allows them to be used in coincidence and timing experiments with very high resolving power. The effective resolu-

TABLE 11.2

Scintillators for Particle Detection

	Relative light yield (β-rays)	α/β %	Decay time 10^{-9} s.
Anthracene	100	9	30
Stilbene	60	9	64
5 g/l Terphenyl in Xylene	48	9	28

It is advantageous to remove oxygen from the solution (e.g. by bubbling nitrogen through it for a time) since oxygen quenches the fluorescent emission.

0·01 g/l. diphenylhexatriene added to the solution improves its efficiency (with respect to glass-windowed photomultipliers) by displacing the wavelength of the emission towards the photocell maximum and away from the region of self-absorption. Birks has shown that this device is less efficient than using terphenyl alone with an ultraviolet sensitive photomultiplier (Cs_3Sb with a quartz window) unless very large volumes of liquid are in use, in which case the self-absorption effect is important. Plastic scintillators usually contain p-terphenyl and commonly a wavelength shifting chemical dissolved in solid polystyrene. They are often convenient in use, though the efficiency is a little lower than that of the liquids.

NaI (1 % Tl)	210	44	$\sim$ 300
LiI (Sn)	12	93	800
LiI (Eu)	75	95	1400
$CaWO_4$	100	—	$\sim$1000

ZnS (Ag, Ni)	Sensitivity high, decay long, not available in larger transparent crystals, so that usefulness confined to α-rays.

The data given are from various sources, and must not be regarded as very accurate. The ratio of the light produced by α and β particles losing equal energies in the phosphor is an indication of how the efficiency varies with rate of energy loss. The LiI phosphors can be used as neutron detectors (p. 365).

tion may in practice be limited by a weak component of the light which decays with a long period (of the order of microseconds) : this effect seems to be absent in liquid scintillators.

Similar difficulties occur because some photomultiplier cells give an appreciable number of afterpulses following a light flash : this effect will probably be reduced by improvements in tube design. A very important limitation arises because of the time spread between the emission of photoelectrons and the collection of their ultimate descendants. As mentioned on p. 373 this effect can be reduced by appropriate design of the electrode system which collects the photoelectrons and multiplies them. In a very good photomultiplier (Mullard 56 AVP) an "infinitely sharp" pulse would be lengthened to about 2 nanoseconds at half height.

As well as affording simple counting response, scintillation detectors can be used to give information about the energy distribution of the events they record. They can be used for β-ray and γ-ray spectroscopy (Bell 1955, see also Sharpe 1955) and the use of activated iodide crystals for γ-ray spectroscopy is particularly important. The property of energy resolution can be used in counting experiments to separate the rays from a particular radio-element or decay process from a background of other events.

TABLE 11.3

Conversion Processes for γ-rays in NaI Crystal

Name and nature of process	Products	Main contributions to pulse spectrum
Photoelectric absorption. For $E_\gamma > 33$ keV this is largely due to K-electrons of iodine.	Photoelectrons X-rays—largely 28 keV iodine K-radiation.	Full energy peak E_γ if X-ray absorbed. Small subsidiary peak at $(E_\gamma - 28$ keV) if X-ray quantum escapes.
Compton scattering	Recoil electron. γ-ray distribution extending nearly to E_γ.	Continuous distribution except in very large crystals.
Pair production	Electron-positron pair, which gives on annihilation two γ-quanta each of 0·51 MeV	Full energy peak. Subsidiary peaks at $(E_\gamma - 0·51$ MeV) and $(E_\gamma - 1·02$ MeV) due to escape of one or two annihilation quanta.

The pulse size is not always linearly related to the energy dissipated in the scintillations, and in organic media the scintillation efficiency decreases markedly with increasing energy loss per unit path (cf. α/β data in Table 11.2).   In β-ray spectroscopy with organic crystals this effect only produces a small departure from linearity in the relation between pulse size and

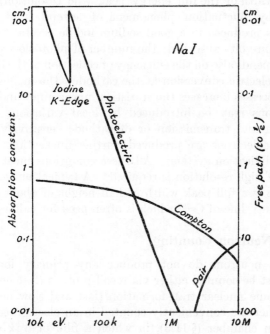

FIG. 11.9 Absorption constants and free paths for different processes in sodium iodide crystal, plotted against energy of γ-rays

energy at low β-ray energies, and a correction can be applied. The departure is less in inorganic crystals, and here the main difficulty in β-ray spectroscopy lies in the fact that many of the incident particle are scattered out of the crystal without giving up all their energy.   The loss can be reduced by special configurations of the scintillator.

When monoenergetic γ-quanta fall on a scintillator, the modes of energy conversion and the corresponding pulse-size distribution are shown in Table 11.3, and the data of Fig. 11.9

P*   429

may be used to estimate the relative importance of different processes. Unless the γ-ray energy is low, or the crystal large, the " full energy " peak contains only a minority of the pulses produced, so that large (and expensive) crystals are advantageous, in particular when it is required to pick out a spectral line against the " Compton tail "* of a more energetic line.

The width of the full energy peak (the resolution) is controlled by fluctuation phenomena of several kinds. One photon is produced in a good sodium iodide crystal for about 35 electron-volts absorbed; the number of photoelectrons produced depends also on the efficiency of collection of the light and of photoelectric conversion at the cathode: the inefficiency of these processes increases the statistical uncertainty and further fluctuations may be introduced by local variations of light collection and transmission or of cathode sensitivity. After the photoelectrons are produced, further fluctuations arise in the multiplication system. All these conditions must be considered if high resolution is required. A typical but good performance is a full peak width at half height of about 8 % for the 661 keV line of Cs^{137} which is often used for calibration.

11.10 Neutron Counting

Since neutrons do not produce any primary ionisation, they must be counted either via recoil protons (fast neutrons), or via some nuclear transformation (fast and slow neutrons). The former are conveniently counted in an electron-collection ionisation chamber (§ 11.3), in which a film of wax or some other hydrogenous material is supported. Hydrogen-filled ionisation chambers are used to measure fast neutron flux : they are relatively very insensitive to gamma rays.

The nuclear reactions available for measuring neutrons include the production of β-radioactivity in Ag, In, the production of fission in U and especially the reaction

$$^{10}_{5}B + ^{1}_{0}n \rightarrow ^{7}_{3}Li + ^{4}_{2}He.$$

The reaction takes place with the liberation of 2·5 MeV at

---

* It is possible to separate either the full energy peak or a well defined part of the Compton distribution by rather elaborate coincidence and anti-coincidence arrangements. Cf. Bell, Sharpe, *loc. cit.*

zero neutron energy, and the α-particle and Li-nucleus will
produce strong ionisation in a gas. Only the ^{10}B nucleus
(abundance 20 %) is effective, and it is therefore advantageous
to use boron enriched in the ^{10}B isotope. The boron can be
used as a solid lining to an ionisation chamber or proportional
counter, or the gas BF_3 can be used to fill a fine-wire proportional counter.*

In practice, counters filled with BF_3 at about 60 cm. Hg
work satisfactorily : as with all proportional counters a
medium-gain amplifier and a well stabilised voltage supply
are required. The purification of the BF_3 represents some
difficulty if electron collection is required (see Tongiorgi *et al*
1951).

Fission counters can be made much less sensitive to γ-rays
than boron counters. They are usually made as cylindrical
electron collection chambers with uranium coated on the
negative electrode. If this is enriched in U^{235} slow reactions
are counted as well as fast. U^{238} responds only to fast neutrons
and with lower efficiency than U^{235}.

The cross-section of boron for slow neutrons is nearly
inversely proportional to neutron velocity over a considerable
range. It may be shown that for this reason the counting
rate is proportional to neutron *concentration* (not neutron
flux). Most of the other neutron detectors show marked
resonances at particular neutron velocities, and it may be
rather difficult to interpret their indications, unless of course
they are used simply to compare neutron intensities under
constant velocity distribution. Slow neutron detectors, in
particular BF_3 counters, may be used to detect fast neutrons
if these are slowed down in a moderator of paraffin wax.
The interpretation of the indications (except in cases of simple
comparison as mentioned above) is then very complicated.
Scintillation counters for slow neutrons may be made to depend
on the nuclear reaction

$$^6_3Li + ^1_0n \rightarrow ^3_1H + ^4_2He(+ 4 \cdot 8 \text{ MeV})$$

The crystal used as a scintillator is LiI activated with Sn or

* The counter should be made of lead glass or of metal. Hard borosilicate
glasses absorb slow neutrons markedly.

preferably Eu.   (Nicholson and Snelling, 1955) : it responds (unfortunately) to γ-rays as well as neutrons.   Fast neutrons produce recoil protons in scintillators containing hydrogen, and may be detected in this way.   One useful detector consists of ZnS crystals suspended in a plastic (which provides the protons).   It is relatively very insensitive to γ-rays.

11.11   Some Special Counting Methods

It is desirable to mention some counting methods which are used occasionally in special investigations or are so new that their full potentialities have not yet been realised.

(1) Secondary electron counting.   When a moderately fast electron, e.g. a β-ray, strikes a suitable surface, it produces a number of secondary electrons which can be accelerated in an electric field and multiplied in turn at another prepared surface.   This phenomenon has been applied as a counting method in β-ray spectroscopy, beryllium copper being a suitable multiplying surface (cf. p. 378) (Allen 1947).   It is also possible to detect positive ions by an appropriate modification of the method.

(2) Solid and liquid ionisation counters.   It has been known for some time that when certain crystals, and also liquid inert gases, are ionised by the passage of fast particles, the ions can be collected as in an ionisation chamber, but these processes have been little used.   The recent development of solid-state counters has proceeded along two main lines: certain solids, particularly the photoconductive crystals of CdS (cf. p. 378) becomes conductive under γ-ray irradiation, and can be used, e.g. in γ-ray monitors.   It is possible to produce superficial potential barriers at the surface of n-type germanium or silicon, and to use the resulting device to detect short range particles (Walter 1960) such as α-particles and fission fragments.   The energy required to produce a hole-electron pair is only a few electron volts, but the effective electrical capacity of the layer is high and the voltage signals obtained are rather small.   The counters give good energy resolution and are of increasing importance in the energy spectroscopy of relatively heavy particles.

(3) Gas scintillation counters. The inert gases are scintillators which can be excited efficiently by heavily ionising particles. The intensity of the scintillations is proportional to the energy lost by the exciting particles, the duration of the light is a few nanoseconds, and the scintillators are little affected by γ-rays. The intensities of the scintillations from Xe, Kr, Ne, He, Ar, appear to decrease in the order given, but the experimental data are confused by the quenching effect of traces of impurities. It has, however, been claimed that helium containing 0·001 % of nitrogen is a particularly good scintillation medium. The emission from all these scintillating gases lies in the ultraviolet and the signals are greatly improved by the use of wavelength shifting secondary phosphors and quartz windows, or both.

(4) Parallel plate counters and spark chambers. A chamber containing parallel plate electrodes and a suitable filling can be used as a Geiger counter. A quenching circuit is required, and the technical difficulties of the device in this form were formidable. Recently the spark counter has been developed into a device (usually in multiplate form) for localising the tracks of ionising particles, and has found considerable application in high energy experiments (Spark Symposium 1961). The new technical features are the application of the high voltage only when the presence of ionising particles has been detected by an auxiliary counter system, and the use of a selected filling gas (Neon, Argon, or mixture of rare gases with a little alcohol vapour), which allows several sparks to develop simultaneously when several ion tracks are present between a particular pair of plates.

(5) It was shown by Cerenkov (1934) that radiation is emitted from charged particles passing through a medium in which the velocity of electromagnetic radiation is less than the particle velocity. If $c\beta$ is the velocity of the particle and n is the refractive index of the medium, the radiated energy is confined to directions making an angle $\cos^{-1}\dfrac{1}{n\beta}$ with the path of the particle. The energy thus emitted in the visible spectrum from a single fast particle can be detected

by a photomultiplier tube, and can be used as a method of detecting particles for which β is high : the angle of emission can be used as an accurate measure of the particle velocity. The special virtues of the Cerenkov detector lie in its very high speed and in its selectivity for particle velocity and direction. It can in principle be made very large since the radiation depends only on the refractive index of the medium, and very transparent substances can be used. A book by Jelley (1958) contains an account of its uses. See also Jelley 1953, Mather 1951.

11.12 Coincidence Counting

Coincidence counting, depending on the detection of simultaneous discharges of Geiger or other counters, is a key technique in cosmic-ray research, since it allows penetrating particles to be detected in the presence of a high background of other events, and since it can be made to detect selectively the presence of showers and other complicated phenomena. In nuclear physics, more strictly defined, it is used to detect the simultaneous or nearly simultaneous production of two particles. The circuit arrangements for detecting coincidences are discussed in § 11.14. The resolving time is the maximum time by which two events are separated if they are to be recorded as a coincidence: the minimum resolving time which can be usefully employed is limited because there are random fluctuations in the time which the counter itself takes to respond to the triggering particle. For a Geiger or proportional counter these fluctuations are rather less than 1 μs ($0 \cdot 1 - 0 \cdot 4$ μs quoted by Sherwin 1948), when the counter is followed by considerable amplification so that the first rise of the pulse can be detected. With the photo-multiplier scintillation counter the fluctuations can be reduced to much less than $0 \cdot 1$ μs (*ca.* 10^{-9} sec. has been obtained).

If two counters give random and unconnected counting rates $N_1 N_2$, it may be shown that the rate of accidental coincidences is $2 N_1 N_2 \tau$, where τ is the resolving time. This relation is often used to find experimentally the resolving time of a counter system. For this purpose N_1, N_2 are preferably made large by using radioactive sources, so that the random nature of most of the discharges is assured.

The corresponding rate for random triple coincidence is $3N_1N_2N_3\tau^2$ but it is necessary to add that this formula is often inapplicable to cosmic-ray experiments, in which the apparent " random triple " rate may be largely due to coincidences between *real double coincidences* (arising, e.g. from showers) and the random discharges of the third counter.

11.13 Anti-Coincidence Counting

There are certain problems which can be solved by including in a coincidence counting system counters which, when actuated, cancel the response. Such systems allow the recording of " anti-coincidences " of the type " response in ABC

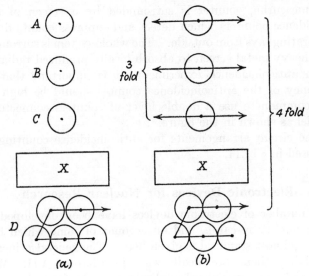

FIG. 11.10   (a) An anticoincidence array
         (b) System for difference counting of anticoincidences

. . . but not in D " for which the usual notation is (ABC − D). Fig. 11.10 shows a simple application to the detection of cosmic-ray particles which pass through ABC and are then absorbed in the lead block X.

435

True anticoincidence circuits are essential if the occurrence of an anticoincidence event is required, e.g. to operate an expansion chamber, but for straightforward counting it is often possible to avoid them by recording simultaneously coincidences of different order. For example, the number of particles absorbed in X could be counted by connecting a fourfold and a threefold coincidence circuit as in Fig. 11.10, and by taking the difference of their readings. It must be noted that the same accuracy could not be obtained by recording the fourfold rate and the threefold rate over separate periods, for the (possibly small) anti-coincidence rate would then be burdened with the statistical fluctuations of the larger numbers of coincidences.

An important application of anticoincidence arrangements is in measuring weak radioactivity as in " ^{14}C dating " studies. The measuring counter is surrounded by a screen of anti-coincidence counters which detect and suppress counts due to penetrating rays from outside. The whole system is surrounded by a heavy metal screen to absorb locally produced radiation.

In anticoincidence experiments it is important that the efficiency of the anticoincidence counter should be high and it is common to use a double layer of counters connected in parallel as shown in the figure.

The circuit arrangements for anticoincidence counting are discussed in § 11.14.

11.14 Electronic Devices for Nuclear Research

A number of electronic devices have been developed for use in nuclear research, and an account of some which have become almost standard is given here. The general principles underlying them are dealt with in Chapter VII. Many devices of more specialised application can be found in papers and in particular in the *Review of Scientific Instruments* from 1946 on. A book on the electronic devices of part of the American Atomic Energy Project has appeared (Elmore and Sands 1949), and a review article has been written by Scarrett (1950). Fig. 11.11 shows typical counting systems and indicates the electronic elements required for them.

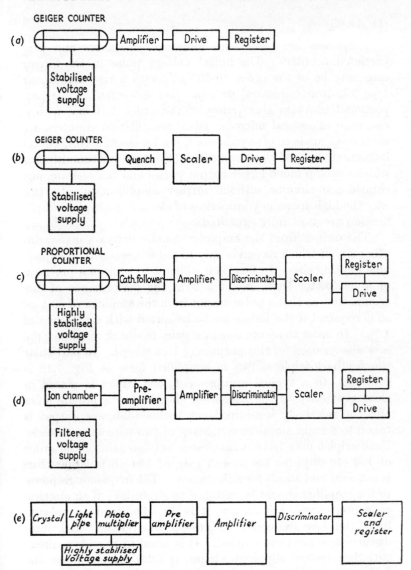

FIG. 11.11 Block diagrams for counting systems, showing electronic devices required

(a) Geiger counter, simplest possible system
(b) Geiger counter with quenching circuit and scaler
(c) Proportional counter
(d) Ionisation chamber
(e) Crystal scintillation counter

(1) *Amplifiers*

Amplifiers are used with ionisation chambers and proportional counters. The initial voltage pulse in the former case may be of the order 10-100 μV, with a rise time about 1 μs (electron collection) or 1 ms (ion collection), while proportional counters give pulses of the order 1-10 mV with a rise time of several microseconds. Scintillation counters are commonly made to give pulses of a few tenths of a volt, but an important line of development is towards photomultipliers which develop much larger output pulses and can operate, e.g. coincidence circuits without further amplification. In this way the high-frequency properties of electron-multiplier amplification are most fully exploited.

The output from the amplifier usually drives a discriminating circuit which responds only to pulses greater than adjustable limiting size. In fact, it is difficult to achieve a precision of much better than, say, 0·5 V in the performance of discriminators, so that a pulse output from the amplifier of 50 V or so is required if the pulses are to be sorted with a precision of 1 %. In order to secure constant gain, feedback amplifiers are now always used for this purpose (§ 7.14 *et seq.*). In particular the feedback-triple shown in simplified form in Fig. 7.18 is suitable. In a typical arrangement, one triplet is placed in close proximity to the ionisation chamber as a pre-amplifier and the relatively low-impedance cathode-follower output is taken to a main amplifier consisting of two triplets in cascade. Each triplet may have a maximum voltage gain of the order of 100 (40 db) and the overall gain of 120 db is larger than is required and allows for adjustment. The frequency response of the amplifier should be matched to its duties ; if an electron collection chamber is in use, it is an advantage severely to limit the low frequency response ; microphonic and hum disturbances are thus avoided. It is usual to provide a differentiating (pulse clipping) circuit (§ 7.23) which limits the L.F. response and an integrating circuit which limits the H.F. response, and to give the rest of the system an amplification band which extends well beyond these limits. In particular, the L.F. response in the other stages is made to go much lower than that of the differentiating stage, for otherwise " overshoots " are generated after the pulse. The frequency limiting circuits must be put early enough in the amplifier to avoid overloading of any stage by components of the signal which are rejected in the filter and late enough to restrict the noise components from any valves which contribute materially to the final noise. In practice it is convenient to put them between the pre-amplifier and the main amplifier.

The noise in these amplifiers is discussed in § 10.9, and fully in Gillespie (1953). It appears that the first grid resistance coupling the ionisation chamber to the amplifier should be

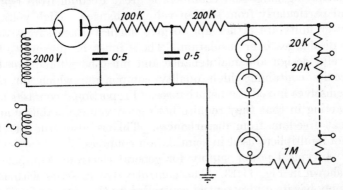

Fig. 11.12 Simple neon-stabilised high-voltage supply for Geiger counters

high, to secure the best ratio of signal to noise, and that the input capacity should be kept low, so as to improve the signal with respect to the anode noise of the first valve. Anode shot noise (and partition noise) may dominate at higher frequencies and grid current shot noise at lower frequencies. Since low grid current in a valve and low anode noise (high g_m) tend to be incompatible, the choice of the first valve and its operating conditions depends on the frequency response desired from the system.

High frequency response is required for resolution in fast counting, but should not be made higher than necessary ; the clipping time (differentiating circuit controlling the L.F. response) should be used to limit microphonic and flicker noise.

It is usually good to make the RC products of the clipping

and integrating circuits alike, and if the amplitude response is to be nearly independent of variations in the collecting time, the RC time constant must be two or three times as long as the longest collecting time.

(2) *Regulated Power Supplies*

Most counting systems need power supplies whose voltage is regulated more or less accurately. Geiger counters do not make stringent demands on voltage stability, and long coincidence experiments have been performed with simple neon-tube stabilisers (Fig. 11.12).

The main requirement for the voltage applied to non-multiplying ionisation chambers is great freedom from ripple and particularly from sudden voltage changes. High voltage power units are rather apt to give small voltage surges due to discharges over insulation. These must be prevented by careful design and maintenance and must be filtered out by circuits containing high quality components which do not themselves introduce disturbances. Proportional counters are exacting in that they require both good voltage stability and great freedom from disturbances. This is also true of the photomultipliers used in scintillation counters.

A typical power supply for general electronic equipment is shown in Fig. 11.13. The control valve in series with the supply has its grid potential controlled by the output of a D.C. amplifier whose input is derived from a balanced circuit which compares a fixed fraction of the output voltage with the voltage across a gas-discharge reference tube. High voltage small current supplies for counters, including proportional counters and photomultipliers, can be obtained from simple neon tube stabilisers which are very satisfactory if special high-stability neon tubes are used: rather larger currents are obtainable from a power unit which uses a high frequency transformer operated from a valve oscillator working at about 100 kc/s. The transformer ouput is rectified by a small diode whose filament is heated by a highly insulated mains transformer or by a winding on the H.F. transformer. The voltage control amplifier now operates to control the amplitude of the H.F. oscillator. A typical circuit is shown in Fig. 11.14.

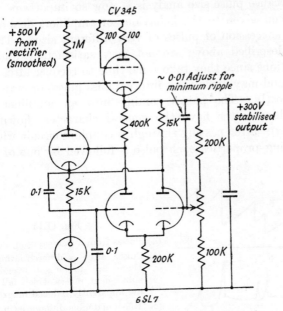

FIG. 11.13   Stabilised power supply for 250–300 volts

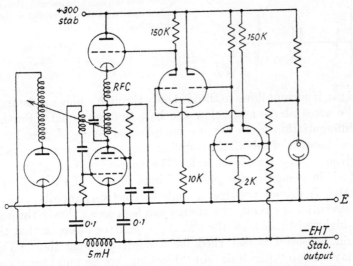

FIG. 11.14   Stabilised (negative) voltage supply from controlled HF oscillator
Applicable to proportional counters and photomultipliers

441

Because pulse size analysis is now so important, attention has been given to the behaviour of amplifiers dealing with a rapid succession of pulses of very different sizes. The amplifiers described above are not very satisfactory under these conditions since they take some time to recover after an overload, and may during this interval miss pulses or amplify them incorrectly. The pulses coming into an amplifier from a particle detector have the general character shown in Fig. 11.15(a); after passing through a coupling circuit with differentiating properties each pulse is followed by one of opposite

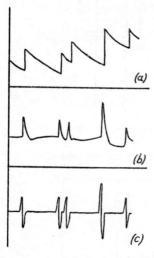

(a)

(b)

(c)

FIG. 11.15

(a) Pulses from a (scintillation) detector

(b) Pulses after a differentiating stage—there are prolonged overshoots and subsequent pulses which fall on them are apparently reduced in size

(c) Effect of double-differentiating amplifier (Fairstein). The overshoots are now quick, and the nearly symmetrical signal pulses can be further amplified without distortion

sign: if current flows to the grid only through a linear resistance, the areas above and below the base line are equal. Further differentiation gives a more complicated series of overshoots and because of this all the coupling stages except one are usually given a long time constant. The successive valves have to deal, in general, with pulses of both signs. If the grid of a valve is driven positive, it collects electrons rapidly, and in conventional circuits the charge can leak away slowly through a high resistance after the end of the positive pulse, so that the grid potential is disturbed for a relatively long time. This may lead to " paralysis " or " blocking " of an amplifier stage. In a discriminator circuit the flow of grid current alters the bias so that the discrimination level depends on the size and rate of the pulses.

Circuits may be designed to reduce these troubles, using the following principles (Chase and Higginbotham 1952, Fairstein 1956):

(1) Direct coupling to the valve grids may be used in place of condenser coupling.

(2) The grid leak resistances may be made small (even less than the anode load of the preceding valve) so that the excursion following a positive overload pulse is quickly over.

(3) Two differentiations may be deliberately introduced so that the pulse acquires the form shown in Fig. 11.16(c).* Providing that grid current does not flow in succeeding stages, a pulse of this shape can be amplified without being lengthened, since it lies nearly equally above and below the zero line.

(4) Long-tailed pairs (§7.16) may replace single valve stages since they can deal with relatively large signals of both signs without the appearance of grid current.

Amplifiers embodying these principles are made commercially.

(3) *Scaling Circuits*

Experiments in nuclear physics may involve the counting of particles at very various rates and there are obvious advantages in counting as fast as possible. If the ultimate counter is a mechanical counter of the Post Office Telephone message register type, the maximum rate of counting is very narrowly limited, for these counters, even when driven by well-designed valve circuits, do not recover from a count in much less than $\frac{1}{5}$ sec. It will be seen in § 11.15 that this restricts them to a random recording rate of 0·05 per sec., if 1 % accuracy is required. Register counters having a better performance than this have been designed in laboratories, and some have been made commercially.†

In order to count faster than the limit of mechanical

* It is advantageous to form these pulses by using delay-line stages instead of simple differentiating stages (see p. 453).

† It is doubtful whether much development along this line is justified, but a version of the telephone register designed for long life is desirable.

counters, it is usual to use an electronic scaling circuit, and very many such circuits have been developed. The valve scale-of-two circuit discussed in § 7.22 and the corresponding transistor circuit (cf. § 7.31) have now become almost standardised elements in such arrangements, and the simplest high speed counting system is a cascade of such circuits followed by a register-driving circuit and a mechanical register. There is no disadvantage in using a binary scaler if the measurement made is the time taken to complete a predetermined number of counts, and this method has the advantage of giving a predetermined statistical accuracy. At the expense of some complication it is possible to make a decade counter by reconnecting the elements of a four-element scale of sixteen scaler. The first three elements count 0-8 as usual; the ninth count trips the fourth circuit in one direction, and the next count, by-passed from the first stage, re-sets it.

Simple scalers have been developed using special tubes in which a gas discharge passes in sequence round a ring of electrodes. The Dekatron counter (Ericsson 1954) is made in several forms—typically a decade tube containing a ring of thirty cathodes connected to three interwoven circuits A, B, C. Normally a local discharge sits on one of the electrodes of group A, but if negative pulses are applied successively to circuits B and C, the discharge moves in two steps and finally transfers to the next electrode of group A. A " carry " pulse is obtained from the " zero " electrode, and this pulse, after amplification and shaping, can be applied to a following decade tube (Fig. 11.16).

The least interval between the pulses counted by these tubes is at present limited to a few hundred microseconds, but this may possibly be reduced in future. For counting very closely spaced pulses, the gas-decade scaler may, of course, be preceded by binary scalers using hard valves.

High vacuum decade tubes are now in use: they are faster and probably more reliable than the gas-filled tubes, though the circuits are more elaborate. A counting tube (E.1.T.) made by Philips is in effect a miniature cathode ray tube in which the electron beam, after deflection, passes through a slotted electrode. A feedback connection from this electrode to one of the deflector plates secures that the electron beam has a series of stable positions in which it passes through one of the slots, but the feedback time constant is such that a properly shaped pulse with sharp rise and slow fall, applied to the other deflector plate, can shift the beam from one slot to the next. When the beam has occupied in turn the ten slots the next pulse brings into action a valve circuit which returns the beam to the first slot and passes a " carry " pulse

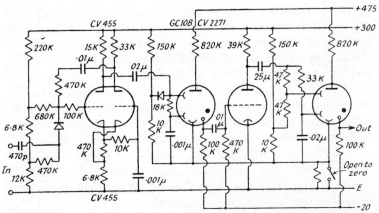

Fig. 11.16. Circuit for a Dekatron scaler. The first valve is a univibrator triggered by 30 V positive-going pulses. The two Dekatron tubes shown are coupled through a triode amplifier, and this sequence of tubes is repeated as required. Circuit details, by permission, from Ericsson Cold Cathode Tube Handbook which gives alternative circuits.

to the next decade tube. These tubes appear to be very reliable: the time resolution depends in practice chiefly on the resetting circuit. With a simple circuit 30,000 equally spaced pulses can be counted per second, but with more elaborate arrangements up to one million pulses per second can be dealt with.

In another type of counting tube (trochotron) electrons from the cathode are deflected by a permanent magnet attached to the tube as well as by the electrostatic fields of the anode and a series of " spade " electrodes. With proper connections to the electrodes there is a set of stable positions which can be occupied by an electron beam, and a pulse applied to the tube will shift the beam from one position to the next in a cyclic series. An intertube valve circuit is again needed to deal with the " carry " pulses.

Scaling circuits using transistors are also coming into use; they have have the advantages discussed in § 7.32, which are quite marked in this application.

(4) *Discriminators and Pulse Height Analysers*

It is usually necessary to pass into a counting circuit only pulses which exceed a definite adjustable size, and this is the function of a discriminator circuit. Such a discriminator excludes amplifier noise and minor disturbances from the count, and by varying the level of discrimination a pulse height distribution may be obtained. With proper precautions in the design of detector and linear amplifier the analysis of the pulses from an ionisation chamber or scintillation counter leads to an energy spectrum of nuclear particles or events.

Discriminator circuits are usually " trigger circuits " derived from the cathode-coupled multivibrator. In the circuit of Fig. 11.17, the valve V_1 is cut off until a positive pulse is applied, big enough to overcome the bias. The circuit then snaps over into a state with V_1 conducting and V_2 cut off, and remains in this condition until the applied voltage drops at the end of the pulse. Any pulse bigger than the set size will therefore produce an output pulse which has a definite, fairly large, amplitude. If necessary this pulse can be differentiated to give a short pulse to the next stage. More elaborate discriminators are in use; it is common to use a discriminator with fixed bias preceded by an amplifier with adjustable bias, which controls the discrimination level.

The accuracy with which these systems discriminate is limited in practice to $0 \cdot 25$-$0 \cdot 5$ V, and large input pulses (e.g. 50 V) are therefore required to preserve high fractional accuracy.

It is often desirable to record pulses belonging only to a particular interval of size, and the simplest instrument for doing this is called a single-channel pulse height analyser.

It consists essentially of two discriminators differentially biased, which receive the pulses in parallel and feed into an anticoincidence circuit, so that only those pulses are finally counted which affect one discriminator and not the other, and which lie therefore in a particular size interval (see e.g. Farley 1956). An extension of this function is the sorting of pulses into a number of size intervals so as to produce in one operation

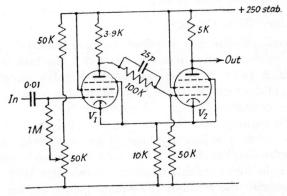

FIG. 11.17   Biased flip-flop discriminator circuit (Higginbotham, 1947)

a size spectrum. Instruments for this purpose, called multichannel pulse height analysers or " kicksorters ", can contain a whole array of discriminators, anticoincidence circuits and storage registers but in practice it is difficult to maintain a series of accurately spaced discriminator settings, and many of the analysers in use depend on other principles.

For example (Hutchinson and Scarrott, 1951) the pulses may be lengthened and the height of the resulting rectangle compared with a regularly rising waveform, the instant at which the voltages coincide being used to decide into which part of a storage system a record shall be placed. Such instruments are not in general capable of analysing pulses at very high repetition rates, and deal with such such rates by random sampling: in this respect they are inferior to systems of stacked discriminators.

Pulse analysers of this kind, with conversion from voltage data to digitally measured time, followed by gates and stores, are really specialised digital computers and can take advantage of developments in computer technique: recent pulse analysers employ transistor circuits to operate stores consisting of matrices of two-state magnetisable cores. There is a clear trend to use computer techniques to deal with the information obtained in nuclear counting experiments: they are used for example in several types of experiment to sort and enumerate pulses according to their time of arrival.

(5) *Register Drive Circuits*

Special circuits are required to give relatively heavy current pulses to drive message registers; the task is made easier if a relay is interposed between valve circuit and register, and a high-resistance Post Office relay is incorporated in some commercial units. A power valve is required to work the register, and this may be preceded by a triggered flip-flop giving a sufficiently long square waveform, or by a linear pulse shaping circuit. This may be a pulse lengthening circuit if the input consists of short pulses. If a scale-of-two stage precedes the register, the square pulses at one of its anodes may be " differentiated " by a circuit of appropriate time constant, amplified and applied to the grid of the power valve. The latter is then turned on for a short time at each alternate transition of the scaling stage.

(6) *Coincidence Circuits*

The use of coincidence circuits is discussed in § 11.12; the circuit usually used for resolving times down to a few tenths of a microsecond is the Rossi arrangement of a number of valves with a common anode load resistance. If large negative pulses are applied simultaneously to all the grids, the valves are all cut off and the potential at the point a rises to H.T.+. If one valve is left without an impulse, it remains conducting and the pulse at a is much smaller than before. It is clear that the discrimination between complete coincidence and " all but one " depends on the remaining valve presenting a low variational impedance, for the cutting off of successive tubes then results in an increase of current to the remaining anodes with a quite small rise of potential at the point a until the last tube is cut off and a rises to the potential of the H.T. supply. The circuit will work with triodes, for which a representative value of the anode impedance is 10,000 ohms, but the best results are obtained with pentodes working under " bottomed " conditions (Fig. 11.18). If pentodes were used over the normal (flat) part of their anode characteristic, the cutting off of successive tubes would give equal voltage steps at a (this property can be used for

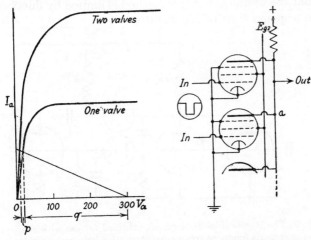

Fig. 11.18 The load-line diagram for the Rossi coincidence circuit. p represents the voltage pulse at the anode when one of two valves is cut off by a negative voltage pulse applied to its grid. q represents the pulse when both valves are cut off. These voltages only develop fully if the pulses are long enough compared with the time constant of the anode circuit

linear mixing of signals), but by using a high anode load resistance (see load line of Fig. 11.18), the valves are caused to work at a point where the anode current varies rapidly with anode voltage. A typical impedance value is 2000 ohms. The anode current of a bottomed pentode is nearly independent of grid voltage above, say, -1 V, but anode current can be cut off by driving the grid a few volts negative, so that these tubes are very suitable for the duty. The point a is connected to a valve biased so that it responds only to the large " coincidence " pulses and ignores the " partial coincidences ".

The resolving time of the arrangement is defined as the minimum separation of pulses which are not registered as coincident. In the Rossi circuit the resolution depends primarily on the shape and duration of the pulses impressed on the grids. Pulses derived, e.g. from a Geiger counter may be sharpened by amplifying them, using circuits designed to give short rise times (cf. § 7.23), and then differentiating them by R.C. circuits of short time constant. It has been pointed out that the usefulness of this method is limited by fluctuations in the response time of the counters.

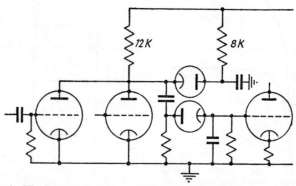

FIG. 11.19 The Rossi coincidence circuit modified for use with short pulses. The upper diode produces greater discrimination between coincidences and singles, the lower diode is part of a circuit to lengthen the coincidence pulses. In practice, germanium crystals are used instead of the diodes

If the Rossi circuit is used for very short pulses (e.g. in connection with electron multipliers), the rise in anode voltage is limited, by the rate of response of the anode circuit, to a value which may be no greater than that produced by a partial coincidence. Under these conditions the circuit fails to discriminate coincidences, but its behaviour may be improved by a diode device, connected in an auxiliary anode feed circuit (Garwin 1950) (Fig. 11.19). The diode has no effect on the pulse obtained when all the anodes are cut off, but in a partial coincidence, the rise in anode voltage is much less than before. Germanium crystal rectifiers are used in this arrangement because of the very low capacity which they add to the anode circuit. Coincidence circuits have been devised which rely entirely on the non-linearity of crystal rectifiers, and for some of these resolving times of 10^{-9} sec. have been claimed. (Bay 1951.)* Many other high-speed circuits depend on making the pulses equal by limiter circuits, then mixing them linearly and discriminating between single and double size pulses. (Lewis and Wells 1954.) Transistors and solid-state diodes are increasingly used in such circuits.

The use of anticoincidence counters was discussed in §11.13. A typical mixing circuit for detecting anticoincidences is the Rossi circuit with the valve connected to the anticoincidence counters biased so that it is normally non-conducting. The pulse from these counters is reversed, so that the pulse on the grid is positive-going. An essential feature of an efficient anticoincidence circuit is that the blocking impulse from the anticoincidence counter must be made to overlap in time the impulse from the coincidence counter. With slowly rising pulses in circuits of low performance it is not difficult to obtain sufficient overlap, but if this requirement is combined with rapid counting and high resolution in the coincidence part of the circuit, fairly sophisticated pulse-shaping circuits are required. For an example see Curran and Craggs 1949.

(7) *High Speed Electronics* (see also § 7.25)

Considerable additions have been made to the electronic techniques of nuclear physics in order to perform coincidence and timing experiments with scintillation, Cerenkov and other fast counters. (Lewis and Wells 1954.) The timing of the interval between two events reduces in principle to the detection of coincidences between signals delayed by known amounts. This may be done by delay lines of one of the types indicated in Fig. 11.20. Suitable coincidence circuits are mentioned above : for high speed work it is desirable to design the mixing stage so that it operates on the signal obtained directly from the detector photomultiplier : amplification may be introduced between mixer and discriminator. Photomultipliers provide wide band amplification (p. 374), but the

*A new " gating tube " for which a high performance is claimed is now in use. See Fischer and Marshall, *Rev. Sci. Instr.*, **23**, 417, 1952.

pulse amplitude conveniently obtainable from them is limited to a few volts, and further amplification is sometimes required. Feedback amplifiers as described in section 2 are not fast

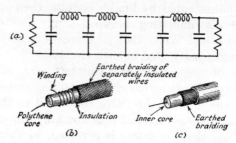

Fig. 11.20. Delay lines.

(a) Circuit with " lumped " elements. Delays of more than 1 μS are obtainable, but there is a definite cut-off at high frequencies, so that pulses are distorted.

(b) Continuously wound delay line. Typical delay 0·01 1 μS per foot. Delay cables of this kind are available with ferrite leading (by Hackethal, Germany); they are very compact for a given delay, giving typically 1 μS per foot.

(c) Coaxial cable. Typical delay 0·001 μS per foot.
All these lines must be terminated in their " characteristic impedance ", or pulses will be reflected from the terminations.

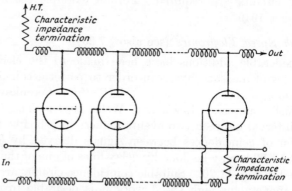

Fig. 11.21. Principle of one stage of " distributed " amplifier. Internal valve capacities form elements of two delay lines which are properly terminated to avoid reflection.

enough : wide-band amplifiers with useful response up to 50 Mc/s or so can be made by introducing inductive frequency compensating elements into the coupling circuits of resistance-capacity amplifiers.   At still higher frequencies it is necessary to use in each amplifying stage several valves connected in such a way that their mutual conductances are additive while their internal capacitances are not.   This can be done by connecting anodes and grids to form parts of two delay lines as indicated in Fig. 11.21.   Distributed amplifiers constructed on this principle can give useful gain up to frequencies of several hundred Mc/s.

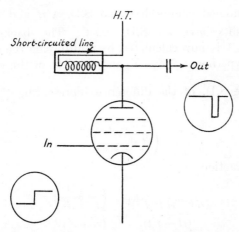

FIG. 11.22   Principle of delay-line circuit for forming a flat-topped pulse of length defined by twice the delay in the line

Another and very important use of delay lines is in pulse forming circuits as shown in Fig. 11.22, where the anode load of a valve is a length of delay line terminated in a short circuit. If a step input is applied to the grid, the output contains a corresponding step followed by its reflection in opposite phase from the short circuited end, and therefore takes the form of a flat topped pulse of defined length.   This circuit is valuable in coincidence and anti-coincidence circuits.   It is used twice to form the symmetrical pulses in the Fairstein amplifier (Fig. 11.15(c)).

11.15   Errors and Statistics in Counting

It is known (§ 2.12) that if n particles are counted, the standard deviation of the result is $\sqrt{n}$ and this is a fraction

Q   453

$\dfrac{1}{\sqrt{n}}$ of the counts. In all counting experiments, therefore, it is a first consideration to reduce this error to an acceptable value. If the "wanted" counts have a background of unwanted counts, the sampling error may be calculated as follows :—

Suppose counts (wanted + background) are recorded at rate r for time t (Experiment 1). The background counts are then recorded separately at rate r' for time t' (Experiment 2).

The combined counts have an S.D. $\sqrt{rt}$ and the background counts have an S.D. $\sqrt{r't'}$. The background of Experiment 1 is now calculated by multiplying the number of counts in Experiment 2 by t/t', and the S.D. of this estimate is $\dfrac{t\sqrt{r't'}}{t'}$. The S.D. of the difference representing the wanted counts is

$$\left(rt + \frac{r't^2}{t'^2}\right)^{\frac{1}{2}}$$

which is a fraction

$$\frac{(rt + r't^2/t'^2)^{\frac{1}{2}}}{(rt - r't)} = \frac{\left(\dfrac{r}{t} + \dfrac{r'}{t'}\right)}{(r - r')}$$

of the wanted counts.

In some experiments we have to decide how best to divide a total time t between counting the "wanted effect + background" and "background only". It may be shown that the percentage error of the "effect" is a minimum (usually flat) when

$$\frac{f}{1-f} = \sqrt{\frac{r'}{r}} \; ; \quad f = \frac{\sqrt{r'}}{\sqrt{r} + \sqrt{r'}}$$

where f is the fraction of t allotted to background counting.

A "count" is usually followed by a "dead" time in some part of the system counter-amplifier-scaler-register, and a systematic error in counting results. The error obviously increases with the counting rate. If random counts occur at an average rate r, and the resolving time of the counter, amplifier, and first scaling stage is σ, then the fractional inefficiency due to the overlapping of counts in these stages is $(1 - e^{\sigma - r})$, which is approximately $r\sigma$ for $r\sigma \ll 1$.*

It is occasionally necessary to use this formula to correct the counting rates obtained with Geiger counters having a long dead time, but it is difficult to obtain accurate dead time data, and the correction should be kept as small as possible. The same formula applies when a register is used without interposition of a scaler, and if a telephone message register, which has a resolving time of about 0·1 sec., is used in this way, the counting rate must be very small if a serious loss of counts is not to occur.

TABLE 11.4

Random Counting Rates for 0·1 % *Loss of Counts*

Scaling factor	2	4	8	10	16	32	64	100
Counts per sec.	0·5	4	20	30	64	172	420	710

The output pulses from a scaling circuit are less random than the input, i.e. very short and very long intervals between pulses are relatively less frequent. The calculation of the counts missed by the register is now fairly complicated (Blackman and Michiels 1948). Table 11.4, adapted from these authors, gives the maximum input rate if the loss is not to exceed 0·1 %. The resolving time τ of the register is taken as 0·1 sec. and the permissible counting rates for other values of τ can be obtained accurately enough by multiplying by 0·1 sec./τ. The loss increases very rapidly if the counting rate is increased above the values given in Table 11.4, and the permissible rates for 1 % loss are only a little higher than those for 0·1 % loss.

* In an accurate calculation it is necessary to distinguish between a system which is unaffected by another pulse arriving during the inactive period following a pulse, and a system which begins its dead time anew in such a case. The quantitative distinction is negligible in practical cases where the loss of counts is small.

Geiger counters often have dead times of the order 10^{-4} sec. ; other counting devices and electronic scaling circuits have dead times of a few microseconds. With high speed counting devices, it will be found that the register limits the counting rate unless unusually high scaling factors are employed.

11.16 The Cloud Chamber

The Wilson cloud chamber, which allows observation of the tracks of individual ionising particles, was for more than forty years an important and versatile tool of research in nuclear physics and cosmic rays. In recent years its use has declined since it is not technically well adapted to the particle accelerators which now dominate research into high-energy particles and the emphasis in cosmic ray investigations has shifted elsewhere. The cloud chamber is therefore treated less fully than in previous editions of this book. A comprehensive account is given in Wilson 1951.

The ions left in the track of an ionising particle act as condensation nuclei for droplets if the atmosphere is supersaturated with a suitable vapour. This condition may be produced in a chamber in which vapour diffuses from a reservoir of liquid near the bottom of the chamber to a strongly cooled region at the top. An intermediate zone of limited depth is then continuously available for track formation by ionising particles (review by Snowden 1953). In the "classical" cloud-chamber, supersaturation is achieved by cooling a mixture of gas and vapour by sudden, nearly adiabatic, expansion. The minimum expansion ratio required depends primarily on the composition of gas and vapour. It is about $1 \cdot 25$ for water vapour in air and $1 \cdot 07$ for a 70 % ethyl alcohol/water mixture in argon. At a rather greater expansion ratio cloud condensation takes place without ions, and the useful range of ratios lies between the "ion limit" and the "cloud limit". When a chamber filled with ordinary dirty gas is expanded, there is a copious deposition of droplets on dust nuclei. The droplets at this stage are small because the condensed liquid is shared between many nuclei; they fall slowly and many of them evaporate before they reach a solid surface. Many of the nuclei are, however, carried to the bottom of the chamber by the falling droplets, and by repeated expansion the chamber may be cleared of dust nuclei, and it is then available to display particle tracks. During the time that the chamber is being cleared and standing waiting, an electric field of the order 10-50 V/cm. is maintained in it to sweep away ions formed by cosmic rays and stray radioactive contamination.* When a chamber is clean, the background of droplets is about 1 per cc. over an appreciable range of expansion ratio: this background deteriorates slowly, for reasons which are rather obscure, and after a day or two the chamber must usually be flushed out with a stream of clean gas, and refilled with the working gas and liquid.

From the moment of formation the trail of ions begins to diffuse. As soon as droplets condense on the gas the rate of diffusion becomes negligible; it follows that trails formed by the passage of a particle *after* expansion are very fine, and that trails formed just before expansion have a width which depends on the diffusion time. Once formed, the droplets must be allowed to grow before they scatter enough light to be photographed. During the period of growth the droplets fall under gravity, and, more important, they are subject to any motion which may agitate the gas. This is the main cause of track distortion, and may be minimised by keeping the temperature in the chamber very uniform except for a slight upward gradient.

After an expansion a chamber shows a background of fine droplets on a second expansion, and it must be cleared by carrying out one or more expansions at reduced expansion ratio, allowing the droplets to settle out before recompressing. It is equally effective and technically more convenient to use slow expansions to the full ratio.

The technical features of a typical cloud chamber are indicated in Fig. 11.23.

* It is usual to suppress the electric field when the particles to be recorded are admitted to the chamber, so that the tracks are not widened or doubled by the motion of ions in the field before their mobility is abolished by condensation.

The chamber is " sensitive ", in the sense that it will give distinguishable tracks, from just before the expansion to just after it. In nuclear research it is usually possible to admit particles to the chamber at the right point in the operating cycle. The sensitive time is, however, only a small fraction of the cycle,

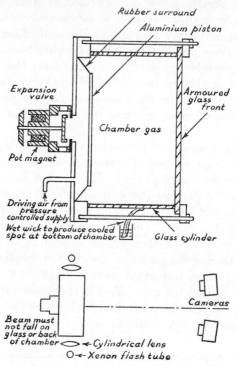

FIG. 11.23   Diagrams of a simple cloud chamber and its arrangement

and where events occur at random as in cosmic ray investigations it is usually necessary to detect the event to be observed and make it initiate the expansion of the chamber.* The design considerations for chambers controlled in this way will be found in Blackett 1934, though the control arrangements there described have been simplified in later work.

* It is then fundamental that the type of event observed is limited by the selection conditions set up, and unforeseen events will not in general be observable.

Besides qualitative observation of such interactions as scattering of particles by nuclei and the production of new particles the cloud chamber has been used for

(1) Quantitative observation of these phenomena including measuring of ranges and scattering angles.

(2) Estimates of the density of ion production along the track of a particle.

(3) Measurements of the momentum of charged particles by the curvature of their tracks in a magnetic field.

Precise measurements of these kinds make special demands on chamber technique, and in particular accurate momentum measurements require special chamber design and operating procedure to reduce the distortion of the tracks.

11.17 The Bubble Chamber

It is found that ions act as nuclei for the formation of bubbles in a superheated liquid obtained by suddenly reducing the applied pressure below the vapour pressure. Unless the chamber containing the liquid is simply shaped and smoothly constructed (e.g. a small glass bulb, in which the metastable state may persist for several seconds), the superheated condition lasts only for a few milliseconds before general boiling takes place, and the ionising particles to be recorded must traverse the liquid in this interval. The lifetime of the nuclei is very short, so that counter-controlled operation of the chamber is not possible: the liquid can, however, be recompressed and decompressed again very quickly (several cycles a second are possible) so that the chamber is sensitive for a fraction of the time larger than can be obtained with cloud chambers. The cycle of operations matches well that of many particle accelerating machines.

The most important advantage of the bubble chamber is that the liquid can contain a high density of the nuclei whose collisions are to be studied, so the probability of interesting interactions is high. Because proton interactions are particularly simple and important liquid hydrogen has been used as a bubble medium despite the formidable technical difficulties. The chamber must then be operated at about 27° K.   Certain hydrocarbons (e.g. pentane at about 150°-160° C. and propane at 50°-80° C.) are technically more convenient and contain high concentrations of protons.

A bubble chamber used in conjuction with an accelerating machine gives an enormous output of data, and at present methods of recovering information from photographs by more or less automatic methods are being actively developed. A review article on bubble chambers is given by Bugg 1959.

11.18 Nuclear Track Emulsions

It has long been known that α-particles produce recognisable tracks in photographic emulsions and several Austrian workers about 1936 found and investigated tracks produced in photographic emulsions by cosmic-ray particles. In recent years the study of tracks in special emulsions has become, largely in the hands of C. F. Powell, a very important tool of investigation in nuclear physics and particularly cosmic rays.

The photographic manufacturers have developed emulsions which are very free from accidental developable grains, and which are very sensitive to ionising particles. Emulsions are now available which will record the tracks of fast particles at the minimum of ionisation, the so-called electron-sensitive plates. Such emulsions acquire a considerable background of developable grains by exposure to cosmic rays ; and, moreover, it is difficult to distinguish between tracks of different grain densities when the densities are well above the minimum. For many purposes, in which heavily ionising particles are recorded, it is therefore preferable to use the older types of emulsion which are insensitive to minimum ionisation particles.

The emulsions display the tracks and interactions of nuclear particles in much the same way as the cloud chamber, with the important advantages of continuous sensitivity and extreme compactness. The disadvantages of the method as compared with the cloud chamber are more subtle. They arise, in cosmic-ray work, partly from the fact that, while it is easy to detect nuclear interactions in a small volume of a medium of high density, the chance of detecting the decay of particles of moderate life is small, unless indeed they are produced in the emulsion with such velocities that they are stopped before they leave the emulsion and decay at rest, as in the case of the π-meson. The continuous sensitivity of emulsion entails the disadvantage that simultaneous events taking place in different parts of the plate cannot be recognised as such.

The purely technical difficulties of the method arise mainly in the processing of the thick layers of emulsion (Dilworth *et al.* 1950) which are sometimes required to give favourable conditions of observation and in the tedious scanning of the developed plates, required to find significant events. Teams of trained scanners (not physicists) have been formed for this purpose in several centres of cosmic-ray research.

Ionising particles lose a given amount of energy in a much shorter distance in the emulsion than in air and the ratio range in emulsion/range in air at N.T.P. is of the order 1/2000. Useful range measurements can be made on tracks which begin and end in the emulsion and the angles between the tracks of particles emitted in an interaction can be measured. In measurements of this kind it is necessary to allow for the fact that the emulsion shrinks in the direction of its thickness during processing, so that distances in this direction measured on the plates are only about $\frac{1}{3}$ of the corresponding distances during exposure. The shrinkage of the emulsion in other directions is effectively restrained by the glass plate.

The scattering of particles, due to multiple small angle deflections in the electrostatic fields of nuclei, can be used as a measure of their momentum ; a statistical measure of the scattering is obtained by dividing a track into a series of cells of definite length and measuring in each cell either the angular deviation or the displacement of the track element from a straight line. These scattering measurements give information comparable with that obtained from track curvature in a magnetic field in the cloud chamber, with the difference that it is not possible to infer the sign of the charge on the particles.*

---

* The deflection of emulsion tracks in a magnetic field has been observed. The deflection in any available field is too small compared with scattering to allow accurate measures of momentum, but the sign ambiguity may sometimes be resolved by the use of a field.

The grain-density along a track may be estimated to obtain a measure of the intensity of ionisation, and in favourable cases this information can be combined with scattering measurements to allow the mass of the ionising particle to be deduced (see below).

The scope of the emulsion technique can be best demonstrated by giving some examples of its use.

The method has been extensively used in investigating the nuclear interactions of cosmic rays. The disintegrations of nuclei by energetic rays appear as " stars " of several heavily ionising particles, and when the electron sensitive plates were introduced, some of these stars were found to contain very energetic, lightly ionising, particles. These latter stars could be identified with the producers of mesons and with the penetrating showers of cloud chamber experiments. Before electron-sensitive plates were available, the emulsion method had revealed the existence of the π-meson— a new fundamental particle (Lattes, Occhialini and Powell 1947). Some of the particles produced in stars showed in the emulsion behaviour which was identified as the decay of a heavier into a lighter meson. The mass of the π-meson was estimated from details of its decay. Later the mass was compared with that of the decay (μ) meson by comparing the ionisation (grain density) of particles of known residual range (Lattes *et al.* 1948). The mass was also estimated in absolute measure from the scattering of tracks of known range (Goldschmidt-Clermont *et al.* 1948).

The production of mesons in the cyclotron by the impact of high-energy (380 MeV) α-particles on targets was discovered by the characteristic interactions of the mesons observed in emulsions.

A systematic study of the masses of the particles produced in stars and showers has been made by observation of the grain density and scattering of the tracks. If these two parameters are plotted against one another, the points lie on a curve characteristic of the mass (Fowler 1950). Mass determinations of cosmic particles have been made by measuring the residual range of the particles and the deflection in the space between two emulsion layers exposed in a magnetic field.

Charged particles heavier than protons have been discovered in the cosmic rays at high altitude. The trails which they produce are far too heavy for grain counting, but they are characterised by a " hairy " appearance due to δ-rays—electrons which are expelled with velocities high enough to produce short branch tracks. By determining the number of δ-rays per unit length of the track, it has in certain cases been found possible to estimate the charge on the particle, and to identify the nuclei of many of the lighter elements.

In a different type of work, the angular distribution of particles scattered from a cyclotron beam can be investigated, and the energy spectra of the particle scattered at any angle obtained from the range distribution of the tracks. A similar method can be applied to study the energy distribution of disintegration products obtained by bombardment. In these applications a great advantage is the amount of data which can be amassed in a short run of the cyclotron or other accelerator. The nuclear track emulsion has been used as a detecting system in an α-ray spectrograph and the advantage of the method is that the particles forming a weak α-ray line may be distinguished from a background of scattered particles by the direction of their tracks.

REFERENCES

AITKEN 1939. *Jour. Roy. Soc. Edinb.* **31**, 44.

ALEXANDER 1946. *J. Sci. Instr.* **23**, 11. Theory of Diffusion Pumps.

ALLEN 1947. *Rev. Sci. Instr.* **18**, 739. Secondary emission counters.

ANDREW 1958. *Nuclear Magnetic Resonance.* University Press, Cambridge.

BARNES and SILVERMAN 1934. *Rev. Mod. Phys.* **6**, 162. Review Article on noise ; references.

BAY 1951. *Rev. Sci. Instr.* **22**, 397.

BAYARD and ALPERT 1950. *Rev. Sci. Instr.* **21**, 571. Ionisation gauge for low pressures.

BEDFORD and FREDENDALL 1942. *Proc. I.R.E.*, p. 440. Square-wave testing.

BELL 1955. Scintillation Counters. Article in Siegbahn *β- and γ-ray spectroscopy.* N. Holland Publ. Co., Amsterdam.

BELLEVUE 1957. Les Progrès récents en Spectroscopie interférentielle. (Conference), *Revue d'Optique*, Paris.

BERG 1948. *Reports on Progress in Physics*, 1946-47, p. 248. Theory of photographic process.

BISHOP and HARRIS 1950. *Rev. Sci. Instr.* **21**, 366. D.C. Amplifier.

BITTER 1936; 1937; 1939. *Rev. Sci. Instr.* **7**, 479, 482; **8**, 318; **10**, 373. Design of magnets for high fields.

BITTER 1951. *Rev. Sci. Instr.* **22**, 171. Ironclad Magnet.

BLACKETT 1934. *Proc. Roy. Soc.* **A146**, 281. The counter-controlled cloud chamber.

BLACKETT 1936, 1937. *Proc. Roy. Soc.* **A154**, 565; **A159**, 1. Cloud chamber curvature measurements.

BLACKMAN and MICHIELS 1948. *Proc. Phys. Soc.* **60**, 549. Loss of counts due to resolving time.

BLEARS 1944; 1947. *Nature* **154**, 20; *Proc. Roy. Soc.* **A188**, 62. Effect of clean-up on readings of ionisation gauges. Vapour pressure of pump oils.

BLEARS and LECK 1951. Vacuum Physics supplement to *J. Sci. Instr.* p. 21. Leak Finding.

BLOCH 1946. *Phys. Rev.* **70**, 460. Nuclear Magnetic Resonance.

BODE 1945. *Network Analysis and Feedback Amplifier Design.* Van Nostrand, New York.

BOMKE 1937. *Vakuumspektroskopie.* Barth, Leipzig.

BOURNE 1948. *Discharge Lamps for Photography and Projection.* Chapman and Hall, London. Extensive tabular data on light sources, including filaments and arcs.

BOUTRY 1946. *Optique Instrumentale.* Masson, Paris.

BOUWERS 1946. *Achievements in Optics.* Elsevier, Amsterdam. Contains a collected account of certain reflecting optical systems.

REFERENCES

BOYS 1895. *Phil. Trans.* **A186**, 1; *Dict. Applied Physics*, **3**, 279. Gravity Apparatus.

BOYS 1923. *Dict. Applied Physics.* **3**, 695. Preparation and use of Quartz Fibres.

BOZORTH. *Ferromagnetism.* Comprehensive treatise on materials, properties and theory. Van Nostrand, New York.

BRADDICK 1960. Reports on Progress in Physics. *Phys. Soc., Lond.* Photoelectric Photometry.

BROWN 1945. *Rev. Sci. Instr.* **16**, 316. Use of silicones in diffusion pumps.

B.S. CODE 1041/1943. Temperature measurement. Comprehensive summary of methods.

B.S.I.R.A. 1924. Report on magnetic behaviour of galvanometer coils. See review in *J. Sci. Instr.* **2**, 270.

BUGG 1959. *Progr. Nuc. Physics*, **7**. Pergamon, London. Bubble Chamber.

BURCH 1929. *Proc. Roy. Soc.* **A123**, 271. Use of petroleum distillate oils in diffusion pumps.

BURCH 1947. *Proc. Phys. Soc.* **59**, 41. The reflecting microscope.

CERENKOV 1934. *C.R. Acad. URSS.* **2**, 451. Radiation from fast particles.

CHAPMAN and BARTELS 1940. *Geomagnetism.* Oxford University Press.

CHAPMAN and COWLING 1939. *The Mathematical Theory of Non-Uniform Gases.* Cambridge University Press.

CHESTERMAN 1951. *The Photographic Study of Rapid Events.* Oxford University Press.

COCKCROFT 1928. *Phil. Trans. Roy. Soc.* **227**, 325. Calculation of Magnetic Coils.

COHEN 1947. *Handbook of Telecommunications.* Pitman, London.

COHEN 1949. *Phys. Rev.* **75**, 1329. Internally controlled cloud chamber.

COMPTON and LANGMUIR 1930. *Rev. Mod. Phys.* **2**, 123. Data on Ionisation and Recombination in Gases.

COMPTON, WOLLAN and BENNETT 1934. *Rev. Sci. Instr.* **5**, 415. Details of Ionisation Chamber (Carnegie Model).

CONRADY. *Dict. Applied Physics.* **4**, p. 221. Distribution of light in optical image.

CONSTANT, FAIRES and LENANDER 1943. *Phys. Rev.* **63**, 441. Treatment of copper to produce non-magnetic behaviour.

COPLEY, SIMPSON, TENNEY and PHIPPS 1935. *Rev. Sci. Instr.* **6**, 265. Comparison of divergent nozzles for diffusion pumps.

COSSULTA and STECKELMACHER 1960. *J. Sci. Instr.* **37**, 404. Helical Mass Spectrometer.

COX 1943. *Optics.* Focal Press, London. Much tabular information on lens types.

COX and GRINDLEY 1927. *J. Sci. Instr.* **4**, 413. Charge and voltage sensitivity of electrometer.

REFERENCES

Cox and Habell 1948. *Engineering Optics*. Pitman, London. Optical instruments applied to engineering.

Cox and Martin 1945. *J. Sci. Instr.* **22**, 5. Critical Review of lens types.

Curran, 1953. *Luminescence and the Scintillation Counter*. Butterworth, London.

Curran, Cockroft and Angus 1949. *Phil. Mag.* **40**, 36, also 53 and 929. Proportional counter at high amplification.

Curran and Craggs 1949. *Counting Tubes*. Butterworth, London.

Deming and Birge 1934. *Rev. Mod. Phys.* **6**, 119. Statistical Theory of Errors.

Dilworth, Occhialini and Vermaesen 1950. *Bulletin 13a du Centre de Physique Nucléaire*. Univ. Libre de Bruxelles. Processing of Nuclear Emulsions.

Dimitrov and Baker 1947. *Telescopes and Accessories*. Blakiston, Philadelphia. Churchill, London.

Dobson, Griffith and Harrison 1926. *Photographic Photometry*. Oxford University Press.

Du Mond and Cohen 1948. *Rev. Mod. Phys.* **20**, 85 ; corrected in **21**, 651, 1949. Best Values for Atomic Constants.

Dunn 1939. *Rev. Sci. Instr.* **10**, 368. Theory of Flux Meter.

Dushman 1949. *Vacuum Technique*. Wiley, New York (Chapman and Hall, London).

Dyson 1949. *Proc. Phys. Soc. Lond.* **62B**, 565. Micro-objective with long working distance.

Edwards. W. Edwards and Co. Ltd. London. Catalogue material on vacuum systems.

Einstein 1906. *Ann. Physik.* **19**, 371. Theory of Brownian Displacement.

Ellett and Zabel 1931. *Phys. Rev.* **37**, 1102. Precision form of Pirani gauge.

Elliot 1949. *Proc. Phys. Soc.* **62A**, 369. Quenching of Geiger Counters.

Elmore and Sands 1949. Division V. Vol. 1 *National Nuclear Energy Series*. McGraw-Hill, New York. Electronic Devices.

Engstrom 1947. *Jour. Opt. Soc. Amer.* **37**, 420. Use of Photomultiplier.

Engstrom, Stoudenheimer and Glover 1952. *Nucleonics*, **10**, 58. Variability of Photomultiplier Performance.

Ericsson, 1954. Cold Cathode Tubes Handbook. Ericsson Telephones Ltd., London.

Espe and Knoll 1936. *Werkstoffkunde der Hochvakuumtechnik*. Springer, Berlin. American Lithoprint, Edwards, Ann Arbor, 1944.

Espley, Cherry and Levy 1946. *Jour. I.E.E.* **93**, IIIA, 1176. Pulse-testing of networks, etc.

Evans 1949. *Jour. Opt. Soc. Amer.* **39**, 229. Interference Filters for Light. (Lyot type.)

Fairstein 1956. *Rev. Sci. Instr.* **27**, 475. Non-overloading amplifier.

REFERENCES

FARLEY 1956. *Elements of Pulse Circuits*. Methuen Monographs, London.

FERRITES 1957. *Proc. I.E.E.* 104B (Supplement).

FLETCHER, MILLER, and ROSENHEAD, 1946. *An Index to Mathematical Tables*. Scientific Computing Service, London.

FOWLER 1950. *Phil. Mag.* **41**, 169. Masses of cosmic-ray shower particles in emulsion.

FRANKELHAUSER and MACDONALD 1949. *J. Sci. Instr.* **26**, 145. Galvanometer amplifier with feedback.

FRAZER, DUNCAN and COLLAR 1946. *Elementary Matrices*. Cambridge University Press.

GAEDE 1947. *Z. Naturforschung*, **2a**, 233. Gas ballast principles for vacuum pumps.

GARWIN 1950. *Rev. Sci. Instr.* **21**, 569. High-speed Rossi circuit.

GARWIN 1952. *Rev. Sci. Instr.* **23**, 755. Liquid Scintillation Counters.

GILLESPIE 1953. *Signal, Noise and Resolution in Nuclear Counter Amplifiers*. Pergamon, London.

GOLAY 1958. *Rev. Sci. Instr.* **29**, 313. Electromagnetic Shims for Uniform Fields.

GOLDING 1961. *Wireless World*, **67**, 329. Transformer Arm Bridge.

GOLDSCHMIDT-CLERMONT 1948. *Proc. Phys. Soc.* **61**, 183. Masses of particles in nuclear emulsions.

GORE, *et al* 1947. *Jour. Opt. Soc. Amer.* **37**, 23. Prisms for the infra-red.

GRAY 1921. *Absolute Measurements in Electricity and Magnetism*. Macmillan, London.

GRAY 1944. *Proc. Camb. Phil. Soc.* **40**, 72. Average energy of ionisation.

GUILD. *Dict. Applied Phys.* 4, p. 767 ; *Proc. Phys. Soc.* **29**, 311, 1917. " Chromatic parallax " in spectroscopy.

GUILD 1956. *Interference systems of crossed diffraction gratings*. Oxford University Press.

GUILD 1960. *Diffraction Gratings as Measuring Scales*. Oxford University Press.

HAGUE. *Alternating Current Bridge Methods*. Pitman, London (1943 and other editions).

HANSEN 1936. *Rev. Sci. Instr.* **7**, 182. Discussion on electrometer.

HARRISON 1929. *Jour. Opt. Soc. Amer.* **19**, 267. Photographic photometry. Comprehensive review article.

HARRISON 1938. *Rev. Sci. Instr.* **9**, 15. Use of preloaded ball bearings in connection with precision screws.

HEALEY and READ 1941. *The Behaviour of Slow Electrons in Gases*. Amalgamated Wireless Ltd., Sydney. *Wireless World*, London.

HEAVENS 1955. *Optical Properties of Thin Solid Films*. Butterworth, London.

HECHT and SCHLAER 1938. *Jour. Opt. Soc. Amer.* **28**, 269. The dark adaptation of the eye.

REFERENCES

HERCOCK 1947. *The Photographic Recording of C.R.O. traces.* Ilford, London.

HEYL 1930. *Bur. Stands. Jour. Research* 5, 1243. (Gravity Apparatus) Fibres for torsion balance.

HIBBERD 1959. *Proc. I.E.E.* 106b 264. Review of Semiconductor Devices.

HICKMAN 1936. *J. Franklin Inst.* 221, 215, 383. Use of Phthalate Esters as pump oils.

HICKMAN 1940. *J. App. Phys.* 11, 303. Fractionating pumps and general pump theory.

HIGGINBOTHAM 1947. *Rev. Sci. Instr.* 18, 706. Electronic Devices for Nuclear Physics.

HILL 1948. *J. Sci. Instr.* 25, 225. Also, Downing, *ibid.* p. 230, and *J. Sci. Instr.* 30, 40, 1953. Moving coil galvanometers.

HODSON 1950. *Phil. Mag.* 41, 826. Internally-controlled cloud chamber.

HUNT 1946. *Electrical Contacts.* Johnson and Matthey, London.

HUTCHINSON and SCARROTT 1951. *Phil. Mag.* 42, 792. Pulse Height Analyser.

JACQUINOT 1954. *Jour. Opt. Soc. Amer.* 44, 161. Efficiency of Spectrometers.

JACQUINOT 1960. *Reports Progr. Phys.* 23, 267. Interference Spectroscopy.

JAFFE 1913. *Ann. Physik.* 42, 303. Columnar recombination of ions.

JELLEY 1953. *Progr. Nuclear Physics* 3, 84. Pergamon, London. Cerenkov counters.

JELLEY 1958. *Cerenkov Radiation and its Application.* Pergamon, London.

JOHNSON 1948. *Astrophysical Journal* 107, 34. Theoretical limits of photocells in astronomical applications.

JOHNSON, MURPHY and MICHELSEN 1949. *Rev. Sci. Instr.* 20, 429. Apparatus for measuring magnetisation of rocks.

JONES 1951; 1955; 1956. *J. Sci. Instr.* 28, 38; 32, 38; 33, 11. Systems of Spring Constraints.

JUDD 1931. *Bur. Stands. Jour. Research* 6, 465. Eye response curves.

KALLMANN and FURST 1950. *Phys. Rev.* 79, 857. Liquid phosphors for scintillation counting.

KANDIAH and BROWN 1952. *Proc. I.E.E.* 99, II, 314. High Gain D.C. Amplifiers (General Discussion).

KENDALL 1945; 1946. *Advanced Theory of Statistics.* Vol. 1 Chaps. 1-16; Vol. 2 Chaps. 16-20. Griffin, London.

KEUFFEL 1949. *Rev. Sci. Instr.* 20, 202. Parallel plate counters.

KODAK. Data sheets on plates for scientific purposes.

KURIE 1948. *Rev. Sci. Instr.* 19, 485. Vacuum Plumbing.

LANDAU 1944. *Jour. Phys. URSS.* 8, 201. Energy loss of fast particles by ionisation (esp. fluctuations).

LANDER and NIELSEN 1953. *Rev. Sci. Instr.* **24**, 20. Angular distribution of light scattered from droplets.

LATTES, OCCHIALINI and POWELL 1947. *Nature* **160**, 453, 486. The π-meson.

LATTES, OCCHIALINI and POWELL 1948. *Proc. Phys. Soc.* **A61**, 173. Masses of mesons by grain counting.

LEE 1946. *Science Progress* **34**, 533. New Optical Glasses.

LEWIS 1942. *Electrical Counting.* Cambridge University Press.

LEWIS and WELLS 1954 ; 1959. *Millimicrosecond Pulse Techniques.* Pergamon, London.

LISTON, QUINN, SARGENT and SCOTT 1946. *Rev. Sci. Inst.* **17**, 194. Contact-modulated amplifier for small D.C. potential.

LIVINGSTONE and BETHE 1937. *Rev. Mod. Phys.* **9**, 245. Properties of ionising particles.

LYOT 1944. *Ann. Astrophys.* **7**, 1-2, 31. Interference filters for light.

MADANSKY and PIDD 1950. *Rev. Sci. Inst.* **21**, 407. Parallel plate counters.

MAKSUTOV 1944. *Jour. Opt. Soc. Amer.* **34**, 270.

MARTIN 1930-32. *Introduction to Applied Optics.* 2 Volumes. (Or Technical Optics 1950.) Pitman, London.

MARTIN and HILL 1947. *Manual of Vacuum Practice.* Melbourne University Press.

MATHER 1951. *Phys. Rev.* **84**, 181. Cerenkov radiation (contains references up to date).

MAZE 1946. *Jour. de Phys.* **7**, 165. External-cathode counters.

MEES 1944. *The Theory of the Photographic Process.* MacMillan, New York.

METCALF and THOMPSON 1930. *Phys. Rev.* **30**, 1498. Analysis and design of electrometer valve.

METSON 1950. *Brit. Jour. App. Phys.* **1**, 73. Valve grid currents—experimental data.

MILNE 1950. *Numerical Calculus.* Princeton University Press.

MITCHELL 1948. *Jour. Ill. Eng. Soc.* Dec. 1948. Very high speed flash lamp.

MOFFATT 1946. *J.I.E.E.* **93**, IIIA, 1335. Diode as an H.F. noise source.

MOLL 1923. *Proc. Phys. Soc.* **35**, 253. Galvanometer Design.

MOLL and BURGER 1925. *Phil. Mag.* **50**, 626. Thermo Relay.

MOND NICKEL COMPANY. *Magnetic Properties of Nickel Iron Alloys.* (Pamphlet giving curves etc. for these materials.)

MORRIS and HEAD 1944. *Phil. Mag.* **35**, 735. Solution of Equations.

MORRIS 1946. *Phil. Mag.* **37**, 106. Solution of Equations.

MOTT and GURNEY 1948 (1940). *Electronic Processes in Ionic Crystals.* Oxford University Press.

MOULLIN 1938. *Spontaneous Fluctuations of Voltage.* Oxford University Press.

469

REFERENCES

MULLARD 1960a. Catalogue Material. Ionisation gauges for use as pumps.

MULLARD 1960b. *Reference Manual of Transistor Circuits.*

NELSON 1945. *Rev. Sci. Instr.* **16**, 273. Hydrogen Ionisation Gauge as a Leak Detector.

NETTLETON and SUGDEN 1939. *Proc. Roy. Soc.* **A173**, 313. Precise calibration of magnetic fields.

NICHOLSON AND SNELLING 1955. *Brit. J. Appl. Phys.* **6**, 104. Scintillation Counters for Neutrons.

NIELSEN 1947. *Rev. Sci. Instr.* **18**, 18. Use of normal valves as electrometer tubes (with reference to earlier work).

NUCLEONICS 1952, 1954. *Symposia on Scintillation Counters.* Scattered through 1952 volume, also March 1954.

NYQUIST 1928. *Phys. Rev.* **32**, 110. Theory of resistor noise.

OWEN 1946. *Alternating Current Measurements* (2nd edit. 1946). Methuen, London (Monographs).

PACKARD 1948. *Rev. Sci. Instr.* **19**, 435. Proton-resonance-controlled magnetic field regulator.

PARTRIDGE 1949. *Glass to Metal Seals.* Socy. of Glass Tech. Sheffield.

PENICK 1935. *Rev. Sci. Instr.* **6**, 115. Electrometer Valve Circuits.

PENNING 1937. *Physica* 4, 21. Cold cathode vacuum gauge.

POLLARD and PHILLIPS 1937. *Engineering*, **143**, 223, 281, 339, 398. Loading of ball-plane contacts.

POLLARD 1929. *Kinematic Design of Couplings in Instrument Mechanisms.* Hilger, London.

PORTER 1950. *Introduction to Servo Mechanisms.* Methuen, London.

POUND 1952. *Progr. Nuc. Physics*, Vol. 2. Pergamon, London. Nuclear Magnetic Resonance.

POWER and CRAWLEY 1954. *Vacuum*, **4**, 415. Backstreaming in Diffusion Pumps.

PRESTON 1946. *J. Sci. Instr.* **23**, 173. Galvanometer amplifier with feedback.

PRINGLE 1950. *Nature*, **166**, 11. Review article on scintillation counting.

PUCKLE 1951. *Time Bases.* Chapman and Hall, London.

PUGH 1958. *Rev. Sci. Instr.* **29**, 1118. Non-Magnetic Alloys.

R.C.A. 1949. *R.C.A. Journal*, Dec. 1949, gives quantitative information on most photomultipliers available in U.S.A. and England at that date.

RING and LISSBERGER 1955. *Optica Acta*, **2**, 43. Interference Filters.

RODDA 1953. *Photoelectric Multipliers.* Macdonald, London.

ROLT 1929. *Gauges and Fine Measurements.* Macmillan, London.

ROSSI and STAUB 1949. Division V. Volume 2 of *National Nuclear Energy Series*. McGraw-Hill, New York. Ionisation Chambers, etc.

SCARRETT 1950. Article on Electronics. *Progress in Nuclear Physics*. Ed. Frisch. Butterworth, London.

SCOTT 1946. *J. Sci. Inst.* **23**, 193. Design of Metal Glass Seals.

SCOTT 1955. *Rev. Sci. Instr.* **28**, 270. Coils for Uniform Field.

SERVO MECHANISMS. *J.I.E.E.* 94, IIA, 1947.

SHARPE 1955. *Nuclear Radiation Detectors.* Methuen Monograph, London.

SHEA 1957. *Transistor Circuit Engineering.* Wiley, New York: Chapman and Hall, London.

SHERWIN 1948. *Rev. Sci. Instr.* **19**, 111. Delays in Geiger Counters.

SMITH, JONES and CHASMAR 1957. *Detection and Measurement of Infrared Radiation.* Oxford University Press.

SNOWDEN 1953. *Prog. Nucl. Physics*, Vol. 3. Pergamon, London. Review of Diffusion Cloud Chambers.

SOMMER 1960. *Optica Acta*, **7**, 121. Photocathodes.

SOUTHWELL 1941. *Relaxation Methods in Engineering.* Oxford.

SPARK SYMPOSIUM 1961. *Rev. Sci. Instr.* **32**, 479 ff. Spark Chambers.

SPILSBURY and WEBB 1945. *J. Sci. Instr.* **22**, 213. Precautions in using flux meter.

STETTER 1943. *Zeit. f. Physik* **120**, 639. Ionisation by α-particles.

STODOLA 1927 and 1945. *Steam and Gas Turbines* (translation). McGraw-Hill, New York, 1927. P. Smith, New York, 1945.

STRONG 1938. *Modern Physical Laboratory Practice.* Prentice-Hall (New York). Blackie, London.

STRONG 1958. *Concepts of Classical Optics.* Freeman, San Francisco. (Appendix on Fibre Optics by Kapany.)

SULLIVAN 1948. *Rev. Sci. Instr.* **19**, 1. Review of vacuum pumps—mainly American.

SURUGUE (ed.) 1947. *Techniques générales du Laboratoire de Physique*, Vol. 1. C.N.R.S. Paris.

SYMONDS 1955. *Rep. Prog. Phys.* **18**, 83. Measurement of Magnetic Fields.

TAYLOR 1952. *Rep. Prog. Phys.* **15**, 49. Range energy relation for protons, etc.

TERMAN 1947. *Radio Engineers' Handbook.* McGraw-Hill, New York.

THOMAS, WILLIAMS and HIPPLE 1946. *Rev. Sci. Instr.* **17**, 368. Mass spectrometer for leak detection.

THOMAS and HUNTOON 1949. *Rev. Sci. Instr.* **20**, 516. Bridge circuits for nuclear magnetic resonance.

THORNESS and NIER 1961. *Rev. Sci. Instr.* **32**, 807. Valves for High Vacuum Systems.

TONGIORGI et al. 1951. *Rev. Sci. Instr.* **22**, 899. Technique of BF_3 counters.

TURNNR, PICKARD AND HOFFMAN 1962. *J. Sci. Instr.* **39**, 26.

TWYMAN 1942. *Prism and Lens Making.* Hilger, London.

TYRRELL 1950. *J. Brit. I.R.E.* May 1950. Performance and Stability of Permanent Magnets.

VALLEY and WALLMAN 1948. *Vacuum Tube Amplifiers.* Vol. 18 of Radiation Laboratory Series. McGraw-Hill, New York.

VASICEK 1960. *Optics of Thin Films.* North Holland Pub. Co., Amsterdam.

WALDEN 1939. *J. Sci. Instr.* **16**, 1. Laboratory Furnaces.

REFERENCES

WALTER 1960. *Rev. Sci. Instr.* **31**, 256. Surface Barrier Counters.

WEST 1953. *Prog. Nucl. Physics*, Vol. 3. Pergamon, London. Use and calibration of proportional counters.

WHITE and HICKEY 1948. *Electronics* **21**, 100. Halogen detector for leaks.

WHITTAKER and ROBINSON 1944. *The Calculus of Observations.* Blackie, London.

WILLIAMS 1946. *J.I.E.E.* **93**, IIIA, 289. Introduction to circuit technique for radiolocation.

WILLIAMS and NOBLE 1950. *J.I.E.E.* **97**, II, 445. Second-harmonic, magnetic modulators.

WILLIAMS and MOODY 1946. *J.I.E.E.* **93**, IIIA, 1188. Time Base Circuits.

WILSON 1951. *The Principles of Cloud Chamber Technique.* Cambridge University Press.

WORCESTER and DOUGHTY 1946. *Trans. Am. Inst. Elec. Eng.* **65**, 946. Mass Spectrometer for Leak Detection.

WORTHING and GEFFNER 1943. *Treatment of Experimental Data.* Wiley, New York; Chapman and Hall, London.

WRIGHT-BAKER (Ed.) 1948. *Modern Workshop Technology.* Cleaver-Hume, London. (Materials and Processes.)

YULE and KENDALL 1945. *Elements of Statistics.* Griffin, London.

VAN DER ZIEL 1955. *Noise.* Prentice-Hall, New York; Chapman and Hall, London.

ZERNICKE 1922. *Proc. Acad. Sci. Amsterdam* **24**, 239. Galvanometer Design.

ZERNICKE 1932. *Zeit. f. Physik.* **79**, 516. Effect of fluctuations on galvanometer readings.

INDEX

INDEX